William Carlos Williams and the Diagnostics of Culture

William Carlos Williams
and the Diagnostics
of Culture

BRIAN A. BREMEN

New York   Oxford
OXFORD UNIVERSITY PRESS
1993

Oxford University Press

Oxford   New York   Toronto
Delhi   Bombay   Calcutta   Madras   Karachi
Kuala Lumpur   Singapore   Hong Kong   Tokyo
Nairobi   Dar es Salaam   Cape Town
Melbourne   Auckland   Madrid

and associated companies in
Berlin   Ibadan

Copyright © 1993 by Oxford University Press, Inc.

Published by Oxford University Press, Inc.,
200 Madison Avenue, New York, New York 10016

Oxford is a registered trademark of Oxford University Press

Library of Congress Cataloging-in-Publication Data
Bremen, Brian A.
William Carlos Williams and the diagnostics of culture / Brian A.
Bremen.
p. cm.   Includes bibliographical references and index.
ISBN 0-19-507226-X
1.Williams, William Carlos, 1883–1963—Criticism and interpretation.
2.Social problems in literature.
3.Medicine and literature.
I.Title.
PS3545.I544Z5766   1993
811'.52—dc20   92–8956

2 4 6 8 9 7 5 3 1

Printed in the United States of America
on acid-free paper

Acknowledgements

This work owes a great deal to a great many people. First and foremost, I want to express my debt to A. Walton Litz. His generosity and wisdom have guided this book from inception to finish, and I hope it reflects some of the lessons I've learned along the way. Sandra Gilbert, who read an early version of the manuscript, has contributed both in comment and in critical example, and I am grateful for her help. Special thanks are extended to Richard Kroll, whose love of ideas and demand for clarity have influenced this work tremendously and are, I hope, evidenced within it. I would also like to thank Barbara Johnson, whose suggestion of Heinz Kohut was timely and valuable, and to Geoffrey Hartman, for getting me started on Kenneth Burke. I would also like to thank Kenneth Burke himself. His letter to me was, in many ways, the gist of this book, and his example in thought and human feeling is monumental one to me.

Several colleagues read various parts of this work and were instrumental in forming the final shape of its argument: Chris MacGowan lent a keen critical eye and a wealth of information on Williams, and Peter Schmidt helped me clarify the critical and literary tradition in which Williams has been read. Ann Cvetkovich, Kate Frost, Michael Hanchard, Barbar Harlow, Elizabeth Hedrick, Kurt Heinzelman, Wayne Lesser, Lora Romero, Ramón Saldívar, and Harvey Teres have all enriched this work through their generous comments and wide variety of critical perspectives. Many more discussions, conversations, arguments, and answers to questions have also found their way way inside these pafes, and I would like to thank those who contributed them: Andrew Barnaby, Hunter Cadzow, Aileen Douglas, John Ferguson, Alan Hepburn, Marjorie Howes, Mike Kowalewski, Jayne Lewis, Robert Mack, Andrew Miller, and Natania Rosenfeld. My special thanks goes to *mio fratello*, Danny Goldberg, who, like Williams, is "the brutal thing itself."

I'd like to dedicate this book to my family. My mother, Ruth Bremen, gave me all the support I could ask for, and my daughter Sara and son Sam are so intimately intertwined within these pages that I'm not sure how best to acknowledge their presence except to say that I love them. Finally, I'd like to thank my late father, Harry Bremen, whose confidence and faith in me made this possible in the first place.

Grateful acknowledgment is given to New Directions Publishing Corporation for permission to quote from the following copyrighted works of William Carlos Williams: The *Autobiography of William Carlos Williams*. Copyright 1948, 1951 by

William Carlos Williams. *The Build-up*. Copyright 1946, 1952 by William Carlos Williams. *The Collected Poems of William Carlos Williams: Volume I, 1909–1939*. Copyright 1938 by New Directions Publishing Coroporation. Copyright © 1982, 1986 by William Eric Williams and Paul H. Williams. *The Collected Poems of William Carlos Williams: Volume II, 1939–1962*. Copyright 1944, 1953, Copyright © 1962 by William Carlos Williams. Copyright © 1988 by William Eric Williams and Paul H. Williams. *The Embodiment of Knowledge*. Copyright © 1974 by Florence H. Williams. *The Farmer's Daughters*. Copyright 1934, 1950 by William Carlos Williams. Copyright © 1957 by Florence H. Williams. *I Wanted to Write a Poem: The Autobiography of the Works of a Poet*. Copyright © 1958 by William Carlos Williams. *Imaginations*. Copyright © 1970 by Florence H. Williams. *Interviews with William Carlos Williams: "Speaking Straight Ahead."* Copyright © 1976 by the Estate of William Carlos Williams. *In the American Grain*. Copyright 1925 by James Laughlin. Copyright 1933 by William Carlos Williams. *In The Money*. Copyright 1940 by Florence H. Williams. *Paterson*. Copyright © 1946, 1948, 1949, 1958 by William Carlos Williams. "Rome." Copyright © 1978 by the Estate of Florence H. Williams. *A Recognizable Image: William Carlos Williams on Art and Artists*. Copyright © 1978 by the Estate of Florence H. Williams. *Selected Essays*. Copyright 1954 by William Carlos Williams. *The Selected Letters of William Carlos Williams*. Copyright 1957 by William Carlos Williams. *Something to Say: William Carlos Williams on Younger Poets*. Copyright © 1985 by William Eric Williams and Paul H. Williams. *A Voyage to Pagany*. Copyright 1928 by the Macauley Company. Copyright © 1970 by New Directions Publishing Corporation. *White Mule*. Copyright 1937 by New Directions Publishing Corporation. Previously unpublished material by William Carlos Williams. Copyright © 1993 by William Eric Williams and Paul H. Williams; used by permission of New Directions Publishing Corporation, agents. Permission to quote from The Edmund Wilson Papers: Letter from John Peale Bishop to Edmund Wilson, October 1922, in the Yale Collection of American Literature, Beinecke Rare Book and Manuscript Library, Yale University, given by Jonathan Bishop. Permission to quote from the Kenneth Burke Collection, Rare Books and Special Collections, The Pennsylvania State University Libraries, given by Kenneth Burke. Grateful acknowledgment is given to the University of California Press for permission to quote from the following copyrighted works of Kenneth Burke: *Attitudes Toward History*. Revised Edition. Copyright © 1984 The Regents of the University of California. *Counter-Statement*. Copyright © 1968 The Regents of the University of California. *A Grammar of Motives*. Copyright © 1969 The Regents of the University of California. *Language as Symbolic Action: Essays on Life, Literature, and Method*. Copyright © 1966 The Regents of the University of California. *The Philosophy of Literary Form: Studies in Symbolic Action*. Copyright © 1973 The Regents of the University of California. *A Rhetoric of Motives*. Copyright © 1969 The Regents of the University of California. I would also like to gratefully acknowledge the University Research Institute of The University of Texas at Austin for its generosity in granting me both a Special Research Award and a Summer Research Award.

Contents

Abbreviations

Works by William Carlos Williams:

A   *The Autobiography of William Carlos Williams.* New York: New Directions, 1967.

BU   *The Build-up.* New York: New Directions, 1968.

CP I   *The Collected Poems of William Carlos Williams: Volume I, 1909–1939.* Ed. A. Walton Litz and Christopher MacGowan. New York: New Directions, 1986.

CP II   *The Collected Poems of William Carlos Williams: Volume II, 1939–1962.* Ed. Christopher MacGowan. New York: New Directions, 1988.

EK   *The Embodiment of Knowledge.* New York: New Directions, 1974.

FD   *The Farmer's Daughters.* New York: New Directions, 1961.

I   *Imaginations.* New York: New Directions, 1971.

IWCW   *Interviews with William Carlos Williams: "Speaking Straight Ahead."* Ed. with an intro. Linda Weishimer Wagner. New York: New Directions, 1976.

IAG   *In The American Grain.* New York: New Directions, 1956.

ITM   *In The Money.* New York: New Directions, 1967.

IWWP   *I Wanted to Write a Poem: The Autobiography of the Works of a Poet.* Reported and edited by Edith Heal. New York: New Directions, 1978.

P   *Paterson.* Rev. ed. New York: New Directions, 1992.

Rome   "Rome." Ed. Steven Ross Loevy. Rpt. in *Iowa Review* 9, 3 (Spring 1978), 1–65.

RI   *A Recognizable Image: William Carlos Williams on Art and Artists.* Ed. with intro. and notes by Bram Dijkstra. New York: New Directions 1978.

SE   *Selected Essays.* New York: New Directions, 1969.

SL   *The Selected Letters of William Carlos Williams.* Ed. by John C. Thirlwall. New York: New Directions, 1984.

SS   *Something to Say: William Carlos Williams on Younger Poets.* Ed. with intro. by James E. Breslin. New York: New Directions, 1985.

VP *A Voyage to Pagany*. New York: New Directions, 1970.

WM *White Mule*. New York: New Directions, 1967.

Works by Kenneth Burke:

ATH *Attitudes Toward History*. Berkeley: University of California Press, 1984.

CS *Counter-Statement*. Berkeley: University of California Press, 1968.

GM *A Grammar of Motives*. Berkeley: University of California Press, 1969.

LASA *Language as Symbolic Action; Essays on Life, Literature, and Method*. Berkeley: University of California Press, 1966.

PC *Permanence and Change: An Anatomy of Purpose*. Berkeley: University of California Press, 1984.

PLF *The Philosophy of Literary Form: Studies in Symbolic Action*. Berkeley, University of California Press, 1973.

RM *A Rhetoric of Motives*. Berkeley: University of California Press, 1969.

RR *The Rhetoric of Religion: Studies in Logology*. Berkeley: University of California Press, 1970.

William Carlos Williams and the Diagnostics of Culture

Introduction

Kenneth Burke opens the first section of *Permanence and Change: An Anatomy of Purpose* (1935) under the subheading *All Living Things Are Critics.* Burke argues that if critics are those who have learned to interpret the signs about them, then even chickens can act critically by being taught to recognize a specific tone as a signal that they will be fed. Of course, as Burke quickly points out, the problem with this critical model (or model critic) is that these chickens can also be gathered together by their food signal only to be slaughtered for someone's dinner. While, for some, this limitation of Burke's chicken-critic may be an absolute boon, Burke himself explains that "Chickens not so well educated would have acted more wisely." He maintains that what separates the live critics from the dead chickens is our ability to move "beyond the criticism of experience to a criticism of criticism" (*PC* 6).

Burke's immediate point here is that signs take on meanings "in accordance with the contexts in which we experience them" and that these contexts include the ways in which we have learned to interpret signs. In this way, Burke reads his chicken-critic's shortcomings as both defect and quality, maintaining that its faulty reading is an inherent part of the chicken's own critical learning. He explains that "the devices by which we arrive at a correct orientation may be quite the same as those involved in an incorrect one." Burke goes on to link this idea with Thorstein Veblen's concept of "trained incapacity"—"that state of affairs whereby one's very abilities can function as blindnesses" (*PC* 6–7). Much like Paul de Man, Burke concludes that all critical orientations contain their respective "incapacities," and the insights gained by any critic are done so by virtue of that critic's "blindness."[1]

I begin with this opening anecdote in order to locate my own critical study of William Carlos Williams—perhaps the most famous poet to write about chickens—within a matrix of thought that includes the relationship between Williams and his critics and the category of criticism in general. Williams's relationship to his critics—both within and outside of universities—has never been a particularly easy one. At its most tendentious, it takes the form of those critics who still read Williams's dictum of "No ideas but in things" as simply meaning "no ideas."[2] But even those more sympathetic to Williams have struggled with both the qualities and the defects of their respective critical approaches. The forms of categorization typical of the "academic" critic have led to the production of many invaluable

3

works on Williams, and there is no question that my own study would have been impossible without the rich body of existing Williams criticism. Still, the "trained incapacities" inherent in any critical approach have seemed especially to limit our understanding of Williams's work by focusing primarily on one particular aspect of his art—i. e., the formal properties of his poetry, its relation to the visual arts, or its enactment of literary theory.

In his own time, Williams was acutely aware of these kinds of critical limitations, and in a 1947 letter to Kenneth Burke he explains that

> the trouble as between me and the "placed" critics is that they think I am fooling or rambling or at best uninformed. To put it in its "academic" light: ignorant. I *am* ignorant but only of inessentials,[*sic*] I haven't had time in my life to bother too much with them.
> But I am neither uninformed nor unguided in the essential matters that concern me as a poet. Rather the others are infants to me and the more so because of their "training," their learning. (which has taken so much of their time)
>
>   (Williams's emphases)[3]

Interestingly, some of the most insightful of Williams's critics outside the academy have been those whose "trained incapacities" have mirrored Williams's own. In particular, Denise Levertov—who early on received training as a registered nurse—reads Williams's use of "things" as part of a practice that perceives "concrete images as the very *incarnation* of thought." "Those images," she explains, "work as Chekovian narrative description; they work as implications of political ideas; *and* they work as analogies for the poet's need to act in society, humbly and with an understanding that in trying to serve the commonweal he will serve his own need for intimate experience of the living mystery" (Levertov's emphases).[4] Kenneth Burke himself—Williams's close friend for over forty years and a similarly autodidactic, specific intellectual—also provides an integrative focus on the kinds of "contact" and the "*tactus eruditus*" particular to the poet-doctor, a focus that intimates a close connection to his own thinking about language, the body, and literary "treatments" (*LASA* 282–91).

Within the academy, there have been many who have read Williams's work in equally enlightening ways. But rather than rehearse the history of the reception of Williams's work—a task already ably done by Paul Mariani, Peter Schmidt, and others[5]—I would like to trace out an example of this "trained incapacity" in one of Williams's most important, and most astute, critics—J. Hillis Miller. As his own critical orientation has shifted over time, Miller's writings on Williams have moved from presenting him as an exemplary "poet of reality" to a writer whose work embodies the "linguistic moment."[6] And, as Terence Diggory points out in *William Carlos Williams and the Ethics of Painting* (1991), Miller's criticism has "advanced our understanding of Williams by revealing the element of interpretation that lies at the heart of the kind of description that Williams practiced." Still, as Diggory argues, Miller avoids a full exploration of the ethical motives inherent in Williams's art.[7] Diggory's book itself argues against the major statements that Miller has made about Williams by emphasizing dialogue, dialectic, and an ideal of nonoppressive desire—arguments that complement my own in this study—and

I refer the reader to his work for a fuller critique of Miller's position than the one I offer below. Instead, I would like to encapsulate my criticism of Miller's criticism in a way that will enable a reconsideration of the term "criticism" itself.

In his 1986 presidential address to the Modern Language Association, Miller begins by "reading" a passage from William Carlos Williams's *In the American Grain* in order to show how "good reading or good criticism" can be as "productive" and "performative" as Williams's own work. "Naming the text rightly," Miller says, "brings the strange phosphorous of the life, what Williams elsewhere calls 'the radiant gist,' back once more above ground. Criticism makes that gist available for present use."[8] Miller argues that the "triumph of theory" in current critical practice has exposed and transformed our understanding of a notion like Williams's "radiant gist," particularly as it applies to that "strange phosphorous of the life" that grounds a culture. Theory has forced us, Miller says, "to recognize that all meanings have a material base," and that the "displacement in literary studies from a focus on the meaning of texts to a focus on the way meaning is conveyed" demands that cultural studies which examine the relationships between the material base and ideological superstructures should recognize the actual linguistic construction of that putative base (PA 282–83).

Despite gestures in his address toward the importance of thinking out the relation between language and history, Miller's reading of Williams here repeats the familiar textualist's engagement with romanticism, one that relies both on the irreconcilability of mimetic and expressive theories of language, as well as on our inability to get beyond an argument's rhetoricity since the "material" ground of any argument is a rhetorical construction.[9] But Miller's "real reading" blinds him to Williams's own awareness of the power of language to construct the material and of the power of rhetoric to persuade, as well as to "erase and inscribe" (PA 291). His view of *In the American Grain,* for example, reduces Williams's idea of American culture into a battle of Puritans against Indians,[10] where figures like Père Rasles and Montezuma lie crushed in the ground that once gave root to a "natural," "magical," heliotrope-like culture. Miller asserts that Williams's cultural ideal "is like Tenochtitlan: rooted in the ground" (PA 281), but in doing so he completely ignores what Williams has Montezuma tell Cortez shortly before Tenochtitlan's destruction:

> He explained that his people were not the aborigines of the land but that they had emigrated there in times past and ended by accepting the Spanish Monarch as his rightful and hereditary master.
>
> (*IAG* 31)

As Montezuma's "rightful and hereditary master," Cortez becomes the next in a line of conquerors beginning with Red Eric and including Montezuma and Columbus. Williams ends this section of *In the American Grain* with the cry "*Viva quien vence!*" and begins the next with the admonition,

> History, history! We fools, what do we know or care? History begins for us with murder and enslavement, not with discovery. No, we are not Indians but we are

men of their world. The blood means nothing; the spirit, the ghost of the land moves in the blood. It is we who ran to the shore naked, we who cried, "Heavenly Man!" These are the inhabitants of our souls, our murdered souls that lie . . .

(*IAG* 38–39)

But the "inhabitants of our souls" are not just the conquered Indians. We "moderns," Williams insists, are also like the Caribs:

the Caribs whom The Great Maker had dropped through a hole in the sky among their islands; they whose souls lived in their bodies, many souls in one body. . . .
    Fierce and implacable we kill them but their souls dominate us. Our men, our blood, but their spirit is master. It enters us, it defeats us, it imposes itself. . . .
    If men inherit souls this is the color of mine. We are, too, the others. Think of them! The main islands were thickly populated with a peaceful folk when Christ-over found them. But the orgy of blood which followed, no man has written. We are the slaughterers.

(*IAG* 39–41)

Williams valorizes the violent energy of both slaughterer and slaughtered in *In the American Grain,* and the valorization of this violence forms the rhetorical grounds for Williams's ideas about history and culture, as it plays an integral part in Williams's poetics. Christopher Columbus, discoverer of the "beautiful thing" that is the new world (*IAG* 26), is also "Christ-over," the bringer of "an orgy of blood." History, for Williams, is not the simple opposition of "natural" to hegemonic cultures, but rather the continuing story of discovery, violence, and enslavement—a story whose analogue in literary history includes the "violent torsions" of Gertrude Stein and James Joyce "to divorce words from the enslavement of the prevalent cliches" (*EK* 143). History and language are inseparable for Williams, and in a way very different from the one proposed by Miller's late colleague Paul de Man, Williams, too, would say that "literary history could in fact be paradigmatic for history in general."[11]

Not surprisingly, Miller's "trained incapacities" mark the limits of his criticism insofar as we take "criticism" to be the equivalent of "theory." But the word "criticism" has its roots in the Latin *criticus*—originally a medical term that meant relating to or involving the crisis of a disease; making a judgment, decision, or diagnosis. This idea, initially from Burke, of Williams as a "medicine man" whose writing is always a form of criticism-as-diagnosis forms the core of my study, and it points out how we need to read Williams's understanding of language less in terms of a textualist analysis and more in terms of a Burkean "symbolic action" that includes certain textualist assumptions. As Burke himself explains in his *Attitudes Toward History* (1937), "the very fact that the work of art is a symbolic act of synthesis makes difficulties for those who would break it down by conceptual analysis." Burke adds that "since the work of art is a synthesis, summing up a myriad of social and personal factors at once, an analysis of it necessarily radiates in all directions at once; . . . the synthetic symbol can be divided into conceptual components *ad infinitum.*" The critic, then, must get "his own pattern of selectivity" from "the pragmatic test of use. Facing a myriad possible distinctions, he should focus on those that he considers important for social reasons" (*ATH* 197–200).

The above assumptions, I would argue, are both Williams's and my own. Burke himself explains these assumptions further by pointing out that as "Bodies That Learn Language," men use "words that tell stories" in order both to "comprehend" their animal condition and to "duplicate the wordless aspects of our environment, greatly expand[ing] the range of *attitudes* by which we relate to one another in keeping with the clutter of concordant and discordant *interests socially rife among us* " (*ATH* 379–85, Burke's emphases). In this way, language functions for Burke both esthetically and *anesthetically* in its relationship to the sheerly physical. In making this argument, Burke recalls

> a remark that my friend William Carlos Williams had made to me in a moment when, as often, his duality as poet and physician spoke as one. . . . in response to his suggestion, I kept remembering: "First, there would be the sheer physicality of life, the human organism as one more species of alimentary canal with accessories . . . digestive tract with trimmings."
>
> (*ATH* 392)

I mention the above not only to substantiate further the close relationship between Burke's and Williams's thinking, but also to point out how naturally Williams's roles as doctor and poet combine with Burke's closely related roles of "Cure" and "Pontificate." If, along with this coincidence, we remember that the word "Semiotic" comes from the Greek meaning "concerned with the interpretation of symptoms" and was used by d'Alembert in his "Tree of Knowledge" to describe that branch of Medicine concerned with diagnosis, we can begin to see how Williams's own concern with history, culture, and the word becomes the way in which he can extend his diagnostics beyond the individual to embrace both the language and the community, providing both with cure and consolation.

My own understanding of Williams as both a theorist and a thinker was made clear by two things in particular: his lifelong fascination and experimentation with the effects of poetry and prose, and his lifelong friendship with Kenneth Burke. In addition, two statements—one by Hugh Kenner, the second by Richard Ellmann—have stayed with me throughout my work. The first is from *The Pound Era,* where Kenner calls Williams "the best theorist the Paris decade had." The second is from Ellmann's biography of James Joyce, where he claims that "we are still learning to be Joyce's contemporaries."[12] What I discovered in the course of working on Williams was that the more seriously I pursued Williams as a theorist, the more it became clear that we are just now learning to be Williams's contemporaries, particularly when we read Williams in relation to Burke's own theoretical ventures. Williams's poetics embrace ideas about literature, history, medicine, gender relations, and politics that are currently finding expression in the contemporary critical enterprise of "cultural studies," and his writing enacts the very kinds of cultural critique that J. Hillis Miller calls for in his address. The aim of this study will be to show how Williams develops these ideas—his diagnostics of culture—in the time between "Spring and All" (1923) and *Paterson,* Books I–IV (1951).

Chapter 1 describes the mechanism Williams develops in seeing prose and verse as both writing. A series of analogues provide the rhetorical, cognitive, and political models needed to clarify Williams's thought from the confused romanticism of *Spring and All* to the methodological empiricism of *Paterson*. In this way, Williams's role as poet also becomes more congenial with his role as doctor—one who uses an analogous methodology to extend his diagnoses beyond the individual to include both language and culture. Chapter 2 shows how the development of Williams's poetics can be better understood by replacing a "textualist" theory of language with a conceptual framework made up of Burke's notion of writing as a form of "symbolic action," Wittgenstein's idea of "language games" and his distinctions between "lines of projection" and "methods of projection," as well as the metapsychological concepts of "empathy," "intersubjectivity," and "narcissistic transformation" proposed by Heinz Kohut and Jessica Benjamin. In this way, we can see how Williams's poetics serves as an alternative psychological model that opposes an oedipal model of development. Using this framework, Chapter 3 explores how we can read Williams's work as an extension of his medical practice—as a kind of homeopathic and allopathic "medicine" that follows from his cultural diagnostics. Here I rely not only on the ideas of Burke, but also on the writings of Philodemus and A. R. Luria. Chapter 4 looks more closely at the cultural models that Williams develops in his writings, first by comparing Williams's notions of "history" and "tradition" in *In the American Grain* and elsewhere with those of T. S. Eliot and Ezra Pound, and then later by examining the Stecher trilogy of novels and seeing how they embody the "proletarian style" that Williams had said he was developing at that time. Chapter 5 returns to *Paterson* to look more closely at how Williams's poetics coincides with his politics in an attempt to restructure epistemological conventions at the level of what Pierre Bourdieu calls the "habitus." By asserting his own dialectical mechanism in opposition to customary forms of representation, Williams engages in a cultural critique that acts as both an engaged diagnosis and a step toward cure, as it also provides the kind of examination of language and history that Miller proposes. Here Williams's design, figured in terms of "the radiant gist," is the promotion of "creative democracy"—in Cornel West's words, "the cultural enrichment and moral development of self-begetting individuals and self-regulating communities by means of the release of human powers provoked by novel circumstances and new challenges."[13]

1

Finding the Poetry Hidden in the Prose

In "How to Read," Ezra Pound distinguishes prose as being "less highly charged" than poetry, yet he sees that "during the last century or century and a half prose has . . . arisen to challenge the poetic pre-eminence."[1] Pound elsewhere asserts "that prose is as precious and as much to be sought after as verse, even in its shreds and patches" and that "one of the finest chapters in English [may be] hidden in a claptrap novel."[2] "Great literature," Pound claims, "is simply language charged with meaning to the utmost possible degree," and those who discover "a mode or process" to do so received Pound's highest praise; they are "the inventors."[3]

William Carlos Williams borrows Pound's terminology in a section of Book II of *Paterson*—his imitation of Pound's Canto 45—in order to extol the importance of invention. Williams writes that "without invention the line / will never again take on its ancient / divisions when the word, a supple word, / lived in it" (*P* 50). Here Williams answers Pound's harangue against usury by focusing our attention on the importance of "invention"—the discovery of new forms and new grammars—and its relationship to the individual word as well as to the individual's unique perceptions of his world. What Williams means here is, in part, explained in his introduction to Byron Vazakas's *Transfigured Night* (1946), a piece written at the same time that he was working on Book II of *Paterson*. Williams praises Vazakas as "that important phenomenon among writers, an inventor" (*SS* 155). Vazakas had discovered a new poetic line, one that broke the bonds of conventional measure and ignored the trite forms in which poetry, for Williams, had been mired. Williams calls Vazakas an American who had "stayed home," "ignored the universities," and found a line that allowed "room in which to develop the opportunities of a new language, a line loose as Whitman's, but measured as his was not . . . resembling, however vaguely, a musical bar . . . since it is not related to grammar, but to *time*" (*SS* 156–59, Williams's emphasis).

Vazakas's line was a jazz-like mix of prose and poetry, and it "came to symbolize for Williams the gist of the new form he had been searching so long for."[4] His discovery of Vazakas in 1944 coincided with his completing *The Wedge*, his having seen MGM's *Madame Curie*, and his continued reading of *Finnegans Wake*, and it catalyzed the wealth of material that Williams had already accumulated for his work—the correspondences with David Lyle and Marcia Nardi, the hundreds of historical documents and newspaper reports about the region, as well as the shorter anticipations of *Paterson* that had appeared throughout Williams's earlier poetry. Now Williams had "a luminosity of elements" that enabled him "to dissect away / the block and leave / a separate metal" (*P* 175) that was to become his own work of invention—*Paterson*. Vazakas's new, more musical measure, his prose/poetic line, and his choice of subject matter struck deep, sympathetic chords in Williams and presented him with a concrete example of what he had been trying to do in his badly stalled epic. Here was a key, a way to give form to the misshapen giant of a man who was a city. Williams's identification with Vazakas and the way in which *Transfigured Night* aided in the delineation of *Paterson* become clearer in the following excerpt from Williams's "Introduction":

> Vazakas doesn't select his material. What is there to select? It is. Like the news-
> paper that takes things as it finds them,—mutilated and deformed, but drops what
> it finds as it was, unchanged in all its deformity and mutilation—the poet, chal-
> lenging the event, recreates it as of whence it sprang from among men and women,
> and makes a new world of it. . . . Night transfigured; this is Vazakas.
>
> (*SS* 158)

As in much of his correspondence during this period, Williams here is talking more to himself than he is about another poet.[5] The words "Night transfigured; this is Vazakas" recall Williams's notion of the "night mind," which he had developed in "The Importance of Place":

> But it is none of these. It is one: all tentatives fit into it, not it into them. It is
> particularly not "the past" out of which knowledge or consciousness going up
> proceeds, leaving it behind. It exists co-incidentally with consciousness, systems,
> is not escaped.
>   Objectified, it is place itself—on which all arguments fall.
>
> (*EK* 133)

The past, place, and chaos is an apt description of the state of *Paterson* in 1944, a "night mind" of subject matter waiting for Williams to transform it. By 1942 Williams had compiled "a hundred pages or so" of prose mixed with verse, and he had written to Robert McAlmon that the first part of *Paterson* should have been "nearly finished now" (*SL* 215–16). By early 1944, Williams had gathered almost all of the materials he would use in *Paterson I,* and most of what would make up the rest of Books II–IV.[6] Still, Williams was unable to coalesce this material into an acceptable form until he had seen what Vazakas had, in part, accomplished. Vazakas's poetry seemed "to occur in the prose as if hidden there," and in using his dialectic between poetry and prose to "recreat[e] the subject matter that is taken as it is found" and in inventing a new line, Williams had found his own way of "challenging the event" and making "a new world of it." Williams had discovered a way to reconcile the poetry with the prose, giving *Paterson* the rich, complicated movement and pattern it required.

Williams's best known statement in *Paterson* is to "Say it! No ideas but in things" (*P* 9), but we need to remember that the second part of Book I ends by

countering this command with "the divisions and imbalances / of his whole con-
cept, made weak by pity, / flouting desire; they are—No ideas but / in the facts"
(*P* 27). As I will begin to show in this chapter, the ways in which "facts" and
"things" are constructed through language in *Paterson* mark the culmination of
Williams's long-developing poetics—a poetics that includes many "ideas" about
language, culture, politics, history, and the ways in which we live our lives. I take
Paterson, Books I–IV, to be not only a work whose construction occupied Williams
throughout his career, but also the text that most successfully embodies his ideas
about writing.[7] The relationship between prose and verse in this work forms the
critical site for the performance of Williams's ideas in a dialectical development
that moves from "facts" that already define objects and people for us within a
given ideology, to "things" whose transformation within the imagination allow
for an "identification" both of and with the object without destroying that object's
unique integrity, to the violence necessary to break those customs and habits that
trap those "things" in historical "facts." In this chapter, by way of introducing
Williams's thought and "naming it rightly," I will explain the mechanism Williams
develops in *Paterson* that shifts his poetics away from the typically romantic ap-
paratus of some privileged site of knowledge to become an operation of "discov-
ery" that is linguistic, cognitive, and political. While much of what Williams says
about his own work sounds at times like a half-failed revision of romantic theory,
we need to recognize that Williams relies not on the performative power of lan-
guage in his poetry, but rather on the power of his poetry as performance to clarify,
to criticize, and even to help "cure" what his close friend Kenneth Burke referred
to as "our human condition as symbol using animals." If we are to "name the
text rightly," we must see the development of Williams's poetics and the achieve-
ment of *Paterson* not as a failed attempt to release that "radiant gist" that will
ground some "natural" culture, but as the successful working out of a dialectic of
poetry and prose that represents, for Williams, both an epistemological and a po-
litical model.[8]

Williams poses a quoted question to the reader of *Paterson* in the work's first
line—" 'Rigor of beauty is in the quest. But how will you find beauty / when it
is locked in the mind past all remonstrance?' " (*P* 3). As Joel Conarroe points out,
the quoted source here is Williams himself, and he answers his question in the
manuscripts of *Paterson*—"It is not in the things about us unless transposed there
by our employment. Make it free, then, by the art you have to enter those starved
and broken pieces."[9] Through the symbolic action of his own poetic performance,
Williams uses his "art" in *Paterson* to recreate a dialectic between the sections of
verse and the sections of prose that establishes a cycle of action whereby language
acts "metonymically" as a necessary reduction of human experience and "synec-
dochically" to recreate that experience within the mind of the reader. Williams
both represents and allows us to participate in what I will call a "grammar of
translation"—a way of seeing, reading, and writing that exposes the rhetorical
construction of the material as it allows for an individual transformation of it
through a process analogous to the one Williams himself uses in revising those
"starved and broken pieces" he lifts from historical sources into *Paterson*. By
taking bits of historical prose from works like Barber and Howe's *Historical Col-*

lections of New Jersey: Past and Present (1868) and Charles P. Longwell's *A Little Story of Old Paterson As Told By An Old Man* (1901) and reshaping them into sections of prose as well as sections of verse, Williams recreates a violent cycle of human thought that dramatically revises and actively participates in what Kenneth Burke calls the "unending conversation" of history.

Williams's notion of writing as a kind of performance, his ideas about the power of poetry to "cure," and his treatment of people as a "symbol using animals," all rely heavily on the work of Kenneth Burke.[10] Williams met Burke in January of 1921 and remained in close contact with him for the next forty-two years. Amazingly, no one has made an extended study of how these two thinkers interacted and influenced each other.[11] Part of my work, then, compares Williams's thought with Burke's. First, however, I look at how Williams moves in his own writing about prose and poetry from the rigid distinctions he sets out in *Spring and All* and *The Wedge* to his recognition in *Paterson* that "prose and verse are both *writing,* both a matter of the words and an interrelation between words for the purpose of exposition, or other better defined purpose of *the art*" (*SL* 263, Williams's emphases). The consequences of this ultimate identification of prose and verse as "both *writing*" are then explained through a series of analogues that provide the rhetorical, cognitive, and political models through which we can clarify Williams's thought from the confused romanticism of *Spring and All* to the methodological empiricism of *Paterson.* In this way, Williams's role as poet will also become more congenial with his role as doctor—one who uses an analogous methodology to extend his diagnoses beyond the individual to include both language and culture. By asserting his own dialectical mechanism in opposition to customary forms of representation, Williams engages in a cultural critique that provides the kind of examination of language and history that recent work in cultural studies has emphasized. Before we can see how the mechanism Williams establishes in *Paterson* operates at this macropolitical level, however, we need to understand how it functions at the level of the individual.

I

In 1929, when Williams wrote to Louis Zukofsky that "My collected things *need* to come out for *us all*" (Williams's emphases), he was mired in one of the low points of his career.[12] Creatively stalled and critically ignored, Williams felt more and more the need to make his poetry available in order to champion the cause of an entire group of poets, as well as to counter the growing influence of T. S. Eliot. As a result, Williams accordingly made "available" a work that had been privately published abroad and circulated only among friends—the 1923 prose-poetry sequence *Spring and All.* This volume contains much of Williams's best, and certainly his most popular, poetry. But when Williams included it in his *Collected Poems, 1921–1931,* he selected only about half of its poems, gave each of them an individual title, and removed all of the prose that he had originally interpolated with the verse. Interestingly, Williams admits in *Spring And All* that: "I think often of my earlier work and what it has cost me not to have been clear. I acknowledge I have moved chaotically about refusing or rejecting most things, seldom accepting

values or acknowledging anything.'' Williams goes on to explain, however, that
he did so "because I early recognized the futility of acquisitive understanding and
at the same time rejected religious dogmatism" (*CP I* 202). This recognition and
rejection is a constant throughout Williams's work, and it forms an integral part
of the way in which the prose in *Spring And All* is meant to interact with the verse.
This attitude also produces both an unwillingness and an inability on Williams's
part to formulate his poetics in a more coherent form—the way Stevens can, for
example, in *The Necessary Angel*.[13] When we combine these factors with the rec-
ognition by Williams that the true power of *Spring And All* was in the verse (*IWWP*
37), along with the growing influence of the New Critics who maintained that
poems must be read as unified wholes, we get the familiar version of *Spring And
All* that appeared in *Collected Poems, 1921–1931*.

In sacrificing the prose, however, Williams also jettisoned his early ideas about
prose and poetry and the ways in which they interact. These distinctions had oc-
cupied a great deal of Williams's thought, and they would continue to do so
throughout his career. In 1906, Williams had read the thirteenth-century Provençal
legend of *Aucassin and Nicolette* with H. D. while he was still in medical school
and remembered discovering "the wonders of . . . the prose and verse alternating"
(*A* 52). Not only *Spring and All* (1923), but also *The Descent of Winter* (1928)
used this alternating prose/verse structure, as did the sequences "From: A Folded
Skyscraper" (1927), and "The Atlantic City Convention, A Composition in Two
Parts: Poem and Speech" (1928). The "Della Primavera Trasportata al Morale"
(1930) began in 1928 as a continuation of the prose/poetry form of *The Descent
of Winter,* but Williams dropped the interpolated prose early on (*CP I* 520). *The
Wedge* (1944)—originally entitled *THE (lang) WEDGE*—was also to have con-
tained both poetry and prose until Louis Zukofsky, in editing the work, removed
all of the prose except for an introduction based on a talk given at the New York
Public Library in 1943.[14] "Written in the most forthright prose," Williams remem-
bered his "Introduction" to *The Wedge* as "an explanation of my poetic creed at
the time—for all time as far as that goes" (*IWWP* 70). In it, Williams restates his
distinctions between prose and poetry:

> To make two bald statements: There's nothing sentimental about a machine, and:
> A poem is a small (or large) machine made of words. When I say there's nothing
> sentimental about a poem I mean that there can be no part, as in any other machine,
> that is redundant.
>
> Prose may carry a load of ill-defined matter like a ship. But poetry is the
> machine which drives it, pruned to a perfect economy. As in all machines its
> movement is intrinsic, undulant, a physical more than a literary character. In a
> poem this movement is distinguished in each case by the character of the speech
> from which it arises.

A bit further on, Williams states:

> When a man makes a poem, makes it, mind you, he takes words as he finds them
> interrelated about him and composes them—without distortion which would mar
> their exact significances—into an intense expression of his perceptions and ardors
> that they may constitute a revelation in the speech that he uses. It isn't what he

says that counts as a work of art, it's what he makes, with such intensity of perception that it lives with an intrinsic movement of its own to verify its authenticity. . . .

There is no poetry of distinction without formal invention, for it is in the intimate form that works of art achieve their exact meaning, in which they most resemble the machine, to give language its highest dignity, its illumination in the environment to which it is native. Such war, as the arts live and breathe by, is continuous.

It may be that my interests as expressed here are pre-art. If so I look for a development along these lines and will be satisfied with nothing else.

(*CP II* 54–55)

In a sense, Williams's "interests" in both 1929 and 1944 were "pre-art." At each of these two crucial stages in his career, Williams decided to revise two separate prose/poetry sequences by removing the prose from each, only to follow these works with substantial experiments involving prose. *Collected Poems, 1921–1931* was followed by collections of short stories, a play, and two novels; *The Wedge* led to the completion of *Paterson*, Book I.

By 1948, Williams was to write to Parker Tyler that the prose in *Paterson*

is *not* an antipoetic device, the repeating of which piece of miscalculation makes me want to puke. It *is* that prose and verse are both *writing*, both a matter of the words and an interrelation between words for the purpose of exposition, or other better defined purpose of *the art*. Please do not stress other "meanings." I want to say that prose and verse are to me the same thing. . . . Poetry does not *have* to be kept away from prose as Mr. Eliot might insist, it goes *along with* prose and, companionably, by itself, without aid or excuse or need for separation or bolstering, shows itself by *itself* for what it is. *It belongs* there, in the gutter. Not anywhere else or wherever it is, it is the same: the poem.

(*SL* 263, Williams's emphases)

Williams's anger at his writing being called "antipoetic" goes back to his displeasure with Wallace Stevens's "Preface" to the *Collected Poems, 1921–1931*, though Stevens probably picked up the term from Williams's own description of his writing's being called "antipoetry" in the opening of *Spring and All* (*CP I* 177). Stevens described Williams's "passion for the anti-poetic" as "a blood passion and not a passion of the inkpot." According to Stevens, the "anti-poetic" was Williams's "spirit's cure. He needs it as a naked man needs shelter or as an animal needs salt. To a man with a sentimental side the anti-poetic is that truth, that reality to which all of us are forever fleeing."[15] Stevens sees the "anti-poetic" in Williams's writing in conflict with Williams's tendency toward "sentimentalization," even though, Stevens says, "What Williams gives, on the whole, is not sentiment but the reaction from sentiment, or, rather, a little sentiment, very little, together with acute reaction."[16]

Stevens reads Williams's *Collected Poems, 1921–1931* as "the conjunction of the unreal and the real, the sentimental and the anti-poetic, the constant interaction of two opposites." In this way, Williams resembles "that grand old plaster cast, Lessing's Laocoön: the realist struggling to escape from the serpents of the unreal."[17] Stevens's use of "the anti-poetic," however, is not wholly pejorative, as it stands for that desire in a poet to embrace reality, that side of one's nature "so attractive to the Furies."[18] At this stage, and throughout his career, Stevens is much more of a skeptic than Williams. For Stevens, the real is always mediated for us by language, and so we are always left struggling with "the serpents of the unreal"—"Another image at the end of the cave, / Another bodiless for the body's slough."[19] Williams, on the other hand, began his career as more of a dogmatic empiricist, believing that the poet could attain the universal through perceptions of the particular,[20] and even as late as 1934, his writing suggests a conflict between his empiricist's desire for contact and his romantic attempt at universals. Stevens calls Williams a romantic in his "Preface," and the term romantic was nearly always used pejoratively by the moderns. But as Stevens explains in "Sailing After Lunch":

> It is the word *pejorative* that hurts.
> .   .   .   .   .   .
> Mon Dieu, hear the poet's prayer.
> The romantic should be here.
> The romantic should be there.
> It ought to be every where.
> But the romantic must never remain,
>
> Mon Dieu, and must never again return.[21]

In his "Review of *Selected Poems* by Marianne Moore," a piece written around the same time he wrote "Sailing After Lunch," Stevens says that "the romantic" does have a pejorative sense when it "merely connotes obsolescence," but the term also "constitutes the vital element in poetry":

> It means, now-a-days, an uncommon intelligence. It means in a time like our own of violent feelings, equally violent feelings and the most skillful expression of the genuine. . . .
>
> The romantic that falsifies is rot and that is true even though the romantic inevitably falsifies: it falsifies but it does not vitiate. It is an association of the true and the false. It is not the true. It is not the false. It is both. The school of poetry that believes in sticking to the facts would be stoned if it was not sticking to the facts in a world in which there are no facts: or some such thing.[22]

Stevens correctly reads Williams as struggling between those "facts in a world in which there are no facts" and a rejection of the "accepted sense of things."[23] The romantic rejection of the "accepted sense of things" is a necessary part of this struggle, and in the early part of his career, Williams uses the "simple continuation of known opinion" as his definition of prose—a "statement of facts concerning emotions, intellectual states, data of all sorts" (*CP I* 219). It is not surprising that in revising *Spring and All* Williams decided to cut its prose in order to "prune down" the "perfect economy" of his poems and avoid the "sentimental." By the time Williams writes *Paterson,* however, he will have greatly refined his ideas about prose and poetry, coming to see them as "both *writing,* both a matter of the words and an interrelation between words for the purpose of exposition, or other better defined purpose of *the art*." By shifting his focus to the ways in which prose and poetry interact, Williams will have recognized both prose and verse as rhetorical structures, but ones whose unequal claims to being "factual" can expose the rhetorical construction of those facts and force into being a moment of "discovery." Interestingly, Williams will also have come closer to Stevens's own recognition that his "essential poetry is the result of the conjunction of the unreal and the real, the sentimental and the anti-poetic, the constant interaction of two opposites." He also will have developed into more of a methodological empiricist—a role more congenial to his role as doctor, whereby one can generate generalizations and inferences for the individual that are highly probable but not necessarily true, and where, through method, "the basic principles of good and bad are established with exactness."[24]

In order to understand these developments more clearly, we need to begin with the way Williams plays with assumptions about poetry and prose in *Spring and All*. In the prose section that follows the poem later titled "To Elsie," Williams says:

> or better: prose has to do with the fact of an emotion; poetry has to do with the dynamization of emotion into a separate form. This is the force of imagination.
>
> prose: statement of facts concerning emotions, intellectual states, data of all sorts—technical expositions, jargon, of all sorts—fictional and other—
>
> poetry: new form dealt with as a reality in itself.
>
> The form of prose is the accuracy of its subject matter—how best to expose the multiform phases of its material
>
> the form of poetry is related to the movements of the imagination revealed in words—or whatever it may be—
>
> the cleavage is complete
>
> Why should I go further than I am able? Is it not enough for you that I am perfect?
>
> The cleavage goes through all the phases of experience. It is the jump from prose to the process of imagination that is the next great leap of the intelligence—from the stimulations of present experience to the facts of the imagination—
>
> the greatest characteristic of the present age is that it is stale—stale as literature—
>
> To enter a new world, and have there freedom of movement and newness.
>
> (*CP I* 219)

Despite this "cleavage" that separates prose, poetry, and "all of experience," Williams is obviously toying here with the imaginative possibilities of prose. As Williams discusses it, prose is a kind of transparent medium through which an author can convey information and facts in a relatively unproblematic way. But when Williams calls attention to the rhetoricity of his own construction in the line "Why should I go further than I am able? Is it not enough for you that I am perfect?" we become aware that what Williams is writing here is not strict prose, according to his own definitions, but a highly charged language that breaks down our traditional notions of prose and yet remains distinct from what he calls "poetry."

He continues to play with these ideas in the prose passages that follow the section of verse that would become his most famous poem, "The Red Wheelbarrow":

> Prose—When values are important, such—For example there is no use denying that prose and poetry are not by any means the same IN INTENTION. But then what is prose? There is no need for it to approach poetry except to be weakened.
>
> With decent knowledge to hand we can tell what things are for
>
> I expect to see values blossom. I expect to see prose be prose. Prose relieved of extraneous, unrelated values must return to its only purpose; to clarity [*sic*] to enlighten the understanding. There is no form to prose but that which depends on clarity. If prose is not accurately adjusted to the exposition of facts it does not exist—Its form is that alone. To penetrate everywhere with enlightenment—
>
> Poetry is something quite different. Poetry has to do with the crystallization of the imagination—the perfection of new forms as additions to nature—Prose may follow to enlighten but poetry—
>
> Is what I have written prose? The only answer is that form in prose ends with the end of that which is being communicated—if the power to go on falters in the middle of a sentence—that is the end of the sentence—Or if a new phase enters at that point it is only stupidity to go on.
>
> There is no confusion—only difficulties.
>
> (*CP I* 226)

While Williams insists here that prose differs from poetry in both form and "intention," the answer to the question "is what I have written prose?" remains both a difficult and a confusing one. I want to suggest, however, that the differences "IN INTENTION" that Williams says separate prose from poetry are analogous to the distinctions that Wittgenstein makes between "lines of projection" and "methods of projection." Wittgenstein makes this distinction in order to explain his shift from an ontology of logical simples in the *Tractatus* to one based on language games.[25] As Charles Altieri explains, "the former privileges a referential correspondence model for assessing meanings, the latter allows us to speak of assessment as dependent on procedures appropriate to the specific activity performed in the discourse." Moving from "lines of projection" to "methods of projection" enables Wittgenstein to embrace an idea of assessable and determinate meanings, without resorting to Kantian notions of a priori mental structures, by appealing to a common world developed from the ways we learn to use language. In order to avoid an extended digression on Wittgenstein,[26] however, I will attempt to explain what I mean here with an analogous moment in Williams.

"Facts," as well as "prose," depend upon a complex cultural grammar for their meaning, and our acceptance of them as unproblematic reflections of reality merely shows how deeply embedded this grammar has become in our construction of our world. The Cotton Mather section of *In the American Grain,* for example, exposes this grammar by presenting the supposedly neutral "facts" of witchcraft within the cultural context of a court of law and eye-witness accounts of "Curiosities" and "Enchantments Encountered"—of which, Mather says, "I shall Report Nothing but with Good Authority" (*IAG* 101). Williams's inclusion of property battles and personal squabbles in these accounts shifts the context in which we read these incidents from that of a legal system that determines right and wrong to a framework of social jealousies that undermines those legal decisions. His incorporation of Mather's comments on "demonic Mexican governors" and on the "fact" that "*Witchcraft* will not be fully understood, until the day when there shall not be one Witch in the World" (*IAG* 89, 101 & 103), not only situates Mather's "facts" historically, but also links Mather's account with Cortez's destruction of Tenochtitlan, further elevating that social framework into the realm of cultural hegemony.

When we approach a piece of prose according to the sense that Williams describes in *Spring and All,* we expect to be able to rely on those "methods of projection"—those conventions of language, grammar, and writing, as well as on social, cultural, and historical frameworks—to enable us to understand the "facts" that prose conveys. Reading "against the grain," however, as we read "Cotton Mather's Wonders," prose now does something different. Like Williams's "poetry," it frustrates or plays with our expectations, "crystallizing the imagination," giving us "new forms as an addition to nature," a "new form dealt with as a reality in itself"—what Wittgenstein would call a "form of life." For Wittgenstein, "to imagine a language means to imagine a form of life" (*PI* 8), and the language Williams asks us to imagine which we read his poems in *Spring and All* is one that both annihilates and recreates the world in "a perfect plagiarism. . . . Only the imagination is undeceived" (*CP I* 181). The distinctions that Williams makes between prose and poetry here reflect two different "methods of projection," two "ways of thinking," whereby the world is either "copied" according to some previously existing set of conventions, or, in Williams's terms, "made anew" by a new way of seeing—"only the imagination is undeceived" that we are examining two different worlds (*CP I* 178–82 & 204–10).

Williams's idea that the imagination can make the world anew is, potentially, his greatest moment of mystification in *Spring and All.* According to Wittgenstein, participating in a "form of life"—participating in a "language game"—means that we still somehow know or sense the rules of that game, even though we may not be able to state them explicitly. Though Williams swears in *Spring and All* that "it is not necessary to resort to mysticism" (*CP I* 207), his own mystification of the imagination's power seems to imply that in entering "the new world naked," we enter a world whose "rules" are completely unknown and unfamiliar. Williams's statement that "only the imagination is undeceived," however, hints at his own awareness of the impossibility of this desire. The remainder of the first "poem" in *Spring and All,* later titled "Spring and All," confirms this awareness:

> They enter the new world naked,
> cold, uncertain of all
> save that they enter. All about them
> the cold, familiar wind—
>
> Now the grass, tomorrow
> the stiff curl of wildcarrot leaf

> One by one objects are defined—
> It quickens: clarity, outline of leaf
>
> But now the stark dignity of
> entrance—Still, the profound change
> has come upon them: rooted, they
> grip down and begin to awaken

(*CP I* 183)

This verse, reminiscent of Pound's "The Return," avoids deifying its subject in part by remaining in the human, quotidian context of "muddy fields / brown with dried weeds" and "the scattering of tall trees // All along the road." The "reddish / purplish, forked, upstanding, twiggy / stuff of bushes and small trees," along with the suggestion of newborn infants, combine to create a context of discovery and renewal that avoids definition and recreation in any essential way but remains within the development of a "new" method of projection appropriate to the "stark dignity of / entrance" and "profound change." The "cold, familiar wind," suggests that this world is not entirely new, but rather is made new by reestablishing relationships between self and object according to some new method of projection. "One by one objects are defined" as these relationships form.

Like Wittgenstein, Williams sees that "*Essence* is expressed by grammar" and that "Grammar tells what kind of object anything is (Theology as grammar)" (*PI* 116). As Williams explains:

That is, the imagination is an actual force comparable to electricity or steam, it is not a plaything but a power that has been used from the first to raise the understanding of—it is, not necessary to resort to mysticism—In fact it is this which has kept back the knowledge I seek—

The value of the imagination to the writer consists in its ability to make words. Its unique power is to give created forms reality, actual existence

(*CP I* 207)

When Williams talks about the imagination's "ability to make words," he means the creation of a new grammar, a new method of projection, that clarifies and "redefines" that word for the reader. As Williams explained in his "Introduction" to *The Wedge,* the poet "takes words as he finds them interrelated about him and composes them—without distortion which would mar their exact significances—into an intense expression of his perceptions and ardors that they may constitute a revelation in the speech that he uses." And while much of what Williams says here sounds like a reworking of romantic theory with its privileging of the imagination as a "force" with the "unique power . . . to give created forms reality," its "revelation" inherent in the speech of the poet, and its seeming desire for subject-object identification, I will show how Williams's poetics moves away from this kind of thinking by developing a series of analogues that establish a framework within which we can see how Williams's ideas about the imagination, the word, and revelation all involve notions of "discovery," "identification," and "empathy" that are very different from an essential "naming" of the world. These analogues will also enable me to show how, by the time he writes *Paterson,*

Williams's ideas about prose and poetry will have blossomed into a dramatic performance of an idea of language that involves writing as a kind of symbolic action—one that moves from prosaic, established grammars that define objects for us, to a poetic cathexis of narcissistic energies that both transforms cultural-objects into self-objects through a process of identity and identification, as it maintains the integrity of both object and self.

II

In *Language and Myth,* Ernst Cassirer borrows Hermann Usener's idea of a "momentary deity" in his explanation of the origins of language. Cassirer says:

> These beings do not personify any force of nature, nor do they represent some special aspect of human life; no recurrent trait or value is retained in them and transformed into a mythico-religious image; it is something purely instantaneous, a fleeting, emerging and vanishing mental content, whose objectification and outward discharge produces the image of the "momentary deity." Every impression that man receives, every wish that stirs in him, every hope that lures him, every danger that threatens him can affect him thus religiously. Just let the spontaneous feeling invest the object before him, or his own personal condition, or some display of power that surprises him, with an air of holiness, and the momentary god has been experienced and created.[27]

It is important in Cassirer, as well as in Williams, that these "momentary gods" are momentary—they appear and they are gone, each revelation of them being unique. It is also important that they are not linked to an apprehension of some ideal essence beyond the immediate moment. Problems arise for Cassirer when a Platonic conception of the world replaces a more Epicurean or Humean one, where the real world is not as important as our sense impressions of it. Platonic thought, of course, relies on a method of projection whereby language as representation becomes an imperfect imitation of thought, which is an imperfect imitation of that ideal essence within or behind reality. Poetry and painting, in this way, become "copies"—a word that Williams uses pejoratively throughout *Spring And All.* Though the connections between Williams and a thinker like Hume may seem a bit forced here, Kenneth Burke once wrote to me that if I "read [his] paragraphs on Hume in [his] *Grammar of Motives,"* I would see where Williams "got *his* 'philosophy' from."[28] While at first I was somewhat doubtful about this connection, thinking of Williams reading Burke reading Hume clarified the point Burke was making. Hume, Burke, and Williams all rely on a denial of "God-terms" in developing an empiricist philosophy that opposes Platonic (and Kantian) *a priori*s with a notion of thought derived from sensory perceptions.[29] Viewed in this way, Williams's dictum of "No ideas but in things" becomes an analogous extension of Hume's writing in the *Enquiry,* which might be restated as "No ideas but in sensation." Of course, in making this extension we need to maintain the crucial difference between these two thinkers that comes about through Hume's privileging, and Williams's censuring, of custom and habit.

Still, by associating Williams with Hume and, by implication with himself,

Burke enables us to place Williams in a tradition of skeptical thought that stands in stark contrast to Williams's usual identification with romantic figures like Whitman and Keats. This tradition has many of its roots in Epicureanism and, before that, in the medical writings of the Hippocratic school,[30] and while it is not clear which, if any, of these works were read by Williams, the Hippocratic tradition and methods of diagnosis were certainly a part of his medical training. Central to this thought is the kind of *tactus eruditus* that Williams mentions in the "Della Primavera" (*CP I* 335) and that Burke stresses in his writings about his friend. Burke himself mentions Philodemus as a link between rhetoric and medicine in his *Rhetoric of Motives,* and discussions of Lucretius, Epicurus, and Diogenes Laertius appear throughout his works.[31] Furthermore, by always appealing to experience and perception as the foundation for all proof, the Epicurean strain of empiricist thought contains the need for "contact" that Williams stressed throughout his career. Finally, since it is based on a methodology that calls for the acceptance of any hypothesis that does not conflict with available evidence when complete verification is impossible, Epicureanism allows for pluralist thought without falling prey to relativism. That is, relations may vary according to situations, but through a kind of "methodological contextualism" we can make inferences about probable truths. As Phillip and Estelle De Lacy point out, while "values may not be absolute in a Platonic sense, yet they are nevertheless real elements in human experience."[32]

Epicureanism relies most heavily on medical practices in drawing inferences about imperceptible things from observable phenomena, and the proof of these inferences can be probabilistically determined by analogy with observable events and objects. In *On Methods of Inference,* Philodemus disputes the Stoic a priori method of inference by contraposition by showing how it is really based on analogy, induction, and experience. In an argument that Burke echoes in his refutation of the *a priori* as the taking of what is temporally antecedent (a conclusion based on experience) and asserting it as logically prior (as a necessary cause), Philodemus asserts that the "reading of signs" and the "construction of inferences" must not be based on "what we *presuppose*" but rather by analogical extension of what we observe to be "similar to those within our experience." He explains that those necessary causes that the Stoics assert *a priori* are in actuality presuppositions based on inferences made from experience.[33]

This denial of the *a priori* and the use of "genetic similarities" from careful observation have an obvious parallel in medical diagnoses, but, more important, they suggest a methodology that fits with the seemingly mystified "crystallization of the imagination" and "new form as an addition to nature" that Williams says poetry provides. The imagination, for Williams, is the locus of that analogical, inferential thought that leads to the construction of what Burke calls a "representative anecdote." By relying on the symbolic reconstruction of context and grammar that bear analogous relationships to observable phenomena, the imagination can "rival nature's composition with [its] own." Like Shakespeare, Williams's greatest avatar of the imagination, we become able to "create knowledge" not through the "conscious recording of the day's experience," but through "the same forces which transfuse the earth" (*CP I* 207–09). In this way nature is the hint to composition not because it is familiar to us and therefore the terms we apply to it have a least common denominator quality which gives them currency—but because it possesses the quality of independent existence, of reality which we feel in ourselves. It is not opposed to art but apposed to it.

(*CP I* 207–08)

Rejecting abstraction and the application of "a metaphor from some unknown object . . . [to] . . . another object equally unknown," Williams's imagistic tendencies share in the Epicurean idea of a language whereby "words refer primarily to objects that are apparent; their cognitive meaning, which is purely extensional, can be determined by specific empirical reference to the objects of experience." According to Epicurus, however, "the only correct language for a philosopher is the language that has been gradually built up by society as a practical means of communication about objects of experience; . . . if this language requires alteration because it is inexact or inadequate, it should never be altered except in strict accordance with empirical facts."[34] What Williams values most highly are those perceptions that involve some "discovery," and while Williams cloaks such an act in the mystified terms of "making new," what he recreates in his poetry is the analogous extension of inference to some previously unobserved object or incident. In these moments of "identification," it is precisely the uniqueness of the phenomena observed that links them to a class of "discoveries." Through the symbolic recreation of these moments where the "new" is "named," Williams is able to give us a "new form as an addition to nature" that must always be "apposed to nature." The language "that has been built up by society," however, will always be inadequate to such a moment, because that language relies on what has been previously "identified" to convey its meaning. Williams forces us to revise Wittgenstein's phrase to read, "to imagine a new form of life means to imagine a new language."

"Making the language new" is a romantic project that goes back at least to Wordsworth and Blake, and, curiously, much of Williams's prose in *Spring and All* feels like Blake's writing in *The Marriage of Heaven and Hell.* Like Blake's, Williams's prose relies on the frustration of a known "grammar of expectations" for its effect. This "grammar," for Williams, is the "straightforward" grammar of science and journalism; for Blake, it is the grammar of prophetic writing.[35] What Williams attempts to achieve in his "discoveries," however, is not some greater apprehension of an *a priori* or transcendental truth, but rather a recognition of "the quality of independent existence, of reality which we feel in ourselves"—an analogous extension of observable phenomena that bears genetic similarity to our own experience. Williams sees language as a form of symbolic action through which he can not only attain this quality, but also recreate that experience for the reader through a kind of performance.

As Kenneth Burke points out, in order to move from the kind of correlation appropriate for "scientific realism," to the "substantial" relations of humans that "poetic realism" seeks to convey, we must recognize that "any attempt to deal with human relationships after the analogy of a naturalistic correlation becomes necessarily the *reduction* of some higher or more complex realm of being to the terms of a lower or less complex realm of being." Left with this strategy of "metonymy," the poet must "convey some incorporeal or intangible state in terms of the corporeal or tangible." The significance of gesture or ostensive definition in early theories of language represent an attempt to ground that reduction from action to word—that act of metonymic "naming"—to some apparent, particular sign. Realizing that "human relations require actions, which are *dramatizations*," poetic "naming"—what Burke elsewhere calls "entitlement"—comes to stand for the dramatic representation of a material scene. " 'Shame,' for instance, is not merely a 'state,' but a movement of the eye, a color of the cheek, a certain quality of voice and set of muscles."[36] These physical states, however, remain only "figures" for the full action. The poet's "terminological reduction" differs from the "real" reduction of the scientist the way that terms of "action" used in psychology differ from descriptions of motion in physics. The poet's "metonymic reduction" is not a "*substantial* reduction," though, because "in 'poetic realism' states of mind as the motives of action are not reducible to materialistic terms" (*GM* 507).

As the reduction of an action to material conditions, poetic naming acts "synecdochically" as well, by aiming to "embody" a state of consciousness in order to produce in the reader a corresponding state. If metonymy is "the substitution of quantity for quality," then poetic realism extends or connects this substitution "both ways"; that is, "the artist proceeds from 'mind to 'body' that his representative reduction may induce the audience to proceed from 'body' to 'mind' " (*GM* 509–10). As Burke explains

> *A terminology of conceptual analysis, if it is not to lead to misrepresentation, must be constructed in conformity with a representative anecdote—whereas anecdotes "scientifically" selected for reductive purposes are not representative.*
>
> (*GM* 510)

In order to be "representative," an anecdote must be both dialectical and ironic. Burke explains that, "Where the ideas are in action we have drama; where the agents are in ideation, we have dialectic" and that "Irony arises when one tries, by the interaction of terms upon one another, to produce a *development* which uses all the terms" (*GM* 512).

As I hope to show in the remainder of this chapter, the dialectical development in Williams's poetics involves the "agents" of prose and poetry in the ironic "development" of what Heinz Kohut calls "wisdom." One way that Williams achieves this "wisdom," and teaches it to his readers, is through the construction of a representative anecdote that, by analogous extension, is what Wittgenstein calls a "perspicuous representation." Wittgenstein explains that

> A main source of our failure to understand is that we do not *command a clear view* of the use of our words.—Our grammar is lacking in this sort of perspicuity. A perspicuous representation produces just that understanding which consists in 'seeing connexions'. Hence the importance of finding and inventing *intermediate cases.*
>
> The concept of a perspicuous representation is of fundamental significance for us. It earmarks the form of account we give, the way we look at things. (Is this a "*Weltanschauung*"?)
>
> (*PI* 49)

We saw briefly how in *In the American Grain* Williams exposed the "way of seeing" that made up a part of the Puritan's *Weltanschauung* by "earmarking the form of account" given by Cotton Mather during a witch trial. This Puritan "grammar"—a "pale negative to usurp the place of that which really they were destined to continue" (*IAG* 66)—is one that denies "independent existence" in what I will call a "grammar of transference." This grammar swallows up anything that lies outside its previously determined "opinion" by imposing its own set, prosaic "way of seeing" on that object or action. The alternative that Williams proposes to this grammar—what I will call a "grammar of translation"—involves the discovery of that "quality of independent existence, of reality which we feel in ourselves" and "in nature." Here we need to "translate" this unique experience inferentially, using both analogous thinking to link it to prior thought and careful observation to maintain that moment's uniqueness as a "new form of life."

This act of "discovery"—what Williams calls "the radiant gist" (*P* 185)— occurs through a perception analogous to Usener's image of the "momentary deity." This "fleeting, emerging and vanishing mental discharge" can be better understood, however, as that cathexis of narcissistic energies that Heinz Kohut calls "wisdom." Kohut's ideas about narcissism[37] rely on a genetic model of consciousness that revises Freud's original model. This concept, Kohut explains, is developed by using both an empathic understanding of the patient and an introspective awareness of the analyst's own condition in order to construct what amounts to a "representative anecdote" of the patient's condition.[38] I will discuss Kohut's ideas and their relationship to Williams more fully in the next two chapters, but here I would like quickly to introduce some of those ideas in order to clarify further what I mean by my "grammars" of "transference" and "translation," as well as to point toward the "development" I see operating at the cognitive level in *Paterson*.

Kohut's theories of narcissism and "narcissistic transformation" go beyond the common, negative associations of narcissism and egotism, and revise the definitions Freud gave to narcissism as certain ego functions related "to the exhibitionistic aspects of the pregenital drives" and to "tensions in the ego as it strives to live up to the ego ideal."[39] Kohut begins his theory under the twin assumptions that: (1) "the self in the psychoanalytic sense is variable and by no means coextensive with the limits of the personality as assessed by an observer of the social field"; and (2) "the antithesis to narcissism is not the object relation but object love." As he explains further, "in certain psychological states the self may expand far beyond the borders of the individual, or it may shrink and become identical with a single one of his actions or aims. . . . [A]n individual's profusion of object relations, in the sense of the observer of the social field, may conceal his narcissistic experience of the object world; and a person's seeming isolation and loneliness may be the setting for a wealth of current object investments" (F&T 429).

What is significant for Kohut is the quality of the individual's psychological state, and in "primary narcissism" that state is characterized by a lack of differentiation between the "I" of the infant and the "you" of the mother. Through the process of maturation, this primary state becomes differentiated into the "idealized parent imago" and the "narcissistic self." The idealized parent imago is a continuation of that originally narcissistic perfection and omnipotence, which gradually emerges as the "ego ideal"—that aspect of the superego which corresponds to the phase specific, massive introjection of the idealized qualities of the object," characterized by "the unique quality of arousing our love and admiration while imposing the task of drive control." This ego ideal—along with the superego, a "vehicle of the ego ideal"—forms the locus of "our standards, ideas and values" (F&T 433–34).

The "narcissistic self," however, is more "closely related with the [narcissistic libidinal] drives and their inexorable tensions," while the "ego ideal is predominantly related to drive control." The "narcissistic cathexis" of the narcissistic self remains within the "nexus of the self," and so this cathexis does not result in idealization, as does the instinctual investment of the "idealized parent imago" and the "ego ideal." For this reason, Kohut says, "the ego experiences the influence of the ego ideal as coming from above, and that of the narcissistic self as coming from below." The difference between the two is the difference between "our ideals and our ambitions." These ambitions, though "derived from a system of infantile grandiose fantasies may become optimally restrained, merge with the structure of the ego's ideals, and achieve autonomy" (F&T 435–38).

Creativity is one of those "healthy directions" that can come from a transformation of narcissism. "Empathy" is another, even more important, transformation that can develop from a "primary empathy" experienced through identification with the mother, to an expanded sense of the self that recognizes its own finiteness in time and space while participating in a concept of a "supraindividual and timeless existence." This "genuine shift of the cathexes toward a cosmic narcissism" is "the creative result of the steadfast activities of an autonomous ego," and "it is accompanied by sadness as the cathexis is transferred from the cherished self to the supraindividual ideals and to the world with which one identifies. The profoundest forms of humor and cosmic narcissism therefore do not present a picture of grandiosity and elation but that of a quiet inner triumph with an admixture of undeniable melancholy." (F&T 455–58).

This stage of "maximal relinquishment of narcissistic delusions" is what Kohut calls "wisdom." As Kohut explains, "Wisdom may thus be defined as a stable attitude of the personality toward life and the world, an attitude that is formed through the integration of the cognitive function with humor, acceptance of transience, and a firmly cathected system of values." Wisdom represents for Kohut "a maximal relinquishment of narcissistic delusions, including the acceptance of the inevitability of death, without an abandonment of cognitive and emotional involvements." It is "the ultimate act of cognition, i. e., the acknowledgment of the limits and of the finiteness of the self"—the victorious outcome of the lifework of the total personality in acquiring broadly based knowledge and in transforming archaic modes of narcissism into ideals, humor, and a sense of supraindividual participation in the world" (F&T 458–9).

I read *Paterson,* Books I–IV, as the "victorious outcome of the lifework" of Williams's total personality, though it will take the remainder of this chapter to show how the mechanism of Williams's dialectic leads to the "ironic development" of this "wisdom." Still, I think we can see how that moment of identification of the "momentary deity" is analogous to an empathic identification with the world around us—the "naming" of an act of narcissistic transformation in a moment of "discovery." This "discovery" not only marks an extension of the self, but also points out its limitations and transience in the necessary ephemerality of that "god." Moreover, the "name" that we use to identify the "momentary deity" is itself cathected with narcissistic libidinal energies, though this energy, this language, needs to be constantly renewed if it is not to lead to the reification of this "God-term."

In Cassirer, as well as in Williams and Burke, it is when those momentary gods we have named become reified, deified, and worshiped that trouble begins. Hierarchies become established, and ways of seeing the world, as well as ways of seeing our self in that world, become the objects of religious devotion to which others must bow down. Language, our way of interpreting the world and our self, if reduced to some calculus (both a symbolic notation for mathematical computation and another name for a kidney stone) runs the risk of becoming at best a stale custom or habit through which we operate unfeelingly in the world or, at worst, a way of seeing the world that has become so set, so "factual," or so "prosaic," that it actually divorces us from reality, and, "Divorce is / the sign of knowledge in our time" in *Paterson*. This is why language and its link to sense impressions and *not* to some reified God-term is so important to Williams, why he says in *The Descent of Winter:*

> God—Sure if it means sense. "God" is poetic for the unobtainable. Sense is hard to get but it can be got. Certainly that destroys "God," it destroys everything that interferes with simple clarity of apprehension.
>
> (*CP I* 312)

Williams's sense of language runs parallel to his sense "that a man in himself is a city" (*P* 253), especially when the language makes the man or, in the case of *Paterson,* makes the city. These relationships between language, man, and city compose a final analogue to Wittgenstein's later philosophy. In the *Philosophical Investigations,* at the end of his discussion of Augustine's ostensive theories of language, Wittgenstein says:

> Do not be troubled by the fact that [the] languages [we have examined] consist only of orders. If you want to say that this shews them to be incomplete, ask yourself whether our language is complete;—whether it was so before the symbolism of chemistry and the notation of the infinitesimal calculus were incorporated in it; for these are, so to speak, suburbs of our language. (And how many houses or streets does it take before a town begins to be a town?) Our language can be seen as an ancient city: a maze of little streets and squares, of old and new houses, and of houses with additions from various periods; and this surrounded by a multitude of new boroughs with straight regular streets and uniform houses.
>
> (*PI* 8)

Those "suburbs of our language" are those traditions, customs, and habits that enable us to play many different sorts of "language games," like those rules of grammar and writing that enable us to read prose. They are those familiar old buildings and streets whose history makes up Wittgenstein's city. But what happens when those rules and preconceptions become so rigid that they no longer allow for any kind of "discovery"? When those familiar old buildings become prison-houses? And most important, what happens when those rules determine who lives where in our city, or even if they're allowed to live there at all? I think we can begin to see both what's at stake in Williams's notion of language and how it connects with notions of culture and politics. Williams's work has always engaged the political, both directly—as he does in examples such as the brief mentions of Woodrow Wilson and "a ramshackle home for millworkers" in *Spring and All* (*CP I* 185 & 180) and his discussion of Social Credit in *Paterson* (*P* 180–85)— as well as theoretically—as he does in his ideas about language, his "dialectic development" of prose and poetry, and his insistence on the avoidance of the "acquisitive understanding" and "religious dogmatism" (*CP I* 202) that form preconceptions. It is for these reasons that a writer like Eliot is anathema to Williams. Eliot's notions of tradition, culture, and community not only embrace "religious dogma," but also value adherence to a code of racial and "religious unity" so highly that "reasons of race and religion combine to make any large number of free-thinking Jews undesirable" in his ideal city.[40]

III

When poetry becomes prose, in Williams's terms, the rules of the game have become so calcified that the "radiant gist" of the extraordinary moment—the discovery of the "beautiful things" and "momentary gods" in this world—threatens to be overwhelmed by set ways of seeing reality, of being locked within a "prison-house of language."[41] Tradition and history combine for Williams to assert this "prosaic" effect. It is that effect which maintains that cleavage between man and city, man and woman, as well as between prose and poetry. It is possible to read the prose passages of *Paterson,* particularly in Books I–II, as simply reflecting this notion of a cleavage between poetry and prose. It seems necessary for both poet and reader to leap successfully from "prose to the process of the imagination" in order to break up the staleness that is "the greatest characteristic of the present age" and to free the language, the city, and the people of *Paterson,* all of whom have become, as Williams says:

> Stale as a whale's breath: breath!
> Breath!
>
> Patch leaped but Mrs. Cummings shrieked
> and fell—unseen (though
> she had been standing there beside her husband half
> an hour or more twenty feet from the edge).
>
> : a body found next spring
> frozen in an ice-cake; or a body
> fished next day from the muddy swirl—
> both silent, uncommunicative.

(*P* 19–20)

To some readers of Williams, it is the prose passages themselves that are the "divisions and imbalances / of his whole concept," as they read these passages as containing "No ideas but / in the facts" (*P* 27). In particular, Ralph Nash, in an article entitled, "The Use of Prose in *Paterson*," classifies the prose passages as either "the prose of Contemporary Fact" or "the prose of Historical Fact," and he sees their function largely in terms of providing "counterpoint" and "documentation" for the rest of the poem.[42] To be sure, these passages do appear as factual documents (bits of "history"), separated from the rest of the poem by a different typography, and Nash's distinctions are significant ones. Moreover, according to Williams's definitions in *Spring and All* and *The Wedge,* the prose passages should "follow to enlighten." Still, Nash takes the prose passages to be "unshaped blocks of foreign material":

> The direct presentation of these fragments, *without their being shaped into the rhythms and diction of the surrounding poetry,* is of course an artistic device. No doubt Williams intends it partly as a forceful marriage of his poem's world with that world of reality from which he is fearful of divorcing himself. But it has also a special effect of presenting the Poet as Recorder, relatively detached and objective, reading his morning mail as he might read a history of Paterson, acting somewhat as the scientist might in checking his guesses against the facts. (my emphasis)[43]

As we will see below, however, these passages *have* been shaped, and while they do provide a kind of counterpoint to the rest of the poem, they also contain the "radiant gist" of the most lyrical passages. *Paterson* asserts that "they are— No ideas but / in the facts," but it also tells us more emphatically to "—Say it, no ideas but in things—" (*P* 6), and the prose passages are both facts and things. We need to see the poetry that seems "to occur in the prose as if hidden there"[44] in order to understand fully the dialectical development that Williams achieves in *Paterson.* As Williams said in *Spring and All,* we must take "the jump between fact and the imaginative reality" and, like Kohut's analyst observing "the living ebb and flow of the analysand's thoughts and feelings," recognize that

> the study of all human activity is the delineation of the cresence and ebb of this force, shifting from class to class and location to location—rhythm: the wave rhythm of Shakespeare watching clowns and kings sliding into nothing.
>
> (*CP I* 221)

For the poet of the poem, the morning mail *is* a history of Paterson, and it discloses the rhythms and measure that make clear the language of the man who is a city. These rhythms in *Paterson* are a "cresence and ebb" from prose to poetry, from fact to thing, from violence to beauty, but none of these forces is pure. Each is "an / interpenetration, both ways," and all are Paterson. As these rhythms amass, "rolling / up the sum, by defective means" (*P* 3), moving from the most prosaic description of an artesian well to the most lyrical evocation of "beautiful thing," we find that, as Williams once said in "Reply to a Young Scientist," "one plus one plus one plus one plus one equals not five but one."[45]

The prose passages in *Paterson,* both documents and letters, fall into four categories: those that Williams quotes verbatim, those that he revises slightly, those that he alters radically, and those that he creates himself (very few in number). Actually, I suspect that we would find some ''factual document'' behind all of the prose passages, as each one seems to have been selected for, or shaped to evoke, a particular rhythm or measure. For example, even the Sarah Cumming passage (*P* 14), quoted nearly verbatim from Barber's *Historical Collections of New Jersey*, contains subtle changes that affect its flow[46]:

> From Alden's Collections, we take the annexed account of the death of Mrs. Cumming, who perished at this spot about 30 years since:

> Mrs. Sarah Cumming consort of the Rev. Hooper Cumming, of Newark, was a daughter of the late Mr. John Emmons, of Portland, in the district of Maine. *She was a lady of an amiable disposition, a well-cultivated mind, distinguished intelligence, and most exemplary piety; and she was much endeared to a large circle of respectable friends and connections.* She had been married about 2 months, and was blessed with a flattering prospect of no common share of temporal felicity and usefulness in the sphere which Providence had assigned her; but oh, how uncertain is the continuance of every earthly joy!

> On Saturday, the 20th of June, 1812, Mr. Cumming rode with his wife to Paterson, in order to supply, by presbyterial appointment, a destitute congregation in that place, on the following day. On Monday morning, he went with his beloved companion to show her the falls of the Passaic, and the surrounding beautiful, wild, and romantic scenery,—little expecting the solemn event which was to ensue.

> Having ascended the flights of stairs, Mr. and Mrs. Cumming walked over the solid ledge to the vicinity of the cataract, charmed with the wonderful prospect, and making various remarks upon the stupendous works of nature around them. At length they took their station on the brow of the solid rock, which overhangs the basin, six or eight rods from the falling water, where thousands have stood before, and where there is a fine view *of most* of the sublime curiosities of the place. When they had enjoyed the luxury of the scene for a considerable time, Mr. Cumming said, ''My dear, I believe it is time for us to set our face homeward;'' and, at the same moment, turned round in order to lead the way. He instantly heard the voice of distress, looked back, and his wife was gone!

> *Mrs. Cumming had complained of a dizziness early in the morning; and, as her eyes had been some time fixed upon the uncommon objects before her, when she moved with the view to retrace her steps, it is probable she was seized with the same malady, tottered, and in a moment fell, a distance of 74 feet, into the frightful gulf!* Mr. Cumming's sensations on the distressing occasion may, in some measure, be conceived, but they cannot be described. He was on the borders of distraction, and, scarcely knowing what he did, would have plunged into the abyss, had it not been kindly ordered in providence that a young man should be near, who instantly flew to him, like a guardian angel, and held him from a step which his reason, at the time, could not have prevented. This young man led him from the precipice, and conducted him to the ground below the stairs. Mr. Cumming forced himself out of the hands of his protector, and ran with violence, in order to leap into the fatal flood. His young friend, however, caught him once more, *and held him till reason had resumed her throne. He then left him, to call the neighboring people to the place.* Immediate search was made, and diligently continued through the day, for the body of Mrs. Cumming; but to no purpose. On the

following morning, her mortal part was found in a depth of 42 feet, and, the same day, was conveyed to Newark.

On Wednesday, her funeral was attended by a numerous concourse of people. Her remains were carried into the church, where a pathetic and impressive discourse, happily adapted to the mournful occasion, was delivered by the Rev. James Richards. Solemn indeed was the scene. A profound silence pervaded the vast assembly. Every one seemed to hang upon the lips of the speaker. In every quarter, the sigh of sympathy and regret echoed to the tender and affecting address.

The italicized sections show the parts of the original that Williams altered, and the most dramatic changes are those omissions he made that change the character of Mrs. Cumming from "a lady of amiable disposition" who suffered from "a dizziness" to a silent, forgotten first wife—a figure of the blocked, divorced, feminine, poetic imagination. But these omissions, along with the more subtle changes in capitalization and the additions of ellipses, also alter the rhythm and the flow of the passage, as well as change the voice of the narrator from the stiff and more knowing tone of the original to a softer, yet still removed, narrator who drifts off into his own brief lapses of silence. Finally, by leaving out the last paragraph, Williams enables the story to join more easily with the verse that follows.

This kind of "metrical shaping" is most apparent in passages like the Ramapos passage (*P* 12), where Williams has successfully copied the "grammar" and rhythms of the historical works he had been reading.[47] The major effect of this shaping is to give this passage a particular voice, and here the voice, as it is in all of the documents, is that of the detached, authoritative observer—a historian or a journalist. This type of writing corresponds to one of the "two phases of language" that Williams discusses in "The Logic of Modern Letters, Primary" in *The Embodiment of Knowledge* (1928–30). There he says

Language is made up of words and their configurations, (the clause, the sentence, the poetic line—as well as the subtler, style); to these might be added the spaces between the words (for measurement's sake) were these not properly to be considered themselves words—of a sort.

Language is again divided according to its use into two main phases. 1. That by which it is made secondary to the burden of ideas—information, what not—for service to philosophy, science, journalism. This includes the gross use of language. And 2. where language is itself primary and ideas subservient to language. This is the field of letters, whence the prevalence of fiction and the preeminence of poetry in this division.

(*EK* 141)

Williams makes two other quick points worth noting here:

These two major uses of language complement each other—or should in a well-adjusted intelligence.

In the modern American world the proper interrelationship between the two is hardly understood at all. The practice of letters is neglected with serious results—sensed but dumbly even by the ablest.

The notion of these "two phases" is echoed in the prose description of the Ramapos, and, consequently, we are forced to consider their "proper interrelation-ship":

> If there was not beauty, there was a strangeness and a bold association of wild
> and cultured life grew up together in the Ramapos: two phases.
>
> $\qquad\qquad\qquad\qquad\qquad\qquad\qquad\qquad\qquad\qquad\qquad\qquad$ (*P* 12)

The two phases here—"a bold association of wild and cultured life"—also have a relationship to the two phases of culture that Williams discusses in "The American Background,"[48] and their later re-presentation in the perverted "Idyl" of Corydon and Phyllis (also from Ramapo) is a significant continuation of both the economic and the sexual themes of the poem—one to which we will return in Chapter 5. When we put these lines back in their immediate context, however, the relationship between these "two phases" and the "two phases of language" becomes clearer, as does the relationship between the prose and the poetry.

The preceding verse, starting with "They begin!" (*P* 11), gives us images of infertility and dissatisfaction, and it ends with

> The language, the language
> $\qquad\qquad$ fails them
> They do not know the words
> $\qquad\qquad$ or have not
> the courage to use them   .
> $\qquad\qquad\qquad$ —girls from
> families that have decayed and
> taken to the hills: no words.
> They may look at the torrent in
> $\qquad\qquad$ their minds
> And it is foreign to them. .
> They turn their backs
> and grow faint—but recover!
> $\qquad\qquad$ Life is sweet
> they say: the language!
> $\qquad\qquad\qquad$ —the language
> is divorced from their minds,
> the language   .   .   the language!
>
> $\qquad\qquad\qquad\qquad\qquad\qquad\qquad\qquad\qquad\qquad\qquad$ (*P* 11–12)

The association between "the language" and the "two phases" may seem a bit tentative here, but we need to recognize the complicated "development" that runs throughout the poem, expanding the thought of Mr. Paterson to include the poly-glottic voices of his city.[49] For example, the immediate antecedent to the pronoun "they" in the lines above is obviously "the girls," but the "them" in "the lan-guage fails them" refers to those "few" who went "to the coast," and the "They" in "They sink back into the loam" seems to refer to the unpollenated seeds that the "tongue of the bee" missed. Moving forward into the prose passage, we see also that the "girls from / families that have decayed and / taken to the hills" could refer to the descendants of "Jackson's Whites" who "ran in the woods" (*P*

12). Further, the "They" in "They begin!" recalls the previous lines—"Around the falling waters the Furies hurl! / Violence gathers, spins in their heads summoning / them"—and here the "they" seems to be the crowd of "They craved the miraculous!" But the intervening prose passages complicate the easy identification of an antecedent. "They" could just as easily be the huge "twaalft," abundant in the Falls basin, or it could be the heterogeneous 1870 population of 33,579.

Fortunately, this "they" in "They craved the miraculous!" has already been somewhat defined in the preceding lines:

> Say it! No ideas but in things. Mr.
> Paterson has gone away
> to rest and write. Inside the bus one sees
> his thoughts sitting and standing. His
> thoughts alight and scatter—
>
> Who are these people (how complex
> the mathematic) among whom I see myself
> in the regularly ordered plateglass of
> his thoughts, glimmering before shoes and bicycles?
> They walk incommunicado, the
> equation is beyond solution, yet
> its sense is clear—that they may live
> his thought is listed in the Telephone
> Directory—
>
> (P 9–10)

The "complex mathematic," the unexplained shift from "thoughts" to "thought" and the mysterious "I" again recall that "equation beyond solution" that Williams gave in "Reply to a Young Scientist"—"one plus one plus one plus one plus one equals not five but one." All of the characters and objects of *Paterson* spill in and out of each other, packed tight with detail like the image of the "multiple seed" (P 4), and ultimately reduce themselves to one: Paterson—the poet, the city, the woman, the crowd, the park, the falls, and so on. The complications in antecedent caused by the intervening prose passages merely add to this list.

Burke points out in his *Grammar* that

> although *all* the characters in a dramatic or dialectic development are necessary
> qualifiers of the definition, there is usually some one character that enjoys the rôle
> of *primus inter pares*. For whereas any of the characters may be viewed in terms
> of any other, this one character may be taken as the summarizing vessel, or syn-
> ecdochic representative, of the development as a whole.
>
> (GM 516)

Paterson, the man who is a city, is just such a "summarizing vessel," and like the Caribs of *In the American Grain* and Kohut's extended "self," he has "many souls in one body" (*IAG* 39). We can begin to see, then, that these prose passages are not only facts or historical information for the rest of the poem, but also "ideas in things." The "two phases" of life that grew up together in the Ramapos, for example, reflect the wildness of the poetic imagination and the culture of prose that is "adjusted" for service to journalism and science, an adjustment that abstracts our sense of reality and, through its own "grammar of transference," reduces people to historical "facts" and economic commodities. Curiously, though, it is in just this "accurate adjustment to the exposition of fact" that these prose documents become parts of the second phase of language, "where language is itself primary and ideas subservient to language." In particular, three ideas central to *Paterson* become subservient to the frozen, historical prose of this passage—the tranquil wildness of the common "things" found at Ringwood, the violence of the hangings of the traitors at Pompton and of the sixty Tuscaroras who had massacred a white settlement in Tennessee, and the economics of slavery and of "providing women" for soldiers. The prosaic "grammar" that Williams recreates here divorces the emotions associated with these ideas from the facts that describe them. Consequently, the prose becomes a kind of poetic line in which the "force of the imagination," the "night mind" of place, remains frozen, much in the same way that the "young and latest" queen is frozen in the *Geographic* picture, or Sam Patch is frozen in a block of ice. The "movements of imagination revealed in words" that are related to the form of poetry here take the form of prose—a prose that overwhelms their ability to crystallize and break free.

Williams's use of the Ramapo document establishes a concrete example of the question posed in the very first line of the poem—" 'Rigor of beauty is in the quest. But how will you find beauty / when it is locked in the mind past all remonstrance?' " The answer provided in the manuscripts of *Paterson*—"It is not in the things about us unless transposed there by our employment. Make it free, then, by the art you have to enter those starved and broken pieces"[50]—reveals that the way in which Williams uses his art to begin to free the beauty is to recreate, through the symbolic action of his own poetic performance, an attempted cathexis of narcissistic energies in which the "self" can "enter those starved and broken pieces" and the reader can participate through his or her own process of "identity" and "identification." In doing so, Williams establishes a cycle of cognitive action that echoes the movement of the Falls and runs throughout the poem.

Having delineated the giants of the place—the poet figures of dogs, Paterson, Peter the dwarf, and Sam Patch; the wife / flower / multiple seed images of Garrett Mountain, Cress, the first wife, and Sarah Cumming—Williams tells us that "Divorce is / the sign of knowledge in our time" and begins this cyclical attempt at freedom:

> Which is to say, though it be poorly
> said, there is a first wife
> and a first beauty, complex, ovate—
> the woody sepals standing back under
> the stress to hold it there, innate
>
> a flower within a flower whose history
> (within the mind) crouching
> among the ferny rocks, laughs at the names
> by which they think to trap it. Escapes!
> Never by running but by lying still—
>
> A history that has, by its den in the
> rocks, boles and fangs, its own cane-brake

> whence, half hid, canes and stripes
> blending, it grins (beauty defied)
> not for the sake of the encyclopedia
>
> Were we near enough its stinking breath
> would fell us. The temple upon
> the rock is its brother, whose majesty
> lies in jungles—made to spring,
> at the rifle-shot of learning: to kill
>
> and grind those bones:
>
> (*P* 21–22)

This "history / (within the mind)" of "a flower within a flower" grins "not for the sake of the encyclopedia." It remains hidden from us, and the violence suggested at its discovery never takes place. Consequently, the "bird alighting . . . falls forward . . . among the twigs," and "The horse, the bull / the whole din of fracturing thought / as it falls tinnily to nothing upon the streets" combine with other "things" in

> Pithy philosophies of
> daily exits and entrances, with books
> propping up one end of the shaky table—
> The vague accuracies of events dancing two
> and two with language which they
> forever surpass—and dawns
> tangled in darkness—
>
> (*P* 23)

The frozen language of the prose history that the beauty of "things" will "forever surpass," the divorce of feeling from fact, and the silence caused by the failure of language, all combine here to thwart the attempt at communion or cathexis:

> we sit and talk
> I wish to be with you abed, we two
> as if the bed were the bed of a stream
> —I have much to say to you
>
> (*P* 23)

But "the stream has no language," and the "silence speaks of the giants / who have died in the past and have / returned to those scenes unsatisfied" (*P* 24). We end this section with the cold, intellectual voice of Edward Dahlberg, who separates himself from Williams and "won't weep over Poe, or Rilke, or Dickinson, or Gogol, while [he] turn[s] away the few waifs and Ishmaels of the spirit in this country." Even though he has said that the "artist is an Ishmael," for Dahlberg, "Ishmael means affliction" (*P* 28).

Still, this "first beauty", this "flower within a flower whose history / (within the mind) crouching / among the ferny rocks, laughs at the names / by which they think to trap it," forces us, I think, to reconsider that name—history—that we have so far used to trap these prose sections. Through his dialectic of poetry and prose, Williams forces us to recognize that history, like prose, must not be considered a clear, transparent exposition of "facts" or an objective presentation of the "truth" about what really happened long ago. History here is a representation, a kind of writing. And as we saw in the Sarah Cumming passage, history is a writing whose cold violence can either annihilate or reify those "momentary gods" within its rational language, imposing a single voice on the man who is a city. These ideas about history can be best understood if we look for a moment at an "anecdote about history" provided by Kenneth Burke. In *The Philosophy of Literary Form*, Burke asks:

> Where does the drama [of human action] get its materials? From the "unending conversation" that is going on at the point in history when we are born. Imagine that you enter a parlor. You come late. When you arrive, others have long preceded you, and they are engaged in a heated discussion, a discussion too heated for them to pause and tell you exactly what it is about. In fact, the discussion had already begun long before any of them got there, so that no one present is qualified to retrace for you all the steps that had gone before. You listen for a while, until you decide that you have caught the tenor of the argument; then you put in your oar. Someone answers; you answer him; another comes to your defense; another aligns himself against you, to either the embarrassment or gratification of your opponent, depending upon the quality of your ally's assistance. However, the discussion is interminable. The hour grows late, you must depart. And you do depart, with the discussion still vigorously in progress.
>
> (*PLF* 110–11)

This "unending conversation" of history, this complicated interweaving of past and present, tradition and change, is evident in Williams's inclusions of these past arguments that have already gone on before us. He even gives us—if we remember that the Sarah Cumming passage in Barber's *Collection* is already taken from Alden's *Collections*—conversations within those conversations. As Burke points out elsewhere

> History in this sense would be a dialectic of characters in which, for instance, we should never expect to see "feudalism" overthrown by "capitalism" and "capitalism" succeeded by some manner of national or international or non-national or neo-national or post-national socialism—but rather should note elements of all such positions (or "voices") existing always, but attaining greater clarity of expression or imperiousness of proportion of one period than another.
>
> (*GM* 513)

Williams's "history" in *Paterson* resists notions of teleological development, and in Chapters 4 and 5 I will discuss how it shares in Pound and Eliot's notions of "contemporaneity" but differs radically from their "definitions of culture." For now, it is important that we see how Williams "enters" these "starved and broken pieces," and through his re-presenting these historical "facts," participates in that "conversation" that makes up history. Moreover, the "tenor" of these arguments—the tone of the detached, authoritative observer—points out the danger of our passively receiving our history from a single voice rather than entering into and uncovering that conversation for ourselves. It shows how the language of *Paterson* can be reduced to a single discourse or tradition (the sad ghost of Eliot should beckon to us at this point), excluding all difference and becoming itself a god to be worshiped. This idea will become clear if, by collapsing our analogues, we locate Burke's "unending conversation" in Wittgenstein's city, within the cozy confines of an exclusive all-male club: a place where no women, no blacks, no Hispanics, no Indians, no Jews—in short, a place where there are "NO DOGS ALLOWED AT LARGE" (*P* 61). Through our "identification" of this particular "grammar of transference," this "perspicuous representation" which forces us to "see connexions" (*PI* 49), we further our identification with Paterson, and say along with him

> .... I cannot stay here
> to spend my life looking into the past:
>
> the future's no answer. I must
> find my meaning and lay it, white,
> beside the sliding water: myself—
> comb out the language—or succumb
>
> —whatever the complexion. Let
> me out! (Well, go!) this rhetoric
> is real!

(P 145)

We also can begin to see, I think, why *Paterson* is such a violent poem. In order to break up the staleness, destroy these old customs and habits, Williams needs to use violence if he is to begin to *change* history. Someone once asked Woody Allen if sex were always dirty, and he replied, "Yes, but only if it's done properly," and I think if we were to ask Williams if making something new, if releasing the "radiant gist" of poetry were always violent, I think the answer would also be, "Yes, but only if it's done properly." Freeing the language, freeing the beauty—the poetry that lies hidden in the prose—always takes place through violence in Williams: through the violence of the white men that leads to the forming of Jackson's Whites, as well as the violent disruption of meter Williams achieves in his "relatively stable foot."[51] In Chapter 2, we will see how this violence functions in a psychic economy of destruction and rapprochement that allows for a mutual recognition of self and other based on the ideas of Heinz Kohut and Jessica Benjamin. For now, however, we need only see that this violence acts as a kind of alternate economy—an irrational, sexual economy of expenditure that Williams opposes to the supposedly rational arithmetic of Alexander Hamilton's SUM plan or the cool reason of the historian reporting a massacre. Consequently, many of the prose documents contain extremely violent events, and this violence becomes all the more brutal in the cold, factual way in which it is related. As Williams writes in "Letter to an Australian Editor"

> Destruction, according to the Babylonia[n] order of creation, comes before crea-
> tion. . . . The same today. We must be destructive first to free ourselves from forms
> accreting to themselves forms we despise. Where does the past lodge in the older
> forms? Tear it out.[52]

The poetry we need to hear in these prose documents is a violent poetry of people divorced from feelings and things: a separation, a dissonance that leads to the most chilling acts of murder. This violence, however, is just as much the violence of the contrast "between the mythic beauty of the Falls and Mountain and the industrial hideousness" of Paterson that leads Williams to invent the "variable foot" of the "three stress line" in writing "The descent beckons" (*P* 78–79)—Williams's "solution of the problem of modern verse" as well as one of the most lyrical and hopeful sections in the entire poem. This "new measure," which begins Book II, is preceded by a short prose piece describing the violence of an earthquake on December 7 (Pearl Harbor Day), 1737, and by Williams's own "reply to the Greek and Latin" of Eliot and Pound "with the bare hands"—a classical justification for a "Deformed verse . . . suited for a deformed morality"— a change in meter "more within the sphere of prose and common speech" that did the "utmost violence to the rhythmical structure" (*P* 40).

The relationship between the frozen violence of the prose documents and the violence needed to free the language, to break up those grammars of language that divorce us from our world, appears explicitly in a scatological joke in the second section of Book IV. In the middle of the verse section about Madame Curie, herself a combination of the science of prose and the poetry of invention, Williams quotes Chaucer's Sir Thopas:

> Namoor—
> Thy drasty rymyng is not
> worth a toord
> —and Chaucer seemed to think so too for he stopped and went
>   on in prose   .
>
> (*P* 176)

Williams follows these prose/verse lines with a verbatim copy of a section of a 1950 *JAMA* article about the reporting of "diarrheal disturbances without fear of economic reprisal," suggesting in a crude way how the "constipated" language could also be made to "flow" more freely (Williams uses these exact words in a 1942 letter to Charles Abbott about the problems he had been having in arranging the material for *Paterson*).[53]

A more serious use of this violent prose comes in the last section of Book IV. In this section, which begins "Haven't you forgotten your virgin purpose, / the language?" (*P* 186), Williams includes the bloody murder of Jonathan Hopper, a brief section urging to "Kill the explicit sentence . . . and expand our meaning" (*P* 188), the exhumed body of Peter the Dwarf (*P* 192), a letter from Ginsburg about a taproom "filled with gas, ready to explode . . . that is really at the heart of what is to be known" (*P* 193), and perhaps the most brutal murder of all, the killing of six-month old Nancy Goodell by her father, who

> told the police he had killed the child by twice snapping the wooden tray of a high chair into the baby's face Monday morning when her crying annoyed him as he was feeding her. Dr. George Surgent, the county physician, said she died of a fractured skull.
>
> (*P* 195)

Williams's question of language and violence is in part the poet's question paraphrased in Allen Tate's translation of *The Vigil of Venus*—"When shall I like Philomena the swallow suffer violence and be moved to sing?"[54]—a question also alluded to at the end of Eliot's *Waste Land.* For Williams, though, this violence is "at the base of modern letters—of modernism"—and it is at the heart of the prose works Williams most admired, those of Gertrude Stein and James Joyce:

> It is to divorce words from the enslavement of the prevalent cliches that all violent torsions (Stein, Joyce) have occurred; violent in direct relation to the gravity and success of their enslavements.
>
> (*EK* 143)

This cycle of prose violence to poetic freedom is nowhere more clear than at the close of Book IV. Just before the newspaper report on the murder of Nancy Goodell, which occurred on Williams's sixty-seventh birthday, Williams "shifts his change" into the prose-like lines he had learned from the young poet Byron Vazakas. This final section, separated from the rest of Book IV by a series of heavy dots, begins with a continuation of what appears to be a mixture of historical and personal reminiscences but in fact is actually a mosaic created from a historical prose document. What Williams has done in these lines is to free the "things" of Longwell's *A Little Story of Old Paterson As Told By An Old Man* by giving them a new measure:

CHAPTER III.
THE OLD GODWIN HOUSE

In the early days of Paterson, the breathing spot of the village was the triangle square bounded by Park street (now lower Main street) and Bank street. Not including the falls, it was the prettiest spot in town, well shaded with trees, with a common in the center where the country circus pitched its tents in the old days. On the Park street side it ran down to the river. On the Bank street side it ran to a roadway leading to the barnyard of the Godwin House, the barnyard taking up part of the north side of the park. When I was a little shaver the circus was an antiquated affair. It was no such head splitting affair as the boy of today sees. It was only a small tent, one ring show. Menageries and shows traveled separately in those days, and they did not allow circuses to perform in the afternoon, because that would close up the cotton mills. Time in those days was

From *Paterson,* pp. 195–96

In the early days of Paterson, the breathing spot of the village was the triangle square bounded by Park Street (now lower Main St.) and Bank Street. Not including the Falls it was the prettiest spot in town. Well shaded by trees with a common in the center where the country circus pitched its tents.
On the Park Street side it ran down to the river. On the Bank Street side it ran to a roadway leading to the barn yard of the Godwin House, the barnyard taking up part of the north side of the park.

The circus was an antiquated affair, only a small tent, one ring show. They didn't allow circuses to perform in the afternoon because that would close up the mills. Time in those days was precious. Only in the evenings. But they were sure to parade their horses about the town about the time the mills stopped work. The upshot of the matter was, the town turned out to the circus in the evening. It was lighted

too precious to allow a circus to inter-
fere with work. They only performed in
the evening, but were sure to parade
their horses about the time the mills
stopped work, and the upshot of the
matter was—well, the town turned out
to the circus in the evening. The cir-
cuses in those days were lighted by
candles especially made for the show.
They were giants and as large as the
shell of a 12-inch gun. They were fas-
tened in boards hung on wires about the
tent—a peculiar contrivance. The giant
candles were placed on the bottom
boards, and two rows of smaller can-
dles, one above the other tapering to a
point, forming a very pretty scene and
giving plenty of light. The candles
lasted during the performance, present-
ing a weird but dazzling spectacle in
contrast with the showy performers.

in those days by candles especially
made for the show. They were giants fastened
to boards hung on wires about the tent,
a peculiar contrivance. The giant candles
were placed on the bottom boards, and two
rows of smaller candles one above the other
tapering to a point, forming a very pretty
scene and giving plenty of light.

The candles lasted during the performance
presenting a weird but dazzling spectacle
in contrast with the showy performers—

Interestingly, it is just this type of line that Randall Jarrell criticized for being
"exactly like the stuff you produce when you are demonstrating to a class that
any prose whatsoever can be converted into four-stress accentual verse simply
by inserting line endings every four stresses."[55] Though Williams nearly does do
just this, particularly in the verses about the circus, the effect of these lines is
much greater than Jarrell assumes. By breaking up the language of Longwell,
Williams reveals the bits of poetry hidden within the sentimental prose. The "old
names" are now remembered, and the beauty of "things" crystallizes in the
images of the circus and its giant candles, and of the birds who no longer fall
"forward nevertheless / among the twigs" (*P* 22), but rather "flutter and bathe
in the little / pool in the rocks formed by the falling / mist—of the Falls" (*P*
197). For Williams, this movement from the measure of prose to the measure
of poetry reveals both a condition of the world in which that measure is found,
as well as a necessary, violent, cyclical action within the world of human thought.
By using the jagged, prose-like lines of Byron Vazakas to transform the language
of Longwell's story, Williams finds a middle ground between the frozen sections
of historical prose and the intense moments of his three stress lines. They become
a moment of calm in the swing from "the exposition of fact" to "the crystal-
lization of the imagination."

By "identifying" his voice with Longwell's, however, Williams does more
than simply enter into the "unending conversation" of "history." Williams em-
ploys a "grammar of translation" in a creative transformation of narcissistic en-
ergies that momentarily "identifies" his voice with Longwell's. Actually, since
the reminiscences retold in *A Little Story of Old Paterson* are supposedly those
of Longwell's grandfather, Williams joins his voice through the action of em-

pathic identification with a string of symbolic recollections that become a temporal and spatial expansion of his "self" into both "city" and "history." Moreover, as part of the movement from prose to poetry, this section begins Paterson's final transformation toward "wisdom" through the use of empathy, introspection, and observation based on the symbolic reconstruction of "personal experience."

This "cresence and ebb" that delineate "the study of all human activity" becomes clear as we slip back into the frozen violence of the murders of John S. Van Winkle and his wife, whose murderer, John Johnson, shows an even further separation of fact from feeling as he has no reaction to the killings other than "an expression of pity, he denying any knowledge of participation in the inhuman butchery" (*P* 197). From this horror we are immediately propelled into the even more disturbing rhythms of Williams's variable foot. Here "hacked corpses," "a sea of blood //—the sea that sucks in all rivers," Iwo Jima, and the escalating war in Korea—"(October 10, 1950)"—all combine ironically in a life-affirming shout that the sea—"our nostalgic/ mother in whom the dead, enwombed again / cry out to us to return"—"the blood dark sea! / . . . is NOT / our home" (*P* 198–201). And so we flow back into the prose/verse lines in which Paterson "rises from the sea where the river appears to have lost its identity and accompanied by his faithful bitch, obviously a Chesapeake Bay retriever, turns inland toward Camden where Walt Whitman, much traduced, lived the latter years of his life and died" (*A* 392). With this turning inland, the section concludes with the suggestion that the cycle will continue, even though John Johnson is hung "in full view of thousands who had gathered on Garrett Mountain and adjacent house tops to witness the spectacle" (*P* 202), and we are told that, despite what Eliot said in "The Hollow Men,"

> This is the blast
> the eternal close
> the spiral
> the final somersault
> the end.
> (*P* 202)

In *I Wanted to Write a Poem,* Williams tells us that "*Paterson IV* ends with the protagonist breaking through the bushes, identifying himself with the land, with America. He finally will die but it can't be categorically stated that death ends *anything*" (*IWWP* 22). In this final acceptance of transience and death, then, Williams displays those qualities of the decathected narcissistic self that Kohut calls "wisdom." Humor, quiet resignation, and a shift from the cosmic identification inherent in his "translation" of Longwell to the recognition of temporal, spatial, and poetic limitations, merge in Paterson's shout that, "the blood dark sea . . . is NOT / our home." In this final scene, Williams swerves from both Whitman's Mother-Sea in "Out of the Cradle Endlessly Rocking" and Pound's own translation of Homer's "wine dark sea" to turn inland after having spit out the seed of some beach plums. At age sixty-eight, melancholy with violent wisdom, Williams heads home.

IV

As an integral part of the poem, the prose documents join the other "voices" in *Paterson* in that sometimes strident conversation of culture and ideas. Economics, for example, comes up not only in the Hamilton / SUM passages, but also in more subtle ways—in the mention that Fred Goodell was a "$40-a-week factory worker" and in suggesting that Johnson's real object was "doubtless money." The constant, adversarial presence of Eliot in *Paterson* juxtaposes a "definition of culture" that leashes its "dogs" to a stone bench within a wall, with one that has to let its "Musty's" run loose (*P* 53–54). And Pound's command to "re read *all* the Gk tragedies in / Loeb" is answered with the contents of an artesian well that follows the statement " . . . The fact that the rock salt of England, and of some of the other salt mines of Europe, is found in rocks of the same age as this, raises the question whether it may not also be found here" with a clichéd quotation from Gray's "Elegy Written in a Country Churchyard" (*P* 138–40). By seeing the prose documents as both "facts" and "things," we discover that movement from prose "with the poetry hidden in it" to poetry that reveals the lyrical, ordinary beauty of "beautiful things" by breaking down the blocks of uranium, the blocks of prose, and the blocks of silence. We also develop our own "grammar of translation" that grounds the "radiant gist" of Williams's American culture.

All of the figures in the poem can be seen as voices that act dialectically toward this development—releasing the radiant gist of poetry that will enable them to free the language or capture that "beautiful thing" in their midst. By "wrenching [herself] free from patterned standardized feminine feelings," even Cress has escaped the life of complete silence and suicide that we see in Sarah Cumming, and her voice is, in part, the feminine voice of the poem made audible. And her attack on Dr. P is more accurate than she knows. "Cress" was "some-*thing* . . . to sit up and take notice of," and as a "thing" she is both "something disconnected from life" and the very essence of it, something which "could be turned by [Williams] into literature."[56] The Cress letters also serve to make clear what Williams sees is the very nature of the poetic process—a process that, in its extreme form of the separation between Dr. P and Cress, is severely blocked.

In an essay entitled "How to Write" (1936), Williams describes the process of writing a poem in terms of "two great phases of writing without either of which the work accomplished can hardly be called mastery." He explains that the poet must "proceed backward through the night of our unconscious past" into the "ritualistic, amoral past of the race," using what he calls the "demonic power of the mind"—its "racial and individual past, . . . the rhythmic ebb and flow of the mysterious life process." Tapping this dark source within the poet enables him or her to release the "unacknowledged rhythmic symbolism" that is poetry's greatest strength and that "makes all prose in comparison with it little more than the patter of intelligence." This process also puts the poet in touch with "voices" that are "the past, the very depths of our being." Once the writing is on paper, however, it enters that other "great phase" and becomes "an object for the liveliest attention that the full mind can give it. . . . It has entered now a new field, that of intelligence." Williams continues:

I do not say that the two fields do not somewhat overlap at times but the chief characteristic of the writing now is that it is an object for the liveliest attention that the full mind can give it and that there has been a change in the whole situation. . . . But lest a mistake occur I am not speaking of two persons, a poet and a critic, I am speaking of the same person, the writer. . . . What I have undertaken is to show the two great phases of writing without either of which the work accomplished can hardly be called mastery. And that, in the phrase of James Joyce, is the he and the she of it.[57]

The parallels between Williams's "two great phases of writing" and his "two phases of language" should be readily apparent. The "night of our unconscious past" becomes the "night mind" of place and "the rhythmic ebb and flow of the mysterious life process" is the "cresence and ebb" that is the force of human activity. The "patter of intelligence" that here is prose is the prose of the first phase of language, and just as it was necessary for Williams to find the poetry that was buried in the prose of the historical documents, so the poet must unite "the intelligence" with the "demonic power of the mind." The poet-figures in the prose letters represent a spectrum of poets who range from the extreme "intelligence" and coldness of "E. D." to the equally extreme "madness" of Cress, and because Dr. P, "E. D.," and even Paterson himself remain separate from the voices of Cress and of Garrett Mountain—from the voices that "are the past, the depths of our very being"—these poets in the poem are unsuccessful at finding the "new language" and "unlocking the beauty." But because he is able to hear all of the voices of *Paterson* and unite both the two phases of writing and the two phases of language, the poet of the poem, Williams, succeeds.

Within *Paterson,* however, Williams still gives us two figures of at least potentially successful poets. As we have already mentioned, Madame Curie is a figure of the successful fusion of a female/mother in the usually male role of the empirical scientist. She mixes the prose of the intellect with the poetry of invention and is able to release the "luminous," "radiant gist" from the block of uranium. Another such figure contained in the letters is "A. G." By this, I do not necessarily mean that Allen Ginsberg is a successful poet in Williams's terms, but that the figure of Ginsberg is the figure of a potentially successful poet in Williams's poem. Ginsberg is himself a kind of "found object" who just shows up in Williams's life, and he, too, is rooted to the place of Paterson.

Ginsberg appears as the true "son of Paterson."[58] A. G. combines both insight and intelligence; he avoided talking with the "Doctor" earlier because he "had nothing to talk about except images of cloudy light, and was not able to speak to [the Doctor] in in his own or [A. G.'s] own concrete terms" (*P* 173). One of his poems "connects observations of *things* with an old dream of the void" (*P* 174), and he shares the poet's vision of "some kind of new speech . . . in that it has to be clear statement of fact about misery (and not misery itself), and splendor if there is any out of the subjective wanderings through Paterson," his "natural habitat by memory" (*P* 173). A. G. sees the same "beautiful thing" that Williams does, and with his "whitmanesque mania & nostalgia for cities and detail & panorama"(*P* 210), he has clearly gotten the "gist" of what Williams has tried to do.

It is significant, however, that we never do see any of A.G.'s poetry, and that

he remains a part of Paterson's larger role of " 'most representative' character.''
Only Williams emerges as the successful creator of poetry, though he allows the
reader to engage in his or her own development toward ''wisdom'' through the
symbolic action of his work. In *Paterson,* Williams gives us both ''fact'' and
''thing,'' ''prose'' and ''poetry,'' ''art'' and ''intelligence,'' and shows us the
complicated rhythms by which they make up our lives. From the detached, cold
measure of the historical documents, to the ''authoritative voice'' of the prose/
poetry fusion of Vazakas and Longwell, to the lyrical explosion of ''the descent
beckons,'' the cycle of the Falls blends with the cycle of the language, spilling
over with a violence to create a new measure, only to be swallowed up again in
silence. To add to Williams's own statement about *Paterson:*

> The Falls let out a roar as it crashed upon the rocks at its base. In the imagination
> this roar is a speech or a voice, a speech in particular; it is the poem itself that is
> the answer.
>
> (*A* 253)

Indeed, it is the poem that is ''the thing itself.'' In Chapter 5 we will return to
Paterson and examine more closely how this mechanism of poetry and prose at-
tempts to subvert customary forms of representation and act as both cultural di-
agnosis and political cure. First, however, we need to ''begin again'' with our
''virgin purpose, / the language'' (*P* 186).

2

The Language of Flowers

Williams's poem "The Flower" (1930) is shot through with the anxiety of a stalled career. As Litz and MacGowan point out, the poem gives Williams's "view" of the stanchions for the then incomplete George Washington Bridge, a view that stands in contrast to "Hart Crane's *The Bridge*, parts of which were being published to great acclaim in *The Dial, The Little Review,* and even T. S. Eliot's *The Criterion*" (*CP I* 518). Williams's poem is, as Paul Mariani writes, a "countercry, a cry of impotency, as he composed his lines out of the despair of knowing that the prize was going to a younger man."[1] "A petal colorless and without form," Williams's "Flower" distances itself not only from Crane's *Bridge*—"Nothing // of it is mine"—but also from Eliot's own "chambers of the sea"—"It is a flower through which the wind / combs the whitened grass and a black dog // with yellow legs stands eating from a / garbage barrel." It also nervously blames some unnamed "they," who "hand you—they who wish to God / you'd keep your fingers out of // their business—science or philosophy or / anything else they can find to throw off // to distract you" (*CP I* 322–23). Williams's desire here is power—the poetic power to construct something as grand as the new bridge—but the demands of his medical practice and of his economic conditions leave him unable to write:

> I plan one thing—that I could press
> buttons to do the curing of or caring for
>
> the sick that I do laboriously now by hand
> for cash, to have the time
>
> when I am fresh, in the morning, when
> my mind is clear and burning—to write.

> (*CP I* 324–25)

Williams's despair is at his being cut off from his immediate surroundings— "the blaze of power // in which I have not the least part"—as well as from the very practice which, as he says in his *Autobiography,* gave him "terms, basic terms with which I could spell out matters as profound as I cared to think of" (*A* 357). In the next chapter we will see exactly how the "terms" of Williams's medical practice form the very "terms" of his poetics, as he shares in Kenneth Burke's ideas about writing as a "homeopathic" or "allopathic form of treatment." For now, we need only to see how in a later poem called "The Term" (1937), the "terms" of Williams's poetry—his "language of flowers"—can come to embody that "blaze" of imaginative "power":

The Term

With the wind over
of brown paper
about the length

and apparent bulk
of a man was
rolling with the

wind slowly over
and over in
the street as

a car drove down
upon it and
crushed it to

the ground. Unlike
a man it rose
again rolling

with the wind over
and over to be
as it was before.

(*CP I* 451–52)

Like Williams's "The Flower," "The Term" is "no more a romance than an allegory" (*CP I* 324). The "rumpled sheet / of brown paper" is "about the length // and apparent bulk / of a man" in that they are both "about" the same size, just as the paper's actions are "about" an equivalent human action. Still, for all that, the paper is "Unlike a man" both in its obvious physical distinctions, as well as in its more significant difference of withstanding potential "destruction" from the car. The "terms" of Williams's poetry move, in both poems, beyond simple notions of allegory or conceit to achieve a suspension of analogical relationships that holds in tension both identity and difference. In doing so, they become both cognitive and psychological models that embody Williams's notions of an empathic imagination. By becoming what he called a "post-Darwinian botanist,"[2] Williams gives his "language of flowers"—the "terms" of his poetry—that power of "identity" and "identification" whose loss he laments in his poem "The Flower."

Historically, the "language of flowers" refers to those "literal" associations that grew up around the giving of flowers—the kinds of associations that Ophelia explains in Act IV of *Hamlet* and that were later codified in nineteenth-century floral dictionaries.[3] Williams's more modern language of flowers moves beyond these simple associations to act as "representative anecdotes" that embody a complex notion of "empathy" and "identification," one that both empowers and even attempts to "cure" the reader. In order to understand what I mean by these admittedly bewildering terms, however, we must first return to Williams's 1923 prose/

poetry sequence *Spring and All* and examine more closely its rhetorical, as well as its metapsychological, implications. Using the mechanism developed in Chapter 1, I will explain how Williams uses his dialectic between "poetry" and "prose" to establish *Spring and All* as a rhetorical, cognitive, and psychological model whose aim is the empowerment of the imagination through the promotion of "empathy" and "intersubjectivity." Williams briefly mentions "Dora Marsden's philosophic algebra" (*CP I* 184) in the beginning of *Spring and All,* and by looking at his 1917 disagreement with the contributing editor of *The Egoist*'s "Lingual Psychology," we will see how Williams develops his own somewhat confusing version of a "male" and a "female psychology."

Next, by using Jessica Benjamin's notions of "destruction" and "intersubjectivity" to further refine Kohut's ideas of "empathy" and "wisdom," I will explain how Williams's thought in *Spring and All* eventually does share in a more feminine, "mother-based" psychology that privileges the "narcissistic" over the "oedipal" and, in doing so, acts as a cognitive and psychological model that allows for the subjectivity of both self and other. I will also show how Williams develops a "poetics" in *Spring and All* that relies on language as a form of symbolic action in order to re-present a kind of "transformation of narcissistic energies" in an empathic "identification" of the other that retains the integrity of both self and object. But because Williams's focus in *Spring and All* is on subject/object relations, the voice of the other in this work remains curiously silent. Consequently, we will have to look to two of his later prose/poetry sequences—"The Descent of Winter" (1928) and "The Atlantic City Convention, A Composition in Two Parts: Poem and Speech" (1928)—as well as to his "Della Primavera Trasportata al Morale" (1930), in order to see how Williams develops his "language of flowers" into a dramatic, dialogic re-presentation of the relationship between self and other. In looking at these works, we will also see how Williams transforms his own "lingual psychology" into a semiotics of both psyche and culture.

I

In *Spring and All,* Williams specifically denigrates the "literal" association of "emotions with natural phenomena such as . . . flowers with love" by calling it, "Crude symbolism . . . Such work is empty." "So long as the sky is recognized as an association," Williams says,

> The man of imagination who turns to art for release and fulfillment of his baby promises contends with the sky through layers of demoded words and shapes. Demoded, not because the essential vitality which begot them is laid waste—this cannot be so, a young man feels, since he feels it in himself—but because meanings have been lost through laziness or changes in the form of existence which have let words empty.
>
> (*CP I* 187–88)

These "demoded words and shapes" are, in part, the result of those "floral dictionaries" that associate flowers and feelings in a "crude symbolism," substituting convention for immediate experience. As Williams says elsewhere in *Spring and*

All, "it is that life becomes actual only when it is identified with ourselves. When we name it, life exists" (*CP I* 202). As a preestablished way of "reading" flowers, these conventions name the world for us, and in doing so they become part of that "constant barrier between the reader and his consciousness of immediate contact with the world" (*CP I* 177). Like those conventions of perspective and "realism" in painting, they are part of "the illusion relying on composition to give likeness to 'nature' " (*CP I* 204). In "La Vie en Fleur" (1921), Anatole France asserts that "Fiction, fable, story, myth—these are the disguises under which men have always known and loved the truth. . . . Without falsehood humanity would perish of despair and ennui,"[4] but in the life of Williams's "flowers," "works of art cannot be left in this category of France's 'lie,' they must be real, not 'realism' but reality itself' " (*CP I* 204).

In "Belly Music," a special, supplemental essay to the July 1919 *Others,* Williams had suggested, albeit somewhat mystically, why writers like France, Mencken, Aldington, and others, confuse the modern "language of flowers" with an older adherence to convention:

It is simply that brains have not passed the mark set by the post-Darwinian botanists, etc. It is important not to ignore the Copernican theory, the voyage of Columbus, not because these things make a damned bit of difference to any one [*sic*], especially to the poet, but because they stick unconsciously in a man's crop and pervert his meaning unless he have them sufficiently at his fingers' tips to be ware of them. And the mark of a great poet is the extent to which he is aware of his time and NOT, unless I be a fool, the weight of loveliness in his meters.[5]

The "post-Darwinian botanist" could be one whose "language of flowers" takes root in the local soil, absorbing the past of Copernicus and Columbus into its own unique, present beauty in a fusion of historical horizons that avoids any notions of teleology or improvement. But I think that Williams's "Darwin" here is not Charles Darwin, but his grandfather Erasmus Darwin, an eighteenth-century doctor and writer whose *The Botanic Gardens* (1791) was an elaborate two-part allegory of sylphs and gnomes designed to "inlist [*sic*] imagination under the banner of Science; and to lead her votaries from the looser analogies, which dress out the imagery of poetry to the stricter, ones which form the ratiocination of philosophy." In a project nearly antithetical, but with some surprising similarities, to the one Williams proposes in *Spring and All,* Darwin sought to "transmute" Linnaeus's system of botanical classification the way that Ovid "did by art poetic transmute Men, Women, and even Gods and Goddesses, into Trees and Flowers."[6] Darwin's work, which contains its own "dialogue" on the use of "poetry" as distinguished from "prose," will be examined more closely in Chapter 3. For now, it is important that we see that Williams's "post-Darwinian botanist" is one whose "language of flowers" must be "ware" of the inherited power of language in all senses of the word—that is, he must not only be aware or conscious of that power of convention to "demode" language, but also be "wary" of that power's potential to "pervert his meaning," as well as be able to shape that language into the product, or "ware," of his own art.

These "demoding" conventions and rules are dangerous not only for artistic reasons, but also for individual and cultural ones, and Williams devotes much of *Spring and All* to their destruction. Though the main emphasis in Williams's work is on the artistic, the cultural is hinted at in poems like "To Elsie" and in sections like the one on "the great furor about perspective in Holbein's day." Here, a painting was considered "realistic" only if it followed the rules of perspective so closely that "it made coins defy gravity, standing on the table as if in the act of falling," or if "one could see 'the birds pecking at the grapes' in it." "Meanwhile," Williams continues,

> the birds were pecking at the grapes outside the window and in the next street Bauermeister Kummel was letting a gold coin slip from his fingers to the counting table.
> The representation was perfect, it "said something one was used to hearing" but with verve, cleverly.
> Thus perspective and clever drawing kept the picture continually under cover of the "beautiful illusion" until today, when even Anatole France trips, saying: "Art—all lies!"—today when we are beginning to discover the truth that in great works of the imagination A CREATIVE FORCE IS SHOWN AT WORK MAKING OBJECTS WHICH ALONE COMPLETE SCIENCE AND ALLOW INTELLIGENCE TO SURVIVE—his picture lives anew.
>
> (*CP I* 199, Williams's emphases)

In paying strict attention to those rules and conventions, we miss the "real birds" outside the window or, more dangerously, the real threats of economic exploitation. Williams elsewhere calls these works "prose paintings" (*CP I* 220), and as such they differ from the art of Juan Gris in the same way that Williams's writing differs from Erasmus Darwin's, or from Pope's dictum, parodied above, that "True wit is Nature to advantage dressed; / What oft was thought, but ne'er so well expressed." Unlike France's "La Vie en Fleur," Williams's "language of flowers" must avoid following that "lie that is art" if it is to become the "pure effect of the force upon which science depends for its reality—Poetry" (*CP I* 225).

In Chapter 1, we saw how Williams plays with assumptions about poetry and prose in *Spring and All* in order to expose that cultural "grammar" that grounds our reading of prose and enables his poetry to "enter the new world naked" in "the perfection of new forms as additions to nature" (*CP I* 183 & 226). Poetry in *Spring and All* breaks free from previously established "grammars" in a new "method of projection" that is a new "form of life"—the poetic cathexis of narcissistic energies in a moment of "discovery" and "identification."[7] This new "grammar"—our "grammar of translation"—must resist codification into a set of rules or conventions that interpret our experiences in advance—becoming a "grammar of transference." It must remain a flexible methodology that allows for new moments of "discovery." As such, this "poetic grammar" differs from those grammars of what Williams calls "prose"—the grammars of science, journalism, and, at least according to Williams, philosophy.

In *Act and Quality,* Charles Altieri explains what Wittgenstein means by a "philosophical grammar":

Philosophical grammar is the process of analyzing the ways in which we make sense of our experiences by relating them to established language games or by modifying language games in accordance with specifiable contexts. Philosophical grammar is the means for analyzing methods of projection—rather than lines of projection—and thus for exploring the activities which constitute a human world.[8]

According to Altieri's Wittgensteinian definition of philosophical grammar, much of Williams's work acts a kind of "philosophy"—one that exposes those cultural/ historical associations that act as "a constant barrier between the reader and his consciousness of immediate contact with the world" (*CP I* 177). A key to the kind of philosophy Williams opposes, however, is contained at the end of the second poem in *Spring and All*. Here, after having entered "the new world naked," and begun that process of discovery whereby subject/object relations are made anew in a world that has been both completely annihilated and exactly duplicated in a "perfect plagiarism"—"only the imagination is undeceived" (*CP I* 178–83)—we are confronted with a poem that Bram Dijkstra has called "a literal rendering into poetry of Demuth's watercolor 'Tuberoses' "[9]:

> Pink confused with white
> flowers and flowers reversed
> take and spill the shaded flame
> darting it back
> into the lamp's horn
>
> petals aslant darkened with mauve
>
> red where in whorls
> petal lays its glow upon petal
> round flamegreen throats
>
> petals radiant with transpiercing light
> contending
>   above
>
> the leaves
> reaching up their modest green
> from the pot's rim
>
> and there, wholly dark, the pot
> gay with rough moss.

(CP I 184)

The problem I have with Dijkstra's description of this poem as a "literal rendering into poetry" of Demuth's painting is the relative lack of recognition it contains of the difficulty inherent in moving from the medium of paint to the medium of language. There can be no more "literal" a rendering of painting to poetry than there can be a "literal" rendering of a flower. At best, both acts are acts of translation, and as such they are prey to the subjectivity of the translator. By adhering to his own "grammar of translation," however, Williams gives us what Kenneth Burke would call a "poetic reduction" of the experience of Demuth's painting—a kind of analogical experience of the flowers themselves. Here Williams relies on an Epicurean notion of language whereby "words refer primarily to objects that are apparent; their cognitive meaning, which is purely extensional, can be determined by specific empirical reference to the objects of experience.''[10] As a "poetic reduction," Williams's "rendering" is also a "dramatization" that involves an act of "entitlement"—Burke's name for the dramatic representation of a material scene.[11] "Pink confused with white" and "leaves / reaching up their modest green" to "the pot / gay with rough moss" are all descriptions that attempt to embody movement and quality through their genetic similarity to previous experience—an "act" Williams also attempts in the poem's physical correspondences to the pot of flowers.[12]

Williams's "poetic grammar" is at its most apparent at the very center of this poem. Here, where the physical layout of the poem attempts to both metonymically re-present the flowers and synecdochically re-create their experience, Williams "literally" uses a new word—"transpiercing"—whose meaning we can discover from both its associations to previous words—"transport," "transparent," and "piercing"—as well as its position within the poem's "grammar." Consequently, we "read" the flowers' petals as somehow not only pierced by, but also shot through and made transparent with, sunlight. Compared with those "prose paintings" (*CP I* 220) that merely copy convention, Williams's "language of flowers" re-presents that "grammar of translation" that allows us our own unique moment of "discovery" and "identification" by "identifying" with that subjectivity that has experienced the flowers. Directly after the poem, however, Williams says:

> A terrific confusion has taken place. No man knows whither to turn. There is nothing! Emptiness stares us once more in the face. Whither? To what end? Each asks the other. Has life its tail in its mouth or its mouth in its tail? Why are we here? Dora Marsden's philosophic algebra. Everywhere men look into each other's faces and ask the old unanswerable question: Whither? How? What? Why?
>
> (*CP I* 184)

Facing a world "made new"—where "EVOLUTION HAS REPEATED IT-SELF FROM THE BEGINNING"—"men look about in amazement at each other with a full realization of the meaning of 'art,' " as they confront the world with no ready-made means of interpreting or naming. Consequently, "[e]mptiness stares us once more in the face" and the "terms 'veracity' 'actuality' 'real' 'natural' 'sincere' are being discussed at length, every word in the discussion being evolved from an identical discussion which took place the day before yesterday" (*CP I* 181). As we will see below, Williams's beginning act in *Spring and All*—where "the imagination, drunk with prohibitions, has destroyed and recreated everything afresh in the likeness of that which it was"—has an important analogue in the narcissistic acts of "destruction" and "rapprochement" that form the core of Jessica Benjamin's metapsychology. As such it is also a vital part of the acts of "empathy" and "identification" that we developed previously, and it holds a key to reading the many acts of violence in Williams's writing. By way of introducing Benjamin's thought, and of seeing how Williams's own acts of "destruction" share in it, we need first to look at what Williams identifies as part of that confused, repetitive discussion—"Dora Marsden's philosophic algebra."

Dora Marsden was one of the founding members of *The Freewoman* (1911–12)—a radical feminist publication that was to become *The New Freewoman* (June–December 1913), and, finally, *The Egoist* (1914–19). Her eighteen-part series, "Lingual Psychology: A New Conception of the Function of Philosophic Inquiry," received the ultimate title of "Philosophy: A Science of Signs," and it began the front page of nearly every issue of *The Egoist,* where Marsden was the contributing editor under Harriet Shaw Weaver. Though little has been written about Marsden, and her contributions to *The Egoist* were very separate from the magazine's literary side, she occupied enough of a place in Williams's thought to prompt an early two-part reaction to her series—entitled "the Great Sex Spiral"—and for Williams to remember her in a philosophical context over thirty years later in a 1948 letter to Louis Zukofsky.[13] To summarize Marsden's project and Williams's disagreements with it briefly, Marsden set out to revitalize the field of philosophy by redefining it away from its currently "impotent" focus on "agnosticism" and "First Principles" toward an empirically verifiable realm of "fact" based on the methodology of "objective science."[14] Marsden hoped to prove that "the function of philosophy is definition"[15] and that it was "the watchdog, censor, guardian, of the universal symbolizing activity." Because "the only comprehensive system of symbols is language, and since every other variety of symbol in exact proportion to its genuineness and intelligibility will debouch into speech and express its specialized function in speech-terms," she called her "new" philosophy "Lingual Psychology."[16] Mixing Berkeley and Nietzsche with Max Stirner's *The Ego and His Own* and Otto Weininger's *Sex and Character,* Marsden's "new philosophy" focused on the sense-experience and psychology of the autonomous "ego" as it constitutes its "world."[17]

Rather than attempt any kind of extended critique of Marsden's thinking, I will focus only on that part of her philosophy that concerns Williams's argument with her and his own ideas about language and psyche. Williams's mention of "Dora Marsden's philosophic algebra" refers, I think, to four particular installments in which Marsden articulated the structure behind her "science" in the form of algebraic equations.[18] Three of these issues contained essays or poems by Williams, the two poems appearing immediately after Marsden's essays. In brief, Marsden takes Berkeley's formulation of "ESSE = PERCIPI" as the basis for an argument that shows the impossibility of investigating questions of ontology (the "ESSE" side of the equation) and asserts the necessity to limit philosophical investigations to the empirically verifiable realm of perception and the "ego" (the psychological or the "PERCIPI" side). In this way, Marsden could counter Otto Weininger— who held that women "have no existence and no essence. . . . Women have no share in ontological reality" because they are psychologically incapable of perceiving Being[19]—by agreeing with his distinctions but reversing their priority, asserting that a "feminine" philosophy of sense perception should replace a worn-out male metaphysics concerned only with unknowable abstractions. Notions like "Truth" and "Reality" could only be agreed upon by providing definitions based on egoistic experience. In fact, for Marsden, it was the project of philosophy, through definition, to fix the relationships between all signs and their referents.

Marsden's "Lingual Psychology" and its close relation to Epicureanism must have appealed to the empiricist side of Williams. However, her reduction of experience to a "philosophical algebra," along with her notion of "fixing" language, would have been anathema to him. In "The Great Sex Spiral: A Criticism of Miss Marsden's 'Lingual Psychology,' Chapter I," Williams makes clear his admiration for Marsden's project, but sees it as both "a magnificent, if perhaps unconscious, piece of irony" and, more significantly, "a covert attack on the 'creative artist.' " Williams explains, in seeming agreement with Weininger, that

> it must not be forgotten that, though male psychology has completely filled the philosophic field heretofore and though it is now past its use and is about to be supplanted by a vigorous and fruitful female psychology, it can only be so supplanted in the realm of practical affairs and not in that of pure knowledge. By overthrowing male psychology as she does Miss Marsden neither accomplishes its destruction nor that of agnosticism, which is inherent in it. She merely glosses over a thing which to her has no reality.[20]

Williams clarifies what he means here in his second installment of "The Great Sex Spiral." As long as philosophy remains the "censor of the universal symbolizing function," Williams says, philosophy acts as the "servant" of "art, religion, objective science, politics, practical affairs, etc." by inventing a "conventionalized speech term" to stand for some "truth" arrived by the coincidence of "several sense experiences of differing sorts." As a "censor," philosophy would "invent nothing," relying wholly on the terms of other activities. Not only is this in itself impossible, Williams asserts, but also should philosophy begin interpreting sense experience, which Williams contends is inevitable, it would "enter the lists beside art, religion, or whatever" and lose its role as censor. "It is in this realm," Williams adds, "that all written philosophy, the 'philosophy' of the past, lies. Written philosophy does not come under her definition."[21]

Admittedly, much of what Williams says in both installments of "The Great Sex Spiral" is very difficult to follow, and, as I said above, my concern is not so much with the particulars of either Marsden's philosophy or Williams's critique. As I think Williams's inclusion of Marsden in *Spring and All* indicates, he sees the fundamental principle behind her philosophy as the paradigmatic position of the artist—making sense of the way we experience our world and expressing that experience by "naming" it. Where "The Great Sex Spiral" interests me most, then, is in what it has to say about Williams's gender-related views on that experience. Williams is in full agreement with both Weininger and Marsden in believing "the psychologic field to be divided into reciprocal halves, the cleavage running roughly with the division into sex." Where he disagrees with Weininger, but agrees with Marsden, is in seeing that "Man is the vague generalizer, woman the concrete thinker, and not the reverse. . . . Man is the indulger in *henids,* and woman the enemy of *henids*"—"*henids*" being Weininger's term for unarticulated, undifferentiated thought and feeling. For Williams, the "male psychology" rules over the realm of vague abstractions, "characterized by an inability to concede reality to fact." The "female psychology," however, is rooted in the earth, "since by her experience the reality of fact is firmly established for her."[22]

Williams thought that the ways in which men and women experienced the world remained discreet, that one sex could never fully understand the other's sense of reality:

> Thus reality—depending on sense-experience—is very different for the male and female. In neither case can one sex concede the reality of the experience that underlies the psychology of the other, since the completely opposed sense-experience of the male on the one hand and the female on the other cannot enter the other's consciousness. Either sex must hold to its own psychology or relinquish its sense of reality. For either sex the other's psychology must always be taken a priori.

While this statement might seem to militate against Williams's valuation of inter-subjectivity and his belief in empathy, we need to keep two things in mind: first, Williams says in the beginning of ''The Great Sex Spiral'' that ''It is the union of these elements, each separately contributed, that gives life to the whole.''[23] What Williams is arguing here is not the impossibility of intersubjectivity, but rather the impossibility of a ''male'' having a ''female'' sense experience. Next, this is an early essay. At least by 1930, Williams will write about the two types of ''mind'' a writer must possess if he or she is to succeed—one that reaches the ''rhythmic ebb and flow of the mysterious life process'' and a second, critical mind, ''the so-called intelligence.'' These ''minds'' are responsible for ''the two great phases of writing without either of which the work accomplished can hardly be called mastery. And that,'' Williams adds, ''in the phrase of James Joyce, is the he and the she of it.''[24] It would seem, then, that Williams had always seen the relationship between these psychologies as at least symbiotic, and that he later came to believe that it was possible for an individual to experience both a ''male'' and a ''female'' psychology.

Williams never plainly states his reasons behind these differing psychologies, and his obfuscation is the essay's downfall. While he does say that ''man's only positive connexion [*sic*] with the earth is in the fleeting sex function,'' and that ''[w]oman is physically essential to the maintenance of a physical life by a complicated and long-drawn-out process,'' what Dr. Williams—the general practitioner, obstetrician, and pediatrician—really means is that women carry, give birth to, and nurture infants; men merely share in engendering the process under the fiction of paternity. It is the experience of birth that ''grounds'' the female psychology, and the experience of his own birth, or rather through it to his connection to his mother, that gives the male his ''connexion [*sic*] to the earth.''[25] Williams's ''psychology'' takes its view from the pre-oedipal stages of nurturing and separation, and by showing how it shares in a great many ways with the feminist metapsychology of Jessica Benjamin, I hope to explain that process by which Williams empowers that ''man of imagination who turns to art for release and fulfillment of his baby promises'' (*CP I* 188). Moreover, I will show how Williams's own ''lingual psychology,'' both in *Spring and All* and in consequent prose/poetry sequences, serves as that ''censor of the universal symbolizing function'' by creating what Altieri and Wittgenstein call a ''philosophical grammar'' that analyzes ''methods of projection . . . exploring the activities which constitute a human world.''

II

Jessica Benjamin begins *The Bonds of Love* with a scene between mother and infant. The mother, cradling her child for the first time, "croons to her baby in that soft, high-pitched repetitive voice (the 'infantized' speech that scientists confirm is the universal baby talk)" and says, "I believe she knows me. You do know me, don't you? Yes, you do." As Benjamin explains:

> To the skeptical observer this knowledge may appear to be no more than projection. For the mother, this peaceful moment after a feeding—often after a mounting storm of cries and body convulsions, the somewhat clumsy effort to get baby's mouth connected to the nipple, the gradual relaxation as baby begins to suck and milk begins to flow, and finally baby's alert, attentive, yet enigmatic look—this moment is indeed one of recognition. She says to her baby, "Hey, stranger, are you really the one I carried around inside of me? Do you know me?" Unlike the observer, she would not be surprised to hear that rigorous experiments show that her baby can already distinguish her from other people, that newborns already prefer the sight, sound, and smell of their mothers.[26]

Beginning with this "recognition" scene between mother and infant, Benjamin constructs a theory of "intersubjectivity"—correcting along the way what she sees to be the failure in Heinz Kohut's theory of "empathy" and "wisdom" to "distinguish between using others as 'selfobjects' and recognizing the other as an outside subject" (*BL* 251). Benjamin takes the concept of "the intersubjectivity of mutual understanding" from the social theory of Jürgen Habermas as a "theoretical standpoint from which to criticize the exclusively intrapsychic conception of the individual in psychoanalysis" (*BL* 20–21). Using D. W. Winnicott's notion of "destruction," Benjamin articulates a pattern of individuation in the pre-oedipal infant that can either lead to a healthy, mutual recognition by two subjects or set the stage for forms of domination. This stage of differentiation and individuation hinges on a process of "mutuality and sharing" that must hold in tension notions of identity and difference. By doing so, this narcissistic phase of development forces a reconsideration of the oedipal complex as the dominant psychological and cultural model, as it exposes the oedipal as a model of domination (*BL* 34–50 & 133–81).

Beginning with Hegel's discussion of "the struggle between 'the independence and dependence of self-consciousness' and its culmination in the master-slave relationship" and noting its similarity to Margaret Mahler's theory of "separation-individuation," Benjamin introduces Winnicott's idea that "in order to be able to 'use' the object we first have to 'destroy' it" (*BL* 31–37). Benjamin argues that both Hegel and Mahler incorporate ideas of domination into their thinking by having the subject first experience himself as absolute and then either demand confirmation of this absoluteness by negating the other (Hegel), or maintain his sense of omnipotence by "taking the mother inside himself" and coming to see her as a "constant object" (Mahler). Using Winnicott's distinction between "relating to the object"—seeing it as part of the subject's mind and not necessarily real, external, or independent—and "using the object"—recognizing it "as *an entity in its own right*" (*BL* 37, Benjamin's emphasis)—Benjamin argues that

Winnicott explains that the recognition of the other involves a paradoxical process in which the object is *in fantasy* always being destroyed. The idea that to place the other outside, in reality, always involves destruction has often been a source of puzzlement. Intuitively, though, one senses that it is quite simple. Winnicott is saying that the object must be destroyed *inside* in order that we know it to have survived *outside;* thus we can recognize it as not subject to our mental control. This relation of destruction and survival is a reformulation of and solution to Hegel's paradox: in the struggle for recognition each subject must stake his life, must struggle to negate the other—and woe if he succeeds. For if I completely negate the other, he does not exist; and if he does not survive, he is *not there* to recognize me. But to find this out, I must *try* to exert this control, *try* to negate his independence. To find out that he exists, I must wish myself absolute and all alone—then, as it were, upon opening my eyes, I may discover that the other is still there.

(*BL* 38, Benjamin's emphases)

The "favorable outcome" of this imagined "destruction" is "pleasure in the other's survival." That is, the other must be affected by the attempt—"so that I know I exist"—but not completely destroyed—"so that I know he also exists." In this way the child receives verification of his independent existence along with the knowledge that the mother exists as her own independent subject somewhere outside that infant's subjectivity. This recognition is a mutual one as well, both mother and infant sharing and reflecting that transformation of primary narcissism in a successful stage of "rapprochement." Complete destruction of the mother by the infant—where all of the infant's grandiose desires are met—results in the mother's ceasing to exist (and not just in fantasy) as a viable other. Refusing to submit—and "destroying" the infant—"inculcate[s] the idea that there is room for only one ego in any relationship." The infant must "obliterate his for now, and hope to get it back, with a vengeance, later. Only through the other's survival can the subject move beyond the realm of submission and retaliation to a realm of mutual respect" (*BL* 38–39).

This stage of development—what Kohut would call the first stage in the relinquishment of narcissistic delusions[27]—is exactly where Williams brings us in the beginning of *Spring and All*. Here, the "imagination, intoxicated by prohibitions, rises to drunken heights to destroy the world" (*CP I* 179). As Williams explains:

This final and self inflicted holocaust has been all for love, for sweetest love, that together the human race, yellow, black, brown, red, and white, agglutinated into one enormous soul may be gratified with the sight and retire to the heaven of heavens content to rest on its laurels. There, soul of souls, watching its own horrid unity, it boils and digests itself within the tissues of the great Being of Eternity that we shall then have become.

(*CP I* 179–80)

The imagination, having exercised its grandiose fantasies of the world's destruction in a "self inflicted holocaust," reaches omnipotence as a "great Being of Eternity," but it does so in a curious "agglutination" of races. Its "unity" is "horrid," and it "boils and digests itself" within its own God-like omnipotence. Consequently, this "destruction" is almost immediately followed by:

It is spring! but miracle of miracles a miraculous miracle has gradually taken place during these seemingly wasted eons. Through the orderly sequences of unmentionable time EVOLUTION HAS REPEATED ITSELF FROM THE BEGINNING.

Good God!

Every step once taken in the first advance of the human race, from the amoeba to the highest type of intelligence, has been duplicated, every step exactly paralleling the one that preceded in the dead ages gone by. A perfect plagiarism results. Everything is and is new. Only the imagination is undeceived.

(CP I 181)

The entire world has been ''recreated'' in a ''perfect plagiarism'' of its former self. It has survived the infantile ''destruction'' of the imagination. ''Everything is and is new. Only the imagination is undeceived.'' Williams leaves us here at that crucial stage of ''rapprochement,'' where either forms of domination begin or feelings of mutuality are discovered. The world has been affected by this ''destruction'' in its being made ''anew,'' but the imagination is ''undeceived'' that the world ever was ''destroyed.'' It is at this point that Williams's ''young man'' can either attain ''release from and fulfillment of his baby promises'' of narcissistic perfection *(CP I* 188), or fall prey to ''THE TRADITIONALISTS OF PLAGIARISM''—that mysterious group who demand adherence to ''Tradition! The solidarity of life!'' *(CP I* 185). Williams gets the phrase ''Traditionalists of Plagiarism'' from Edgar Allan Poe's essay, ''Mr. Longfellow and Other Plagiarists,'' in which Poe accuses Longfellow of merely imitating (if not actually stealing from) the worn-out styles of previous poets.[28] To follow the ''Traditionalists of Plagiarism'' would be to adhere to those ''rules and conventions'' that make up ''prose paintings.'' The choice here—between some more genuine, original ''contact'' involving mutuality (or at least *avoiding* forms of domination) and an adherence to a rigid ''law'' that subsumes individual identity—is analogous to the distinctions Benjamin makes in comparing her model of ''intersubjectivity'' based on ''rapprochement'' with the model of the oedipal complex.

In discussing the inevitable conflict involved in the infant's act of individuation, Benjamin asserts that

what is not inevitable is that this confrontation will be resolved only by splitting, and that this splitting will be conventionalized as gender opposition. It is not inevitable that the knowledge of difference be reduced to the complementarity of male and female—a parallel to the split between subject and object, good and bad, doer and done-to. It is this complementarity which, even as it appears to idealize sexual difference, recasts the knowledge of difference as invidious comparison.

(BL 222)

''Splitting'' here refers to ''a defense against aggression, an effort to protect the 'good' object by splitting off its 'bad' aspects that have incurred aggression'' *(BL* 63). As a psychic mechanism, it is used to explain the ''relieving of tensions'' that occurs in relationships of domination where ''each partner represents one pole in a split unity'' in a desire to retain that original narcissistic perfection. ''Splitting'' can also occur in a failed act of ''destruction'' where ''facing an environment that doesn't respond to the infant's actions makes it seem as though it is impossible to affect the 'not-me' strictly through the action of the self. The rage that ensues" from this failed confrontation forms the beginning conditions for "splitting," where the "key to the resolution of splitting is the establishment of externality" (*BL* 263).

Benjamin extends the use of "splitting," along with her model of mutuality, to counter the dominant oedipal model, which she sees as a culturally and historically specific means of legitimating gender domination. Benjamin contends that in the formation of identity, the oedipal construction of difference leads to the devaluation of the mother—whose relegation to a role of selfless "nurturing" denies her subjectivity—and to the idealization of the father—whose role is defined in opposition to the mother as the active, vital subject. This culturally sanctioned "splitting" of roles organizes gender identity into irreconcilable differences, symbolically centering on the possession or lack of the penis. As opposed to the conflict inherent in "destruction" and "rapprochement," the oedipal conflict leaves no room for maternal identification. For the male, "separation takes precedence over connection," and "the two central elements of recognition—being like and being distinct—are split apart. Instead of recognizing the other who is different," the male must "repudiate" rather than "renunciate" the feminine, which is now constituted as "whatever is opposite to masculinity." "Recognition is thus reduced to a one dimensional likeness"—and we need to remember here Williams's disparaging that "Crude symbolism . . . typified by use of the word 'like' " (*CP I* 188). Finally, Benjamin adds that "as distinct from early childhood, where any likeness will do, this likeness is sexually defined" (*BL* 170).

Benjamin cites recent evidence that shows the coincidence of "rapprochement" with gender identity during the second year of life. She then argues that the culturally approved roles of the active male and the nurturing mother set up the father as the recipient of an "ideal love" that "resolves the paradox of the rapprochement phase, the paradox of the child needing to be recognized as independent by the very person he depends on." The ambivalence between the need for recognition and the desire to control his world can be met by "splitting" this ambivalence between his parents—where "each parent may represent one side of the mental conflict between independence and dependence." Since gender identity is also forming at this stage, my use of the masculine pronoun here is purposeful, as Benjamin argues that it is by "identification" with "the magical father" that the male child receives his recognition and sense of omnipotence. For the female, since "identification" with the father is at best problematic, the need for "identificatory love" is met by an identification with the mother as "an object of desire," turning inward her "aspirations for independence and her anger at non-recognition." Moreover, Benjamin explains, "the pre-oedipal girl's identificatory love becomes the basis for later heterosexual love; when the girl realizes she cannot *be* the father, she wants to *have* him" (*BL* 100–10, Benjamin's emphases).

With the male child locked in a system of identity that hinges on repudiating the feminine as the other, and the female child experiencing a "lack" that is in actuality a "gap in her subjectivity," Benjamin proposes that the only way out of this dilemma is by opposing the notion of "gender polarity":

It is possible . . . that in a context of different gender arrangements, the girl's identification with the father and symbolic appropriation of the phallus might well be constructive. To envision such an alteration we must reject the assumptions underlying the psychoanalytic account of early gender development. These are: That mothers cannot offer their daughters what fathers offer their sons, a figure of separation and agency; that little girls do not need such a figure because they might just as well remain identified with the mother of early attachment and merging; that fathers cannot offer their daughters what they offer their sons. These assumptions are, at best, no more than descriptions of our culture. I believe that, given substantial alteration in gender expectations and parenting, both parents can be figures of separation *and* attachment for their children; that both boys *and* girls can make use of identifications with both parents, without being confused about their gender identity.

(*BL* 112)

I do not wish to imply that these ideas of gender redefinition are present in *Spring and All*. "These assumptions" that Benjamin lists are even more so descriptions of Williams's culture, as his own assertions of gender polarity and exclusive use of the male as active subject show. Still, as we will see by the end of this work, Benjamin's assertion that "individuals ideally should integrate and express both male and female aspects of selfhood (as culturally defined)" (*BL* 113) is not only one that Williams states openly in "The Great Sex Spiral," but also one that he will develop even more dramatically in *Paterson*. Moreover, as we will see in Chapter 4, Benjamin's belief that "the deep source of discontent in our culture is not repression or, in the new fashion, narcissism, but gender polarity," along with her assertion that under this oedipal model of gender polarity "freedom means fleeing or subjugating the other" (*BL* 171 & 221), will find an important expression in *In The American Grain* and Williams's other cultural critiques.

Benjamin admits that the "interpsychic" forms only a part of the problem, and that the "intrapsychic"—which she condenses as "the splitting of tensions into complementary forms: subject and object, idealization and repudiation, good and bad, doer and done-to"—poses many problems for interpersonal relations (*BL* 221–22). Still, as I will argue in the rest of this chapter, her ideal of a mutual recognition between equal subjects that can only be maintained in the logic of a paradox—like the need for recognition and independence—that sustains the tension between contradictory forces is very much Williams's ideal, and in his dialectic between "poetry" and "prose," he seeks to release the "radiant gist" of recognition in just such a paradox of "identity" and "identification." Rejecting a simple reversal like the assertion of the priority of a "female psychology," Williams's dialectic—whereby we need to "find the poetry hidden in the prose," as well as the "prose hidden in the poetry"—recreates an act of "empathy" and "recognition" whereby we see the self in other, as well as the other in the self. By creating a "philosophical grammar" that acts as what Burke calls a "representative anecdote" and as what Wittgenstein calls a "perspicuous representation," Williams's desire for the "radiant gist" actively engages in Benjamin's search to find "the point at which breakdown occurs and the point at which it is possible to recreate tension and restore the condition of recognition" (*BL* 223).

By quickly returning to *Spring and All,* we can begin to see how Williams develops an analogous version of the idea that "the intersubjective view . . . finally enables us to confront the painful aspect of external reality—its uncontrollable, tenacious otherness—as a condition of freedom rather than of domination" (*BL* 48). Immediately before he "destroys" the world, Williams calls for an act of empathic "identification" between "author" and "reader":

> In the imagination, we are henceforth (so long as you read) locked in a fraternal embrace, the classic caress of author and reader. We are one. Whenever I say "I" I also mean "you." And so, together, as one, we shall begin.
>
> (*CP I* 178)

As I mentioned above, Williams is very much a victim of gender polarity in this work, and the "fraternal embrace" between "author and reader" stands in opposition to the feminine objectification that occurs throughout the "poetry" in *Spring and All.* The male remains the active subject, the vital user of imagination. Still, Williams asserts that "Only through the agency of this force can a man feel himself moved largely with sympathetic pulses at work—" and that a "work of the imagination which fails to release the senses in accordance with this major requisite— the sympathies, the intelligence in its selective world, fails at the elucidation, the alleviation which is—" (*CP I* 192). The "alleviation which is—" is the alleviation from those "tensions" that Benjamin called "the painful aspect of external reality—its uncontrollable, tenacious otherness" (*BL* 48). The imagination gives us a sense of oneness to the world in a feeling only *analogous to* that "oceanic feeling" of primary narcissism that Freud feared,[29] as we devour the "ocean" but "acknowledge that the ocean we would drink is too vast . . . the stomach is full, the ocean no fuller, both have the same quality of fullness." The imagination "gives the feeling of completion by revealing the oneness of experience" (*CP I* 194), by providing us with genetic experience on which we can base an empathetic understanding of the other in a *transformation* of narcissistic energies. In this way, "it is that life becomes actual only when it is identified with ourselves. When we name it, life exists" (*CP I* 202). Relying on rules and conventions, or on Marsden's "definitions," to interpret our world for us denies that sympathetic, mutual relationship between subject and object and, instead, recreates that "splitting" whereby we "identify" with the "ideal father," subsuming the uniqueness of the other into our "definition" of it. Williams avoids our own such idealization of his "author" by forcing the reader to "recreate" this imaginative activity for himself, to "discover" the "rules" on his own.

This idea of "discovery" is Williams's goal in *Spring and All,* and as such it takes the form of a "philosophical grammar" that clarifies—but never codifies— "the process of analyzing the ways in which we make sense of our experiences by relating them to established language games or by modifying language games in accordance with specifiable contexts."[30] This "process" takes place in the "crystallization of the imagination . . . the dynamization into a separate form" that Williams calls "poetry" in *Spring and All* (*CP I* 226 & 219)—a "process" that completes "science and allow[s] intelligence to survive" (*CP I* 199) by restoring the tensions between identity and difference. Williams achieves this maintenance of tension between subject and object, as well as hints at reasons for its failure, in two separate poems in *Spring and All.* In the final poem of the work, Williams's "language" is once again a "language of flowers":

> Black eyed susan
> rich orange
> round the purple core
>
> the white daisy
> is not
> enough
>
> Crowds are white
> as farmers
> who live poorly
>
> But you
> are rich
> in savagery—
>
> Arab
> Indian
> dark woman

(CP I 236)

Like both "The Flower" and "The Term," Williams's "object"—the black eyed susan—is neither "like" an "Arab, Indian, dark woman," nor *is* it an "Arab, Indian, dark woman." Unlike "farmers / who live poorly," Williams's flower resonates between identity and difference as "Arab," "Indian," and "dark woman" hang both in opposition and in likeness to the first stanza's "Black eyed susan / rich orange/ round the purple core." Williams as "the artist figure of / the farmer—composing /—antagonist" (*CP I* 186) avoids overwhelming the object in an agonistic act of romantic identification and instead hangs his composition of the flower in sympathetic proximity to the "Black eyed susan."

Still, the object here is feminized; the farmer is presumably masculine. But Williams has already exposed both these and other cultural impediments to "mutuality" in "The pure products of America / go crazy" (*CP I* 217–19), the poem that he later entitled "To Elsie." James Clifford cites "To Elsie" as the "pretext" for his book *The Predicament of Culture,* calling the poem the embodiment of the "predicament of ethnographic modernity." Clifford sees Williams here as "off center among scattered traditions" in the common, "modern condition of rootlessness and mobility." "Elsie," Clifford continues,

> stands simultaneously for a local cultural breakdown and a collective future. To Williams her story is inescapably his, everyone's. Looking at the "great / ungainly hips and flopping breasts" he feels things falling apart everywhere. All the beautiful, primitive places are ruined. A kind of cultural incest, a sense of runaway history pervades, drives the rush of associations.[31]

But Clifford sees more than just an empathic "identification" that escapes an objectification of the feminine here, and his comments deserve to be quoted at length:

[Elsie's] very existence raises *historical* uncertainties undermining the modernist doctor-poet's secure position. . . . If authentic traditions, the pure products, are everywhere yielding to promiscuity and aimlessness, the option of nostalgia holds no charm. . . . Such authenticities would be at best artificial aesthetic purifications. Nor does Williams settle for two other common ways of confronting the rush of history. He does not evoke Elsie and the idiocy of rural life to celebrate a progressive, technological future. He shares her fate, for there really is "no one to drive the car"—a frightening condition. Nor does Williams resign himself sadly to the loss of local traditions in entropic modernity—a vision common among prophets of cultural homogenization, lamenters of ruined tropics. Instead, he claims that "something" is still being "given off"—if only in "isolate flecks."

In the discrepancy between "this emergent, dispersed 'something' and the car in which 'we' all ride," Clifford sees that ambivalence between attraction and repulsion, appropriation and freedom that marks those qualities held in tension by Williams's "author." "An inarticulate muddle of lost origins," Elsie is "going nowhere," but then neither are "we."[32] There is "No one / to witness / and adjust, no one to drive the car" (*CP I* 219). Clifford's description of this poem as both "ethnography" and "modern history" is one to which we will return later. Clifford is correct in noting those near-violent cultural and historical ambivalences that permeate this poem. As Clifford also observes, "Elsie is still largely silent here, but her disturbing presences—a plurality of emergent subjects—can be felt,"[33] and while Williams never does give the other a "voice" in *Spring and All*, he begins to expose those cultural conditions that doom the other to silence. Denied subjectivity for reasons of race, gender, and economic condition, "Elsie" occupies a threatening position not only within Williams's "poetry," but also within the confines of his own domestic space. Moreover, Williams's empathic "identification" with "Elsie"—"a girl so desolate / so hemmed round / with disease or murder" (*CP I* 218)—marks an act of "recognition" that both breaks down notions of gender polarity, as it allows for the possibility of "rapprochement" in the threatened "destruction" that Elsie could cause. As such, Williams's "philosophical grammar" reveals those "methods of projection" that both entrap Elsie and that, potentially, hold the key to her freedom. In order to understand the ways in which Williams develops this "grammar," however, we need to return to Kenneth Burke.

III

Almost immediately after Williams met Kenneth Burke in January of 1921,[34] Williams convinced him to contribute to the little magazine that he and Bob McAlmon had started called *Contact,* and for the next forty-two years the two continued to exchange manuscripts, insults, opinions, admiration, and theories. In that first year alone, Williams was to write to Burke that he was amazed at Burke's "lightning like penetration," though he was just as likely to be left baffled by Burke's "damned theorizing about—about—about—Well, what the hell do I care whether you theorize or not so long as you occasionally write something I like." Williams also told Burke that "you fairly illustrate what Bob [McAlmon] and I mean by contact. . . . Damn it man you encourage me . . . THERE IS HOPE! It's a damned lie. There is BURKE."[35] As he wrote Burke in 1924, "If we practice on each other, trying to knock each other's blocks off, we'll be ready one day to knock a few real blocks into the discard" (*SL* 65). As I hope to show throughout this study, Burke's "damned theorizing" is an essential means of understanding Williams's writing, just as Williams's writing provides an important critique of Burke's work. In particular, Burke's ideas about language as a kind of symbolic action form the backdrop against which Williams's dialectic of "poetry" and "prose" performs most dramatically.

In his opening essay to *Language as Symbolic Action,* Burke explains the paradox he sees as inherent in language and its relationship to the "nonverbal":

> . . . In being a link between us and the nonverbal, words are by the same token a screen separating us from the nonverbal—though the statement gets tangled in its own traces, since so much of the "we" that is separated from the nonverbal by the verbal would not even exist were it not for the verbal (or for our symbolicity in general, since the same applies to the symbol systems of dance, music, painting, and the like).
>
> A road map that helps us easily find our way from one side of the continent to the other owes its great utility to its exceptional existential poverty. It tells us absurdly little about the trip that is to be experienced in a welter of detail. Indeed, its value for us is in the very fact that it is so essentially inane.
>
> (*LASA* 5)

People are more complicated than road maps, and yet both rely on symbolic constructions for much of their "identity." Road maps, through their simple correspondence to a nonverbal reality, are extremely useful for simple functions, but they fall far short of providing the kinds of history and information that text like a Bædeker, for example, provides. In his letter to me, Burke wondered whether "the esthetic or poetic aspects of *Paterson* by a 'medicine man' like Williams might in effect *complete* his ideal of 'contact' " by making his poem act like a kind of "Bædeker . . . informing the reader, as *tourist,* of what is going on in *Paterson* as both a *place* and a *poem.*" The jump from Burke's road map to his "conceit of the Bædeker"[36] includes with it the kinds of complicated functions that both Williams and Burke see language as performing, and much of the remainder of this work, in a way, will be an untangling of Burke's gnomic sentence to me. For now, I want to look at that "paradox" of language that Burke describes above and examine its implications for seeing language as a kind of symbolic action.

"Language referring to the realm of the nonverbal is necessarily talk about things in terms of what they are not," and for Burke even the strict referentiality of a road map does not escape "the fact that such terms are sheer emptiness, as compared with the substance of the things they name." As such, man as "the symbol-using animal" is doomed to "abstraction," since even the "rich imagery of Keats" and a "bodily form of expression" like a "dance" are both abstracted symbols (*LASA* 5–6). Burke goes on to ask, when we use these "symbols," just who or what is doing the using?

When a bit of talking takes place, just what is doing the talking? Just where are the words coming from? . . . Do we simply use words, or do they not also use us? An "ideology" is like a god coming down to earth, where it will inhabit a place pervaded by its presence. An "ideology" is like a spirit taking up its abode in a body: it makes that body hop around in certain ways; and that same body would have hopped around in different ways had a different ideology happened to inhabit it.

(*LASA* 6)

Burke's notion of "ideology" is a complex one, and I will discuss it along with Williams's ideas about "history" in Chapter 4. For now, we need only to see Burke's "ideology" as a kind of "grammar"—one that influences expression in certain determining ways, though a variety of "expressions" are possible within it. In this way, language as a kind of symbolic act becomes a dual notion, observable in the typical Burkean shift between substantive and qualifier. That is, it is a symbolic *act* in that it proceeds from some sort of motive according to some "strategy," and it is a *symbolic* act in that it is subject to the paradox inherent in all symbols of being a "substantial abstraction" that both links us to and separates us from our "world." Together, as "symbolic act," language acts ambivalently, potentially controlling as much as it is controlled.

Burke's notion of language as symbolic action might be better understood if we see that, for Burke, a "symbolic act" is also a "textual act." As Fredric Jameson points out, "Burke's pioneering work on the tropes mark[s] him as the precursor of literary theory," though Jameson is quick to add that "Burke's stress on language, far from reinforcing . . . the ideologies of the intrinsic and of the anti-referential text, had on the contrary the function of restoring to the literary text its value as activity and its meaning as a gesture and a response to a determinate situation."[37] Jameson values Burke's work precisely for this insistence on seeing the "literary or aesthetic gesture" always standing in "some active relationship with the real, even where its activity has been deliberately restricted to the rather sophisticated operation of 'reflecting' it. Yet," Jameson continues,

> in order to act on the real, the text cannot simply allow reality to persevere in its being outside of itself, inertly, at a distance; it must draw the real into its own texture, and the ultimate paradoxes and false problems of linguistics, and in particular of semantics, are to be situated here, in the way in which language and the texts of language carry the real within themselves as their own "intrinsic" subtexts. Insofar, in other words, as symbolic action—Burke will map it out as "dream," "prayer," or "chart"—is a way of doing something to the world, to that degree what we are calling "world" must inhere within it, as the content it has to take up into itself in order to give it form. The symbolic act therefore begins by producing its own context in the same moment of emergence in which it steps back over against it, measuring it with an eye to its own active project. The whole paradox of what we are calling the subtext can be measured by this, that the literary work or cultural object itself, as though for the first time, brings into being that situation to which it is also, at one and the same time, a reaction.[38]

Jameson explains that by positing a notion of symbolic action as a "theory of verbal *praxis*," Burke is able to avoid the irresolvable problem of having intention coincide with expression by "setting forth at a point before the fall, and positing a place of emergence that precedes the breach which so many mechanical models have proved unable to heal." By focusing on the symbolic *act,* Burke can locate his criticism at that point in which "not only is human intention still inseparable from its scene or situation, language and the mental or structural categories which govern it are still at one with the raw material, the facticity, the data it is in the process of organizing."[39] Moreover, Jameson contends, if "narrative is one of the basic categorical forms through which we apprehend realities in time and under which synchronic and analytic thinking is itself subsumed and put in perspective, then we no longer have to be defensive about the role of culture and the importance of its study and analysis,"[40] since "culture" itself would act as what Jameson calls a "subtext."

Jameson has serious reservations about Burke's criticism in this last regard, and I will explain later how both his notion of the "subtext" and his criticism of Burke's "ideological analysis" join, in part, with the ways in which Williams's work critiques that of his close friend. Still, Jameson's explanation of a symbolic act as a "textual act," along with his criticism of Burke's system as having "no place for an unconscious,"[41] provides us with an important means for our own critique of Burke's notions of "identity" and "identification." As Burke explains in *Attitudes Toward History:*

> Bourgeois naturalism in its most naive manifestation made a blunt distinction between "individual" and "environment," hence leading automatically to the notion that an individual's "identity" is something private, peculiar to himself. And when bourgeois psychologists began to discover the falsity of this notion, they still believed in it so thoroughly that they considered all collective aspects of identity under the head of pathology and illusion. That is: they discovered accurately enough that identity is *not* individual, that a man "identifies himself" with all sorts of manifestations beyond himself, and they set about trying to "cure" him of this tendency.
>
> *(ATH 263)*

This tendency can't be "cured," Burke says, because it is an intrinsic part of the way we construct our sense of who we are. "The so-called 'I,' " says Burke, "is merely a unique combination of partially conflicting 'corporate we's.' " As such, we form our "identity" through a process of "identification with" that Burke sees as "hardly other than a name for the *function of sociality*" (*ATH* 264–67). Through our "identification with" particular dramatic characters—and for Burke a philosophical term can be as dramatic as *Hamlet*—we both are given and "earn" our "corporate identities" (*ATH* 264). As a form of symbolic action, the construction of identity becomes another "textual act" whereby we would "draw" the other into the "texture" of the "self" with the "instrumental design" of making it our own "intrinsic subtext."

But we need to remember that we use symbols as much as symbols use us, and the ways in which we "organize" that "subtext" of "identity" would involve the degree to which either we determine its construction, or it determines ours. In this way we can use Jessica Benjamin's concept of splitting to see how an unconscious could be included in Burke's system. Here, an "organization" that involved the "splitting of tensions into complementary forms" would lead to possible forms of domination by both "subtext" and "self." "Identifying with" some "ideal father" would involve our being determined by the rules or "grammar" of that ideal (or "ideology"), just as we would determine, through repudiation, the "identity" of the rejected mother. Ideally, then, we would want to "organize" our "selves" around some sense of "mutuality" that sees that "subtext" as both part of us and different from our "selves" at the same time. In other words, with no intrinsic notion of identity, our sense of who we are would involve maintaining the paradoxical distinction that we are "like" certain people, things, or ideas, but also unlike any of them. As such, this notion of "identity" would entail "as a condition of freedom" a "painful" sense of our own "uncontrollable, tenacious otherness" (*BL* 48).

This sense of "our own otherness" finds its expression in the first entry of Williams's *The Descent of Winter* (1928), where Williams asks:

> *"What are these elations I have*
> *at my own underwear?*
>
> *I touch it and it is strange*
> *upon a strange thigh."*

(*CP I* 291)

Here Williams's use of quotation marks and italics makes a strange beginning even stranger. Certain only of the ownership of his underwear and the fact that he is touching it, Williams's voice remains detached from any sure point of reference, including his sense of himself. This idea of referentiality is picked up in the very next entry, as the "steward" removes the bed to which the sign for "Berth No. 2" referred, and

> only the number
> remains
> · 2 ·
>
> on an oval disc
> of celluloid
> tacked
>
> to the white-enameled
> woodwork
> with
>
> two bright nails
> like stars
> beside
>
> the moon

(*CP I* 291–92)

The sign—"· 2 ·"—divorced from its referential surrounding enters the realm of what Jameson elsewhere calls the "schizophrenic," becoming "ever more material—or, better still, literal—ever more vivid in sensory ways" even though "meaning is lost." Using Lacan, Jameson explains that "the experience of personal identity over months and years—this existential or experiential feeling of time itself—is also an effect of language" in that language "has a past and a future" and "because the sentence moves in time." Because the schizophrenic has no knowledge of "language articulation" in this way, "schizophrenic experience is an experience of isolated, dislocated, discontinuous material signifiers which fail to link up into a coherent sequence. The schizophrenic thus does not know personal identity in our sense, since our feeling of identity depends on our sense of the persistence of the 'I' and the 'me' over time."[42]

The materiality of the signifier, however, shifts our experience of language toward being that of a "*substantial* abstraction," and as such the material receives Williams's emphasis in the image—"an oval disc / of celluloid / tacked // to the white-enameled / woodwork / with // two bright nails." Immediately, however, this isolated "image" is made continuous with the simile—"like stars / beside // the moon." I think we need to read this simile—perhaps an attempt to posit meaning in order to "relieve the tension" of this "schizophrenic state"—as a projection by the authorial subjectivity that completely "destroys" the original object. As Williams says later in *The Descent*, the "realization" of poetic vividness "has its own internal fire that is 'like' nothing. Therefore the bastardy of the simile" (*CP I* 302). The use of simile is a resort to that "crude symbolism" of given associations, and so Williams criticizes himself in his next entry (as it appeared in *The Exile* in 1928):

> There are no perfect waves—
> Your writings are a sea
> full of misspellings and
> faulty sentences. Level. Troubled.
>
> A center distant from the land
> touched by the wings of nearly
> silent birds that never seem
> to rest, yet it bears me
> seriously—to land, but without
> you.
>
> This is the sadness of the sea—
> waves like words all broken—
> a sameness of lifting and falling mood.
>
> (*CP I* 515–16)

With "me" and "you" being carried farther apart, with writing that is "a sea / full of misspellings and / faulty sentences," Williams's second simile—"waves like words all broken"—forms part of yet another "faulty sentence" that begins now to work against a smooth understanding of the analogy. With this confusion of "waves" and "words," Williams returns to the scene's materiality—"watching the detail / of brittle crest"—holding out hope for the formation of some "coral island" that will rescue him, only to confront the reader in the next entry with the following image:

and there's a little blackboy
in a doorway
scratching his wrists

The cap on his head
is red and blue
with a broad peak to it

and his mouth
is open, his tongue
between his teeth—

(*CP I* 292–93)

Unlike the sign "· 2 ·" the "little blackboy" remains free of any associated ideas or images, and so maintains his own materiality to both reader and author. What Jameson referred to as the "schizophrenic image" is here an other who maintains his own "tenacious otherness" against Williams's subjectivity. In other words, by maintaining that tension between "I" and "me," between sign and suspended referent, Williams also maintains the separation of subject and object. In this way, Williams says, "I will make a big serious portrait of my time." By fitting together these "blocks" of poetry—like the "brown and creamwhite block of Mexican onyx" or the "rock shingles of Cherbourg"—Williams confronts the reader with the unsituated materiality of his own poems, "like stones fitted together and that is love." Williams explains that, "there is no portrait without that has not turned to prose love is my hero who does not live, a man, but speaks of it every day" (*CP I* 295). By presenting his "portrait" in a "prose" that defeats codification and simple understanding, Williams enables his "hero" to live in the dialectic he creates between his "prose" and his "poetry." A "hero who does not live, a man"—Williams's "love" here is very much like Benjamin's mother who in "reflecting" her baby's behavior, provides that "recognition" needed by the infant. Williams's poetry, in "reflecting" his world with as little subjective imposition as possible "speaks" of the need for that love "every day" in the datelines of each separate entry.

Moreover, this "schizophrenia"—which as Jameson explains is a descriptive and not a diagnostic term[43]—is characterized by the same lack of identity and intense experience of the present that Williams valorizes throughout the work, most notably in his several discussions of Shakespeare, whose poetry Williams confronts in the "yellow leaves / and few" that are juxtaposed with "a young dog" jumping "out / of the old barrel" (*CP I* 294). In the entry entitled "Shakespeare," Williams explains this "schizophrenic" style:

The difficulty of modern styles is made by the fragmentary stupidity of modern life, its lacunæ of sense, loops, perversions of instinct, blankets, amputations, fulsomeness of instruction and multiplications of inanity. To avoid this, accuracy is driven a hard road. To be plain is to be subverted since every term must be forged new, every word is tricked out of meaning, hanging with as many cheap traps as an altar.

The only human value of anything, writing included, is intense vision of the facts, add to that by saying the truth and action upon them—clear into the machine of absurdity to a core that is covered.

(CP I 312)

"To be plain" is to speak according to known conventions, and the purpose of Williams's "terms" is to expose that "machine of absurdity" to its impenetrable "core." Cut loose from these conventions, a "poem is a soliloquy without the 'living' in the world" and the poet must learn to defeat his own sense of subjectivity and "be nothing and unaffected by the results, to unlock and flow, uncolored, smooth, carelessly—not to cling to the unsolvable lumps of personality (yourself and your concessions, poems) concretions—" *(CP I* 314–15). Like the "sagas," Williams's poems must "seem to have been made on the spot" *(CP I* 302), and by lifting his "signs" literally from their surroundings, Williams can achieve saga-like magnification:

> And in runningpants and
> with ecstatic, æsthetic faces
> on the illumined
> signboard are leaping
> over printed hurtles and
> "1/4 of their energy comes from bread"
>
> two
> gigantic highschool boys
> ten feet tall

(CP I 303)

But, as Williams asserts, "this is modern, not the saga. There are no sagas—only trees now, animals, engines: There's that" *(CP I* 302). The condition of "schizophrenia" is still a painful one, and it remains far removed from that state of "intersubjectivity" that Benjamin asserts.

The "context" of commercial exploitation forms the grounds that rob the modern of "the old dignity of life," and most often the "schizophrenic" signs that Williams presents are connected either with buying and selling, or with the political, as in "Coolidge" saying "let there be imitation brass filigree fire fenders behind insured plateglass windows and yellow pine booths with the molasses-candygrain in the wood instead of the oldtime cake-like whitepine boards always cut thick their faces!" *(CP I* 296). By uprooting the "grammars" that enable us to connect signifier and signified, Williams juxtaposes abstract nouns with concrete images in order to resituate the meanings of "abstractions" such as:

> The justice of poverty
> its shame its dirt
> are one with the meanness
> of love
>
> its organ in a tarpaulin
> the green birds
> the fat sleepy horse
> the old men

      the grinder sourfaced
          hat over eyes
      the beggar smiling all open
          the lantern out

      and the popular tunes—
          sold to the least bidder
      for a nickel
          two cents or

      nothing at all or even
          against the desire
      forced on us

                                                                  (*CP I* 300–01)

This "subtext" of convention and economic exploitation—along with the ideal of forming some new relationship beginning in that schizophrenic split between sign and signifier, subject and object—all coincide to "organize" the context in which we must read both "A Morning Imagination of Russia" and the story of the poem's "hero." The "hero" of *The Descent*, of course, is "Dolores Marie Pischak . . . born, September 15, 1927, 2nd child, wt. 6 lbs 2 ozs" (*CP I* 296). Williams once remarked that he got his poetry "out of the mouths of Polish mothers" (*A* 311), and the sections describing "Pischak's place" mix the broken, Polish accents of its inhabitants with "the feeling of Fairfield" that is neither romanticized nor nostalgic. "Here one drinks good beer," and "the stupefying monotony of decency is dead, unkindled even by art or anything—dead: by God because Fairfield is alive, coming strong." But even "A dell with a pretty stream in it below the garden and fifty feet beyond," is right next to "the board fence of the Ajax Aniline Dye Works with red and purple refuse dribbling out ragged and oily under the lower fence board." Dolores's older sister "has jaundice," and her father— "A man who might be a general or president of a corporation, or president of the states. Runs a bootleg saloon. Great!" Still, "This is the world. Here one breathes and the dignity of man holds on. . . . Peace is here—rest, assurance, life hangs on. Oh, blessed love, among insults, brawls, yelling, kicks, brutality—here the old dignity of life holds on—defying the law, defying monotony" (*CP I* 296–98).

As in "To Elsie"—"something is given off," in Fairfield even if it is "only in isolate flecks"—and Williams hints at the "love" that could potentially "cure" the "fragmentary stupidity of modern life" (*CP I* 312) in his visit to Dolores's home. Here, at the heart of "Pischak's place" is Benjamin's "recognition scene"—the infant Dolores nursing in her mother's arms:

> She lies in her mother's arms and sucks. The dream passes over her, dirt streets, a white goose flapping its wings, and passes. Boys, wrestling, kicking a half inflated football. A grey motheaten squirrel pauses at a picket fence where tomato vines, almost spent, hang on stakes.
>   O blessed love—the dream engulfs her. She opens her eyes on the troubled bosom of the mother who is nursing the babe and watching the door. And watching the eye of the man. Talking English, a stream of Magyar, Polish what? to the tall man coming and going.

>   (*CP I* 298)

Williams's "female psychology" of the concrete focuses on the event that "grounds" both his and Benjamin's psychologies—the act of nurturing and "recognition" by baby and mother. The "eye of the man . . . [t]alking English" is the figure of Williams as doctor in *The Descent,* and his empathic "contact" with mother and child is echoed in the "contact" he achieves throughout the work, suggesting that "intersubjectivity" that will serve as "remedy."

This empathic "intersubjectivity" is achieved on a larger scale in "A Morning Imagination of Russia," and it is here that we see clearest the relationships between the "subtexts" of the "culture" and the "individual." The opening lines make clear that interplay between the individual and his surroundings, as Williams says:

> The earth and the sky were very close
> When the sun rose it rose in his heart.
> It bathed the red cold world of
> the dawn so that the chill was his own
> The mists were sleep and sleep began
> to fade from his eyes, below him in the
> garden a few flowers were lying forward
>
> (*CP I* 303–04)

Gone are "the walls / against desire save only for him who can pay / high, there were no cities—he was / without money" (*CP I* 304). This condition of economic poverty and existential richness will be later echoed in Williams's own statement that "I make really very little money. / What of it?" (*CP I* 315), and the relationship between subject and city here is nearly as complex an empathic "identification" as we will find in *Paterson:*

> The very old past was refound
> redirected. It had wandered into himself
> The world was himself, these were
> his own eyes that were seeing, his own mind
> that was straining to comprehend, his own
> hands that would be touching other hands
> They were his own!
>
> (*CP I* 305)

Gone also is the "schizophrenic" estrangement that began *The Descent*—" *'what are these elations I have / at my own underwear?'* "—as the subject here "recognizes" both self and other, as well as the "self in the other." Moreover, his next act will be one of communication and cooperation, as "He would go / out to pick herbs . . . He would go out / and ask that old woman, in the little / village by the lake, to show him wild / ginger. He himself would not know the plant" (*CP I* 305). Jameson sees that "schizophrenic" condition of the "floating, material signifier" as "consonant with" the conditions of late capitalism, where commodity production is closely tied in with styling changes that obviate against notions of continuity in "a perpetual present and in a perpetual change that obliterates traditions of the kind that all earlier social formations have had in one way or another to preserve.''[44] While I am by no means making a case for Williams's Marxism in ''A Morning Imagination''—he later called the poem merely a ''sympathetic human feeling—non-political—roused by thoughts of Russia'' (*CP I* 517)—Williams does make this connection to capitalism and style in the lines:

> Cities are full of light, fine clothes
> delicacies for the table, variety,
> novelty—fashion: all spent for this.
> Never to be like that again:
> the frame that was. It tickled his
> imagination. But passed in a rising calm
>
> (*CP I* 304)

The ''frame that was'' is an ''ideology'' whose ''grammar'' determines the meaning (and price) of ''this''—a floating signifier that remains open to perpetual redefinition according to the economic ''grounding'' it receives. Williams calls America a ''Soviet State decayed away in a misconception of riches. The states, counties, cities are anemic Soviets,'' saying that ''Russia is in every country'' and that ''The United States should be in effect, a Soviet State'' (*CP I* 306–08). While we will discuss Williams's politics more specifically later, we need to keep two things in mind here: first, Williams's ''Soviet'' is a participatory form of government that allows for full ''identification'' in an uncertain, local, cooperative effort—''he was himself / the scales. The local soviet. They could / weigh. If it was not too late. He felt / uncertain many days. But all were uncertain / together and he must weigh for them out / of himself'' (*CP I* 305). Next, I think Williams shares in the then common, progressive perception of Russia as a site for the achievement of democratic ideals. As Noam Chomsky has pointed out, the immediately perceived threat of the Bolshevik revolution by the leadership of the United States was that it would lead to greater democratic reforms:

> Woodrow Wilson's Secretary of State Robert Lansing warned that the Bolshevik disease, were it to spread, would leave the ''ignorant and incapable mass of humanity dominant in the earth.'' The Bolsheviks, he warned, were appealing ''to the ignorant mentally deficient, who by their numbers are urged to become masters, . . . a very real danger in view of the process of social unrest throughout the world''; it is, as always, democracy that is the fearful threat. When soldiers' and workers' councils made a brief appearance in Germany, Woodrow Wilson expressed his concern that they might inspire dangerous thoughts among ''the American negro [soldiers] returning from abroad.'' Already, ''negro'' laundresses were demanding more than the going wage, saying ''that money is as much mine as it is yours,'' Wilson had heard. Businessmen might have to adjust to having workers on their boards of directors, he feared, among other disasters if the Bolshevik virus were not exterminated.[45]

Williams's position with regard to the Left is a vexed and confusing one, and I think ''A Morning Imagination of Russia'' is just that: an ''imagination'' of the soviet, and not a substantial relationship to Communism. The appeal, as I think it always is for Williams, is to a more democratic form of government, one that will erase "the feeling / that there is a piece of glazed paper / between me and the paper—invisible / but tough running through the legal / process of possession—a city, that / we could possess—" (*CP I* 306). What one gets from "A Morning Imagination of Russia" is "touch. The eyes and the ears / down on it. Close." (*CP I* 306)—that "*tactus eruditus*" that Williams mentions in the "Della Prima-vera" and that Burke calls attention to in nearly all his writings about his friend. As Williams explains in "A Morning Imagination"—"It's in art, it's in / the French school"—but it is also potentially in America—"Russia is every country, here he must live, this for that, loss for gain. Dolores Marie Pischak" (*CP I* 306). As Williams continues:

> . . . Loss and gain go hand in hand. And hand in hand means my hand in a hand which is in it: a child's hand soft skinned, small, a little fist to hold gently, a woman's hand, a certain woman's hand, a man's hand. Thus hand in hand means several classes of things. But loss is one thing. It is lost. It is one big thing that is an orchestra playing. Time, that's what it buys. But the gain is scattered. It is everywhere but there is not much in any place. A city is merely a relocation of metals in a certain place.—He feels the richness, but a distressing feeling of loss is close upon it. He knows he must coordinate the villages for effectiveness in a flood, a famine.
>
> (*CP I* 307)

The "mutuality" of "hand in hand" means "my hand in a hand which is in it": a child's hand, a woman's hand, a man's hand. It also means "loss and gain," and I read Williams's melancholy here as that kind of melancholy that Heinz Kohut says results from the transformation of "narcissistic energies," as "the cathexis is transferred from the cherished self to the supraindividual ideals and to the world with which one identifies."[46] The sense of "time" that it "buys" is that sense of continuity over time that might "heal" Jameson's "schizophrenia." "It is a pure literary adjustment," Williams says, but it is not the sense of tradition that is the "supremacy of England" (*CP I* 307). Rather, it is a sense of identity and difference one gets from "The very old past . . . refounded / redirected" (*CP I* 305). And so Williams ends *The Descent* with a reminiscence about his own family—his grand-mother and grandfather, his brother, and, most important, his greatest avatar of the imagination after Shakespeare, his own mother.

Williams explains his "poverty" in the rich recollection of his family's history. Here economic distrust and betrayal mix with pride, love of Paris, and "identifi-cation":

> When my brother was happy he would sing, walking up and down kicking out his feet: *Si j'étais roi de Bayaussi-e, tu serais reine-a par ma foi!* You made me think right away of him.
>
> (*CP I* 317).

The Descent of Winter ends in the middle of winter—"12/18"—and it is only in the "imagination" of Russia that an empathic act of "identification" actually oc-curs, although the act remains potential in the scene between the infant Dolores and her mother. Ultimately, though, the environment we face here is one that "does not respond'' (*BL* 263), and so we are left with images of ''splitting'' and ''schizo-phrenia.'' One kind of ''splitting,'' for example, occurs between the implied ''I'' that identifies with Mrs. Pischak and the bigoted ''you'' of ''you sit and have it waved and ordered.... And nothing to do but play cards and whisper ... of the high-school girl that had a baby and how smart her mama was to pretend in a flash of genius that it was hers.... Or lets us take a run up to the White Mountains ... Not Bethlehem (New Hampshire) any more, the Jews have ruined that like lice all over the lawns'' (*CP I* 299). The kind of ''intersubjectivity'' that Benjamin pro-poses is never fully accomplished in this work, and the ''mutuality'' that is Wil-liams's ''desire'' and ''love'' never fully remedies the ''schizophrenia'' of separation. Still, Williams's ''philosophical grammar'' exposes those conditions of poverty and power that cause this lack of communication. The exposed ''subtexts'' of ''culture'' and ''identity'' are organized too fully, however, to allow ''rap-prochement'' to occur. The ''signs'' of Fairfield remain in their schizophrenic state of materiality (*CP I* 315–16), and Williams remains as separate from his ''self'' and world as he was from his wife Flossie when he wrote *The Descent* (*CP I* 515).

The dialectic between poetry and prose that Williams creates in *The Descent of Winter* offers even fewer distinctions between the two forms of writing than the one in *Spring and All*, forcing the reader even more to find the ''poetry hidden in the prose'' and the ''prose hidden in the poetry.'' In this freer exchange, the voice of the other gains expression as we hear those ''Polish mothers'' speak for them-selves. Through our own empathic ''identification'' of and with the voices of the poem, we begin that process of ''rapprochement'' that Williams sees as ultimately frustrated in his world. In ending this chapter, then, I'd like to look at two more works from around the same time as *The Descent* and examine more closely both the forms of domination that Williams sees as responsible for this sense of sepa-ration, as well as some of the conditions that allow for both the possible achieve-ment and the re-presentation of an act of ''intersubjectivity.''

IV

''The Atlantic City Convention, A Composition in Two Parts: Poem and Speech'' (1928) is as bald a work of male desire and domination as Williams ever wrote. Consisting of a ''poem''—''The Waitress''—and a prose ''convention speech'' called ''The Conservation of the Human Sub-Species,'' Williams's sequence moves from a seemingly appreciative meditation on an uncommon waitress's ''momentary beauty'' (*CP I* 281) to a ''speech'' about the ''instincts governing a proper use of the male sperm'' (*CP I* 284). The temptation in this work is to read ''The Waitress'' as pitting the hushed admiration for another ''Beautiful Thing'' like the ''belle chose'' of ''Paterson: Episode 17'' (1937) against the vulgar desire to impregnate ''vigorous girls'' for the dehumanized, political purpose of continuing ''the race.'' Instead, I want to suggest that Williams's ''subtext'' of desire and domination in both ''speech'' and ''poem'' acts dialectically to expose what Jessica Benjamin called ''that point at which breakdown occurs and the point at which it is possible to recreate tension and restore the condition of recognition'' (*BL* 223). By marking out both the site and the conditions for even the subtlest forms of gender domination, Williams exposes the "grammar" of domination inherent in a "male psychology" that abstracts and commodifies the feminine.

"The Waitress" centers on the desire for the male speaker to have a particular waitress "Wait on us. / Wait on us"—a desire sparked by his admiration for "the silence of her ways, grey eyes in / a depth of black lashes—" and "the hair held back practically / by a net, close behind the ears, at the sides of / the head. But the eyes—/ but the mouth, lightly (quickly) / touched with rouge." The poem contains the kinds of appreciation for the woman's "fallen" condition that we saw in "To Elsie"—"The benefits of poverty are a roughened skin / of the hands, the broken / knuckles, the stained wrists"—along with an unsentimental observation of the waitress's qualities:

> There is a mole under the jaw, low under
> the right ear—
>
> And what arms!
>
> The glassruby ring
> on the fourth finger of the left hand.
>
> (*CP I* 279–80)

But the speaker's "appreciation" of the things that separate this waitress from the others—"All the rest are liars, all but you"—is radically undercut by the contents of the "speech" that follows—"The Conservation of the Human Sub-Species." Here the convention's speaker makes the argument that

> as elsewhere throughout nature the human fertilizing agent is in great measure
> scattered and destroyed during the series of acts leading up to impregnation and
> that therefore only the part of it can be considered to exist which has final access
> to the ripe ovum . . . so hedged about by social and other impedimenta that the
> quantity which does finally come into contact with the mature egg is in many
> instances rapidly approaching the vanishing point.
>
> (*CP I* 281)

The consequence of this horrifying situation is that "qualitatively certain vastly important strains of men may die out due to lack of the penetration of their highly specialized reproductive material into adequate receptors" (*CP I* 282). The "social and other impedimenta" that have led to this point involve an increasing democratization that must be opposed by more "selective laws":

> A democracy of understanding has certain prerogatives which it will exercise:
> accessibility of sentiment, an appreciation for the material thrown up by the break-
> down of discipline in the lower classes; but it has this glaring defect, that it cannot
> discover a satisfactory selective mechanism by which to discriminate in favor of
> the higher biologic types. Unless it find a way to learn from its lesser freedoms
> to gain a tolerance by which to liberate its more specialized members for a full
> fertilization of the mass the vulgus will grow more lacking in the seeds of these
> types as time passes, or the types themselves will depreciate in effectiveness.
>
> (*CP I* 283–84)

Our "speaker" assures us that what he says is "sound logic and of great psychic importance. . . . It is sound heredity, sound biology . . . inescapable from the viewpoint of Mendelian law" and that there is even a "natural attraction" between "men of power" and "vigorous girls" (*CP I* 282–84). The real "psychic importance" of this speech, however, is the way in which it embodies that male psychology that Williams described in "The Great Sex Spiral," taking its abstractions to the extremes of eugenics and racial superiority. There Williams argued that man's only connection to the "objective world" was through the "fleeting sex function" and that once having obtained his "objective," the male is doomed only to "further pursuit"—"that is, not toward the earth, but away from it—not to concreteness, but to further hunting, to star-gazing, to idleness"—and to the realm of "abstraction."[47] In his speech, Williams's "abstract" male tries to argue the clear, "logical facts" of totalitarianism in a call for the "lawful" domination of the female that would even meet their own "desires," as—"Girls desire distinguished men as sires for their children and do not (necessarily) expect to hold them in leash except as economic requisites make it important" (*CP I* 284).

In this speech, Williams has raised male "abstraction" to the level of what Burke has called a "God-term"—an "ideology" that causes the body to "hop around in certain ways" (*LASA* 6). As such, we need to return to "The Waitress," remembering from *Spring and All* both that "Prose may follow to enlighten" and that "Prose, relieved of extraneous, unrelated values must return to its only purpose: to clarity to enlighten the understanding" (*CP I* 226). The ways in which Williams's prose "enlightens" his poem is to make us see "the prose hidden in the poetry." That is, by returning to "The Waitress," we can now see that the inclusion of "convention speech" within the poem itself makes the connection between the two speakers more than casual and anything but oppositional:

> The Nominating Committee presents the following
> resolutions, etc. etc. etc. All those
> in favor signify by saying, Aye. Contrariminded,
> No.
>   Carried.
>   And aye, and aye, and aye!

Moreover, this "carried motion" follows the most sexually explicit "appreciation" in the poem:

>   —and the movements
> under the scant dress as the weight of the tray
> makes the hips shift forward slightly in lifting
> and beginning to walk—
>   (*CP I* 280)

The "subtext" of domination that is the speaker's "ideology" invades the poem, forcing us to re-read its initial lines as an act of domination and submission:

> No wit (and none needed) but
> the silence of her ways, grey eyes in
> a depth of black lashes—
> The eyes look and the look falls.
>   (*CP I* 279)

"The eyes look and the look falls" under the male gaze that fixes those eyes in the position of a desirable body with "No wit (and none needed)" and no voice. Consequently, I think we can read the scene in which Williams relates the "organization" of the poem as a kind of Lacanian "mirror stage"—one that asserts the autonomous subjectivity of the male by "destroying" the female within the "substantial abstractions" of his poem. Here, beginning with a romantic apostrophe to the "unlit candle," Williams begins to "write" the poem he has already written:

> O unlit candle with the soft white
> plume, Sunbeam Finest Safety Matches all together in
> a little box—
>
>   And the reflections of both in
> the mirror and the reflection of the hand, writing
> writing—
>   Speak to me of her!
>
>   —And nobody else and nothing else
> in the whole city, not an electric sign of shifting
> colors, fourfoot daisies and acanthus fronds going from
> red to orange, green to blue—forty feet across—

(*CP I* 280–81)

This "mirror scene" reflects more than the speaker's desire—metynomically expressed by the phallic matches in their "little box." It also exposes the ways in which Williams's "speaker" has reduced his waitress to the level of the material signifier in its use of the reflected image—"Sunbeam Finest Safety Matches"— thus also reducing her to the level of the commodity. Williams's "language of flowers" here is a set of "electric signs" magnified to the "saga-like" level of the "two / gigantic highschool boys" in *The Descent* (*CP I* 303). But Williams's "schizophrenic" reduction also extends to his own speaker, as the speaker's arm is also "cut off" and reflected in the mirror. Perhaps this is why from the beginning of the poem there was "no way, no way," and why the "speaker" ends with:

> Wait on us, wait
> on us with your momentary beauty to be enjoyed by
> none of us. Neither by you, certainly,
>   nor by me.
>   *CP I* 281)

By exposing a "male psychology" based on the "ideology" of domination, Williams makes clear a "context" in which neither waitress nor speaker can enjoy "beauty." In doing so, Williams also exposes that "point at which breakdown occurs'' (*BL* 223) under the ''schizophrenic,'' detached male gaze that adheres only to ''abstraction.'' This ''point of breakdown'' occurs most explicitly when Williams's ''speaker'' evades the waitress's own eyes and focuses instead on her silenced lips—''But the eyes—/ but the mouth, lightly (quickly) / touched with rouge'' (*CP I* 279). As such, this ''point of breakdown'' also marks ''the point at which it is possible to recreate tension and restore the condition of recognition'' by suggesting that the waitress's own eyes must be granted the power to gaze (and perhaps it is this power that the speaker's eye needs to avoid), just as her lips must be given their own ''speech.''

While we must wait to hear this ''voice of the other'' in Williams's writing, the ''Della Primavera Trasportata al Morale'' (1930) gives us an example of how a ''male'' and a ''female psychology'' are united in Williams's own mind. Written shortly after he had finished *The Descent of Winter,* the ''Della Primavera'' appears to have been initially considered the actual work for which *The Descent* was merely ''an introduction,'' and Williams's removal of sections of prose from the final version does reflect the work's more ''poetic'' emphasis (*CP I* 520). As such, the united ''psychologies'' of the ''Della Primavera'' act as an embodiment of that ''remedy'' for the ''schizophrenia'' that infects *The Descent.* Here, that ''touch'' that was the result of the price paid for the ''soviet'' in ''A Morning Imagination''—''The eyes and the ears / down on it. Close.'' (*CP I* 306)—becomes that ''*tactus eruditus*'' that Burke once called the ''platform'' of Williams's poetics (*LASA* 283). Williams had written to Zukofsky around the time he was writing the ''Della Primavera'' that ''I'm out of my slump—in a way. But our family affairs are still in bad shape,'' and I would argue that this work reflects both an emodiment of the unification of Williams's ''psychologies,'' as well an example of his continued problems with recognizing the other as independent subject, as reflected in his problems with his wife, Flossie.[48]

The ''Della Primavera'' begins with ''April,'' marking the poem as yet another answer to Eliot's *The Waste Land,* as well as another act of revolt against ''The Plagiarists of Tradition'' found in *Spring and All* (*CP I* 182–86) and the ''supremacy of England'' mentioned in *The Descent* (*CP I* 307 & 315). Williams's work is filled with the rain and rebirth that Eliot's poem lacks, and it openly opposes the ''myths'' of both Eliot and Anatole France:

> There never were satyrs
> never maenads
> never eagle-headed gods—
> These were men
> from whose hands sprung
> love
> bursting the wood—
> (*CP I* 338)

Williams also opposes Pound's ''Ancient Music'' (1916)—which begins ''Winter is icummen in, / Lhude sing Goddamm''—with his ''the bounty / of . . . and Spring / they say / Spring is icummen in—'' (*CP I* 343 & 527). The answer to both

Pound's medieval "Winter" and his own *Descent,* Williams's "Moral Interpretation of Springtime" acts materially and spiritually in opposition to all forms of poetic, cultural, and psychic restraint.

In addition, and perhaps most important, Williams's work attempts to oppose the "Law of the Father" in his inclusion of his own father's death—"He's dead // the dog won't have to / sleep on his potatoes / any more to keep them / from freezing // he's dead / the old bastard—" (*CP I* 346). The Father—Benjamin's embodiment of the oedipal model of domination—is presented here as the impediment to "love":

> Love's beaten. He
> beat it. That's why
> he's insufferable—
>
> because
> he's here needing a
> shave and making love
> an inside howl
> of anguish and defeat—
>
> He's come out of the man
> and he's let
> the man go—
>   the liar
>
>   (*CP I* 347)

Despite the "shrunken" corpse of his English/Spanish father, the "Law of the Father" is literally "disembodied" as a potential deathly force at the end of this poem. But Williams's response in the following lines is significant. Rather than enter into an agonistic relationship with the father—one that would only serve to continue the model of domination—Williams instead "buries" the Father with "love":

> Dead
>   his eyes
> rolled up out of
> the light—a mockery
>   which
> love cannot touch—
>
> just bury it
> and hide his face—
> for shame.
>   (*CP I* 347–48)

Williams's father, who had stressed the value of "an English liberal tradition," was a late Victorian socialist about whom Williams was, as Mariani says, "deeply ambivalent."[49] Still, I think we can read "Death" as an attempt to lay the corpse of the father to rest in act of love whose touch the oedipal Father can never feel. While I am not suggesting that Williams here is openly rejecting the oedipal Father to embrace the narcissistic Mother, Williams's act in this poem is an act of "rapprochement," and as such it begins to leave the realm of domination for the embrace of "mutuality."

In *The Descent of Winter* Williams had said that "the art of writing is to do work so excellent that by its excellence it repels all idiots but idiots are like leaves and excellence of any sort is a tree when the leaves fall the tree is naked and the wind thrashes it till it howls" (*CP I* 295), and the "movement" of the "Della Primavera" imaginatively embodies the action described in Williams's statement. Taking the reader from "April" to "Full Moon" to "The Trees," Williams then moves to "The Wind Increases," "The Bird's Companion" (originally a part of the previous poem), "The House," "The Sea-Elephant," "Rain," and "Death," to finally come to rest at "The Botticellian Trees." For reasons I will make clear below, I would add "A Marriage Ritual"—the next poem in Volume I of *The Collected Poems,* and written at the same time as the rest of the sequence—as a final coda to Williams's work, especially as it contains that "one leafless tree" that Williams describes as "excellence of any sort." In reading this movement from poem to poem, I will show how, with the inclusion of "A Marriage Ritual," Williams's writing achieves its "excellence" from a unification of his two "psychologies," as it openly acknowledges the impediments to full "intersubjectivity."

"April" begins with "the dress / in which the veritable winter / walks in Spring—" (*CP I* 329–30), but the profusion of "buds," "onion grass," and "iris blades" is quickly interrupted by the detached "sign"—"BUY THIS PROPERTY" (*CP I* 330). "April" contains several such "signs" transposed into its verse, and the need to "ground" these "substantial abstractions" in the "loose flow" of the verse is part of the project of unifying those "male" and "female" psychologies. For example, the ability to "BUY THIS PROPERTY" is immediately described as "—the complexion of the impossible / (you'll say) // never realized—/ At a desk in a hotel in front of a // machine a year / later—for a day or two—" (*CP I* 330–31). The kind of sexual union achieved in hotels (perhaps even "bought" from a prostitute) is unlike the "reality" that "trembles" at its own likeness to this economic exchange:

> Whereas the reality trembles
> frankly
> in that though it was like
> this
> in part
> it was deformed
> even when at its utmost to
> touch—as it
> did
> and fill and give and take
> —a kind
> of rough drawing of flowers
> and April

(*CP I* 331)

The ability to maintain "identity" and "difference" in a paradoxical tension is part of the project of the "Della Primavera," just as we must balance the list of concrete "Morals" with its counterpart—Williams's abstracted list of "Beliefs." As Williams explains, "—the moral is love, bred of / the mind and eyes and hands—// But in the cross-current // between what the hands reach / and the mind desires // and the eyes see / and see starvation, it is // useless to have it thought / that we are full—" (*CP I* 332–33). The "cross-current" that separates "mind" from "eyes and hand" is suggested in the set of "I believes" that follow—a curious combination of political slogans and detached signs that represent the "abstract" male psychology. Williams's list—which includes "progressive Mulish policies . . . honest law enforcement . . . giving the farmer and / land owner adequate protection . . . [and] equality for the negro"—gives way to even more abstract "signs" such as—"ICE—and warehouse site // No parking between tree and corner" to a list of ice cream flavors and prices. The problem here is a lack of connection between these "abstractions" and some "grounding" in a feminine "reality." Consequently, even Williams's "*tactus eruditus*"—here another detached "sign"—gives way to the vulgar, "Maple, I see you have / a squirrel in your crotch—// And you have a woodpecker / in your hole, Sycamore" (*CP I* 334–35). The "fat blonde" and the "POISON!" sign (complete with skull and crossbones) suggest that this kind of desire—a male, abstract desire—is indeed "POISON!" and the very next "signs"—"WOMAN'S WARD" and "PRIVATE" with two arrows underneath each, pointing in opposite directions—make clear in their "schizophrenic" detachment the separation inherent in this masculine ideology that keeps women lumped together in a single ward, separate from the "PRIVATE," autonomous male "identity" (*CP I* 335–36).

These ideas, I would contend, are concentrated in the next lines—"The soul, my God, shall rise up /—a tree." Here we need to remember two things: first, that the "soul" was posited by Otto Weininger as a purely male possession, one that marked the proof of male ontology and the absence of feminine "essence." In "The Great Sex Spiral," Williams called this move Weininger's "most palpable error," saying that "to save him from the inevitable charge of futility . . . Weininger borrows the worn-out term 'soul,' with which he proceeds to endow man, meanwhile disparaging woman's practical symbolization."[50] Next, in *The Descent,* Williams had said, "God—sure if it means sense. 'God' is poetic for the unobtainable. Sense is hard to get but it can be got. Certainly that destroys 'God,' it destroys everything that interferes with simple clarity of apprehension" (*CP I* 312). The "tree" that "rises up" here, described as both Williams's "soul" and his "God," is not that "tree" that is "excellence of any sort," but rather one whose "branches" must be "lashed" by the "mortal wind" before it can recognize the "You" it opposes:

> But who are You?
> in this mortal wind
> that I at least can understand
> having sinned willingly
>
> The forms
> of the emotions are crystalline,

> geometric-faceted. So we recognize
> only in the white heat of
> understanding, when a flame
> runs through the gap made
> by learning, the shapes of things—
> the ovoid sun, the pointed tress
>
> (*CP I* 336)

In order to "recognize . . . the shapes of things," Williams must become the kind of poet who can join in "mutuality" male abstraction with feminine materiality, or, as he says in "The Wind Increases"—"a man / whose words will / bite / their way / home—being actual / having the form / of motion // At each twigtip // new // upon the tortured body of thought // gripping // the ground // a way / to the last leaftip" (*CP I* 339). Williams's attention to the "material" can be found throughout the "Della Primavera," but even more significant are Williams's many changes in the "materiality" of the actual poems. This sequence appeared in different forms in the *Imagist Anthology* (1930), *Blues* (Fall 1930), *The Miscellany* (Nov. 1930), *An "Objectivists" Anthology* (1932), and the *Collected Poems, 1921–1931* (1934), where the poems' spatial form on the page received as much attention as their content (*CP I* 520–31). In these changes, Williams's was searching for several kinds of "recognition"—not only for his poetry, but also within it. Most important, Williams hoped to "recognize" that kind of "love" that he calls— "Unworldly love / that has no hope // of the world // and that / cannot change the world / to its delight—" (*CP I* 345). Rather than continue with my reading of the sequence, then, I would like to jump to its final poem—"The Botticellian Trees"— and show how Williams's "tree" that is "excellence" of any sort embodies those ideals of "mutuality" and "paradox" that make up this "love."

In "The Botticellian Trees," Williams has moved beyond the "experiences" of wind, rain, and the death of the Father, to present the reader with his final "tree." Here Williams creates that kind of poem that is "no more a romance than an allegory" (*CP I* 324) with which we began this chapter. Williams's "language of flowers" is now "The alphabet of / the trees" that "is fading in the / song of the leaves" (*CP I* 348). The male desire that was so deadly in "The Atlantic City Convention" is now contained in the "tree" itself. Having first been parodied in "The Sea-Elephant" as a "wallow of flesh" with an "appetite stupidity / cannot lessen" and put on display in the circus (*CP I* 341–43), this "love from the sea" was embodied in "Rain" in the trees washed by "the spring wash / of your love // the falling // rain—":

> The trees
> are become
> beasts fresh-risen
> from the sea—
> water
>
> trickles
> from the crevices of
> their hides—

So my life is spent
                    to keep out love
with which
she rains upon

                    the world
of spring

                    drips
so spreads

                    the words
far apart to let in

                            her love
And running in between
the drops

                    the rain
is a kind physician

                    the rain
of her thoughts over
the ocean

                                        (*CP I* 344–45)

By stretching the space of his lines, Williams tries in "Rain" to re-create physically that space of "mutuality" where male and female desire can coexist, and at the end of "The Botticellian Trees," Williams potentially achieves this kind of "intersubjective space" in his "post-Darwinian botanist's language of flowers" that holds in paradoxical suspension woman, poem, and tree:

        until the stript
        sentences

        move as a woman's
        limbs under cloth

        and praise from secrecy
        quick with desire

        love's ascendancy
        in summer—

        In summer the song
        sings itself

        above the muffled words—

                                        (*CP I* 349)

The "kind physician" has stopped "running in between // the drops" (*CP I* 345), and his "stript sentences" metonymically re-present that "one leafless tree" in the physical shape of the poem itself. But the poem and woman are still objects here: that is, they still have no voice. Only the voice of the poem is heard, though that other "song" that "sings itself // above the muffled words" exists as the grammar of mutuality that has determined this poem. While the reconciliation of male abstraction and female grounding is realized in the materiality of Williams's signs by rescuing them from that schizophrenic detachment of "April" and *The Descent,* the ideal of "intersubjectivity" remains unrealized though an "intersubjective space" has been created.

Consequently, in "A Marriage Ritual," Williams can achieve an empathic "identification" with both "city" and "flower," but the act of "recognition" or "rapprochement" remains incomplete:

> Above
> the darkness of a river upon
> winter's icy sky
> dreams the silhouette of the city:
>
> This is my own! a flower,
> a fruit, an animal by itself—
>
> It does not recognize me
> and never will. Still, it is my own
> and my heart goes out to it
> dumbly—
>
> (*CP I* 349)

The symbolic action of Williams's "language of flowers" has blossomed to allow his poetry to act as a "grammar of translation" that provides both release and fulfillment of the narcissistic "baby promises" of that "young man" of imagination, but it has yet to allow for its feminine fulfillment. As such, mutual recognition cannot occur, just as Williams remains unrecognized both by and for his own poetry. Notions of gender polarity still contaminate the attainment of intersubjectivity in the full, mutual "recognition" of two subjectivities in Williams's work, though, as we will see in the next chapter, Williams's methods of diagnosis hold the key to "curing" this condition. But the potential for this achievement is also contained in the final image of "A Marriage Ritual," where a Polish woman— reminiscent of Dolores Marie Pischak and her mother—fights with another "young man" for possession of "a stout metal drum":

> The woman and the boy, two
> thievish figures, struggle with
> the object . . . in this light!
>
> And still
> there is one leafless tree
> just at the water's edge and—
>
> my face
> constant to you!
>
> (*CP I* 350)

But until we hear the voice of both "the woman and the boy" in their "struggle with / the object," Williams's "language of flowers" will remain "one leafless tree" facing a silent other.

3

Modern Medicine

The relationship between Williams's medical practice and his career as a writer has typically been described in the complementary terms Williams himself provides in his *Autobiography:*

> ... As I say, often after I have gone into my office harassed by personal perplexities of whatever sort, fatigued physically and mentally, after two hours of intense application to the work, I came out at the finish completely rested (and I mean rested) ready to smile and to laugh as if the day were just starting.
>
> That is why as a writer I have never felt that medicine interfered with me but rather was my very food and drink, the very thing which made it possible for me to write. ... Oh, I knew it wasn't for the most part giving me anything very profound, but it was giving me terms, basic terms with which I could spell out matters as profound as I cared to think of.
>
> (*A* 357)

Somehow, Williams explains, "I could always find the time to bang out 10 or 12 pages. In fact, I couldn't rest until I had freed my mind from the obsessions which had been tormenting me all day" (*A* xiv). Just as Williams's writing revives him from the long hours of his practice, the prosaic "humdrum, day-in, day-out, everyday work that is the real satisfaction of the practice of medicine" (*A* 356) gives Williams the raw material in which he can discover the "radiant gist" of his poetry. Interacting with his patients, he finds "the actual words, as we hear them spoken under all circumstances, which contain it. It is actually there, in the life before us, every minute that we are listening, a rarest element—not in our imaginations but there, there in fact" (*A* 362).

But the "facts" of his medical career enabled Williams's poetry in more ways than just providing material that he could reshape into his writing. From the very start, Williams had pursued medicine because "only medicine, a job I enjoyed, would make it possible for me to live and write as I wanted to" (*A* 51). Obviously, Williams's decision to practice among the working class of Rutherford shows that "living and writing as he wanted to" meant something other than economic security and the artistic independence it would provide. Neither did it mean that Williams wanted to play the starving artist—"I would not court disease, live in the slums for the sake of art, give lice a holiday. I would not 'die for art,' but live for it, grimly! and work, work, work (like Pop), beat the game and be free (like

Mom, poor soul!) to write'' (*A* 51). Instead, his decision to practice medicine among the poor immigrants of his home town gave him both the modicum of material security he needed to survive and the wealth of artistic material he needed for his writing by giving him the opportunity to make an empathic contact with some romantically more "authentic" member of the human community through an act of diagnosis. Williams explains:

> I lost myself in the very properties of their minds: for the moment at least I actually became *them,* whoever they should be, so that when I detached myself from them at the end of a half-hour of intense concentration over some illness which was affecting them, it was as though I were reawakening from a sleep. For the moment I myself did not exist, nothing affected me. . . .
>
> I knew it was an elementary world that I was facing, but I have always been amazed at the authenticity with which the simple-minded often face that world when compared with the tawdriness of the public viewpoint exhibited in reports from the world at large. The public view which affects the behavior of so many is a very shabby thing compared with what I see every day in my practice of medicine.
>
> (*A* 356–57)

The possibility of an empathic identification with some other returns us to the confusion with romantic thought that pervades Williams's writing. But as we have already seen, Williams's methodological empiricism, his attitudes toward language as symbolic action, and his acknowledgment of the dangers inherent in the act of empathy all combine to defeat a too-easy reading of Williams as a failed romantic. In this chapter I will argue that it is precisely Williams's role as a doctor and its symbiotic—not merely complementary—relationship to his role of poet that provides the clearest model of Williams's aspirations for his writing. Specifically, it is the act of diagnosis that is at the core of both Williams's medicine and his poetry. From his early fascination with the neurologist Spiller in medical school— where "diagnosis was Spiller's forte" (*A* 52)—through his portrayal of doctors in his fiction and poetry, to the description of his own practice in the *Autobiography,* Williams returns again and again to the act of diagnosis as that part of the "daily practice of medicine" that allows him "to catch the evasive life of the thing, to phrase the words in such a way that stereotype will yield a moment of insight" (*A* 359).

The ways in which Williams performs his diagnoses and his attitude toward them as verbal embodiments of those moments when "the inarticulate patient struggles to lay himself bare for you" and, in doing so, "reveals some secret twist of a whole community's pathetic way of thought" (*A* 359) mark an important moment in both modern medicine and modern writing. Williams's writing about medicine in his short stories, novels, and plays exposes the inadequacy of an increasingly paternalistic, predominantly scientific model of diagnosis established as far back as the Enlightenment. Williams shows how limiting a diagnosis to a reading of the physical signs of disease ignores those psychological and cultural symptoms that extend the notions of sickness and cure beyond the physical realm of the body and into the more symbolic realms of both the self and the social. More important,

Williams's use of his writing as a form of symbolic action extends his ideas on writing *about* medicine to include notions of writing *as* medicine. In both *Kora in Hell: Improvisations* (1917–20) and "Rome" (ca. 1924), as well as in his correspondence with Kenneth Burke, Williams develops a notion of writing as medicine that Burke later incorporates into his shared theory of the poet as a kind of "medicine man"—one who employs either a "homeopathic" or an "allopathic strategy of cure" (*PLF* 64–66).

Beginning with d'Alembert's use of the word "semiotics" to describe that branch of medicine "concerned with the interpretation of symptoms," I will show in this chapter how Williams's writing-about-medicine exposes the limits of the predominantly algebraic, scientific model of diagnosis prevalent around the turn of the century. Specifically, I will compare Williams's writing with that of an earlier doctor/writer, S. Weir Mitchell—one of the leading nerve specialists in America, who practiced in Philadelphia around the time that Williams entered medical school at the University of Pennsylvania. Mitchell was also the diagnostician to both Charlotte Perkins Gilman and Edith Wharton, as well as the author of a great many short stories and novels. By comparing Mitchell's diagnostics with Williams's, I hope to show how Williams's method marks the need for a more dialectical relationship between nomothetic and idiographic approaches to medicine. In resituating the importance of this interplay between the regulatory law and the unique case, Williams emphasizes the necessity for a more "narrative" understanding of the patient that echoes the concerns of contemporary medical writers such as A. R. Luria, Oliver Sacks, and Richard Seltzer. Specifically, Williams opens the scope of his diagnoses to focus on the unique psychological, sexual, and political conditions of each patient in an act of empathy that stresses the dialogic and chastises the monologic gaze of the all-knowing doctor.

The importance of empathy in Williams's diagnostics brings out questions of transference and identification that I will try to answer through a return examination of Williams's method with that of Heinz Kohut and Jessica Benjamin. Using Benjamin's and Kohut's ideas about narcissistic transformation and empathy in both the therapeutic relationship and the establishment of object love, I will show how Williams develops a "grammar of translation" for his diagnoses whereby he can achieve empathic contact with an other and still maintain the integrity of both subject and object. Through this process of "discovery" and "identification," Williams's diagnoses become "representative anecdotes" (in Burke's terms) of the patient's condition, as well as "perspicuous representations" (in Wittgenstein's terms) that expose the established, social grammars that define objects for us. In this way, Williams's poetics incorporates Burke's early notions of writing as a form of "homeopathy," "allopathy," "cure," and "education," as it extends his diagnostics beyond the individual to embrace both the language and the community. Williams performs these "diagnostic treatments" by using language as a form of symbolic action that serves two important functions: first, it allows us to "identify" what Williams calls in *Spring and All* that "quality of independent existence, of reality which we feel in ourselves" (*CP I* 208) through the analogous extension of observable phenomena that bear analogical similarity to our own experience. Next, it symbolically recreates that experience for us through the work's own linguistic performance, allowing us our own moment of empathic "contact" and "identification." This "modern medicine" that Williams first mentions in *Kora in Hell* will become the primary strategy through which we can understand more fully the cultural diagnostics at work in Williams's writings.

I

Williams's short story "The Use of Force" has become a near-standard text in the field of literature and medicine, though at least one critic sees it as the site where these two fields become incompatible. David B. Morris explains that "At least in imagination and in sensibility, Williams's poet frequently occupies a place so far removed from the doctor's world of professional duties and of ethical obligations that conflict is inevitable." Morris argues that at times, "doctor and poet . . . are like two contrary spirits trapped within a single flesh" and that Williams's poetic act of "destruction" is diametrically opposed to his medical duty to cure. By acting "like a poet," Morris says, the doctor in Williams's story loses all sense of responsibility and sees his patient as " 'material' for a work of art." Morris reads Williams's doctor here as "confusing the boundaries between literature and medicine," abusing his power as medical man by poetically seeking a moment of "spontaneous, pure, undisguised being, when individuals seem to live with an unrestrained intensity which precludes dissemblance or practiced wisdom."[1]

Morris's reading of Williams's story relies on notions of poetry and medicine that, I will argue, Williams himself redefines. If anything, Williams's figure in "The Use of Force" is all too much the overpowering, paternalistic doctor and not enough the empathic poet, as we will see in our comparison of Williams's story with S. Weir Mitchell's "The Moral Management of Sick or Invalid Children" in section III below. Here I will read the story as a "diagnostic treatment" of an act of diagnosis, one that shows the complicated interplay between Williams's notions of poetry and medicine. The act of diagnosis holds a central position in both Williams's practice as well as his poetics. For Williams, an act of diagnosis is as much a poetic act as it is a medical practice, and as such he moves his diagnoses away from a model established in the Enlightenment to an understanding of diagnostics more in line with recent medical practices. In order to see how this shift comes about, we need to look at the development of the act of diagnosis itself and see what historically has caused the "conflict" between doctors and poets that Morris claims above.

In his *Preliminary Discourse to the Encyclopedia of Diderot* (1751), D'Alembert describes agriculture and medicine as the "principal causes" of the birth of "the vast science generally called Physics, or the study of Nature." At once "both our most primitive knowledge and the source of all other knowledge," medicine and agriculture provided those initial sites of "useful knowledge" that grow out of a need to maintain and support the body. As such, these originary forms of knowledge give birth to the methodology behind all science. D'Alembert is quick to point out, however, that these branches of knowledge have been "stifled and overshadowed" by the "physico-mathematical sciences" because they can not be reduced to algebraic or geometric "truths." Though "some have tried to reduce

... the art of curing to calculations, and the human body, that most complicated machine, has been treated by our algebraic doctors as if it were the simplest or the easiest one to reduce to its component parts," such reductions are merely "intellectual games to which Nature is not obliged to conform."[2]

Because of the inability to reduce the body to general law, d'Alembert confines medicine to "the history of the human body, of its maladies and their remedies" and locates it along the zoological branch of "Particular Physics." The four branches of "Medicine—Hygiene, Pathology, Semiotics, and Therapeutics"—concern the prevention, causes, indications, and healing of the sick body, and all are limited in their scope by the skeptical empiricism inherent in an "Experimental Science." In other words, if the scientist can know nothing beyond perceptions, then that science must be reduced to "mere experience and practice, without the formulation of any theoretical principles."[3] "Semiotics," which "has for its object the indications of life, of health, of *sicknesses,* their diagnosis and prognosis" (original emphasis), becomes particularly limited in this scheme to a record of physical signs and the diseases, or states of health, to which they refer.[4]

In essence, d'Alembert marks the codification of the "Science of Medicine," begun in the late seventeenth century by Sydenham, by limiting it to a "General and Experimental Science" and removing it from its previous association with very different forms of knowledge.[5] As Robert Darnton points out, in "trimming the tree of knowledge," d'Alembert and Diderot attempt "to root knowledge in epistemology" by consigning to the "unknowable" all forms of knowledge that lay outside of the rational sensationalism of the *philosophes.*[6] As such, the newly defined fields of "Medicine" and "Semiotics" become epistemologically limited to the recognition of previously observed physical "signs" of health and disease, morphologically consistent with the rest of the "Natural Sciences," and historically relocated to a position anterior to the development of "History, Logic, and Ethics." Through these three strategies, d'Alembert confines "Medicine" to the realm of the observable and completely severs "Medicine" from its far more ancient ties to the realm of the insensible and to the arts of "Rhetoric" and "Poetics."

In his preface to *Samson Agonistes,* Milton discusses tragedy as a kind of homeopathic "physic" intended to "purge the mind" of pity and fear, just as "things of melancholic hue and quality are used against melancholy, sour against sour, salt to remove salt humors." Before him, George Puttenham described a "forme of poetic lamentations" as allowing the poet to play physician to his readers in a way analogous to the "Paracelsians" by "making the very greef it selfe (in part) cure of the disease." These Renaissance examples mark the continuation of a connection between medicine and rhetoric that goes back to the ancient Greeks. Above the door of the Library at Thebes was inscribed the words "Medicine for the Soul," and, as Philip de Lacy points out, the methodology of Greek empiricism and of Epicureanism was first formulated in the Hippocratic writings of the fifth to fourth centuries B.C.[7]

In Epicurean rhetoric, medicine provides a methodology of inference and probability that relies on apparent signs as the indicators of "unperceived objects, some of a determinate existence, some of non-existence, some of the absence of a determinate existence."[8] As such, both medicine and rhetoric rely on a methodological empiricism whereby conjecture based on genetic similarity to previous experience can provide probable arguments of both cause and effect. "For just as the physician knows what is probable in disease, and the pilot knows what is probable in weather, so the rhetor considers the course of political events, when something is going to occur in the state, and from this knowledge he says he is going to persuade the people."[9] Medicine and rhetoric become analogous arts that consider all perceptions to be true and ultimately derive all knowledge from perceptions. Moreover, they treat apparent signs as the indicators of unobserved, though by no means unintelligible, objects.

As Keith Hutchinson points out, it is just this distinction between unobserved and unintelligible phenomena that marks a crucial redefinition that takes place during the scientific revolution. Briefly, Hutchinson explains how Descartes' rejection of manifest qualities as being just as insensible as occult qualities marks the "acceptance of insensible agencies into the scope of natural philosophy" and moves the meaning of the word "occult" away from its earlier connotation of "insensible" to its modern meaning of "unintelligible."[10] By recognizing that no qualities are ever directly perceived, Descartes rejects as unknowable those *qualitates* that Aristotle used to explain occult qualities and replaces them with mechanisms that were also insensible, but still intelligible. Medically, these mechanisms became the explanations behind those signs observed by the diagnostician. In this way, the body became the site of a new "concrete knowledge" to be gained by "bringing to light" the previously invisible realm of subcutaneous, localized symptoms. No longer was disease considered a disorder of the "whole body"; instead, diseases became categorized as specific afflictions of particular organs. As Foucault explains in *The Birth of the Clinic,* by the end of the eighteenth century, "a reorganization of the elements that make up the pathological phenomenon" had occurred—"a grammar of signs [had] replaced a botany of symptoms." The question that began the medical examination was no longer "How do you feel?" but rather "Where does it hurt?"[11]

With this relocation of disease into what Foucault calls "a space of projection without depth, of coincidence without development," the "Science of Medicine" concerned itself more and more with the observable and the probable, gradually separating itself from the insensible and the "occult"—a word that, beginning in the eighteenth century, took on its more modern associations with the unknowable and the supernatural.[12] In another kind of "grammar of transference," medicine now reduces the particulars of a sick individual to those particular signs of disease that are made coincidental with the disease itself according to a "grammar" of diagnosis, based on statistical correspondence. But as F. G. Crookshank points out in his "Supplement" to Ogden and Richards'ss *The Meaning of Meaning,* "medical statistics relate to the usage of symbols for general references, whether or no the symbolisation is correct and the references adequate, rather than to things, occurrences, or happenings." By collapsing the signs of disease with the name of the disease itself into this "space of projection without depth, of coincidence without development," the diagnosis that proceeds according to this "grammar of signs" does two things: first, it reduces the individual patient to that set of signs that best corresponds to some known set of universals, or names of diseases. In this way, Crookshank says, "an accurate appreciation of a patient's 'present state' is often treated as ignorant *because* it is incompatible with the sincere use of one of the few verbal symbols available to us as Proper Names for Special Diseases" (original emphasis).[13] Next, by ignoring the value of these signs as having analogical similarity to other forms of disease—by ignoring their value as a "botany of symptoms"—certain diseases can actually be treated incorrectly because of a faulty identification based on a too-narrow reading of signs. In both cases, the idiographic qualities of the unique individual or unique incident get sacrificed in the "scientific reduction" of that person or occurrence into a set of signs that adhere strictly to some nomothetic law or "Proper Name."

Obviously this methodology would not appeal to Williams, who described the poet's business as "Not to talk in vague categories but to write particularly, as a physician works, upon a patient, upon the thing before him, in the particular to discover the universal. John Dewey had said (I discovered it quite by chance), 'The local is the only universal, upon that all art builds' " (*A* 391). As we will see by the end of this chapter, it is just such a "spatial coincidence" as the one described above that Williams plays with in a poem like "Queen Anne's Lace"—making tenor and vehicle, woman and flower, indistinguishable and transforming the "field / of the wild carrot taking / the field by force" (*CP I* 162) into the spatial field of his modern diagnostics. In this way, Williams's poetic "botany of symptoms"— an "identification" based on analogical similarity—acts dialectically with the more "scientific," medical "grammar of signs" to form an epistemological field very different from either the field of vision open to the gaze of the scientist or the romantic ideal of the poetic as some privileged field of knowledge. In order to see how Williams's writing opens up that discursive space that both Foucault and Crookshank associate with the "Science of Medicine" and resists, if not redefines, its epistemological boundaries, we need first to see how Williams's sense of language as symbolic action—that "post-Darwininian botanist's language of flowers" discussed in Chapter 2—situates that field by allowing his writing to act metonymically as a reduction of experience, but does so in such a way that his "diagnostic treatments" of his patients are no longer a reduction of that person into a "grammar of signs."

Williams's diagnoses become, in Kenneth Burke's terms, a "material reduction" that is not a "*substantial* reduction" such as the "correlation" appropriate for "scientific realism," because "in 'poetic realism' states of mind as the motives of action are not reducible to materialistic terms." As Burke explains, "scientific reductions" work in "one direction"; that is, they allow for the substitution of *either* "quantity for quality, or quality for quantity (since either side could be considered the sign, or symptom, of the other)" (*GM* 507–10). And as Williams explains in "Belly Music" (1919), in order to "pass the mark set by the post-Darwinian botanists," we need to remember that previously established "facts" like "the Copernican theory" and "the voyage of Columbus" cannot become a "grammar of signs" through which we interpret our experience. In other words, we cannot allow a "scientific reduction"—a "grammar of signs"—to become our sole epistemological field. Even d'Alembert realized that "the human body" cannot be reduced by "algebraic doctors . . . to its component parts," and Williams's epistemology, as embodied in his poetics, avoids such a reduction to the "nomothetic" by emphasizing its necessary interaction with the "idiographic"—the unique case explainable only through its analogical similarity to previous experience. In this way, by maintaining those analogical relationships between particulars, Williams avoids the scientific reduction of a unique occurrence into a single universal, or nomothetic law, even though this law, of course, still plays a part in the diagnosis. Additionally, Williams resists having his "botany of symptoms" calcify into a "grammar of signs" by having his writing act "synecdochically," aiming to "embody" a state of consciousness in order to produce in the reader a corresponding state.[14] In this way, Williams's diagnoses become what Burke calls "representative anecdotes"—the dialectical, ironic re-presentation of human experience.

To appreciate more fully what it means for our understanding of Williams to see his diagnoses as "representative anecdotes," as well as to understand the historical relationship of his diagnoses to the hastily sketched shifts in the science of medicine described above, I will conclude this section with another compressed, historical look at two works by two more doctor/writers in an attempt to clarify the historical distinction between doctor and poet that David B. Morris relies on for his reading of Williams. Published in 1791, Erasmus Darwin's *Botanic Gardens* and P. P. Price's *A Treatise On the Diagnosis and Prognosis of Disease*[15] together mark out the discursive space in which a "scientific" diagnosis was made distinct from a "poetic" description. Price's work, in fact, is cited by the *OED* as the first modern use of the term "diagnosis"—the "identification of a disease by careful investigation of its symptoms and history"—a definition that solidifies d'Alembert's limitation of "Semiotics" to the realm of the sensible and the intelligible and that resituates the word's etymological root of "to know thoroughly." What can be known, according to Price, is only that which falls under the gaze of the doctor, and treatment depends upon correctly classifying the disease and following that course of action which, historically, has proved most successful. As such, Price helps to distinguish the "Science of Medicine" from other "Medical Arts"—such as Physiognomy, Physiology, and Homeopathy—that involve vitalistic qualities or causes that are either insensible or now declared unintelligible.

Erasmus Darwin—grandfather of Charles Darwin, and initially a famous physician in Scotland—states in his "Advertisement" for *The Botanic Garden* that his design is "to inlist [*sic*] Imagination under the banner of Science; and to lead her votaries from the looser analogies, which dress out the imagery of poetry, to the stricter ones which form the ratiocination of philosophy."[16] His project in both "The Economy of Vegetation" and "The Loves of the Plants" is to "transmute" Linnaeus's botanical system of classification into a fanciful allegory of plant life, the way that Ovid "did by art poetic transmute Men, Women, and even Gods and Goddesses, into Trees and Flowers." As Darwin explains in his "Advertisement" for "The Loves of the Plants":

> In the first Poem, or Economy of Vegetation, the physiology of Plants is deliver'd; and the operation of the Elements, as far as they may be supposed to affect the growth of Vegetables. But the publication of this part is defer'd to another year, for the purpose of repeating some experiments on vegetation, mentioned in the

notes. In the second poem, or Loves of the Plants, which is here presented to the Reader, the Sexual System of Linnaeus is explain'd, with the remarkable properties of many particular plants.[17]

The Botanic Gardens is an elaborate allegory of sylphs, nymphs, and gnomes, designed to animate and extend Linnaeus's botanical system. A part of the literature involving "Newton's Rainbow," Darwin's allegory—like James Thompson's *The Seasons*—"puts back into the . . . phenomena the sensuousness and drama—even, in the implied figure of the scientist as a magician, the mystery and enchantment— which Newton [here Linnaeus] had methodically excluded from his experimental observations." Darwin's poetry acts as a kind of "grammar of translation," expanding the "scientific reduction" inherent in Linnaeus's systems of classification by using mythological and fantastic figures as "hieroglyphs" of particular plants. But Darwin's motives are far from fanciful. He did not believe, as Keats later did, that "the goblin is driven from the hearth, and the rainbow is robbed of its mystery" by the scientific explanations that reduced perceptual phenomena to something more elementary.[18] Instead, Darwin seeks to incorporate in his allegory those occulted qualities and causes in nature that were implicit in, but excluded from, the stricter scientific thought of Linnaeus. Darwin returns to a more Epicurean reading of manifest signs, explained above, as indicators of "unperceived objects, some of a determinate existence, some of non-existence, some of the absence of a determinate existence." In particular, Darwin's allegory includes a "big bang" theory of creation, an early account of evolution (which influenced his grandson's theories), and a use of figures from "the Rosicrucian doctrine of Gnomes, Sylphs, Nymphs, and Salamanders" because it was "probable, that they were originally the names of hieroglyphic figures representing the elements" and were designed to explain early "discoveries in philosophy and chemistry before the invention of letters."[19]

Darwin presents the reader with images from a "Camera Obscura . . . in which are lights and shades dancing on a whited canvas, and magnified into apparent life!"[20] These "lights and shades," like Williams's own images, represent "ideas in things." In his own discussion of poetry and prose, Darwin as the "Poet" explains to the "Bookseller" in his first "Interlude"

> next to the measure of the language, the principal distinction appears to me to consist in this; that Poetry admits of very few words expressive of perfectly abstracted ideas, whereas Prose abounds with them. And as our ideas derived from visible objects of our other senses, the words expressive of these ideas belonging to vision make up the principal part of poetic language. That is the Poet writes principally to the eye, the Prose-writer uses more abstracted terms.[21]

By interpolating long, abstract, "scientific" footnotes into the text of his allegory, Darwin provides those ideas behind his figures while maintaining a "voluntary suspension of Reason" in the action of his verse. As the "Bookseller" says to the Poet/Botanist/Author at the beginning of this "Interlude," "Your verses, Mr. Botanist, consist of *pure description*, I hope there is *sense* in the notes" (original emphasis). By putting the "sense" in his notes and the "sensual" in his poetry, Darwin can expand Linnaeus's classifications with those less "reasonable" qualities and causes explored by "occult" philosophers like the Rosicrucians and even by Darwin himself. Moreover, the "imaginative" quality of Darwin's text also acts synecdochically to recreate those sensations of pleasure and power that Darwin associates with plant life by acting in the same way as nightmares and tragedies.[22]

Darwin's work attempts to extend Linnaeus's botany beyond its "scientific" limits, while Price's work situates diagnostics confidently within the bounds of the observable and the probable. P. P. Price remains the preeminent doctor in his work; Dr. Darwin becomes the "poet" in his. Yet Darwin insists, however playfully, that he is simply setting up a "Camera Obscura" before our eyes and that his focus remains on what is visible to all. His "botany of symptoms" is as true as Price's "grammar of signs." Still, the anxiety toward science produced by such an assertion is alleviated by Darwin's acknowledging the distinctions between art and science, imagination and fact, poetry and prose. By going beyond the epistemological limits set for "science" and "diagnosis," Darwin "sees" beyond the collapsed field open to the gaze of the doctor, but what he "sees" is only available to the imagination, and consequently not strictly a part of Linnaeus's work.

But *The Botanic Gardens* is more than just a comment on the disparity between imaginative and scientific observation. It attempts to open up that "space of projection without depth" in which a writer like Price locates his "diagnoses." As such, Darwin's work is a precursor to the romantics' debate with science. More important, though, Darwin situates that point at which science itself becomes anxious about that which it "sees"—that point at which medicine in particular must declare itself an "art." By collapsing the symptoms of disease and the name we give it into a "space of projection without depth, of coincidence without development," the doctor/scientist makes manifest what is essentially occult. There is no more visually verifiable "reality" behind the "Proper Names of Special Diseases" than there is behind the "loves of the plants." The gaze of the doctor/scientist that describes an illness "sees" no more accurately than the poet/botanist: his "descriptions" only conform more precisely to the ideals of "scientific realism." The difference is one of methodology and epistemology. The doctor/scientist's "grammar of signs" anxiously maintains a "stricter" correlation than that loose "botany of symptoms" developed by the poet/botanist. As we shall see below, this anxiety extends for at least the next hundred years, and it appears prominently in the "art" of our next doctor/writer—S. Weir Mitchell.

II

In *The Autobiography of a Quack* (1900), S. Weir Mitchell gives a fictional, "first-hand" account of the dissolute career of that greatest of "scoundrels," the fake doctor.[23] Prophetically named Ezra Sandcraft by a family with a penchant for biblical names, Mitchell's protagonist was born into a bourgeois Philadelphia family but soon rose above his parents. His mother—though "a Fishbourne, and a lady"—had married beneath her station and died when he was an infant; his "common" father owned a legal stationery store in Philadelphia, doubled as the bell ringer of Christ Church, and was "born somewhere in New Jersey . . . he was once angry because a man called him a Jersey Spaniard." Ezra attends Princeton, develops a "fatal . . . liking for all the good things in life," and is expelled for stealing to support his refined tastes. When his father's death—"while training his bell ringers in the Oxford triple bob"—leaves him a legacy of two thousand dollars, Ezra enters medical school in Philadelphia and graduates by "attend[ing] the quizzes, as they call them, pretty closely, and, being of a quick and retentive memory, was thus enabled to dispense with some of the six or seven lectures a day which duller men found it necessary to follow" (*AQ* 4–13).

Sandcraft is a quick study with no morals—one of that most American breed of characters that practices what Poe, in one of Williams's favorite short stories, calls "the most important of the Exact Sciences . . . Diddling." Picaresque in plot, *The Autobiography of a Quack* is a typical story of the downfall of a fascinating but reprehensible young man. Dying of "Addison's disease," Sandcraft is told by his doctor (whose diagnosis Sandcraft does not believe) that "if you were to write out a plain account of your life it would be pretty well worth reading. If half of what you told me last week be true, you must be about as clever a scamp as there is to be met with." Sandcraft does so, though under the pretense that "no one will ever see these pages" (*AQ* 2–3). He soon interrupts his narrative, however, to say:

> I find just here that I am describing a thing as if I were writing for some other people to see. I may as well go on that way. After all, a man never can quite stand off and look at himself as if he was the only person concerned. He must have an audience, or make believe to have one, even if it is only himself. Nor, on the whole, should I be unwilling, if it were safe, to let people see how great ability may be defeated by the crankiness of fortune.
>
> (*AQ* 7–8)

My fascination with Mitchell's story, and with this section in particular, is twofold. *The Autobiography of a Quack* is a confessional narrative on two important and distinct levels. First, and most obviously, it is Ezra Sandcraft's ironic confession of a "good mind gone bad." Drunk with desire for the "all the good things in life," Ezra lies, cheats, steals, nearly kills his Aunt Rachel while stealing money from her Bible, and betrays the only person who loves and believes in him—his sister Pen. My real interest in Mitchell's story, however, concerns the betrayal of another "pen"—Sandcraft's and Mitchell's "pen" that produces a narrative that betrays its own author. Throughout his "confession," Sandcraft shows almost no remorse. The closest he comes to regret is when, in Henry James fashion, he sees the ghost of his former self as a young boy, during a bout of delirium tremens in the church where his father used to be a bell ringer. Even then, Sandcraft says only, "I do not know why he [the young boy] was worse to me than snakes, or the twitchy old woman [a vision of his Aunt Rachel] with her wide eyes of glass, and that jerk, jerk, to right" (*AQ* 96). The only other incident that brings Sandcraft close to regret is a nightmare he has about his sister Pen, who appears in his dream as "a shameless, worn creature, with great sad eyes." Remembering "what she had been been, with her round, girlish innocent face and fair hair," Sandcraft resolves that if he lives, he will burn "this pleasant history . . . and as soon as I get a little money I will set out to look for my sister" (*AQ* 112). He dies, however, immediately after he tells us about the dream.

Sandcraft's "pen" betrays him as boldly as he betrayed his sister Pen, as we easily read the occulted immorality behind his manifest assertions of necessity and ingenuity. When Sandcraft first explains his stealing to pay his debts at Princeton, for example, we read his protestations with a knowing eye—"I borrowed from two or three young Southerners; but at last, when they became hard up, my aunt's uncounted hoard proved a last resource, or some rare chance in a neighboring room helped me out. I never did look on this method as of permanent usefulness, and it was only the temporary folly of youth" (*AQ* 9). Poe is only half-kidding when he calls "diddling" one of the "Exact Sciences" and defines it as "a compound, of which the ingredients are minuteness, interest, perseverance, ingenuity, audacity, *nonchalance,* originality, and *grin*" (the diddler always grins privately after a successful diddle).[24] As a "diddler"—a con man and a quack—Sandcraft is an extraordinarily insightful semiotician. His "diagnoses" rely on a cunning ability to read the manifest signs of human behavior, see what the "illness" is (or at least see what the patient *thinks* the illness is), and prescribe the "remedy" that will best satisfy the patient's *expectations* of treatment. Sandcraft's semiotics relies almost wholly on the idiographic—the individual case—as well as on the occult— both the insensible and, during his brief stint as a fake spiritualist, the "supernatural." In fact, at the height of his career as a quack, Sandcraft attempts to combine "in one establishment all the various modes of practice which are known as irregular." He goes on to say:

> This, as will be understood, is really only a wider application of the idea which prompted me to unite in my own business homeopathy and the practice of medicine. I proposed to my partner, accordingly, to combine with our present business that of spiritualism, which I knew had been very profitably turned to account in connection with medical practice. As soon as he agreed to this plan, which by the way, I hoped to enlarge so as to include all the available isms, I set about making such preparations as were necessary.
>
> (*AQ* 73)

By adding spiritualism, the most "occult" of the practices associated with late nineteenth-century medicine, Sandcraft manages to practice all of those kinds of treatment that had been occulted from the "strict" practice of medicine—homeopathy, electromagnetism, "pill-pushing," spiritualism, and even, as we shall see below, writing.

If Sandcraft's pen betrays his immorality, Mitchell's pen betrays his own anxiety toward his practice as the leading nerve specialist in The United States. Mitchell is perhaps best known today as the diagnostician to Charlotte Perkins Gilman, whose "The Yellow Wallpaper" chronicles her treatment under Mitchell's "rest cure." While a great deal has already been written about Mitchell and Gilman,[25] I would like to call attention to two aspects of Mitchell's "cure." The first has to do with the "scientific" nature of Mitchell's diagnostics; the second with the act of writing itself. In *The Genesis and Development of a Scientific Fact,* Ludwik Fleck discusses how knowledge, and specifically medical knowledge, inevitably involves some interplay between what he terms "*active association of the phenomen*"—cultural, historical associations that combine to form a "thought style which determines the formulation of every concept"—and *"passive associa-tions"*—observations "not explicable in terms of either psychology (both individ-ual or collective) or of history" (original emphases).[26] As Elaine Showalter and others have shown, the treatment of female "nervous diseases" in the nineteenth century is a complex mass of "cultural, historical associations" raised against women. As such, it is not difficult to see Mitchell's diagnoses as heavily reliant on "active associations." His treatment of women participates in a [Charles] "Dar-winian psychiatry" that views the female as a backward, if not infantilized, member of the species whose "natural" development toward reproductive specialization has left her inferior to man in "courage, energy, intellect, and inventive genius."[27] Consequently, Mitchell has his sufferers from "hysterical motor ataxia" learn to crawl on kneepads before attempting to walk. "Following nature's lesson with a docile mind," Mitchell writes, "we have treated the woman as nature treats an infant."[28]

In his adherence to the "natural" and his insistence on the "true nature of medicine" as opposed to "quackery," Mitchell remains blind to the degree that his ideas are determined by "active associations." In his "Introductory" to *Doctor and Patient* (1888), Mitchell writes:

> Scarcely a fact I state, or a piece of advice I give, might not be explained or justified by physiological reasoning which would carry me far beyond the depth of those for whom I wrote. All this I have sedulously avoided.
>
> What I shall have to say in these pages will trench but little on the mooted ground of the differences between men and women. For me the grave significance of sexual difference controls the whole question, and if I say little of it in words, I cannot exclude it from my thought of them and their difficulties. The woman's desire to be on a level of competition with man and to assume his duties is, I am sure, making mischief, for it is my belief that no length of generations of change in her education and modes of activity will ever really alter her characteristics. She is physiologically other than man. I am concerned with her now as she is, only desiring to help her in my small way to be in wiser and more healthful fashion what I believe her Maker meant her to be, and to teach her how not to be that with which her physiological construction and the strong ideals of her sexual life threaten her as no contingencies of man's career threaten in like measure or like number the feeblest of the masculine sex.[29]

During his "spiritualist/homeopath" phase, Mitchell's "quack," Sandcraft, has his accomplice disguise himself as a patient, take a place in the waiting room, and talk about his "illness" with the rest of the patients. Based on what his assistant learns, Sandcraft is able to amaze his patients with immediate, Sherlock Holmes/Dr. Charles Bell–like diagnoses of their maladies. This is obvious quackery, but how different is it from Mitchell's own reliance on the "active associations" of "phys-iological reasoning" to make his own diagnoses "factual," "natural," and even "divinely correct"? Do Mitchell's "active associations" act as a kind of invisible accomplice that shuttles "knowledge" back and forth between doctor and patient? How much, I wonder, did Mitchell's "successes" with women rely on his telling the patient what she *thinks* the illness is and his prescribing the "remedy" that most satisfies her *expectations* of treatment? How far away is the methodology and epistemology of Mitchell's "exact science of medicine" from the "exact science of diddling"?

Mitchell's blindness toward "active associations" leads to my second interest in his "diagnostics treatments." Obviously, one of the most fundamental activities that Mitchell sees as part of a woman's "physiological construction and the strong ordeal of her sexual life . . . [that] threaten her as no contingencies of man's career threaten . . . [even] the feeblest of the masculine sex" is the act of writing. For both Ezra Sandcraft and S. Weir Mitchell, writing is a means of self-justification, if not an out-and-out act of self-creation. But Sandcraft's own admission that "a man never can quite stand off and look at himself as if he was the only person concerned" (*AQ* 7), betrays more than the immoral "quack" that Mitchell hoped to show. Both authors remain blind to the power of writing as an act of self-discovery. Consequently, both authors' writing soon betrays itself and its author in an attempted act of repression that reveals what it had hoped to conceal. Sandcraft's cruelty, Mitchell's anxiety, and the "active associations" that lie behind both texts—those previously determined "facts" that constitute the "grammars" of both the "science of medicine" and the "science of diddling" all come into view as boldly, and nearly as madly, as the unnamed woman steps out from behind Gilman's "Wallpaper."

For Charlotte Perkins Gilman, of course, writing was a forbidden activity that could only worsen her already depressed condition. She followed Mitchell's advice for nearly three months in 1887 and "came so near the borderline of utter mental ruin that I could see over." She recovered her "power" only after she had "cast the noted specialists advice to the winds" and began, again, to read and write. She sent Mitchell a copy of the story, and while "[h]e never acknowledged it," Gilman was later told "that the great specialist had admitted to friends of his that he had altered his treatment of neurasthenia since reading 'The Yellow Wallpaper.' "[30] Mitchell's alterations, however, still betray his "active associations." In "Out-door and Camp-Life for Women"—the last essay in *Doctor and Patient*—Mitchell does recommend that "nervous women" spend time outdoors and "lead a man's life" in a tent; once she has "overcome her dread of sun and mosquitoes," of course, and even then, "only until the snow falls." Women are also allowed to do "light reading" while camping, though letters from home are forbidden. She can even write brief "word-sketches" of nature, providing she "learns first" to be properly "methodical and accurate." Mitchell even provides a few "objective" examples from his own notebooks as instructive guides; Ruskin is suggested as another exemplary writer.[31]

I focus on Mitchell because it is his blindness toward and unconscious reliance on "active associations" that gives him both national prominence and scientific authority in the field of American medicine from just after the Civil War to 1914— four years after Williams had graduated with a medical degree from the University of Pennsylvania, completed his internship at the French Hospital in New York, and studied pediatrics for a year in Leipzig. Yet their writing about, and practice of, medicine couldn't be more antithetical. Mitchell's "diagnoses," both in his fiction and his practice, unconsciously rely on "active associations" to give their insistence on the nomothetic its scientific, "objective" authority. These "active associations," which Mitchell admits he "cannot exclude . . . from my thought of [women] and their difficulties," determine that "physiological reasoning" that Mitchell "sedulously avoided" in *Doctor and Patient* because it "would carry [him] far beyond the depth of those for whom [he] wrote." What Mitchell writes "applies and must apply chiefly to the leisured class,"[32] and his "Darwinian psychiatry" helps constitute a "grammar of signs"—the nomothetic, regulatory laws—to which those individuals were often ruthlessly subsumed, but most times willing submitted. This insistence on the nomothetic situates these women in that "space of projection without depth" that falls under the gaze of the all-knowing doctor who simply "sees" the manifest signs of illness and ignores all "occult" forms of knowledge. His "diagnostic treatments" are simply reductions to a "scientific realism" that correlates to the "grammar of signs" that defines disease and prescribes the "proven" remedy.

As I will show in the next two sections, Williams's writing about medicine in his short stories takes an antithetical stance to nearly every statement I just made about Mitchell. His writing is preeminently a space of self-discovery that openly exposes the inadequacy of the nomothetic, tightly focuses on the individual, and consciously reveals those "active associations" that ground the seemingly objective. Moreover, by establishing a dialectical relationship between the nomothetic and the idiographic, Williams's "diagnostic treatments" avoid the reductions inherent in Mitchell's brand of "scientific realism" and act as a kind of "botany of symptoms" not unlike Erasmus Darwin's *Botanic Gardens*. But Williams's "post-Darwinian botanist's language of flowers" moves beyond *The Botanic Gardens* in an attempt to act synecdochically as its own form of "homeopathic" and "allopathic" treatment, relying on "passive associations" to animate and extend the unique moment of empathic "identification." Taken together, Williams's and Mitchell's writing about medicine, like the works of Price and Darwin in the previous section, mark a shift in the discursive space in which a "diagnosis" is performed. Also like Price and Darwin, Mitchell remained the preeminent doctor during his lifetime and Williams was primarily known as the "poet." Still, by challenging that discursive space of diagnosis, Williams's writing remains closer to more recent shifts in medical diagnostics proposed by doctor/writers such as A. R. Luria, Oliver Sacks, Gerald Weissmann, and Richard Seltzer. By establishing a strategy of "identity" and "identification" that focuses on the need for "empathy" and for a "transformation of narcissistic energies," Williams transforms his diagnoses into "representative anecdotes" which more fully re-present the particular patient's condition, allowing that patient both to maintain his or her uniqueness and still be "representative." In this way, as we will see in our own reading of "The Use of Force," the roles of poet and doctor become analogous. By emphasizing the idiographic and "passive associations"—"the actual words, as we hear them spoken under all circumstances"—Williams is able "to catch the evasive life of the thing, to phrase the words in such a way that stereotype will yield a moment of insight." As Williams goes on to say, it is in these acts of writing, these "diagnostic treatments," that "the inarticulate patient struggles to lay himself bare for you . . . [and] reveals some secret twist of a whole community's pathetic way of thought" (*A* 362 & 359).

III

Mitchell begins "The Moral Management of Sick or Invalid Children" (1888) with the following anecdote:

> Not long ago a pretty little girl of ten was brought to me from a long distance to get my advice as to a slight paralysis of one leg. The trouble had existed for several years. I soon saw that the child was irritable, sensitive, and positive, and I was, therefore, careful to approach her gently. The moment it was proposed to show me the leg, she broke into a fury of rage, and no inducement I could offer enabled me to effect my purpose. An appeal to the parents, and from them to force, ended in a distressing battle. She bit, scratched, kicked, and at last won a victory, and was left sullen and sobbing on the floor. Next day the same scene was repeated. It is true that at length they were able to undress her, but neither threats nor persuasion would keep her quiet long enough to enable me to apply the simplest tests. The case was obscure, and demanded the most careful study. Their time was limited, so that they were obliged to take her home in despair, without any guiding opinion from me, and with no advice, except as to her moral education, concerning which I was sufficiently explicit. I have seen many such illustrations of a common evil, and have watched the growth to adult life of some of these cases of wretched character, and observed the unpleasant results which came as they grew older. I have used an extreme case as a text, because I desire to fix attention on the error which parents and some doctors are apt to commit in cases of chronic ailments in children.

I have quoted this "extreme case" also "as a text," but not a text designed "to fix attention on the error" that Mitchell says "parents and some doctors are apt to commit in cases of chronic ailments in children." Mitchell's message is that "the spoiled, over-indulged child is a doubly unmanageable invalid" because she "lose[s] self-restraint," while she learns "to exact more and more, and to yield less and less." According to Mitchell, "when in illness the foolish petting of the mother continues, the doctor, at least, is to be pitied."[33]

Mitchell's case is typical of his writing, and it again betrays the detached, cold, clinical gaze of the paternalistic, all-knowing doctor. Always in control, he patiently struggles with the young girl but is simply never "enabled" either "to effect [his] purpose" or "to apply the simplest tests." The young girl may have "at last won a victory," but she has clearly lost the war. Unwilling to submit to the doctor (or to "enable" him), the young girl, whose own experience is completely effaced from the account, is sent home with her despairing parents. Pity the poor doctor.

Williams ends "The Use of Force" (1933) with the following account:

> Get me a smooth-handled spoon of some sort, I told the mother. We're going through with this. The child's mouth was already bleeding. Her tongue was cut and she was screaming in wild hysterical shrieks. Perhaps I should have desisted and come back in an hour or more. No doubt it would have been better. But I have seen at least two children lying dead in bed of neglect of such cases, and feeling that I must get a diagnosis now or never I went at it again. But the worst of it was that I too had got beyond reason. I could have torn the child apart in

my own fury and enjoyed it. It was a pleasure to attack her. My face was burning with it.

The damned brat must be protected against her own idiocy, one says to one's self at such time. Others must be protected against her. It is social necessity. And all these things are true. But a blind fury, a feeling of adult shame, bred of a longing for muscular release are the operatives. One goes on to the end.

In a final unreasoning assault I overpowered the child's neck and jaws. I forced the heavy silver spoon back of her teeth and down her throat till she gagged. And there it was—both tonsils covered with membrane. She had fought valiantly to keep me from knowing her secret. She had been hiding that sore throat for three days at least and lying to her parents in order to escape just such an outcome as this.

Now truly she *was* furious. She had been on the defensive before but now she attacked. Tried to get off her father's lap and fly at me while tears of defeat blinded her eyes.

(*FD* 134–35)

While people have had a wide range of reactions to Williams's story, few that I know of have suggested that "the doctor, at least, is to be pitied." Williams's account has been "dubbed *the* paradigmatic example of literature and bioethics in a close marriage. . . . [A]nthologized in the two major collections in the field of literature and medicine, . . . [i]t is one of the most frequently taught core texts . . . and has made its way into the ethics curriculum at several medical schools."[34] "The Use of Force" is Williams's "diagnostic treatment" of an act of diagnosis. As such, it brings into the reader's "gaze" conflicts involving paternalism and the rights of patients, loss of control on the part of the doctor, barely displaced feelings of sexual attraction and violence—if not out-and-out rape—and it calls into question the status, power, and fear of the medical profession. And it does these things openly. Rather than attempt to conceal the power he commands, as Mitchell does by using the weak passive verb "enabled," Williams is all too aware of his "force." Even though Williams tries to adopt a stance similar to Mitchell's in the story—"I would not insist on a throat examination so long as [the parents] would take the responsibility"—the dread of diphtheria in the minds of both doctor and parent makes the choice inevitable. Obviously, Williams's act of writing is no simple act of self-justification, and it is more than an act of self-discovery. Not only is he aware of what "one says to one's self at these times"; he knows what we're hiding when we say it. Williams stretches his story into an act of self-exposure, a moment of public revelation.

In terms of bioethics, the greatest difference between these two accounts for me is this: Mitchell's "pretty little girl of ten" refuses to submit to the gaze of the doctor, and she is sent home with "no advice, except as to her moral education." Williams gives in to his "feeling of adult shame, bred of a longing for muscular release" and makes the diagnosis that will save the life of a "savage brat" that he "had . . . fallen in love with," admiring the "magnificent heights of insane fury of effort bred of her terror of me." Williams exposes his doctor to the complications that Mitchell refuses to display openly. Mitchell's "distressing battle" ends in a Pyhrric victory for his "over-indulged" young girl, who is suitably punished, "left sullen and sobbing on the floor." Williams is shamefully aware of the defeat suffered by his "unusually attractive little thing. . . . She had fought valiantly to keep me from knowing her secret" (*FD* 131 & 135). The overwhelming "use of force" by the doctor is presented as both a necessary act and a willed, perversely pleasurable choice. Both doctor and patient are scarred by the battle.

In terms of "diagnostic treatments," the two stories also make clear the difference between what Kenneth Burke calls a "material reduction" such as the "correlation" appropriate for "scientific realism" and a "representative anecdote." Mitchell's story provides the manifest signs for his nomothetic conclusion—"The spoiled, over-indulged child is a doubly unmanageable invalid" whose "foolish petting . . . mother" has made pitiful both patient and doctor. But since, as Burke also says, "states of mind and motives for action are not reducible to materialistic terms" (*GM* 507), we can read those "occulted qualities" behind Mitchell's anecdote and "see" what his nomothetic law excludes from the story. Williams's "treatment" is an attempt at "poetic realism," and as such it provides that "paradigmatic example of literature and bioethics in a close marriage" by emphasizing the idiographic qualities of this unique case. It is "ironic" in that it presents the reader with a "dramatic, dialectical development." As Burke explains:

> Irony arises when one tries, by the interaction of terms upon one another, to produce a *development* which uses all the terms. Hence, from the standpoint of this total form (this "perspective of perspectives"), none of the participating "subperspectives" can be treated as either precisely right or precisely wrong. They are all voices, or personalities, or positions, integrally affecting one another. When the dialectic is properly formed, they are the number of characters needed to produce the total development.
>
> (*GM* 512, Burke's emphasis)

Williams's "total development" achieves its paradigmatic status by refusing to be reduced to a series of manifest "symptoms" that correlate to some "grammar of signs." Instead, insensible and potentially unintelligible qualities like the young girl's fierce pride in "keeping her secret" and the doctor's irrational fury and pleasure in his "attack" all contribute to the total "condition." We hear all of the voices involved, including the parents' embarrassed, fumbling concern and, most important, the young girl's hysterical shrieks. In this way, and unlike Mitchell's account, the symbolic action of Williams's "diagnostic treatment" acts as a "representative anecdote" of an act of diagnosis that lies outside the boundaries set by P. P. Price and the medical profession in general. The nomothetic law—the discovery of the signs of diphtheria—is made intentionally inadequate to explain all that we see and hear.

Two more aspects of Williams's "diagnostics" are worth mentioning here. First, Williams at least begins his diagnostic procedure in a way that both adheres to accepted principles and demonstrates the shrewd superiority of the general practitioner. Based on the information he receives from the parents—"fever for three days . . . a lot of sickness around"—the doctor takes "a trial shot at it as a point of departure" and asks "Has she had a sore throat?" The doctor knows that "we had been having a number of cases of diphtheria in the school to which this child went'' and so despite her parents response that ''No . . . No, she says her throat don't hurt her,'' the doctor demands visual verification—''Have you looked?'' (*FD* 131–2). Williams's doctor relies on knowledge obtained by ''close contact'' with his surroundings in order to generate what are called ''prior probabilities.'' As K. Danner Clauser explains, the general practitioner could often ''best the specialists'' because ''[h]e knew the incidence of . . . disease in his population; and he knew the incidence of symptoms that existed independently of that disease.''[35] Williams's doctor relies on the idiographic to focus immediately on the most probable, as well as the most dangerous, possibility. Computer simulation of this diagnostic procedure is currently being developed.[36]

But Williams's doctor also demonstrates a more significant, and more occulted, form of knowledge in his empathic understanding of both the girl and her parents. He recognizes the pain, the embarrassment, and the terror of the parents, although, like Mitchell, he chastises the over-indulgent mother and directs most of his understanding toward the father. Consequently, even though the doctor recognizes that ''both the mother and the father almost turned themselves inside out in embarrassment and apology,'' it is the father who is described as being torn between ''the fact that she was his daughter, his shame at her behavior, and his dread of hurting her,'' along with ''his dread also that she might have diphtheria'' (*FD* 133). The doctor also knows that the child knows he could hurt her, and he grinds ''his teeth in disgust'' when the mother uses the word ''hurt'' as he coaxes the child to open her mouth (*FD* 132). And, in his most complex act of empathy, he knows and admires Mathilda's own ''use of force'' in trying ''valiantly'' to ''keep her secret,'' even as he feels pleasure in his violent, inexcusable attack.

This empathic ''knowledge'' combines with a social reading of occult causes behind manifest signs to complete the ''total development'' of this ''representative anecdote.'' The parents' poverty as a contributing factor in the disease is hinted at when the mother apologizes for her daughter's being back in the kitchen because, ''It is very damp here sometimes.'' Poverty also mixes with pride when the doctor understands why the parents ''weren't telling me more than they had to . . . that's why they were spending three dollars on me'' (*FD* 131). Williams's use of empathy is oddly as insistent as his use of force, and it forms one of the sites of his own resistance to the reduction inherent in the ''diagnostic space.'' Moreover, as we saw in S. Weir Mitchell's writing above, ''occult'' forms of knowledge mark that point at which science becomes most anxious about itself. For Williams, however, this ''occult'' knowledge, which consists of the psychological, the sexual, the cultural, and the political, marks the complete diagnosis.

The significance of the psychological is the primary focus of ''the Insane'' (1950), a brief conversation between ''the old Doc'' and his son, a ''senior in medical school.'' Here the son relates a case history encountered during his rushed study of psychiatry, which lasted only ''a few weeks.'' Briefly, the son relates the case history of ''a funny-faced little nine-year-old guy with big glasses'' who ''has lost weight, doesn't sleep, [suffers from] constipation and all the rest,'' and whose mother ''brought him in for stealing money.'' The son explains that his job was ''to get the history, do a physical, a complete physical—you know what that means,

Dad—make a diagnosis and prescribe treatment'' (*FD* 288–90).

The son's point in the story is this: the boy's psychological case history yields a far more significant diagnosis than any physical examination. The boy's problems are a means of compensating for the love he lost when his alcoholic father, who showered him with attention, leaves his mother, who transfers her hatred of the father onto the boy and shows greater attention to his younger brother—the off-spring of a different father. As the son explains:

> And then he began to steal—from his mother—because he couldn't get the love he demanded of her. He began to steal from her to compensate for what he could not get otherwise, and which his father gave him formerly. . . .
> The child substitutes his own solution for the reality which he needs and cannot obtain. Unreality and reality become confused in him. Finally he loses track. He doesn't know one from the other.
>
> (*FD* 190)

More significant than the quality of the son's diagnosis, although he is confident that when he ''explain[s] the mechanism to the mother . . . and if she follows up what she's told to do the boy is likely to be cured,'' is the final reaction of both father and son:

> But what gets me, said his son. Of course we're checked up on all these cases; they're all gone over by a member of the staff. And when we give a history like that, they say, Oh those are just the psychiatric findings. That gripes me. Why, it's the child's life.
> Good boy, said his father. You're all right. Stick to it.
>
> (*FD* 190)

''The child's life''—the case history—cannot be reduced to the ''space of projec-tion'' that locates the diagnosis obtained from just the physical examination. Both disease and cure lie outside that space, in the psychological and the verbal. The symptoms are a form of symbolic action that must be read and treated as such. ''A history like that'' cannot be reduced to the ''grammar of signs'' that the son's medical superiors respect; they are a ''botany of symptoms'' whose value both father and son recognize.

''A history like that'' is the kind of ''clinical biography'' that A. R. Luria and Oliver Sacks have recently asserted as giving a complete ''picture of disease.'' They are ''unimagined portraits'' that Luria models after Walter Pater's *Imagined Portraits*. These ''pathological narratives'' give ''symptomological or behavioral facts that have been selected, arranged, and interpreted within a diagnostic frame-work,'' and, as such, they conform to the idea of a ''representative anecdote'' developed above. Moreover, these ''portraits'' result from Luria's own reformu-lation of the nomothetic and the idiographic, or, as Luria calls them, borrowing from Max Verworn, ''classical and romantic science.'' As Anne Hunsaker Hawkins goes on to explain, ''Both approaches are, theoretically, necessary in the biomedical sciences, for an individual is both a physiological organism governed by objective laws and causal explanations, and also an experiencing human being with beliefs and feelings and thoughts about himself or herself.[37]

Oliver Sacks argues that to "restore the human subject at the center—the suffering, afflicted, fighting, human subject—we must deepen a case history to a narrative or tale; only then do we have a 'who' as well as a 'what', a real person, a patient, in relation to disease—in relation to the physical." Sacks explains that in neurology in particular these narratives—a form of "poetic realism"—are essential as "the study of disease and of identity can not be disjoined" and that his own studies hope "to bring us to the very intersection of mechanism and life, to the relation of physiological processes to biography."[38]

Hawkins also points out the "representative" value of these "particular" cases

> in that they are histories about another human being, they function as reflections about ourselves. According to the eighteenth-century biographer Samuel Johnson, the unique appeal of biography consists in its presentation of "those parallel circumstances and kindred images to which we readily conform our minds."[39]

Dr. Johnson also once called tragedy "a true Medicine, which Purges the Passions" and praised Shakespeare—Williams's avatar of the imagination—saying that "he who mazed his imagination, in following the phantoms which other writers raise up before him, may here be cured of his delirious extasies, by reading human sentiments in human language."[40] In seeing tragedy and Shakespeare's use of "human language" in terms of symbolic actions, Dr. Johnson brings us back to those ideas of "empathy" and "identification" associated with Heinz Kohut and Jessica Benjamin and explored in the previous two chapters.[41] Briefly, both Kohut and Benjamin propose a "mother-based" psychology where the original undifferentiated relationship between mother and child forms the basis for the relationship between self and world by means of (in Kohut's terms) a "cathexis" of "narcissistic energies" from the "cherished self" to the "supraindividual ideals and to the world with which one identifies."[42] Kohut, in particular, sees empathy as "the operation that defines the field of psychoanalysis," and he defines the analyst's act of empathy as " 'vicarious introspection' or, more simply, as one person's (attempt to) experience the inner life of another while simultaneously retaining the stance of an objective observer."[43] For the analysand, empathy is part of that way in which we develop a sense of "identity" by establishing object relations through "the expansion of the self beyond the borders of the individual" by means of the "antithesis to narcissism"—"object love."[44] The "cathexis of narcissistic energies" and the "relinquishment of narcissistic delusions" are crucial components of this act of empathy, but rather than repeat previous arguments, it will be enough for now to define empathy not only as the ability to see the self in the other, but also as the ability to see the other in the self.

For Williams, the act of empathy defines the field of diagnosis where, as he explains in the *Autobiography,* "I lost myself in the very properties of their minds: for the moment at least I actually became *them* . . . And my 'medicine' was the thing which gained me entrance to these secret gardens of the self. It lay there, another world, in the self. I was permitted by my medical badge to follow the poor, defeated body into those gulfs and grottos" (*A* 356 & 288). But Williams's "field" of diagnosis stands at odds with that "space of projection" that was the "scientific" diagnostic space. In order to see this opposition more clearly and recognize its relationship to an act of empathy, I will use as a kind of negative example, the story "Jean Beicke" (1933). Here, the doctor's lack of empathy combines with his failure to diagnose the illness properly in a reduction of the infant Jean onto the autopsy table where, only after she has died, will she yield her "secret."

Williams's doctor in "Jean Beicke" works in the children's ward of a hospital in Paterson, and his lack of feeling is not hard to understand. He deals daily with starving, malformed, abandoned infants—products of the Depression—in an ill-equipped, understaffed clinic:

> The ones I mean are those they bring in stinking dirty, and I mean stinking. The poor brats are almost dead sometimes, just living skeletons, almost, wrapped in rags, their heads caked with dirt, their eyes stuck together with pus and their legs all excoriated from the dirty diapers no one has had the interest to take off them regularly.
>
> (*FD* 159)

It becomes obvious from the beginning of the story that the doctor refuses to feel empathy, and the reasons for his refusal are complicated. More than just a "hard-boiled" submersion of feeling, the doctor's refusal to feel empathy—to see himself in the other, or to see the other in himself—stems from a refusal to implicate himself in the world around him because of that world's horror, treachery, and complexity. Consequently, the doctor reacts to a couple's being "habitual drunk-ards" by saying, "No fault of theirs, maybe," and his comment on crooked doc-tors—"Men we all know too"—is only, "Pretty bad. But what can you do?" (*FD* 159–60).

The doctor's lack of empathy stands in contrast to the feelings of the nurses who "grow attached" to the children. One nurse reacts to a child's being abandoned twice by her mother by saying, "I couldn't speak to her . . . I just couldn't say a word I was so mad. I wanted to slap her" (*FD* 158–59). A second nurse refuses to watch Jean's autopsy—"I may be a sap, she said, but I can't do it, that's all. I can't. Not when I've taken care of them. I feel as if they're my own." The doctor, however, reduces nearly all of his reactions to the diagnostic space of "lumbar punctures," "x-rays," and "broncho-pneumonia with meningismus" (*FD* 161–63). Even his kidding has a reductive, automatic quality to it—"Give it an enema, maybe it will get well and grow up into a cheap prostitute or something. The country needs you, brat. I once proposed that we have a mock wedding between a born garbage hustler we'd saved and a little female with a fresh mug on her that would make anybody smile" (*FD* 160). And after "the older sister of Jean's mother" tells him the history of Jean's father, who left Jean's mother twice, and of the mother-in-law who stole away her nine-year-old son, the doctor responds:

> Listen, I said, I want to ask you something. Do you think she'd let us do an autopsy on Jean if she dies? I hate to speak to her of such a thing now but to tell you the truth, we've worked hard on that poor child and we don't exactly know what is the trouble. We know that she's had pneumonia but that's been getting well. Would you take it up with her for me, if—of course—she dies.
>
> (*FD* 164–65)

The doctor can only "know what is the trouble" with Jean in that "space without depth" that she will occupy as a corpse on the autopsy table. Immediately after she dies, and the autopsy is delayed until the next morning, she becomes an object—"They packed the body in ice in one of the service hoppers. It worked perfectly." The older sister had said that "I guess the condition she [the mother] was in was the cause [of Jean's illness]," but the doctor doesn't want to understand the causes of desertion, infidelity, and kidnapping. Even when he does consider what could have been done to save Jean, he only lists diagnostic options that weren't followed. At the autopsy, however, "the diagnosis all cleared up quickly" (*FD* 165), and the story ends with the recounting of the postmortem findings, followed by:

> I called up the ear man and he came down at once. A clear miss, he said. I think if we'd gone in there earlier, we'd have saved her.
> For what? said I. Vote the straight Communist ticket.
> Would it make us any dumber? said the ear man.
>
> (*FD* 166)

Voting "the straight Communist ticket" is as great a social reduction of Jean's condition as her autopsy findings are a reduction of her disease, and it wouldn't make Williams's doctor any dumber or any less limited. To be fair, the doctor's limitations stem from being overworked and overwhelmed by forces far beyond his control, and his primary motivation for the autopsy is to learn to recognize Jean's condition when he sees it in another patient. Still, his inability to comprehend the physical, the psychological, or the social aspects of Jean's condition shows the limitations of, if not the lethal qualities inherent in, that "scientific" diagnostic space. His constant reduction of the idiographic situation to the nomothetic law— both diagnostically and socially—shows the severe limits of the diagnostic space and suggests a relationship between these limits and a lack of empathy.

The ways in which Williams resists the limits of this diagnostic space have significant consequences for both his poetry and prose, and, even more significantly, for his prose/poetry sequences. In the next section, I will examine the theory of writing as a form of "homeopathic" and "allopathic cure" that Williams develops along with Kenneth Burke. I would like to close this section, however, with a quick look at how Williams's resistance to that "deadly space" that describes the epistemological field of the "scientific diagnosis" takes the form of a new kind of spatial representation in his poetry that, as such, represents an epistemological shift.

In a 1939 letter to Frances Steloff, Williams describes "the poet's task":

> The poem being made of words the form itself becomes a "word." An 8th century form, that is, *means* in some measure the whole conceptual world of the 8th century which invented it and to which it is fitted whereas a 20th century form should embody, if possible, something of the astro-physical, chemical, sociological make up of its day. . . .
>
> Poetry should be the synthesis of its time in passionately communicable form.[45]

"the synthesis of its time" embodying "something of the astro-physical," Williams's answer to the diagnostic space of the scientific revolution has a great deal in common with the "hyper-space" of contemporary science fiction, as well as with the "postmodern space" that Jameson discusses in "Postmodernism, or The Cultural Logic of Late Capitalism,"[46] though I will leave off developing these comparisons here. For now, however, we can call this shift in spatial representation a "space of projection *with* depth, of coincidence *with* development" and we can see it at work in a poem like "Queen-Anne's-Lace" (1921):

> Her body is not so white as
> anemone petals nor so smooth—nor
> so remote a thing. It is a field
> of the wild carrot taking
> the field by force; the grass
> does not raise above it.
> Here is no question of whiteness,
> white as can be, with a purple mole
> at the center of each flower.
> Each flower is a hand's span
> of her whiteness. Wherever
> his hand has lain there is
> a tiny purple blemish. Each part
> is a blossom under his touch
> to which the fibres of her being
> stem one by one, each to its end,
> until the whole field is a
> white desire, empty, a single stem,
> a cluster, flower by flower,
> a pious wish to whiteness gone over—
> or nothing.

(CP I 162)

Originally entitled "Queenannslace" when it was first published in *Others for 1919,* Williams's poem begins by distancing itself historically from an earthy, anti-extravagant love song like "My mistress' eyes are nothing like the sun"—" Her body is not so white as / anemone petals nor so smooth—nor / so remote a thing"—only to turn away from simile altogether. Instead, Williams's "post-Darwinian botanist's language of flowers" avoids becoming a simple "grammar of signs" for his wife Flossie by obscuring distinctions between tenor and vehicle. More than simple analogies of each other, flower and wife occupy that "field" both simultaneously and separately—"until the whole field" is a projection of "white desire." The "Queen-Anne's-Lace" is neither simple conceit nor Darwinian allegory. "It is a field / of the wild carrot taking / the field by force"; the pedestrian "grass / does not raise above it." "It" is an epistemological field that generates analogous situations without reducing one—flower or wife—to the terms of the other. Williams's "diagnostic treatment" here acts within a "grammar of translation" that maintains the particulars of both woman and flower in their analogous relationship to the poet.

Both flower and wife become "representative anecdotes" for each other in the "development" of their relationship to the poet's "hand" that measures and caresses the particulars of each as it re-presents the other. Additionally, in the same way that empathy can only be generated by an appeal to previous experience, neither "development" can be understood alone. Both are a part of that "space of projection *with* depth, of coincidence *with* development" that is the space of *Williams's* diagnostics. The particular signs of the flower are read analogously with the particulars of the woman, and in doing so Williams avoids the spatial reduction of one in terms of the other. Instead, Williams creates that "intersubjective space" that we explained in Chapter 2. And, in the unfolding of the development of this analogical relationship, Williams gives the coincidence of his particulars a temporality that rescues them from the detached condition of "schizophrenia" that we also saw in the previous chapter. As a projection of desire, however, Williams's poem shows the danger of having its "grammar of translation" become a "grammar of transference" in its recognition that "Wherever / his hand has lain there is / a tiny purple blemish." This kind of poem is what Thom Gunn, in his reading of "The Term," called "a completely new poem."[47] Neither allegory, nor conceit, image or object, Williams's creates a "field" that is, in part, all of these things, as well as "a pious wish to whiteness gone over—/ or nothing." In Chapter 5, we will see how Williams uses this "diagnostic field" as a part of his "modern medicine," but first we need to understand Williams's method of "cure."

IV

Williams tells his readers in *Kora in Hell: Improvisations* (1920) to "call on modern medicine to help you" (*I* 66) and says elsewhere that this medicine is "an inverted sort of horticulture. Over and above all this floats the philosophy of disease which is a stern dance. One of its most delightful gestures is bringing flowers to the sick." This "pathology," which is "literally speaking a flower garden," follows a strange section where disease, politics, and plants all get thrown in together:

> Damn me I feel sorry for them. Yet syphilis is no more than a wild pink in the rock's cleft. I know that. Radicals and capitalists doing a can-can tread the ground clean. Luck to the feet then. Bring a Russian to put a fringe to the rhythm. What's the odds? Commiseration cannot solve calculus. Calculus is a stone. Frost'll crack it. Till then, there's many a good backroad among the clean raked fields of hell where autumn flowers are blossoming.
>
> (*I* 77–78)

Along with the familiar figure of the dance, Williams uses the notion of a cyclical change in nature that brings relief, here the violent relief of frost cracking the hard stone of "calculus"—both a "grammar of signs" for mathematical computation and another name for a kidney stone. This combination of thought and body recalls another section of *Kora* where Williams explains:

> *That which is known has value only by virtue of the dark. This cannot be otherwise. A thing known passes out of the mind into the muscles, the will is quit of it, save only when set into vibration by the forces of darkness opposed to it.*
>
> (*I* 74)

According to Williams here, a thought, passing into the body and leaving the realm of the active will, can still be set into motion by "the forces of darkness" and become a part of "the aggregate of all those experiences which have taken form in [our] imagination" and which would become a part of our counter-response to those forces. Or, that thought could harden within the body, blocking the smooth flow of its functions, and become a set "calculus" with which we formulate our responses in advance. Williams combines the processes of the body here with the processes of social action in the symbolic action of what James Breslin calls Williams's "prose of pure process."[48] Marianne Moore, in her review of *Kora* printed in the Summer 1921 issue of *Contact,* links Williams's ideas about this "process" with Kenneth Burke's:

> Burke speaks of the imagination as the most intensive province of pleasure and pain and defines it is [*sic*] a creative power of the mind, representing at pleasure the images of things in the order and manner in which they were received by the senses or in combining them in a new manner and according to a different order. Dr. Williams in his power over the actual, corroborates this statement. Observe how, by means of his rehabilitating power of the mind, he is able to fix the atmosphere of a moment.[49]

It is interesting, in this regard, that, in her review of *Kora,* Marianne Moore refers to Williams's "rehabilitating power of the mind" and the ways in which it corroborates Burke's Coleridgean statements about the imagination. As we shall see below, Williams's use of the body, his call for a "modern medicine of flowers," his mentioning of syphilis, and his connecting these ideas with the political "can-can" of "radicals and capitalists," also combine in Burke's description of the role of the writer as "Cure."

Burke explains that the writer can act as a kind of "medicine man" in providing either "homeopathic or allopathic styles of treatment." The "homeopathic" style is based "on the feeling that danger cannot be handled by head-on attack, but must be *accommodated*" (*ATH* 45, Burke's emphasis). Part of this accommodation would involve "bringing flowers to the sick," which is "one of [the] most delightful gestures" of the "philosophy of diseases" that Williams says "floats over" this "modern medicine" (*I* 77). As Burke explains elsewhere, the writer "in his pious or tragic role, would immunize us by stylistically infecting us with the disease" (*PLF* 65), and the act of "commiseration" inherent in the giving of flowers becomes a symbolic, empathic act of "suffering with." It serves to "coach an attitude" of "pious awe" by presenting an "attenuated variant" of the disease or, Burke would add, of "the sublime" (*PLF* 62).

Another homeopathic aspect of the "gift of flowers" lies in Williams's statement that "syphilis is no more than a wild pink in the rock's cleft." As he goes on to explain in the "note" that follows, "Pathology literally speaking is a flower garden. Syphilis covers the body with salmon-red petals. The study of medicine is an inverted sort of horticulture" (*I* 77). Pathology "literally speaking" here is closer to "Semiotics"—d'Alembert's term for the diagnostic branch of medicine, and the reading of the signs of disease is identical for Williams with the reading of the "language of flowers" that is "literally" the language of his poetry. As such, Williams's "language of flowers" becomes the site of both diagnosis and cure in its re-presentation of a "diseased" situation that allows the reader to experience empathically an "attenuated variant" of the illness. The imaginative reading of the signs of disease becomes, in part, a kind of homeopathic "cure."

Homeopathy, as a science, was developed by the nineteenth-century German physician Samuel Hahnemann, a figure with whom Williams had to be familiar in medical school at the University of Pennsylvania. At the very least, Williams knew a great deal about homeopathy after his study in Vienna in 1924, as he writes about it specifically in "Rome"—the improvisational work written during his stay in Europe in 1924. Interestingly, as Burke explains, Hahnemann "tried also to deduce all diseases from three principal stocks, psora (the itch), *syphilis,* and sycosis (figwart disease)" (*ATH* 47, my emphasis). "Syphilis" is also the disease that Ludwik Fleck focuses on in his *Genesis and Development of a Scientific Fact,* because its formulation was particularly influenced by "active associations."[50] Moreover, while the "cure" for syphilis was mercury, many of Hahneman's remedies came from various plants and flowers whose "signature"—that is, their physical, "observable" properties—resembled parts of the body or other vitalistic signs of the disease involved.[51] Though Williams's use of the word "syphilis" is obviously meant to imply a diseased sexuality, its connection to Hahnemann, to his homeopathic "language of flowers," and to "active associations," is still significant. Moreover, Burke insists that even though Hahnemann's " 'integrative' zeal . . . for a kind of 'nosological trinity' " caused his followers a great deal of embarrassment and was later abandoned, this *"integrative attitude towards life"* is "much akin to the 'tragic integration' in Mann's assertion that one must 'contain his enemies.' We question whether Hahnemann could have made his admittedly valid contributions to medicine without his admittedly invalid vision of nosological genesis" (*ATH* 47, Burke's emphasis). Williams specifically denigrates this "integrative zeal," however, in his discussion of the imagination in his "Prologue" to *Kora.* It is not surprising, then, that Williams rejects the homeopathy of commiseration and containment for the "allopathy" of "frost."

In a letter marked "re: W.C.W. on art as disease," Burke notes just such a distinction between their respective attitudes on poetry and health:

> his indignation with those who wd. call art a disease.
> he himself a physician—his poetry as avocation—in his equation, quite understandably, art equals health.
>
> .   .   .
>
> an artist will certainly at least deal with that which most compellingly concerns him; and nothing quite concerns one more intensely and with more fertility than one's burdens, particularly when one has discovered a means of using them by the devices of symbolic transformation. vive ever the prosperity of poverty, vive ever the aspera which seem to be the first condition of one's advance ad astra.[52]

Williams's "allopathic style" "confronts the threat of danger with an antidote of assurance" (*ATH* 45), seeking to abolish a problem through direct confrontation, achieving "health" through effects different from those produced by the disease. In the section from *Kora* quoted above, Williams abandons the homeopathy of commiseration for the allopathic "frost" of nature that will crack the hard stone of "calculus." Additionally, Williams's improvisational prose acts allopathically to "cure" the "lack of imagination" in the reader, assuring against his use of a "set calculus" of interpretation by using that "prose of pure process," which "lacking explicit connectives" forces the reader to "fill in the gaps," abandoning "whatever fixed point of view we bring to the work."[53]

Burke regards all "manifestations of symbolic action as *attenuated variants* of pious awe (the sublime) and impious rebellion (the ridiculous)," and Williams's allopathic style here approaches the impious dance of "a satyr-play" (*PLF* 62, Burke's emphasis). His "can-can dance" of radicals, Russians, and capitalists echoes Burke's insistence that these "styles" are as much political and religious styles as they are real styles of medicine. As Burke explains:

> Western optimism, that began its formal career with the attacks made by the bourgeoisie upon the style of the church (based homeopathically on the "prosperity of poverty") was superbly direct in the development of allopathic hygiene. The change had much to do with the rationalization of the revolutionary attitude, as it stimulates people under disaster to begin grumbling *early*. Particularly in America, where we have been trained to take prosperity as the *norm*, any interference with the acquisition of commodities creates immediate resentment (a response further stimulated by the fact that "justification by the acquisition of commodities" has been written into the whole texture of the productive-distributive mechanism). Hence, our "conscientious" business leaders are up against a basic contradiction. To uphold a structure based upon sales and advertising, they would coach a return to religion. When the "economy of plenty" cannot abide by its own norms, they would "take up the slack" by restoring the "prosperity of poverty." They can recommend the church's homeopathy with some plausibility because it is adequate *insofar as disease, sorrow, frustration, and death are ineradicable.* And they would try to extend the area of such plausibility so that men would resign themselves even to situations for which remedies must be sheerly "economic."
>
> (*ATH* 45–46, Burke's emphases)

I quote this rather long explanation not because I think that somehow all of these ideas are compacted into Williams's brief "can-can," but rather to show how homeopathy and allopathy as forms of political action involve what Burke calls "moving in on the symbols of authority." By first "moving in on" and then reinstating the religious ideology of the "prosperity of poverty," the " 'conscientious' business leaders" take over an existing "texture of beliefs"—a set of "active associations"—that can accommodate in its own ideology the radical contradictions of an "economy of prosperity" and a "prosperity of poverty" by making "sheerly 'economic' " problems as inevitable as death and frustration.

Williams's "can-can dance" impiously suggests this intricate interweaving inherent in the formation of ideology, but he lacks the power himself in *Kora* to "move in on the symbols of authority" of history and culture. He makes an attempt at this act, however, in a 1921 essay entitled "Yours, O Youth," where he argues that it has been by paying naked attention to the thing itself that American plumbing, American shoes, American bridges, indexing systems, locomotives, printing presses, city buildings, farm implements and a thousand other things have become notable in the world. Yet we are timid in believing that in the arts discovery and invention will take the same course.[54]

The problem here is that Williams is trying to achieve a "perspective by incongruity" that is simply too incongruous to be bridged so quickly. As Burke points out, "we mean by 'transcendence' the adoption of another point of view from which [A and B] cease to be opposites. This is, at present, the nearest approach we can make to the process by verbal means" (*ATH* 336). Williams's attempted act of "transcendence" in "Yours, O Youth" lacks that "point of view" whereby "the arts" and "plumbing" can "cease to be opposites." Williams must "invent" a "texture of beliefs" that is both a literary history of "real literary values" and a history of American culture in order to "transcend" the set of active associations that control his culture's "symbols of authority" and keep them separate from its "art." The "symbols of authority" that Williams can "move in on" are, paradoxically, ones that he will also have to "invent" himself in *In the American Grain.* In order to understand how Williams achieves this act of "transcendence," however, we must once more examine his attitudes toward history, literature, and medicine, and see how they combine with his notions of "cure."

In his essay "Gloria", which appeared in the July 1919 issue of *Others,* Williams explains the paradoxical sort of limbo he finds himself in:

> We older can compose, we seek the seclusion of a style, of a technique, we make replicas of the world we live in and we live in them and not in the world. And THAT is Others. The garbage proved we were alive once, it cannot prove us dead now. But THAT is Others now, that is its lie.[55]

What Williams means by the word "lie" here is explained in another 1919 piece, "Notes from a Talk on Poetry," where he discusses the "lie of the scientist" using the example of Madame Curie, who was later to become a figure of "transcendence" in her own right in Williams's use of her in *Paterson.* Williams explains that the scientist "seeks the emotion of stability, of fixity, of truth! But he thinks the things he finds are that truth. And he teaches this to others and it becomes law—i.e., a lie." Any language that relies on the nomothetic, on a "grammar of signs," to interpret an experience in advance, robs that experience of its emotion and discovery and, consequently, becomes a "lie" in the face of the "facts" of an artist who "knows the fleeting nature of his triumphs before they come."[56] The artist, using a "fresh language" that relies on the "passive associations" of "the actual words, as we hear them spoken under all conditions" (*A* 362), embodies in his work "the fundamental emotional basis of all knowledge"—the expression of an idiographic moment of sensual discovery. This empathic "knowledge," however, can just as easily become a lie if we allow it to solidify into a "calculus"— a predetermined form in which we fit our discoveries in advance that acts like a kidney stone in blocking both the processes of the body and the process of discovery.

As we have seen already from Burke, "words are not puppets. They have more than mere 'delegated power.' They also command.'' We use words, and they use us with the power they have accumulated through ''active''—historical/cultural—''associations.'' Williams is by no means unaware of this power of language, however. In ''Belly Music,'' a special, supplemental essay to the July 1919 *Others* containing ''Gloria,'' Williams makes that somewhat mystical declaration we have already, in part, explained:

> It is simply that brains have not passed the mark set by the post-Darwinian botanists, etc. It is important not to ignore the Copernican theory, the voyage of Columbus, not because these things make a damned bit of difference to any one [*sic*], especially to the poet, but because they stick unconsciously in a man's crop and pervert his meaning unless he have them sufficiently at his fingers' tips to be ware of them. And the mark of a great poet is the extent to which he is aware of his time and NOT, unless I be a fool, the weight of loveliness in his meters.[57]

The ''post-Darwinian botanist'' is one whose ''language of flowers'' takes root in the local soil, absorbing the past of Copernicus and Columbus into its own unique, present beauty in a fusion of historical horizons that avoids any notions of teleology or improvement and occupies that ''diagnostic space'' of ''projection with depth.'' In being ''aware of his time,'' he is aware of those ''active associations''—those cultural, historical associations that, according to Fleck, ''combine to form a thought style which determines the formulation of every concept.'' In other words, as Williams wrote to Frances Steloff, he is ''aware'' that ''a 20th century form should embody, if possible, something of the astro-physical . . . make up of its day,'' just as Erasmus Darwin's poem embodies Linnaeus's thought. But the ''post-Darwinian botanist'' must also be ''ware'' of the inherited power of language in all senses of the word—that is, he must not only be aware or conscious of that power, but also be ''wary'' of that power's potential to ''pervert his meaning,'' as well as be able to shape that language into the product, or ''ware,'' of his own art. Williams himself, however, must become more aware of the ''lie that is art'' in order for him to move beyond the paradox he presents in ''Gloria.'' As he explains there, ''the garbage proved we were alive once, it cannot prove us dead now.'' Williams needs to construct his own ''transcendental frame of acceptance'' that will allow his ''replicas of the world we live in'' to live—as he will go on to say in *Spring and All*—''as pictures only can: by their power TO ESCAPE ILLUSION and stand between man and nature as saints once stood between man and sky'' (*CP I* 199).

If all this seems a bit too mystical for Williams, we must remember that he once wrote to Burke in 1921 saying, ''I suppose I am at heart a mystic. But who isn't until he clarifies his meaning or dies trying to?'' (*SL* 54), and Williams's search for clarity, both in his writing and in his roles as ''Cure'' and ''Pontificate,'' was at its most intense in the years 1921–24. In another letter to Burke, written in 1924 after Williams had returned from a six-month sabbatical in Paris, Vienna, and Rome, Williams adds this postscript:

> P.S. We must all grow clearer, we must work in, together—not for comfort but for training and by bunching our candles to get more light. Join to gain head. I don't mean for consolation, no sect! No creed but clarity. Work in, in, in—by

bringing in all we can gather—trying, testing, scrapping together—with an eye open for an opportunity to use our stuff in the open when we can.

If we practice on each other, trying to knock each other's blocks off, we'll be ready one day to knock a few real blocks into the discard.

(SL 65)

Williams's concern here is not consolation, but cure. His command—"No creed but clarity"—must be read, I think, as an early formulation of what will become a large part of that "cure": his famous, and often misunderstood, dictum to "Say it, no ideas but in things" *(CP I* 263), which was to appear in the poem "Paterson" (1927). Clarity was also the ideal pursued in a manuscript that Williams had included with the above letter, saying that "it was just to show you that I was alive; the manuscript had no other value; if it is lost so much the better" *(SL* 65). Williams can only mean here that he had sent Burke the manuscript of the journal of improvisations that he had kept while in Europe. While parts of this work found their way into *A Voyage to Pagany* (1928), it remained unpublished and unseen until 1978, when Steven Ross Loevy edited it for publication in the *Iowa Review* under the title "Rome."

Part of the reason why Williams did not care whether Burke lost the manuscript of "Rome" is this work's own lack of "clarity" despite its violent assertions that we must achieve this ideal at all costs:

> To BE uppermost. The knowledge, talent, force and verve all in one.
>
> That was ROME. It killed them.
>
> Be it as it may, it is that that is clarity of life, that alone.
>
> (Rome 28)

"Rome" remains an act of improvisation designed more to free Williams's own imagination and allow it once again to follow "a more flexible, jagged resort" *(I* 14) than it is meant for our own clarification. Still, "Rome" contains the crystallization of Williams's ideas about the body, medicine, history, and writing that enables him to combine his chthonic ideal with the "philosopher's stone" of the imagination. Read alongside *Spring and All* (1923), this work continues to refine Williams's ideas about language and writing into a kind of *jouissance,* released through the pleasure inherent in the dramatic form of the text.[58] Read as a prelude to *In the American Grain,* "Rome" shows how Williams has clarified his notions of history and writing. No longer satisfied simply to present his ideas about history as he did in *Kora,* Williams now recognizes the need to re-present historical figures and texts within the grain of his own writing. "History is our possession," he declares, "we are it. We own it—it is to use, they are our *servants*" (Rome 19, Williams's emphasis). Williams's full attention here is with the *act* of writing— with the recognition that "There is no writing but a moment that is and dies and is again wearing the body to nothing" (Rome 12). Williams knows that in order to "bridge" history and modernity in this way, he must "break the habit of self":

> There is escape only by moments in walking out from a self and in saying it was.
>
> Not said, God it cannot be said, that's why it is not said. That's why it is said.

To say is Marcus Aurelius—sayings that came whence? There is no sense in this save in grapes and silks and long thin bricks.

These are not the sayings of Marcus Aurelius—but they say only we are Marcus Aurelius—he was a saying, made of words by shop keepers who ran his place—Bombastic lawyers whose brains were carts of dung being dumped into the Tiber. This is the meaning.

(Rome 12–13)

"To say" is to be like Marcus Aurelius, who has disappeared into the "sayings" that serve the "shopkeepers" and "bombastic lawyers" of the Roman Empire. "In saying it was," we are formulating in a phrase a moment of discovery—a release from the "calculus" of the self—that can never adequately be reduced to language—"Not said, God it cannot be said, that's why it is not said." Another reason, however, "why it is said" is so that others can "move in on" these "sayings" in an act of hegemony designed to get or maintain power—much in the same way that the "truths" of science were turned into "laws" in "Notes from a Talk on Poetry." Williams, by leaving these moments of clarity "not said," is able to maintain the "motion" inherent in their discovery as well as escape the calcification that occurs in the "lies" of a "technique."

Opposed to the "sayings" that are Marcus Aurelius is the vivid, sexual action of Praxiteles, whose lost statues of Eros, an Apollo Sauroctonus, and the Aphrodite of Cnidus—here combined with the city itself and remembered as "Venus Capitolenus"—are "buried in the sand, lost, returned to light or there new" (Rome 12). Historically, Praxiteles was a sculptor whose work "showed, at its best, the tendency of the Greek sculptors of the fourth century to abandon the more reverent and dignified style of the fifth century for the expression of softer and finer shades of form and feeling,"[59] yet this information is scrupulously left *unsaid* by Williams in "Rome." Instead, he relies on the vivid motion of his writing to convey in explicit sexual terms the *jouissance* of Praxiteles's actions. As Williams explains, "Clarity is motion that is under way" (Rome 58), and Williams's re-presentation of the motion that is Praxiteles achieves its clarity in the reader's own discovery of him.

Interestingly, the only surviving statue of Praxiteles's is one of Hermes with the infant Dionysius on his arm (Rome 20),[60] and the coincidence here of these two mythical figures makes Williams's empathic identification with Praxiteles an extremely complex one. Hermes was the inventor of the lyre and a figure of fertility, and his caduceus is the symbol for medicine. Dionysius is connected with ecstasy and the earth, and his name was used by Williams as the middle name for his thinly disguised autobiographical figure "Evan Dionysius Evans" in a "sample prose piece" called "The Three Letters" (1921)[61]—a name he later changed to Dr. "Dev" Evans for the book that described his stay in Rome, *A Voyage to Pagany* (1928). The relationship between Williams, these mythical figures, and Williams's "identification" of himself within these figures corresponds with the extremely complicated historical consciousness that Williams has arrived at in this work—an act of "projection with depth, of coincidence with development" that we will examine more fully in Chapter 4. This relationship, while not at all clear, achieves its clarity in the endless motion it contains.

While Marcus Aurelius remains fittingly trapped in the things said about him, Williams's figure of Praxiteles comes alive through the works he created that once again have "returned to light" as a kind of absent center in Williams's writing. Even here, however, Williams comes close to "saying" more about Praxiteles than he shows us, and he relies heavily on the shock value of the explicit sexual language used in order to "free" the figure of the sculptor. An even more "dramatic" re-presentation in "Rome" involves Williams's use of the banker J. P. Morgan. Williams reprints, verbatim, a letter by Morgan that appeared on the front page of the *New York Times* on Saturday, July 26, 1924 (Rome 31 & 64). The letter concerns the sale of German bonds to American investors, and though the letter was written while Morgan was "sailing for my annual holiday," he assures his reader that "my trip has nothing to do with the London conference" that was being held then to discuss this issue. Morgan goes on to insist that "We have no desire, nor is it within our province, to make any political suggestions, much less to attempt to enforce any political views." Still, Morgan concludes the letter by explaining that:

> It goes without saying that as bankers we should not ask the American investor to buy German bonds unless and until the Allies have in their own time, in their own way and for their own reasons determined upon a policy which will, in our opinion, give security to the bondholders. If this very simple and obvious fact is borne in mind it will, I think, be found that most of the questions now under discussion answer themselves.
>
> (Rome 31)

The questions do indeed "answer themselves," and it equally "goes without saying" that, despite his denials, Morgan's involvement in the creation of both economic and political policy is re-presented here in the successful act of exposing Morgan's own frozen "sayings." Williams explains a bit further on that the "poet he sees through, language, history, all in a flash, country, districts, mistakes, habits—all contribute to his delight—" (Rome 35). By literally re-presenting Morgan's letter, Williams allows the reader to participate in his own "poetic" act of seeing through the language it contains and the history it creates. In this way, the reader performs his own "diagnostic" reading of the occulted meanings behind Morgan's manifest words. This technique of "literally" incorporating the "language of history" also allows Williams to "move in on" a previous historical discourse while it retains the "clarity" of the modern that "is motion under way" by forcing the reader to reconstruct Williams's "act" through his own "act of seeing," or here of "seeing through," language. Williams will return to this technique often in *In the American Grain,* and it will become a vital part of *Paterson.*

Equally important to this technique, however, is the writing with which Williams surrounds this "language of history." In immediate proximity to Morgan's letter, Williams includes subtle allusions to the historical "language of poetry" of Emily Dickinson—"It will come as a snake in the grass" (Rome 30)—as well as of Wordsworth and Keats—"THAT KNOWLEDGE IS ABSOLUTELY NOTHING * BUT PLEASURE. an *ENDLESS* / pursuit. Diana, a chase, / a love pursuit. It has an ENDLESS vista/ leads to NOTHING but the instant of its pleasure"

(Rome 32). The most important inclusions, however, come in Williams's repeated calls for "Education, learning—!" (Rome 32) and his statement that "The solution is in—aesthetic—moral or in / ERDHEIM:" (Rome 30). Jacob Erdheim was one of Williams's instructors at the Children's Hospital in Vienna, where Williams studied in order to "check up on his diagnostic technique" (*VP* 143; Rome 64). Earlier in "Rome," Williams includes sections about a Viennese doctor explaining his techniques of diagnosis and, most significantly, of the allopathic treatment of "brain lesions" by injecting the patient with small doses of "a malaria vaccination" (Rome 23–26). Notions of diagnosis, the body, cure, education, and even pontification are made explicit in connection with Morgan when Williams follows the letter with this statement:

> ***** take [Erdheim's] explanation of liver degeneration, the lobule with its central vein and its peripheral arteries—the flow is from the periphery toward the center. Then, from an impoverished blood, the outer part gets all the nourishment and the center degenerates.
> (see the similarity between this and Morgan's statement?)
>
> (Rome 32)

By reading the signs of the body we can also learn how to read, analogically, the signs of a society, and the "clarity" of medicine and poetry can teach us to do both:

> he sees it—in all places, or in any one spot. he may be a doctor—if he chooses no special life is needed—physical occupation is a delight often—but he is a poet—so he takes that from his   teachers is poetry—as from a stone the organization, the perfection of clarity in the men as here—Vienna, chooses the poem they make in the air—which doctors feel perhaps—in that they too are poets— not doctors
>
> (Rome 34)

As Williams will go on to say about the doctors in *A Voyage to Pagany*, "There was a strong sense of the priest in all these men, a priest presiding over a world of the maimed, living in the hospital, pondering and dreaming—a great sense of beauty over this sordid world" (*VP* 155). In "Rome," Williams conflates the priestly, the poetic, and the medical with his notion of education, an idea which he explains somewhat obscurely in his statement that the "solution of the school lies in the bad boy who is expelled" (Rome 28).

As we should expect by now, the "solution" to Williams's statement is to be found in Burke. In an early configuration of what he will call "John Dewey's . . . distinction between 'education as a function of society' and 'society as a function of education' " (*ATH* 331), Burke explains part of his "program" in "the service of the aesthetic in keeping the practical from becoming too hopelessly itself":

> Indolent school children. Beating did little good. They remained indolent. Then it was found that by improving the ventilation one made them less indolent. After which it was found that under a changed curriculum and new methods of instruction many of these school children not only ceased to be indolent but showed an exceptionally keen interest in their studies. So a pandemic of indolent school

children might indicate that something is wrong with the school? And the most receptive children might be the ones most depressed by a faulty system? Then might indolence, under certain conditions, be symptomatic of a virtue in the indolent? Such is the roundabout defense for the aesthetic side of the conflict.

(*CS* 112)

Williams, of course, replaces "indolence" with sexual energy and violence, but his ideas about education are identical to Burke's:

The vicious things all schools teach is that knowledge is complicated. It is vicious because it creates barriers to knowledge, defeats its own end—ends in disappointment, disgust, restriction—and force.

But this is mere trickery, a glass between the object the [*sic*] the man—reach and be blocked off by that through which we can look—

Schools should teach that pleasure is endless—often austere, the greatest always so

.   .   .

(the [*sic*] teach confusion with a purpose, to hold children so as to hold men, by deliberate maiming of the mind as chinese women's feet are maimed—we think this funny in the papers)

(Rome 17–18 & 33)

The site of Williams's education "in the service of the aesthetic," like Foucault's education of "discipline," occurs at the site of "the body." Foucault explains how under the detached gaze of the master the student's body becomes objectified and placed within a system of "knowledge" and "punishment" that "normalizes" that student within a rigorously controlled system of power.[62] Williams's solution to this situation, therefore, lies within the "bad boy" who opposes this system and, by being "expelled," is saved from its effects while he also reveals the faults of that system of power. Like Burke's "changed curriculum and new methods of instruction" that revive the indolent student, Williams's education of knowledge through pleasure and clarity would presumably show the "virtue" in the bad boy who formerly received only discipline and punishment.

The same objectifying gaze that is so troubling in Foucault is equally disturbing in Williams when it takes the form of the clinical detachment shown toward the body in the act of diagnosis. However, an *empathic* act of diagnosis that does not attempt to reduce or punish the body is essential to Williams's ideas of "cure," as Williams makes clear throughout the improvisations of "Rome" in his conflations of the body, the sexual, and the city, with the notions of education, writing, and cure. In particular, Williams uses the repeated image of the "Cloaca Magna" (Rome 15) and the "Cloaca Vernalis" (Rome 55) to link together in the diagnostic space of his improvisations the ideas of writing and release, the sewers of Rome, the chamber within a body into which the intestinal, urinary, and generative canals discharge, and the suggestion of springtime and youth. He demands, for example, that we "Make perfect sentences and *pleasure* in writing. Don't take findings for my end—but the writing: Cloaca Vernalis (Rome 55, Williams's emphasis). Williams insists that

it must be clear and it must be a whole: like this book which is clearly and wholly
a motion: CLOACA: in which there is so perfect pleasure: perfect sex

(Rome 56)

To Williams, the Romans "weren't fools, they knew what they had, they had
a clarity THE BODY, the fucking, feeding body, with a planted cock shooting it
between the legs—" (Rome 28). Through the pleasure and clarity of a "cloacal
release" gotten through the "motion" of his writing, Williams can discover "a
logos that is completely satisfying" (Rome 33). "Thus the hidden genius of the
land will be freed. Not by what is done in mines or fields but by the inspiration
of clarity, a logical carrying through of the thing that is, the American logos"
(Rome 41).

Williams's "cure" and "education" of America, the discovery of this "Amer-
ican logos," never occurs in "Rome." As Williams explains:

There is a great cultural discovery, far more significant than a machine (where the
superficial American genius lies) immanent—that will shoot out rays into EVERY
department of life NOT KNOWLEDGE—rearranging it into CLARITY—so that
its complications will grow plain—grouped, bagged—for pleasure, leisure—
     It will break the rubber neck of a french culture which
clamish [*sic*], reaches out to pull everything into its maw or finds it bad if it can't
reach it.

(Rome 21)

Williams begins to clarify here his own "grouping" and "bagging" that will occur
in his next work. With his recognition that:

A modernist is he who sees through the modern—to an essential and continuous
organization that exists in it, perfectly so that to him there is no confusion, no
necessity to go back, or to look ahead—he gets his pleasure, here, now—
     His work is made of the modern whatever bit he chooses—there will be pas-
sionate choices—this taken, that neglected—it makes no difference, that is race
and time—but it will be all modern always—the success is the joy of self pos-
session and a perfect present use of material—through the seemingly apparent
brokenness of the life about him

(Rome 34)

Williams will be able to make his own "passionate choices" in a "perfect present
use of material" by "seeing through the modern" to that "unending conversation
of history" in which America must participate. By re-presenting American history
in the service of the modern and the aesthetic, Williams will combine his roles of
doctor, poet, teacher, and pontificate in a writing that can at last "bridge" the
problems of history, literature, and modernity. By exposing those "active associ-
ations" that normalize the regulation of power, and by creating his own "tran-
scendental frame of acceptance," Williams will "invent" his own American
tradition that will allow for the empathic "identification" of an American
"identity."

In a final explanation of the problems of education, Williams declares near the end of "Rome" that:

> I say the schools today do actually teach subservience to the actual leaders. They are not for knowledge but to keep children from knowledge—with their fastening on remote historical examples and training in petty mechanical business details. They breed stupidity as surely as under a higher policy they would breed light.
>
> (Rome 62)

As we shall see in Chapter 4, in the "clarity" that is the "motion" of *In the American Grain,* Williams will begin to embody that "higher policy" within his own "historical examples," bringing to America that "light" into which Praxiteles' statues have returned. In doing so he, like his hero Columbus, will discover America.

4

Attitudes Toward History

Williams's constant attention to historically specific political actions in nearly all of his works—from his section on "Paterson—The Strike" in his first version of "The Wanderer: A Rococo Study" (1914) to his collaborative "translation" of Mao Tse-Tung's "Spring in the Snow-Drenched Garden" (1960)[1]—indicates his abiding concern with the political and its integral position within his poetics. But Williams politics are no less complicated than his poetics, and they are intimately connected with what Williams's sees as the role of the artist. Williams held a contentious relationship to the Left in both the thirties and the forties, and his opinions about Stalinist Russia and schemes of Social Credit often alienated him from its most vocal members. Consequently, Williams's active political role with regard both to writers on the Left as well as to critics such as the New York Intellectuals was at best strained and at worst adversarial. Still, Williams's contact with both Kenneth Burke and Louis Zukofsky led him to a consideration of leftist thought that infuses his writing with an "attitude toward history" that locates him, along with Burke, within a tradition of pragmatism concerned with "creative democracy."[2] As we will see in this chapter, Williams combines an Emersonian emphasis on the individual with a concern for the creative powers of the imagination as it confronts the determining forces of ideology—what Burke calls the "symbols of authority"—in a politics designed to empower the dispossessed, allowing them to participate within Burke's "conversation of history" as fully "recognized" subjects.

Explaining how Williams develops this "attitude," however, will necessitate something of a critical, historical leap. Beginning with Williams's early poem entitled "History" (1917), I will show how Williams's desire to express the "modern" confronts the de Manian paradox of history and modernity. Here, where history depends on the modern for its duration and modernity is prey to a "regressive historical process," Williams remains trapped within the textuality of his own writing. It is only after Williams's "attitudes toward history" begin to share in Kenneth Burke's "theory of verbal praxis" as articulated in his *Attitudes Toward History* (1937) that Williams becomes able to "use" history against itself by "moving in on" historical texts in response to his own determinate, cultural situation. Using Jameson's notions of the "subtext" and of "ideological analysis," I will show how Williams provides us with the kind of "history lesson" that Jameson says Burke promises but never delivers. By seeing the literary text as "a gesture and response to a determinate situation," I will explain how Williams's own "theory of verbal praxis" begins to articulate a mode of cultural criticism in order to promote an "Emersonian culture of creative democracy."[3]

In 1936 Williams wrote to Louis Zukofsky that "What we must have in poetry today is not propaganda for the proletariat—but a proletarian *style*,"[4] and this chapter aims to explore the development of that style along with the ways in which Williams envisioned it as providing a form of both cultural capital and political empowerment for the dispossessed. In both *In the American Grain* (1925) and his Stecher trilogy of novels (1937, 1941, and 1952) Williams develops this "proletarian style" in forms that will allow his dialectic between poetry and prose to serve as a political model. Though neither work actually employs the kinds of interaction between prose and poetry that we have looked at thus far, they do articulate an "attitude toward history" that responds to forms of political domination and gender polarity in a way that will enable *Paterson* to act as a "cognitive map," one that both exposes and attempts to correct the epistemological, psychological, and political limitations of Williams's America.

I

In 1958, when Williams commented on his early poem "History" (1917), he recalled it as "the first example of a studied poem . . . I was self-consciously talking about history and it showed" (*IWWP* 25). For a poet like Williams, nearly obsessed with the invention of the modern and the destruction of old forms, "History" betrays a dependence on the poetic past in its somewhat high-flown diction and overwrought style. Still, Williams's self-conscious talk about history in the poem takes the form of a tension between the desire to display the modern and the inexorable pull of the past, and it is just this self-conscious tension that makes "History" into something much more than a celebration "of the indestructibility of the imagination."[5] Instead, "History" explores the complex, paradoxical relationship between history and modernity, a problem with which Williams grappled throughout his career.

In order to "express the modern"—a term that I will define more carefully at the end of this section—Williams first had to come to grips with this paradox, and he shows in the poem "History" that he recognizes that "if history is not to become sheer regression or paralysis, it depends on modernity for its duration and renewal; but modernity cannot assert itself without being at once swallowed up and reintegrated into a regressive historical process."[6] In this early poem, Williams attempts to free the modern from the bonds of the historical only to recognize the failure of his attempt in the figuration of the poem's final section. As we shall see later, it was only after he had come to share in Kenneth Burke's reworking of the Nietzschean recognition that "history itself must resolve the problem of history"[7] that Williams began to use history against itself in the service of the modern in works like "Rome" and *In the American Grain*.

"History" begins with an ironic deflation of the modern world of the poem itself in the gnomic statement that "A wind might blow a lotus petal / over the pyramids—but not this wind.'' Williams continues to compare the fineness of the past with the vulgarity of the present by noting the ''clay fetish-faces'' of the ''worshippers'' who have thronged to the Metropolitan Museum of Art in New York to see the late Egyptian sarcophagus of Uresh-nofer, a priest of the goddess Mut[8] and by revealing that:

> I come here to mingle faïence dug
> from the tomb, turquoise-colored
> necklaces and wind belched from the
> stomach; delicately veined basins
> of agate, cracked and discolored and
> the stink of stale urine!
>
> (*CP I* 81)

Williams continues this confusion of temporality in the poem's second section by juxtaposing the statement that ''This sarcophagus contained the body / of Uresh-Nai'' with the command ''Run your finger against this edge!'' Here Williams begins to counter his deflation of the modern by giving the present the power to animate the past. This power becomes manifest in the poem's quoting the disembodied voice of the priest in a fusion of past, present, and future:

> ''The chisel is in your hand, the block
> is before you, cut as I shall dictate:
> This is the coffin of Uresh-Nai,
> priest to the Sky Goddess,—built
> to endure forever!
>   Carve the inside
> with the image of my death in
> little lines of figures three fingers high.
> Put a lid on it cut with Mut bending over
> the earth, for my headpiece, and in the year
> to be chosen I shall rouse, the lid
> shall be lifted and I will walk about
> the temple where they have rested me
> and eat the air of the place:
>
> Ah—these walls are high! This
> is in keeping.''
>
> (*CP I* 82)

The ''temple'' where the priest now rests is the museum, and the priest's own ancient temple, his coffin, and the modern museum all combine in the ambiguous line—''these walls are high!'' By reading ''what is writ for you in these figures / hard as the granite that has held them,'' we become somehow able to unlock the letter of the sarcophagus and mingle our own flesh which ''has been fifty times / through the guts of oxen'' with ''I who am the one flesh.'' Like a lover, we are meant to mix our desire with the desire of the spirit of the priest, who in the poem's greatest moment of temporal confusion, echoes Whitman's closing in ''Song of Myself'' by projecting a future that both coincides with and is already beyond the present of the reader:

> Here I am with head high and a
> burning heart eagerly awaiting
> your caresses, whoever it may be,
> for granite is not harder than
> my love is open, runs loose among you!
>
> (*CP I* 83–84)

Our sense of time is restored in the poem's final section, as we are told that "it is five o'clock. Come!" But now the spirit of the poem, the spirit of the modern, has replaced the voice of the priest as it demands that we:

> . . . Look! this
> northern scenery is not the Nile, but—
> these benches—the yellow and purple dusk—
> the moon there—these tired people—
> the lights on the water!
>
> Are not these Jews and—Ethiopians?
> The world is young, surely! Young
> and colored like—a girl that has come upon
> a lover! Will that do?
>
> (*CP I* 84)

Paul de Man points out in "Literary History and Literary Modernity" that "as soon as modernism becomes conscious of its own strategies—and it cannot fail to do so if it is justified . . . in the name of a concern for the future—it discovers itself to be a generative power that not only engenders history, but is part of a generative scheme that extends far back into the past."[9] Williams's own concern for the future is made clear in a statement that appeared on the dustjacket of *Al Que Quiere!*, the 1917 volume that contained "History," where he declares that "we have the profound satisfaction of publishing a book in which, we venture to predict, the poets of the future will dig for material as the poets of today dig in Whitman's *Leaves of Grass*" (*CP I* 480). Consequently, Williams's final gesture in the last section of the poem becomes both an immediate statement of the present and a writing—like the writing on the sarcophagus as well as like Whitman's own writing in "Song of Myself"—that depends on future generations to give it life. But Williams's final assertion of the modern in the poem's last nine lines does more than simply embody this impulse, it also figures its failure.

By emblematizing the "young world" in the figure of "a girl that has come upon / a lover," Williams forces an immediacy onto the modern that attempts to wrestle free from the anteriority of the museum and the ancient Egyptian past it contains. This immediacy is even more emphatic in Williams's ostensive gestures toward a present "reality" that lies outside the language of the poem, as he forces us to regard "these benches," "that moon there," and "the lights on the water." Still, the lover's encounter repeats our own encounter with the sarcophagus, pulling this figure back into the past and linking it with the figure of Mut "bending over the earth," carved on the coffin's lid. The "reality" that exists outside the poem remains trapped in the language that constitutes its representation. Even more subtly, however, Williams epitomizes the impossibility of the modern to assert itself through his use of simile.[10] The modern can never be fully present to itself, and in the assertion that it is "like" a young girl, Williams expresses an anteriority that exposes the dependence of the immediate on the prior while it simultaneously attempts to break free of that dependency in the movement inherent in the indefinite temporality of "has come upon." In the end, however, the voice of the modern becomes as ghostly a phantom as the voice of Uresh-Nai, and the answer to Williams's final question—"Will that do?"—is an already anticipated "No."

For de Man this problem of modernity is one of the distinctive characters of literature in general. As he explains:

> The continuous appeal of modernity, the desire to break out of literature toward the reality of the moment, prevails and, in its turn, folding back upon itself, engenders the repetition and the continuation of literature. Thus modernity, which is fundamentally a falling away from literature and a rejection of history, also acts as the principle that gives literature duration and historical existence.

This insight leads de Man to the conclusion that "literary history could in fact be paradigmatic for history in general, since man himself, like literature, can be defined as an entity capable of putting his own mode of being into question." This new "literary history," which is both a kind of literary interpretation and feature of the self-conscious literary text, helps explain de Man's now somewhat tainted idea that "the bases for historical knowledge are not empirical facts but written texts, even if these texts masquerade in the guise of wars or revolutions." What de Man calls "good literary interpretation" is able to "maintain the literary aporia throughout, account at the same time for the truth and falsehood of the knowledge literature conveys about itself, distinguish rigorously between metaphorical and historical language, and account for literary modernity as well as for its historicity."[11]

Conceived in this way, a literary history that both accounts for the modern while it serves as the basis for historical knowledge would, as de Man claims, radically revise both "the notion of history and, beyond that . . . the notion of time on which our idea of history is based."[12] But de Man's own idea of the modern relies on a too-selective reading of Nietzsche's *The Use and Abuse of History*. While the antihistoricism implicit in Nietzsche's powerful call to engage in a "forgetting" of the past in order to serve "life" does lead to the kind of aporia that de Man describes as the predicament of "our own modernity,"[13] Nietzsche's overall aim in this work is to rescue us from "the disease of history" and show us how we "may again become healthy enough to study history anew, and under the guidance of life make use of the past in that threefold way—monumental, antiquarian, or critical." The active man, says Nietzsche, is the one who "avoids quietism, and uses history as a weapon against it."[14] While there may be some bad faith, as de Man points out, in Nietzsche's delegating the power of modernity to his mythical "youth,"[15] we can also read this move toward the future as part of Nietzsche's recognition that the creation of history should always involve this paradoxical interrelationship between past and present. Nietzsche knows that his own text can only continue as one more historical document that must be made use of in "that three-fold way," just as Williams recognizes that *Al Que Quiere!* must become an archaeological site in which future poets must dig. While I do not want to engage in an extended critique of either Nietzsche's text or de Man's use of it,[16] it will be important to remember that as a text—as a product of language—the past in either case becomes an opportunity for the "historian" to invent his own "ingenious 'melodies,' "[17] whether this means Nietzsche, de Man, or Williams.

This de Manian recognition of history as a rhetorical phenomenon also appears in Williams's poem in another curious and probably unintentional way in Williams's use of Egypt and the Pyramids as the scene of the recalled past of "History." As de Man points out elsewhere with regard to Baudelaire's "Spleen II":

> Egypt, in Hegel's *Aesthetics,* is the birthplace of truly symbolic art, which is monumental and architectural, not literary. It is the art of memory that remembers death, the art of history as *Erinnerung.* The emblem for interiorized memory, in Hegel, is that of the buried treasure or mine (*Schacht*), or, perhaps, a well. Baudelaire, however, fond though he is of well-metaphors, uses "pyramid," which connotes, of course, Egypt, monument and crypt, but which also connotes, to a reader of Hegel, the emblem of the sign as opposed to the symbol. The sign, which pertains specifically to language and to rhetoric, marks, in Hegel, the passage from sheer inward recollection and imagination to thought (*Denken*), which occurs by way of the deliberate forgetting of substantial, aesthetic, and pictorial symbols. Baudelaire, who in all likelihood never heard of Hegel, happens to hit on the same emblematic sequence to say something very similar.[18]

Williams, like Baudelaire, probably never read much Hegel but still uses this emblematic sequence in much the same way. Perhaps in their mutual admiration of Poe, both poets have come to regard the crypt and the Egyptian as the scene of both a recollection and a forgetting inscribed in a rhetorical figuration and, in doing so, have come to share in Hegel's use of them as emblems for the sign.[19] Certainly Williams would have been familiar with Kandinsky's condensation of Hegel and other German thinkers in his use of pyramids in *Concerning the Spiritual in Art.*[20] Whatever the connection, Williams's desire to express the "new" in his poem, to wrestle free of the bonds of the historical and read the "signs" of the modern in all their immediacy, ultimately lies entombed within the signs of his own poetic inscription. The problems of history, of language, and of the sign remain entangled within the "little lines of figures" of the image of Uresh-Nai's death, carved inside the coffin, marked inside the poem. The winds of inspiration, unable to "blow a lotus petal over the pyramids," are equally insufficient to allow Williams to compose his own "ingenious melody" of the modern. They are strong enough, however, to provide him with a wealth of reflection on the difficulties inherent in that melody's construction.

Still, Williams's use of the sign as an emblem of thought and his engagement with the dialectic between history and the modern recalls the ways in which his poetic language—his "language of flowers"—resists reduction to simple allegory by attempting to compress within the "diagnostic space" of its writing a "poetic reduction" that holds in tension both identity and difference. What I have hoped to show in the condensed example of "History" is Williams's concern with the temporal limits of poetic language as just such a language of signs. On the one hand, the poetic act of communication always occurs for Williams within the historical and social continuum of particular receptions.[21] At the same time, however, what has become known as the play of the signifier[22] acts dialectically to negate any such reception, allowing for the fleeting possibility of escape from the historical through the rhetorical dimension of language. The maintenance of this "intersubjective space" becomes impossible in "History" when the forces of historicity itself ultimately draw the present into the past. As such, Williams's poem dramatically re-presents this dilemma in the poem's temporal confusion. "History" acts as a kind of representative anecdote for that "generative power" released "in a concern for the future" that discovers itself to be merely a "generative scheme that extends far back into the past."

The question Williams asks here, and throughout his work, is the one that his muse "had put on to try" him in "The Wanderer: A Rococo Study," his well-known poem of poetic initiation that closes *Al Que Quiere!*—"How shall I be a mirror to this modernity?" The answer, for now, lies in a failed attempt to "express the modern"—a term we can now define as an act of self-creation, the articulation of "identity" within the textual matrix of history. As such, "History" becomes a representative anecdote of this failure in the poem's re-creation of an act that is both a birth and a death, a forgetting and a remembrance. In order for Williams to move beyond the mere re-presentation of these tensions, however, the paradoxical relationship between modernity and history must begin to combine with this antagonistic interdependence of history and literature in an "attitude toward history" that is more adept at engaging the historical in a critical fashion. In "America, Whitman, and the Art of Poetry," another work published in 1917, Williams discusses this relationship of modern poetry to the poetry of the past in more generous terms than he will acknowledge in any of his later writings. Williams asserts that

> Whitman created the art in America. But just as no art can exist for us except as we know it in our own poetry even our own art cannot exist but by grace of other poetry. Nothing comes out of the air, nor do we know whence anything comes but we do know that all we have receives its value from that which has gone on before.
>
> There is no art of poetry save by grace of other poetry. So Dante to me can only be another way of saying Whitman. Yet without a Whitman there can of course be for me no Dante. Further than that: there is no way for me to talk of Whitman but in terms of my own generation—if haply such a thing may be.
>
> To speak of the art there is no way but to speak in terms of my own generation whereby, touching the art today, I touch it everywhere and at all times or failing to find my own terms I fail to find the means to speak.[23]

Williams's attitude toward historical understanding here seems an unproblematic expression of Hans-Georg Gadamer's notion of a "fusion of horizons." I say "seems" because later in the essay Williams does reveal hints of anxiety toward Whitman when he makes statements like "The only way to be like Whitman is to write *unlike* Whitman" (Williams's own emphasis), and the question of influence always complicates Williams's readings of the past, though as we will see below, Williams's attitude towards his predecessors shares more in a feeling of "mutuality" than it does in an agonistic need to overcome another "strong poet."[24] Still, Williams is aware that the only way in which he can begin to understand that past is through his understanding of the present, just as he is aware of the burden that the past places on the present. As Gadamer points out, "every encounter with tradition that takes place within historical consciousness involves the experience of the tension between the text and the present."[25] By projecting a historical horizon that differs from the continually forming horizon of the present and by consciously bringing out this tension, we test the "prejudices" that make up the "horizon of a particular present" which we bring with us to the text, while we gain an "understanding of the tradition from which we come." Additionally, Gadamer feels, we avoid becoming paralyzed by the past—by what Nietzsche called "the historical disease"—by projecting a historical horizon that is only "a phase in the process of understanding, and does not become solidified into the self-alienation of a past consciousness, but is overtaken by our own present horizon of understanding." In this way, "historical consciousness is aware of its own otherness and hence distinguishes the horizon of tradition from its own. On the other hand, it is itself . . . only something laid over a continuing tradition, and hence it immediately recombines what it has distinguished in order, in the unity of the historical horizon that it thus acquires, to become again one with itself."[26]

These ideas about the need for a flexible, revisionary relationship between these horizons and the importance of "recognizing" the "otherness" inherent in historical consciousness have their analogues in both Williams's own "flexible" methodological empiricism, as well as in his sharing in Jessica Benjamin's notion of "mutuality." These ideas get compressed in "America, Whitman, and the Art of Poetry" in Williams's recognition that, "the only freedom a poet can have is to be conscious of his manoevres [*sic*]." Williams argues that we need to distinguish "new verse, in a new conscious form" from the verse of Whitman or Dante, while we also need to recognize that "we can expect to invent nothing of our materials." While the poetry of Whitman and Dante is at once something other than modern verse, our modern consciousness is itself made up of the tradition which includes Whitman and Dante. Consequently, as Williams tells us, one can "be a Whitman, if you will, only please, if you love your kind, *don't write like Whitman*" (Williams's emphasis).[27] In this fusion of historical horizons, what Gadamer calls "the task of effective-historical consciousness,"[28] Williams sees that we can both animate the modern and preserve the historical:

> Our age isolate will fall apart from sheer surrounding emptiness. To live, our poetry must send roots into the past. To live freely it—as we—must live free of time. To be free of time it must live for all time, past and future. It must have the common interlocking quality that establishes it in its environment. It must live or be capable of living from the beginning to the end.

Williams differs radically from Gadamer, however, in his assertion that through this fusion of horizons we somehow gain access to "the democratic groundwork of all forms, basic elements that can be comprehended and used with new force." Williams continues in his description of these elements, claiming that "being far back in the psychic history of all races no flavor of any certain civilization clings to them, they remain and will remain forever universal, to be built with freely by him who can into whatever perfections he is conscious of. It is here that we must seek."[29] This chthonic ideal—nearly always expressed in terms of the feminine from the goddess Mut of "History" to the Kora / "Core" / Persephone of *Kora in Hell* (1920) to the "Beautiful Thing" of *Paterson* (1946–58)—takes on Platonic overtones here that are always problematic in Williams's early writing. As we have already seen, however, by the time Williams wrote *The Descent of Winter* (1928), he said of this "core":

> The only human value of anything, writing included, is intense vision of the facts, add to that by saying the truth and action upon them,—clear into the machinery of absurdity to a core that is covered.
>
> God—Sure if it means sense. "God" is poetic for the unobtainable. Sense is hard to get but it can be got. Certainly that destroys "God," it destroys everything that interferes with simple clarity of apprehension.
>
> (*CP I* 312)

This "democratic groundwork of all forms" is apprehended through historical understanding, and it somehow stands in opposition to those "aristocratic" forms of the past it lies behind.[30] As we will see by the end of this chapter, this "democratic groundwork" is analogous to the acts of "discovery" and "identity"—acts of self-articulation within the matrix of history and tradition. Williams's unique brand of historical consciousness and its connection with tradition and "God-terms" will become clearer, I think, if we compare it briefly with the early ideas of two other modernists concerned with historical understanding—Pound and Eliot.

In *Modernist Poetics of History,* James Longenbach borrows Fredric Jameson's term "existential historicism" to describe the historical perspectives of such thinkers as Dilthey, Croce, Collingwood, Gadamer, and—Longenbach adds—Ezra Pound and T. S. Eliot.[31] As Jameson explains, "existential historicism"

> does not involve the construction of this or that linear or evolutionary or genetic history, but rather designates something like a trans-historical event: the experience, rather, by which *historicity* as such is manifested, by means of the contact between the historian's mind in the present and a given synchronic cultural complex from the past.[32]

Williams, too, can be included among these "existential historicists" in his recognition that history as such is a result of the historian's interrogation of the past in terms of the present. Like Jameson, he knows that history is "the experience . . . by which *historicity* as such is manifested." Moreover, as we shall see, Williams will come to depend on the historian's ability, in effect, to "invent" history. As Williams will go on to say in "Rome" (1924), "History is our possession—we are it. We own it—it is to use, they are our *servants*" (Rome 19, Williams's emphasis).

Longenbach explains how both Pound and Eliot share in a matrix of historical thought made up, primarily, of the ideas of Wilhelm Dilthey and Benedetto Croce and of the direct influences of Jacob Burckhardt on Pound and F. H. Bradley on Eliot. In particular, Dilthey, Croce, Pound, and Eliot all believe in "the individual's ability to transcend his own historical limitations" and, like Odysseus's revival of the ghost of Tiresias in Pound's final version of Canto 1, "give new life to the bloodless shadows of the past."[33] As Longenbach points out, even though Eliot claims in "Tradition and the Individual Talent" (1919) that he proposes to "halt at the frontier of metaphysics or mysticism," both Pound and Eliot cross this boundary in the philosophical foundations of their "sense of the past."[34] They share in a tradition of transcendental philosophy and mystical belief that includes such esoteric thinkers as Richard of St. Victor, Evelyn Underhill, and Louis de Bonald. Both poets were "simultaneously profoundly *visionary* and rigorously *skeptical*" historicists. Their skepticism, however, not only "led to their rejection of nineteenth-century positivistic historical beliefs," it also couched their visionary tendencies in less than mystical terms. As Longenbach states:

> they were very much children of their age: in *Consciousness and Society: The Reorientation of European Social Thought 1890–1930*, Stuart Hughes notes that although the period is best described as a time of 'neo-romanticism or neo-mysticism,' the greatest thinkers of the time . . . sought to curb the mystical tendencies of their work.[35]

So far, I think we can safely see the Williams of 1917 as yet another "child of his age." Williams's "mysticism," though nowhere near as pronounced as either Pound's or Eliot's, does share in a privileging of "imagination," "intuition," and "spirit"—key terms for all of the above thinkers. Williams's greatest swerve from Pound and Eliot, however, lies in the way each poet views the relationship of the present to the tradition of the past. Both Pound and Eliot share in a profound sense of contemporaneity between the modern and the historical. Pound had asserted as early as 1910 his belief that, "All ages are contemporaneous. . . . This is especially true of literature, where the real time is independent of the apparent, and where many dead men are our grandchildren's contemporaries." Eliot explains in his famous statement in "Tradition and the Individual Talent" that the "historical sense"

> involves a perception, not only of the pastness of the past, but of its presence; the historical sense compels a man to write not merely with his own generation in his bones, but with a feeling that the whole of the literature of Europe from Homer and within it the whole of the literature of his own country has a simultaneous existence and composes a simultaneous order. This historical sense, which is a sense of the timeless as well as of the temporal and of the timeless and of the temporal together, is what makes a writer traditional. And it is at the same time what makes a writer most acutely conscious of his place in time, of his contemporaneity.[36]

Both Pound and Eliot are Americans-in-exile who have readily absorbed a vast European literary tradition and who wish, themselves, to be absorbed into continental culture. It should be no surprise, then, that they see that the "existing monuments" of the literature of the past "form an ideal order among themselves"— an order that "is complete before the new work arrives" and which is "ever so slightly" altered "after the supervention of novelty." In this shifting of the "*whole* existing order," the relations, proportions, values of each work of art toward the whole are readjusted; and this is conformity between the old and the new. Whoever has approved this idea of order, *of the form of European, of English literature,* will not find it preposterous that the past should be altered by the present as much as the present is directed by the past. And the poet who is aware of this will be aware of great difficulties and responsibilities. (my emphasis)[37]

Williams's concern, of course, is with *American* literature, and with this concern he is aware of a very different set of "difficulties and responsibilities." As late as 1948, the London critic George Barker asserts that "American poetry is a very easy subject to discuss for the simple reason that it does not exist"—a statement that Williams will later incorporate into Book Three of *Paterson* (1949), right after a letter from Pound exhorting him to "re read *all* the Gk tragedies in / Loeb.—plus Frobenius, plus / Gesell plus Brooks Adams / ef you ain't read him all,—/ Then Golding 'Ovid' is in Everyman lib." followed by Williams's "reply . . . with the bare hands" to Pound's "Greek and Latin"—"the tabular account of the specimens found" in the substratum of an artesian well at the Passaic Rolling Mill, Paterson in 1880 (*P* 138–40).[38]

Williams's chthonic ideal, the "democratic groundwork of all forms," had to be "built into" a modern American poetry with "the common interlocking quality that establishes it in its environment." Unfortunately, the American soil of 1917 was as barren of literary tradition as the Passaic Rolling Mill's artesian well was of water. Still, at the end of the description of the well, Williams includes this bit of text:

> At this depth the attempt to bore through the red sandstone was abandoned, the water being altogether unfit for ordinary use. . . . The fact that the rock salt of England, and some of the other salt mines of Europe, is found in rocks of the same age as this, raises the question whether it may not also be found here.

This text, found along with the description of the well, is taken from William Nelson's *Geological History of the Passaic Falls* (1892),[39] both a piece of historical writing and a piece of history in its own right. As we saw in Chapter 1, Williams incorporates it into his epic to serve both of these roles. Williams was sure in 1917 that the "rock salt" of England and Europe could be found in the soil of America, and he was equally sure that "terms of [his] own generation—if haply such a thing may be" could only be found in a distinctly American tradition. For Williams, these "terms" had to occur in a distinctly American form. Pound and Eliot were working within the already firm bedrock of a literary tradition thousands of years old. Their work remains rooted in "the aristocratic forms of past civilizations," and, in Williams's opinion, they were among those who "have cleverly taken up old forms and as cleverly refurbished them." Williams goes on to add, however, "Not all are unconscious of the necessity for new canons."[40]

Obviously by 1919, Eliot was not "unconscious of the necessity for new canons" either, but both Eliot's "Tradition and the Individual Talent" and Williams's "America, Whitman, and the Art of Poetry" need to be read in terms of their roles in a larger modernist project of literary redefinition, as well as in the context of their respective milieux. Eliot, writing in *The Egoist,* merely wants to reshuffle an

"already existing order" of English and other European literature into new rela-
tionships. Williams, to paraphrase Blake, must create his own order or be enslaved
by another country's. The incongruity between Eliot's "historical sense" and Wil-
liams's is evident not only in the increased anxiety Eliot shows toward his pred-
ecessors (note how many times Eliot refers to "dead poets" in his essay), but also
in the very first words of the titles of their respective essays—"Tradition" as
opposed to "America"—the one firmly established, the other barely defined. This
issue of America, literature, and history was summed up most forcefully by Van
Wyck Brooks in his now famous piece that appeared in *The Dial* in 1918, "On
Creating A Usable Past":

> The present is a void, and the American writer floats in that void because the past
> that survives in the common mind of the present is a past without living value.
> But is this the only possible past? If we need another past so badly, is it incon-
> ceivable that we might discover one, that we might even invent one?[41]

The decade between 1915 and 1925 saw an unprecedented attempt literally to
"invent" the American past. Beginning with Brooks's own "America's Coming
of Age" and ending with Williams's *In the American Grain,* this intense search
to assemble an American tradition in opposition to the then-dominant Puritan tra-
dition of capitalism included influential books by Waldo Frank, Harold Stearns,
Paul Rosenfeld, H. L. Mencken, and Lewis Mumford.[42] Though my focus here
will be exclusively on Williams, all of these authors were engaged in an attempt
to articulate a cultural criticism that would not only expose the ways in which the
production of "culture" involves the material forces and relations of production,
but also create texts that would directly influence that production.[43]

In Williams's case, this attitude toward history and history making took two
directions. The first was in his poetry and experimental prose, through his desire
to "cleanse the language," identify an "American idiom," and establish "contact"
with his local environment. The other was in his many novels, essays, and other
prose pieces which both explained and surrounded his verse—sometimes literally
in his long prose/poetry sequences. The refinement of Williams's ideas about lan-
guage and culture gradually takes shape during this decade in response to this
opportunity to "invent America," and his ideas reach an initial fulfillment in
"Rome" (1924) with the recognition that "History is our possession—we are it.
We own it—it is to use, they are our *servants*" (Rome 19). As we saw in Chapter
3, Williams uses this "recognition" in his re-presentation of historical figures in
order to re-create that "clarity [that] is motion under way" (Rome 58) that leads
to an act of "discovery" and "identification." Here—particularly in his conflation
of Jacob Erdheim's "explanation of liver degeneration" with J. P. Morgan's 1924
letter about the sale of German bonds to American investors—Williams incorpo-
rates his medical "Semiotics" with a cultural "diagnosis" in order to provide
those "homeopathic" and "allopathic forms of treatment" that Burke elsewhere
develops. Williams combines the roles of poet, doctor, and educator in the dynamic
act of "seeing through the modern" in order to re-create a "clarity" that is also
"a great cultural discovery" (Rome 21), though as I argued then the actual em-
bodiment of that "American logos" was to wait until *In the American Grain.* In

order to understand fully the mode of cultural criticism that Williams develops in this work, however, we must first examine Kenneth Burke's own *Attitudes Toward History* (1937) and see both the goals and the limitations of Burke's historical project.

II

I want to focus in this section on one of Burke's early works—his *Attitudes Toward History* (1937)—as a clear expression of the kind of "historical sense" that both he and Williams were moving toward back in the early twenties. Burke himself wrote in "Curriculum Criticum" (his 1953 addendum to the 1931 work, *Counter-Statement*) that all three of his early books—*Counter-Statement, Permanence and Change,* and *Attitude Toward History*—represent a working out of ideas that he had been developing since "early manhood" and that they form "a graph of his responses to the veerings of history" (*CS* 213–15). Burke's entire œuvre, in fact, becomes, in retrospect, an elaborate expansion of his definition of man:

> Man is
> the symbol-using (symbol-making, symbol-misusing) animal
> inventor of the negative (or moralized by the negative)
> separated from his natural condition by instruments of his own making
> goaded by the spirit of hierarchy (or moved by the sense of order)
> and rotten with perfection.
>
> (*LASA* 16)

Burke's thought in *Attitudes Toward History* is very much a product of the thirties in its direct concern with the social order. As he explains, it stands in relation to its predecessor, *Permanence and Change,* "as Plato's *Republic* is to his *Laws*. That is, just as the *Republic* deals with the ideal State, and the *Laws* deals with the real one, so *P&C* thinks of communication in terms of ideal coöperation, whereas *ATH* would characterize tactics and patterns of conflict typical of actual human associations." Taking his cue from the end of Emerson's "Experience," Burke points out that its more "realistic emphasis reflects the fact that the author had begun to get a closer view of the ways in which projects for social amelioration work out practically" (*CS* 216). Even with its historical specificity, however, *Attitudes Toward History* remains both timely and timeless in its exploration of how "men build their cultures by huddling together, nervously loquacious, at the edge of an abyss" (*PC* 272).

Burke begins *Attitudes Toward History* by presenting his own American literary tradition of "meliorism," which he traces back from William James through Whitman to Emerson. All writers, Burke argues, "act in the code of names by which they simplify or interpret reality" by creating " 'frames of acceptance' . . . the more or less organized system of meanings by which a thinking man gauges the historical situation and adopts a role with relation to it." Burke demands that we see all writing as an "act"—a complicated kind of praxis that necessarily both engages in and is engaged by the world around it, and he introduces the three "transcendental" frames of acceptance of James, Whitman, and Emerson as "the three most well-rounded, or at least the most picturesque" of these engagements (*ATH* 4–5). Burke's Emerson, for example, operates within his world by affirming "a doctrine of 'polarity,' " whereby the difference between good and evil is also a compensatory difference within: " 'For everything you have missed you have gained something else.' A bad government creates the resistances that cure its badness. The swindler swindles himself." Burke's Emerson avoids the sentimentality of a too easy acceptance of the "indifferency [sic] of circumstances" by introducing the "transcendental doctrine of the soul . . . the vast affirmative, excluding negation, self-balanced, and swallowing up all relations, parts and times, within itself." Through this ontological variant "of the same device that Hegel developed, and that Marx proposed to secularize," Burke explains that Emerson gives us a "project for living by the extending of cosmos farther into the realm of chaos, the reclaiming of chaos for cosmic purposes" (*ATH* 18–19).

Burke's reading of Emerson is neither quietistic nor sentimental, and it subtly enacts its own self-consciously forged comic frame. Burke is not only aware of the tendency of literature to be discernibly on edge about its own rhetorical status, he depends upon its "undecidability." As Frank Lentricchia has pointed out, this undecidability does not mark "the sign of literature's social and political elusiveness" for Burke. Instead, it points to the ground of both "its historicity and its flexible, but specific, political significance and force."[44] Burke recognizes that "the very fact that the work of art is a symbolic act of synthesis makes difficulties for those who would break it down by conceptual analysis," and that "since the work of art is a synthesis, summing up a myriad of social and personal factors at once, an analysis of it necessarily radiates in all directions at once; . . . the synthetic symbol can be divided into conceptual components *ad infinitum*." The critic, however, must get "his own pattern of selectivity" from "the pragmatic test of use. Facing a myriad possible distinctions, he should focus on those that he considers important for social reasons" (*ATH* 197–200). Burke's Emerson acts as a kind of "pontificate" who, by creating his transcendental frame of acceptance, gives us our ritualistic, imaginative, "symbolic" means for participating in history, and Burke himself, as critic, aids this social function by elucidating Emerson's "act."

The line between Burke's Emerson and Burke himself is a purposefully thin one. Burke recognizes Emerson as one of the "symbols of authority" of our culture, and he consciously "moves in on" the Emersonian discourse for his own social, historical reasons. History, as Burke explains in *Attitudes Toward History*, is just such a series of similar dialectical "symbolic mergers," which Burke then "discounts" by showing how a particular doctrine behaves "when released into a social texture" (*ATH* 244–45). This idea will become clearer if we look again at Burke's anecdotal description of history that he provides elsewhere:

> Imagine that you enter a parlor. You come late. When you arrive, others have long preceded you, and they are engaged in a heated discussion, a discussion too heated for them to pause and tell you exactly what it is about. In fact, the discussion had already begun long before any of them got there, so that no one present is qualified to retrace for you all the steps that had gone before. You listen for a while, until you decide that you have caught the tenor of the argument; then you put in your oar. Someone answers; you answer him; another comes to your de-

fense; another aligns himself against you, to either the embarrassment or gratifi-
cation of your opponent, depending upon the quality of your ally's assistance.
However, the discussion is interminable. The hour grows late, you must depart.
And you do depart, with the discussion still vigorously in progress.

(*PLF* 110–11)

The debate, having already begun before us and always continuing after us,
shapes our participation in it even while we contribute to its shape with our ar-
guments. Two of Burke's most radical assumptions about this debate—assumptions
that alienated Burke from both the left and the literary elite of the thirties but that
would find several "allies" today—involve the ways in which a symbolic act is
also a textual act and how this textuality allows for manipulation of this "conver-
sation of history." Burke argues, for example, that

> children decree by *naming the essence* of their play objects, assigning names that
> violate realistic identity: thus, picking up a block of wood, the child decrees by
> legislative fiat: "This is a train"—or "This is a house." The child "transcends"
> the material reality by "discounting." Like Whitman, it sees "unseen existences"
> in the object—and this is its prayer.
>   An adult may do the same in adult ways when, looking at the welter of the
> world, he "sees" the class struggle there. You can't *see* the class struggle. It is
> an *interpretation* of events.
>
> (*ATH* 322–23, Burke's emphases)

These "interpretations" act as a "secular prayer"—"the *coaching of an attitude*
by the use of mimetic and verbal language." These acts "transcend" material
reality by "discounting," or "like Whitman, it sees 'unseen existences' in the
object" (*ATH* 322–23, Burke's emphases). This "shaping of attitudes" through
what is essentially the creation of texts is performed by adopting and re-forming—
"moving in on"—previous texts. Consequently, while there is a necessarily end-
less intertextuality to the "debate" of Burke's "history," we paradoxically rely
on the terms of this intertextuality—the terms we "name" in these texts—to pro-
vide us with participation and even our own "names" within history.

Burke denies the idea of a stable self and posits instead the idea that we are
made up of a "Babel of voices." "The so-called 'I,' " Burke argues, "is merely
a unique combination of partially conflicting 'corporate we's' " (*ATH* 264).
Through our identification with particular dramatic characters we both are given
and "earn" our "corporate identities," and the "organized systems of meaning"
found in various "frames of acceptance" help to ground this passive/active self.
Additionally, while Burke does destabilize man as subject, he does not deny his
efficacy as agent. Consequently, our action within history is real, though our un-
derstanding of that history is at best an imperfect interpretation of an imperfect
interpretation.

Burke recognizes that the comic frame that he constructs is just such an inter-
pretation of an interpretation, but he posits this construction as the inevitable way
of responding to what he terms the "bureaucratization of the imagination"—a
" 'perspective by incongruity' for naming a basic process of history" whereby
words are "wrench[ed] loose" from one category and applied "metaphorically"

to another" (*ATH* 308). As Burke goes on to explain, "an imaginative possibility (usually at the start Utopian) is bureaucratized when it is embodied in the realities of a social texture, in all the complexity of language and habits, in the property relationships, the methods of government, production and distribution, and in the development of rituals that re-enforce the same emphasis" (*ATH* 225). This "bureaucratization," he argues, is necessarily limiting, and those who are dispossessed by it need to avoid "being driven into a corner" by "transcending" this conflict through "symbolic mergers." Those who control these "symbols of authority" maintain their power both through systems of discipline and education, as well as by "moving in on" the symbols of the opposition.

For Burke, the literary is always a form of social action, and he would recognize an act of "literary production" as the invocation of a "secular prayer" by which one can "move in on" literature. His response to this act, however, is already embodied in and performed by his work. Burke actively re-forms the scientific, religious, and economic terms that both shape and reflect our own "attitudes" toward the "symbols of authority" of our culture. Because of man's "spiritual" stake in the reigning structure of authority, even in opposition to it, Burke insists that

> our own program, as literary critic, is to integrate technical criticism with social criticism (propaganda, the didactic) by taking the allegiance to the symbol of authority as our subject. We take this as our starting point and "radiate" from it. Since the symbols of authority are radically linked with property relationships, this point of departure automatically involves us in socio-economic criticism. Since works of art, as "equipment for living," are formed with authoritative structures as their basis of reference, we also move automatically into the field of technical criticism (the "tactics" of writers).
>
> (*ATH* 331)

Burke's most subtle performance of this program appears in his "Dictionary of Pivotal Terms" (*ATH* 216–338), an abecedarian project that takes the reader from "alienation" to "transcendence" within the "attitude" of Burke's own "comic frame of acceptance." But while Burke believes that symbols can be "moved in on," he also knows that "Words are not puppets. They have more than mere 'delegated power.' They also command." At the same time, however, "words are public properties, and the individual 'has a stake in' their public ownership. . . . He uses them, and they use him" (*ATH* 332–33). Burke's "Dictionary" formulates a vocabulary that creates a frame of acceptance by defusing and reshaping the language of his culture into a new attitude, keeping the reigning symbols of authority intact while he extends their "convertibility."

Burke situates the critic/writer in the role of "Pontificate"—a "terministic" enterprise whose main function is to provide "Consolation" and "to minister in terms of a 'beyond.' " Closely related to the role of "Cure"—the role primarily of medicine and hygiene—the Pontificate ministers to those situations beyond which there can be no consoling: "the inevitable sorrows of separation, suffering, and death." Burke also lists under "Pontificate" duties that "are clearly connected with a priesthood"—providing the terms by which an occasion "is *interpreted,* and thereby *'sanctioned'* . . . often in terms of an ultimate eternal or supernatural ground (a 'beyond')'' (*ATH* 358–66, Burke's emphases).

If, as Burke claims, much of our action in and understanding of the world is done symbolically through various kinds of texts and language, then the Pontificate's main role is to answer the question posed by another contemporary of Williams's—Wallace Stevens—who asks in his "Adagia": "How has the human spirit ever survived the terrific literature with which it has had to contend?" We might answer that question, along with Burke, with yet another of Stevens's notes:

> The relation of art to life is of the first importance especially in a skeptical age since, in the absence of a belief in God, the mind turns to its own creations and examines them, not alone from the aesthetic point of view, but for what they reveal, for what they validate and invalidate, for the support that they give.[45]

Burke demands that we share "The maker's rage to order words of the sea, / Words of the fragrant portals, dimly-starred, / And of ourselves and of our origins, / In ghostlier demarcations, keener sounds." If, for Stevens, "the poet is the priest of the invisible,"[46] then, for Burke, the critic must join the poet in that priestly function, engaging in "the difficultest rigor" to bring us that "vivid transparence that . . . is peace."

Unlike Stevens, however, Burke's mystification takes place not only in the imagination but also in a kind of metabiology that privileges the body. As "Bodies That Learn Language," men use "words that tell stories" in order both to "comprehend" their animal condition and to "duplicate the wordless aspects of our environment, greatly expand[ing] the range of *attitudes* by which we relate to one another in keeping with the clutter of concordant and discordant *interests socially rife among us*" (*ATH* 379–85, Burke's emphases). In this way, language functions for Burke both esthetically and *anesthetically* in its relationship to the sheerly physical. In making this argument, Burke recalls

> a remark that my friend William Carlos Williams had made to me in a moment when, as often, his duality as poet and physician spoke as one. . . . in response to his suggestion, I kept remembering: "First, there would be the sheer physicality of life, the human organism as one more species of alimentary canal with accessories . . . digestive tract with trimmings."
>
> (*ATH* 392)

I mention the above not only to differentiate Burke and Williams from Stevens, but also to point out how naturally Williams's roles as doctor and poet combine with Burke's closely related roles of "Cure" and "Pontificate." If, along with this coincidence, we remember that the word "Semiotic" comes from the Greek meaning "concerned with the interpretation of symptoms" and was used by d'Alembert in his "Tree of Knowledge" to describe that branch of medicine concerned with diagnosis, we can begin to see how Williams's own concern with history, culture, and the word becomes the way in which he can extend his diagnoses beyond the individual to embrace both the language and the community, providing both with cure and consolation.

Burke's work is not without its problems, however. His terms are often very slippery, just as he relies on the slipperiness of language for the effectiveness of his program. Frank Lentricchia's own *Criticism and Social Change,* for example, provides an interesting instance of how Burke's own terms can be "moved in on" in a Burkean fashion.[47] In addition, Burke makes several claims that are at best questionable—he implies the best values, for example, will always "enlist the most vigorous and original craftsmen" (*ATH* 335). Even with these problems, however, Burke's insistence on John Dewey's distinction between "education as a function of society" and "society as a function of education" in order to formulate an active, vital cultural role for the literary critic marks a strong response to those who—from T. S. Eliot to William Bennett—would use literature hegemonically. Still, Burke's "program"—by "taking allegiance to the symbol of authority as [its] subject" and by proceeding along a "pattern of selectivity" that is closer to William James's less "engaged" form of pragmatism than it is to Dewey's own historically specific forms of intervention—is left open to the kinds of criticism that Fredric Jameson levels at it.

In "The Symbolic Inference; or, Kenneth Burke and Ideological Analysis," Jameson critiques Burke's writing in an attempt "to determine whether his work can be reread or rewritten as a model for contemporary ideological analysis"— what Jameson himself prefers to call "the study of the ideology of form."[48] Seeing "Burke's conception of the symbolic as act or *praxis*" as constituting a critique of "theory," Jameson asserts that "Burke's stress on language" has "the function of restoring to the literary text its value as activity and its meaning as a gesture and a response to a determinate situation" (SI 508–09). Jameson explains that in analyzing the symbolic act as a textual act, Burke's "theory of verbal praxis" takes on two inseparable roles recognized in the typical Burkean shift between substantive and qualifier: that is, it is a *textual* act in that it "begins by producing its own context in the same moment of emergence in which it steps back over against it, measuring it with an eye to its own active project," and it is a textual *act* in that it maintains "an active, well-nigh instrumental, stance . . . towards the new reality, the new situation, thus produced; . . . accompanied immediately by gestures of praxis—whether measurements, cries of rage, magical incantations, caresses, or avoidance behavior" (SI 512). Since this "textual act" is exactly what Jameson means by "ideological analysis," he takes pains in its articulation that make his writing nearly as difficult as Burke's own. But Jameson's analysis of Burke is an acute perception of Burke's limitations, and, as such, it also marks out the ways in which Williams's writing joins in Jameson's critique of Burke and performs its own "ideological analysis."

Jameson remarks that Burke's description of the symbolic act as *textual* act presupposes those "acts" of textual theorists in observing how all texts call into question their own rhetoricity by creating the "material grounds" on which they rest. As Jameson says, the text "articulates its own situation and textualizes it, encouraging the illusion that the very situation itself did not exist before it, that there is nothing but a text, that there never was any extra- or con-textual reality before the text itself generated it" (SI 512). Burke's genius, according to Jameson, is to link this observation inextricably with the notion that the symbolic act is still also a textual *act*—that it is designed to perform some action according to some purpose. It is here—in Burke's slighting of "Purpose" in his "dramatistic pentad" of Act, Scene, Agent, Agency, and Purpose—that Jameson locates the ideological downfall of Burke's writing. According to Jameson, in terms of "strategy" Burke either avoids "that vaster social or historical or political horizon in which alone the symbolic function of those symbolic acts which are the verbal and literary artifacts become visible to us" (SI 515), or he develops his own "strategy of containment" that flees "ideological analysis" by taking refuge in "the notion of art as ritual, the appeal to the bodily dimension of the verbal act, and the concept of the self or of identity as the basic theme or preoccupation of literature in general" (SI 518). When Burke does engage the political, as Jameson notes of both the *Grammar* and the *Rhetoric of Motives,* he does so in an attempt to "endow American capitalism of the thirties and early forties with its appropriate cultural and political ideology." Jameson explains:

> We are here after all in the thick of a New Deal and Deweyan rhetoric of liberal democracy and pluralism, federalism, the "Human Barnyard," "the competitive use of the coöperative," and the celebration of political conflict in terms of what the motto to *A Grammar of Motives* calls the "purification of war": from the nostalgic perspective of the present day, the perspective of a social system in full moral and civic dissolution, what seemed at the time a shrewd diagnosis of the cultural and ideological conflicts of the capitalist public sphere and an often damaging critique of the latter's strategies of legitimation must now come to have implications of a somewhat different kind. The very forms of legitimation have been dialectically transformed, and consumer capitalism no longer has to depend on conceptual systems and abstract values and beliefs to the same degree as its predecessors in the social forms of the immediate past; thus, what tends to strike us today about the *Grammar* and *Rhetoric of Motives* is less their critical force than Burke's implicit faith in the harmonizing claims of liberal democracy and in the capacity of the system to reform itself from within.
>
> (SI 520)

Jameson's critique of Burke is, in part, Williams's critique of Burke, but with some significant differences. Williams too, I think, ultimately believes in the "claims of liberal democracy and in the capacity of the system to reform itself from within." But the kinds of restructuring that Williams sees as necessary for this reformation involve going beyond the limits that Jameson rightly sees in Burke's notions. In particular, they involve that kind of "history lesson" that Jameson says Burke avoids teaching us—"the narrative of that implacable yet also emancipatory logic whereby the human community has evolved into its present form and developed the sign systems by which we live and explain our lives to ourselves" (SI 523). In Chapter 3 we saw how Williams develops the "diagnostic techniques" that enable him to begin this "lesson," noting along the way how Williams anticipates the kind of "dialectic transformation" of "the forms of legitimation" that Jameson himself argues in "Postmodernism, or The Cultural Logic of Late Capitalism."[49] In the remaining sections of this chapter, I will show how Williams's writing shares in Burke's project of "diagnosing" the "cultural and ideological conflicts of the capitalist public sphere" by exposing those "forms of legitimation" on which its "psychology" depends. In particular, my focus will be on how Williams highlights both "gender polarity" and the rhetoricity of "prose" as "strategies of limitation." Moreover, I will show how by using the "strategies" inherent in the symbolic action of his own writing to construct and expose what Jameson calls "subtexts," Williams's call for "intersubjectivity" and "mutuality" oppose his own culture in fundamental ways—ways that will ultimately demand an epistemological, economic, and political restructuring. As such, Williams's "language of flowers" will grow into his own form of "ideological analysis."

III

In "The Virtue of History"—one of the final sections of *In the American Grain,* dedicated to Aaron Burr—Williams gives the following conversation on his own ideas about the "use and abuse of history":

> If history could be that which annihilated all memory of past things from our minds it would be a useful tyranny.
>
> But since it lives in us practically day by day we should fear it. But if it is, as it may be, a tyranny over the souls of the dead—and so the imaginations of the living—where lies our greatest well of inspiration, our greatest hope of freedom (since the future is totally blank, if not black) we should guard it doubly from the interlopers.
>
> You mean tradition. Yes, nothing there is metaphysical. It is the better part of all of us.
>
> *(IAG* 189)

Williams begins *In the American Grain* by explaining that "In these studies I have sought to re-name the things seen, now lost in chaos [*sic*] of borrowed titles, many of them inappropriate, under which the true character lies hid" (*IAG* v). Unfortunately, much of the "true character" of this work has remained hidden under the "names" critics have borrowed from Williams himself, linking them together to form two violently opposed traditions of either Puritan vs. Indian, Hamilton vs. Burr, or "natural" vs. "imposed" cultures. As one voice in the above "conversation of history" explains, however, "You violate your own concept of what history should be when you speak so violently." Although these extreme appropriations of historical "fact" may be necessary because—as Williams goes on to explain—"The pendulum must swing. Is it not time that it swung *back* ?" (*IAG* 195, Williams's emphasis), these simple notions of opposition and distortion are not what Williams's "concept of history" is about. For Williams, history *should be* a "conversation" composed of as many voices as there are in a country. What history *is,* however, is revealed in his discussion of Burr. Williams asserts that

> Burr's account in history is a distortion. The good which history should have preserved, it tortures. A country is not free, is not what it pretends to be, unless it leave a vantage open (in tradition) for that which Burr possessed in such remarkable degree. This is my theme.
>
> *(IAG* 197)

Too often Williams has been read merely in his attempt to "swing back the pendulum," and so his ideas have often been left in their own incomplete, exaggerated state. Certainly this is true of his ideas about tradition, particularly as they were formulated negatively in opposition to Eliot. Rather than see tradition in purely negative terms, however, Williams viewed it as "nothing" inherently "metaphysical,"—potentially, "It is the better part of all of us." When, for example, Rebecca West charged that "Mr. James Joyce is a great man who is entirely without taste," Williams replied that Joyce merely lies beyond the confining boundaries of an "English tradition," but that "there is an American criticism that applies to American literature—all too unformed to speak of positively. This American thing it is that would better fit the Irish of Joyce" (*OE* 181). This "American thing," in part, is what Williams begins to develop in *In the American Grain*—an American tradition in line with John Dewey's project of "creative democracy." It is important to note, though, that Williams avoids the narrowness of Dewey's relatively homogeneous communal model by including the voices of blacks, Indians, Puritans, women, writers, and politicians in his "conversation of history."[50]

Both "history" and "tradition" are inescapable "textual acts" for Williams. By this I do not mean that "history is a text," but that—as Jameson asserts and, I think, Williams would agree—history is only accessible in textual form. "Tradition" then is merely a selective reduction of that larger "text" that *is* "history." As such, "tradition" both constitutes and is constituted by those "symbols of authority" that are, in effect, Burke's notion of "ideology." As Burke explains, this "term" is perhaps his most fluid, as it is "better designed for pointing-in-the-direction-of-something than for clear demarcation of that-in-the-direction-of-which-we-would-point" (*ATH* 329). What it "points-in-the-direction-of" are those attitudes, allegiances, things, and ideals with which we "identify" and which constitute our "identity." In "America, Whitman, and the Art of Poetry," Williams argued that "just as no art can exist for us except as we know it in our own poetry even our own art cannot exist but by grace of other poetry. Nothing comes out of the air, nor do we know whence anything comes but we do know that all we have receives its value from that which has gone on before." As such, both "tradition" and "history" become that "what-has-gone-on-before" that determines the value of poetry as well as of people and things. As Williams was to go on to say in "The Poem as a Field of Action" (1948)—"It may be said that I wish to destroy the past. It is precisely a service to tradition, honoring it and serving it that is envisioned and intended by my attack, and not disfigurement—confirming and *enlarging* its application" (*SE* 284, Williams's emphasis).

As "texts," as "symbols of authority," both "tradition" and "history" can be "moved in on"—incorporated within the "organized system of meaning" found within some "frame of acceptance" (*ATH* 322–23). This act of "moving in on" is that "textual act" that is analogous to what Jameson calls "ideological analysis"—'the rewriting of a particular narrative trait or seme as a function of its social, historical, or political context," or

> the rewriting of the literary text in such a way that it may itself be grasped as the rewriting or restructuration of a prior ideological or historical subtext, provided it is understood that the latter—what we used to call the "context"—must always be (re)-constructed after the fact, for the purposes of the analysis.
>
> (SI 511)

In this way, Williams "moves in on" historical texts such as Cotton Mather's *The Wonders of the Invisible World,* Kip's *The Early Jesuit Missions in North America,* Olson and Bourne's *The Northmen, Columbus, and Cabot, 985–1503* and the *Narratives of the Career of Hernando De Soto, Conquest: Dispatches of Cortez from the New World,* Franklin's *Poor Richard's Almanac* and *Autobiography,* along with the papers and memoirs of Burr, Hamilton, Washington, and Poe. And in doing so, Williams performs a complicated act of "ideological analysis" in *In the American Grain* that is at the same time a re-formation of American "history" and "tradition." Williams's project here is to "rewrite" historical texts in order both to expose what history *is* by revealing a Puritan tradition of domination and subversion at the textual level, and to suggest what history *should be* by including those voices that tradition has repressed or silenced. In doing so, Williams's "history lesson" re-presents "the task of effective-historical consciousness" in an effort to enlarge that discursive space in which self-creation can occur.

Williams dramatically re-presents what Gadamer called "the task of effective-historical consciousness" in the conversation he re-creates in "The Virtue of History." The two "voices" Williams uses bring out that "tension" between the "horizon of a particular present" that sees Burr in his generally received historical position of being a "dangerous man, one who ought not to be trusted with the reins of government" (*IAG* 190) and the "text" made vocal by Burr's defender. In presenting this section in the form of a conversation, literally the "conversation of history," Williams makes clear several of Gadamer's points about the "fusion of horizons." First, and perhaps most readily visible in this "conversation," are the "prejudices" that Gadamer says are brought out in this tension between historical horizons, along with the "otherness" of "historical consciousness." In this way, the two voices are both "something laid over a continuing tradition" and act dialectically to "recombine what . . . [is] distinguished" in the "unity of the historical horizon" thus acquired.[51]

This final "fusion of horizons"—what Gadamer calls the "task of effective-historical consciousness"—is finally left up to the reader, however, as Williams ends this section with the two "voices" in disagreement:

> But passion will obscure our sense so that we eat sad stuff and call it nectar. Burr was heavily censured by his time, immoral, traitorous and irregular. What they say of him, I still believe.
>
> Believe it if you will but listen to this story: Near the end of his life a lady said to him: "Colonel, I wonder if you were ever the gay Lothario they say you were." The old man turned his eyes, the lustre still undiminished, toward the lady—and lifting his trembling finger said in his quiet, impressive whisper: "They say, they say, they say. Ah, my child, how long are you going to continue to use those dreadful words? Those two little words have done more harm than all others. Never use them, my dear, never use them."
>
> (*IAG* 207)

While Williams's "conversation" is admittedly weighted against the "swing of the pendulum" in favor of Burr's "textual" defender, it is important to note that the disagreement itself is still recorded. What "they say" is still a part of history, shaping the "tradition." What's added here is Burr's own voice, which has always been apart from that tradition. Moreover, Burr (and Williams) only admonish against the unquestioned acceptance of what "they say," and this notion of interrogating both the "facts" as well as the very consciousness with which we interrogate those facts is acted out in Williams's text. We need to be aware of both voices in the conversation. Moreover, this interrogation is grounded neither in foundationalist thinking, nor in some "hermeneutics of suspicion." Williams gives us instead the voices of two suspicious hermeneuticists. Finally, by forcing the reader to mediate between these "voices," Williams also forces an empathic act of the imagination analogous to the one he creates in his prose/poetry sequences by creating the opportunity for our own "identification" of and within the conversation. "The Virtue of History" (both as a title and as a quality) is an act of "engaged diagnosis" like the ones we discussed in Chapter 3. Here, a fluid exchange needs to be maintained between the nomothetic law—what "they say"—and the idiographic—the unique case of Aaron Burr—in an act of empathic "identification" that enlarges the tradition of American "identity" by leaving "a vantage open (in tradition) for that which Burr possessed in such remarkable degree" (*IAG* 197).

The "history" that Williams wants us to "identify" here marks an important corrective to what Williams sees are the dominant "symbols of authority"—the workings of Washington, Hamilton, Jefferson, and the rest of the "Virginia Junto" (*IAG* 202)—just as, we will see in Chapter 5, the "virtues" that Williams "coaches" in this "history" mark an important adjustment of Pound's more metaphysical notion of "virtú." In particular, Williams enlarges the notion of "the individual" from the pursuit of "self-interest" as embodied in Hamiltonian Federalism to Burr's "sense of the individual"—"the basis on which the war was fought, instantly the war was over began to be debauched" (*IAG* 194). The "individual" is the cornerstone of Williams's "history lesson," though Williams's notion of the individual shares almost nothing with the bourgeois ideal of autonomous, rugged individualism. This notion, we will see below, relies on an act of forgetting that is antithetical to Williams's project. Rather, Williams's "individual" is a "humanity, his own, free and independent, unyielding to the herd, practical, direct" (*IAG* 204). As such, the "individual" constructs his "identity" within the discursive space of what *should be* history from a firmly cathected set of values. These values grow out of the "transformation of narcissistic energies" in their sense of "identifying with" others but maintaining an integrity between self and other. A crucial part of these values is a near-Stoic notion of "servitude" that, Williams says, is "foreign to us: a trick for foreigners, a servant's trick. We are afraid that we couldn't do it and retain our self-esteem. . . . Thus we see of what our self-esteem is made" (*IAG* 176). This sense of "self-esteem" is constructed on "self-interest" and depends on structures of domination for its sense of "identity." Consequently it rejects "servitude" out of fear and replaces it with "service," which Williams explains as "Sending supplies to relieve the cyclone sufferers in Indiana" (*IAG* 176). This "self-esteem" also relies wholly on notions of difference, and so structures of racial, sexual, and ethnic prejudice all become a vital part of this structure and its need to reject "servitude." As Williams puts it, "Do not serve another for you might have to TOUCH him and he might be a JEW or a NIGGER" (*IAG* 177, Williams's emphases).

Williams's notion of self-creation is neither unrestrained nor reliant upon a stable notion of self. Self-creation always takes place for Williams within the discursive space of a tradition. As Williams says of Samuel de Champlain, "Is it merely in a book? So am I then, merely in a book" (*IAG* 69), and the "textual act" of self-creation depends on those "books" that make up the tradition in which we "find" ourselves. The American "identity" is made up of that "Babel of voices," that "corporate we" that Burke "identifies" in *Attitudes Toward History*. Consequently, Williams's struggle with Eliot over the the demarcation of tradition—over the "symbols of authority"—is a very real struggle for political power. We will examine Eliot's tradition more fully in the next chapter; for now it should be clear that a tradition that rigorously excludes the voices of women and minorities effectively relegates these groups to a subordinate silence, while it also denies them both active subjectivity and the possibility of "identifying" themselves with their own voices within its "conversations."

Williams asserts early on in *In the American Grain* that we are like

> the Caribs whom The Great Maker had dropped through a hole in the sky among their islands; they whose souls lived in their bodies, many souls in one body. . . .
>
> Fierce and implacable we kill them but their souls dominate us. Our men, our blood, but their spirit is master. It enters us, it defeats us, it imposes itself. . . .
>
> If men inherit souls this is the color of mine. We are, too, the others. Think of them! The main islands were thickly populated with a peaceful folk when Christ-over found them. But the orgy of blood which followed, no man has written. We are the slaughterers.
>
> (*IAG* 39–41)

"We are, too, the others," and this "recognition" of both the self in the other and the other in the self may be the most vital part of Williams's notion of self-creation. As such, no one individual or group is either wholly valorized or condemned in this work. Christopher Columbus is both the discoverer of the "beautiful thing" that is the New World (*IAG* 26) and "Christ-over," the bringer of "an orgy of blood." Williams's discursive space of tradition and self-creation operates within the larger textual realm of history, whose narrative is one of power and domination:

> History, history! We fools, what do we know or care? History begins for us with murder and enslavement, not with discovery. No, we are not Indians but we are men of their world. The blood means nothing; the spirit, the ghost of the land moves in the blood, moves the blood. It is we who ran to the shore naked, we who cried, "Heavenly Man!" These are the inhabitants of our souls, our murdered souls that lie . . . agh.
>
> (*IAG* 39)

Even Montezuma, generally valorized in critical descriptions, explains that "his people were not the aborigines of the land but that they had emigrated there in times past and ended by accepting the Spanish Monarch as his rightful and hereditary master" (*IAG* 31–32).

Williams's notions of "self" and of the "individual" follow along closely with the notion of "mutuality" and "narcissistic transformation" that we looked at in the first two chapters, and we can see them operate "dramatically" here in Burr's relationship to women. One of the charges "they say" against Burr was that he was "immoral," and Williams sees this charge as the "only defense" against the kind of "liberating force" that Burr's relationship to women possessed. Burr's "defender" argues that "He was perhaps the only one of the time who saw women, in the flesh, as serious, and they hailed and welcomed with deep gratitude and profound joy his serious knowledge and regard and liberating force—for them" (*IAG* 204–05). While Williams is guilty of idealizing the feminine as the embodiment of the imaginative and sensual "spirit" of the land, particularly in the De Soto section, we need to remember that for Williams the "feminine psychology" was "grounded" in an empirical relation to the "real," and unlike a "male psychology" of abstraction, it remained firm in its relationship to the concrete. Consequently, we need to "read" Williams's valorization of the feminine against the Puritan's "unofficial sexual indulgence and the plight of [their] women" (*IAG* 119).

Burr is praised in his regard for women because

> he kept their secrets; no man has a better record. Asked his opinion he could say of women: all seriousness, yet you must speak light nothings to them. The rest were frivolous with women. The rest denied them, condoned the female flesh, found them helpmates at the best and at the worst, horses, cattle, provincial accessories, useful workers to make coffee and doughnuts—and to be left to go crazy on the farms for five generations after—that's New England, or they'd hide the bull behind the barn, so that the women would not think it knew the cows were—Bah, feudal dolls gone wrong, that's Virginia. Women? necessary but not noble, not the highest, not deliciously a free thing, apart, *feminine,* a heaven;— afraid to delve in it save like so much dough. Burr found the spirit living there, free and equal, independent, springing with life. Or did he? I say if he did he was before his time. Surely they drank of him like water.
>
> (*IAG* 205)

Williams's own "identification with" Burr is nearly as complete as his "identifications with" Père Rasles and Poe, and in all three cases Williams's "exaggerations" are attempts to "swing back the pendulum" of commonly held opinion. But even Williams's idealization of the feminine here avoids the "aestheticization" of women into lifeless objects. Instead, the feminine is valued as "free and equal, independent, springing with life." Williams's greatest avatar of the feminine in this work—Jacataqua (who briefly meets Burr)—is valued for her active role as "Sachem" and as "poetically" giving "form" to "the positives that . . . give character and dignity to the damp mass of the overpowering but characterless resistance" (*IAG* 186).

Burr's relationship with women is an act of empathic identification that maintains the identity of "spirit" along with both the difference of sexuality and a relationship to the "real" that was immediate and open. This second difference is also, paradoxically, an "identity" for both Williams and Burr, as it forms the "ground" of both men's ideal of "creative democracy." It is here in his notion of "democracy" that Williams's own "frame of acceptance" approaches the "transcendental," marking the site where Williams's notions of writing coincide with his relations to women and the "common people." As Williams continues his "conversation," he explains,

> Burr knew what a democracy must liberate.
> What then?
> Men intact—with all their senses waking. He had, raised to a different level, the directness of "common people" which reformers, that is to say, schemers, commonly neglect, misname, misapprehend as if it were anything but to touch, to hear, to see, to smell, to taste.
> Transcendental theory, my dear countryman.
> What is; the delicious sincerity of pioneer people? In Burr this aristocratic strain, straight out of the ground, was *seeing* its own ground belied. To maintain the truth up through the scale is the hard thing.
>
> (*IAG* 206, Williams's emphasis)

Williams's "other" openly questions the "transcendental" nature of his own belief both in his ideal of "contact" and in his romantically locating this "quality" in the "common people." It is this same quality that Williams will "quote" in "The Advent of the Slaves" as the only way that blacks—who are socially determined as "*nothing*" and "NOBODY"—come to be " 'ME' . . . That's SOMETHIN'. . . . There is a racial solidity, a racial irreducible minimum, which gives them poise in a world where they have no authority—" (*IAG* 209). And it is vital to note that Williams not only gives blacks the authority of having voiced their own language in this section, but also respects the integrity of that authority in voicing a desire to "write a play in collaboration with" a black man in his town (*IAG* 211). Most significantly, though, he records these African-American "voices" in his "conversation of history," making them a crucial part of his "tradition." This tradition is allied with Burr in the above section as Williams links Burr's valuation of the "common people" with the very source of Williams's poetry:

> A while ago, just here, I heard a Polish woman saying to her daughter: "you bust your coat with your fifty sweaters."
> What's that: You bust your coat with your fifty sweaters?
> Its immediacy, its sensual quality, a pure observation, its lack of irritation, its lack of pretense, its playful exaggeration, its repose, its sense of design, its openness, its gayety, its unconstraint. It frees, it creates relief. In the great it is the same, or would be if it ever existed, a delicious sincerity (in greater things of course) not a scheme, nor a system of procedure—but careless truth.
>
> (*IAG* 206)

Williams's poetics are his politics, and just as, as Williams himself once said, his poetry comes from "the mouths of Polish mothers" (*A* 311), his politics includes the voices that other writers either omit, repress, or seek to silence. But

Williams's politics, like his poetics, are not a sentimental over-valuation of some "transcendental" ideals. Williams's matrix of "history" and "tradition" operates in a fluid realm of power, domination, and resistance, though Williams retains the possibility of human agency in the determination of that matrix. In this same way, Williams's poetry operates in a similarly textual realm of dominant traditions that can likewise be resisted and re-formed. To remain with the political, however, Williams's understanding of the forces of "history" and "tradition" demonstrates the complicated ways in which—while we can never exist outside of either one— we can influence both. In this way, Williams combines the "task of effective-historical consciousness" with Jameson's notion of "ideological analysis" by "the rewriting of the literary text in such a way that it may itself be grasped as the rewriting or restructuration of a prior ideological or historical subtext" (SI 511). In particular, by exposing the ways in which the dominant Puritan tradition subsumes alternate traditions in its own rewriting of history, Williams can effectively create his own historical subtext of buried voices, making those alternate traditions once again available in order to enlarge the "corporate we" of American "identity."

But just as Burr was "the essence of the schemes the others made" (*IAG* 207), Williams himself embodies those "qualities" that make up part of the Puritan's contribution to the "American Grain," though it takes a Frenchman, Valéry Larbaud, to point this out to Williams in yet another "conversation of history" in the "Père Sebastian Rasles" section:

> This interests me greatly because I see you brimming—you, yourself—with those three things of which you speak: a puritanical sense of order, a practical mysticism as of the Jesuits, and the sum of all those qualities defeated in the savage men of your country by the first two. These three things I see still battling in your heart. This interests me greatly—and it pleases me still more that you show a taste for books. Does this indicate, I say to myself, a new force in your country? Are you today presenting me with a new spectacle, a man, no matter what his qualities may be, who has *begun* to reach a height but who still retains his warmth; that moment when all greatness is conceived. It is no more than a moment, it is the birth of a civilized interest in the world.
>
> No, no, no, I cried. I speak only of sources. I wish only to disentangle the obscurities that oppress me, to track them to the root and to uproot them—
>
> Continue, he said. Adding with a smile, You wish to uproot history, like those young men of the Sorbonne.
>
> No, I seek the support of history but I wish to understand it aright, to make it SHOW itself.
>
> Continue, continue.
>
> (*IAG* 116, Williams's emphases)

Larbaud is "a student" while Williams is "a block . . . the brutal thing itself" (*IAG* 107), and the "history lesson" he gets from Larbaud is a sense of his own "otherness"—a "recognition" of the other in the self. Again, both sides of the "conversation" make up the "lesson":

> By the strength of religion alone, [the Puritans] surmounted all difficulties in which science has degraded us again today; all things they explain, with clarity and

distinction. It is firm, it is solid, it holds the understanding in its true position, not beneath the surface of the facts, where it will drown, but up, fearlessly into a clear air, like science at its best, in a certain few minds. For our taste, it is perhaps a little grotesque, this explanation—but firm. There is vigor there—and by that a beauty.

(IAG 110)

As Williams will later say, "If history could be that which annihilated all memory of past things from our minds it would be a useful tyranny. But since it lives in us practically day by day we should fear it" (*IAG* 189). What Williams recognizes here is the inescapability of history. Williams, as the "brutal thing itself," is as much orderly Puritan as he is mystical French Jesuit, and sensual Indian. As Larbaud says in his conversation with Williams, "As with all histories, it begins with giants—cruel but enormous, who eat flesh. They were giants" (*IAG* 113), and the three giants of English Puritans, French Jesuits, and American Indians all stake their claim in the discursive space of Williams's own identity.

The Puritans were "the first American democracy," but it was also "they, in the end, who would succeed in making everything like themselves" (*IAG* 63), and their determination to make the new world over in their own likeness is anathema to Williams's notion of self-creation. This distinction is analogous to those differences between an oedipal model of domination and a narcissistic model of mutuality that we discussed in Chapter 2, where the oedipal model divides the world into active self—modeled after the dominant father—and passive (m)other. The narcissistic model allows for both identification and difference with mother and father, holding this paradoxical relationship in tension.[52] All people, then, become potentially both self and other while, strictly defined, they are also always other. In this way notions of "identification" and "empathy" maintain this paradox of identity and difference by moving beyond power relations to achieve greater intersubjective understanding.

This ideal is embodied in the "Père Rasles" section in the example of Père Rasles himself, who sees the Indians as "his children" and yet respects the integrity of both their language and their ways. He shares with Burr the quality of being a "great listener," and "his generous spirit" is the "moral source" that Williams wants to "make Americans see" (*IAG* 122–23). But Williams admits that "much the Puritans complained of in the Jesuits was justified"—just as "much that Père Rasles might have said against the Puritan-English was also true"—leaving us with "two flaming doctrines" (*IAG* 127–28). Both Puritans and Jesuits are figured in the section using religion as a means of dominating and exploiting the Indian, and Puritanism and Catholicism both act as kinds of grammars for interpretation. The Puritan "grammar" is in effect a "grammar of transference"—like the one developed in Chapter 1—that remains within its own set "lines of projection" in order to read signs. Williams elsewhere calls it "this pale negative to usurp the place of that which really they were destined to continue" (*IAG* 66). Consequently, Williams says,

the Puritan, finding one thing like another in a world destined for blossom only in "Eternity," all soul, all "emptiness" then here, was precluded from SEEING

the Indian. They never realized the Indian in the least save as an unformed PU-
RITAN. The *immorality* of such a concept, the inhumanity, the brutalizing effect
upon their own minds, on their SPIRITS—they never suspected.

(IAG 113, Williams's emphases)

Catholicism is equally a "grammar of transference," but, Williams argues, it at
least offers "ALLEVIATION" from "lack of sensual application, removed from
without by an authority that represents mystery itself" (*IAG* 129) in its emphasis
on ritual and the mystical.

Père Rasles combines this mystery and ritual within his own "grammar of
translation" that seeks to maintain and appreciate the integrity of the other. As
such, Rasles is described in terms of an empathic identification with the Indian—
"In Rasles one feels THE INDIAN emerging from within the pod of his isolation
from eastern understanding, he is released AN INDIAN. He exists, he is—it is an
AFFIRMATION, it is alive" (*IAG* 121, Williams's emphases). But a "grammar
of translation" is nonetheless a "grammar"—one that relies on the subjectivity of
the translator to give as "true" a translation as possible by eliminating "preju-
dices" from his act. It is for this reason that the ideals of translation, mutuality,
and identification all rely on the vehicle of conversation if they are to avoid be-
coming "grammars of transference." Only by recognizing the "otherness" of his-
torical consciousness, as well as the subjectivity of the other itself, can we ensure
against having translation or identification become forms of domination.

Consequently, an even more vital way the "Père Rasles" section embodies
Williams's ideals of intersubjectivity and mutuality, which are intimately allied to
his ideals of both democracy and the individual, is in the very act of conversing
with Valery Larbaud about books. Larbaud and Williams reveal each other's "prej-
udices" during the course of their talk, with Williams noting Larbaud's relatively
detached, analytical appreciation of American history—"Cotton Mather's books,
to you an enchanting diversion, a curious study" (*IAG* 116)—and Larbaud bringing
out not only the three forces within Williams, but also an awareness of Williams's
own "theoretical interests":

> It is good that you struggle to appreciate it. Proceed. Mather. *What* a force, still
> to interest you; it is admirable. But I find your interest "très théorique."
>
> What! I cried. Wait a bit. These men are not the only ones of these times.
>
> It is of books that we were speaking.
>
> It is of books that I wish to tell you.
>
> Then they live still, those books?
>
> I could not assure him that they did, those books of Mather's. As books, no,
> I said to him. But what is in them lives and there hides, as in a lair from whence
> it sallies now and then to strike terror through the land.
>
> And you would be the St. George? Are they then in such a bad state in
> America, in such a swamp? I thought—
>
> As always, I answered him. This fiery breath, as of a dragon, is to us a living
> thing. Our resistance to the wilderness has been too strong. It has turned us anti-
> American, anti-literature. As a violent "puritanism" it breathes still. In these
> books is its seed.

(IAG 115–16)

Williams "cannot merely talk of books" here, and his "wish to drag this THING out by itself to annihilate it" (*IAG* 115) is the part of his "theory" of history that needs most to be reconsidered. Williams claims in this section that he speaks "only of sources. I wish only to disentangle the obscurities that oppress me, to track them to the root and to uproot them—" and that he seeks "the support of history but I wish to understand it aright, to make it SHOW itself." Williams knows that the American construction of identity most often takes place in an act of forgetting—"the fools do not believe that they have sprung from anything: bone, thought and action. They will not see that what they are is growing on these roots. ... Their history is to them an enigma" (*IAG* 113). But the mere exposure of these "roots" will not alter that textual matrix of tradition in which self-creation occurs. Only by effectively "moving in on" these texts—by rewriting them in such a way that their own historical subtext of domination is revealed in an attempt to enlarge that tradition—can Williams get beyond his "theoretical interests" in them and effectively alter that matrix of history, making audible those voices that these texts would leave silent. Consequently, a section like "Cotton Mather's Wonders of the Invisible World" both reveals the effaced voice of Mather himself in a supposedly "neutral" account of the facts of witchcraft and makes visible the property squabbles and sexual jealousies beneath the accusations. "The May-Pole at Merry Mount" compares various accounts of the "incident of the May-pole at Merry Mount" to reveal the conscious burying of Thomas Morton's punning, sexual story beneath both Bradford's limited understanding of the forces at work in the incident and A. C. Adams's modern preface to Morton's *The New English Canaan,* which describes Morton as "a vulgar, loyalist libertine" (*IAG* 75).

But Williams's story here also embodies his historical project in an even more significant way by re-producing Williams's own historical conditions around the time of the work's production. The section begins with a string of names of artists that Williams met during his six week stay in Paris in 1924, the year before *In the American Grain* was published. The similarities between this opening and Williams's 1926 "Poem"—a list of figures from American history—makes clear the kinds of conflations between poetics and politics that we discussed above, as it also hints at Williams's differences with other modernists. Williams describes them as "*warily* conscious of a newcomer, but wholly without inquisitiveness—No wish to know; they were served" (*IAG* 105–06, original emphasis), and Williams's own "servitude" combines here with his desire to articulate an American tradition to begin to suggest both political and aesthetic distinctions between himself and writers like Pound and Eliot that we will examine more closely in Chapter 5. By incorporating his own history within the dialectic of his conversation with Larbaud, Williams embodies that paradoxical tension between identity and difference with an equally complicated tension between the living and the dead. Larbaud, a Frenchman, lives at "the bottom of an alley which opened out into a court, as of a decayed cloister" (*IAG* 107). Williams, "the brutal thing itself," would also "be the St. George" (*IAG* 107 & 115). In this way, Williams makes clear both what history *is* and what history *should be* through the textual construction of his own "identity" in a fusion of historical horizons that involves both the texts of the past and the text of Williams's present.

In the American Grain may be Williams's most successful fusion of prose and poetry not only in its alternating historical prose and lyrical passages, but also in its understanding of the prosaic force of what history *is* and its attempt to discover poetically what history *should be.* As such, however, it also calls into question the efficacy of equating poetics with politics. The mere inclusion of black voices, for example, does not guarantee that an act of translation avoids becoming an act of appropriation, though the ideals of a "grammar of translation" that attempts to reproduce those voices as accurately as possible, giving them the authority of their own language, does militate somewhat against such an act of domination.[53] In my final section, then, I would quickly like to examine the ways in which Williams's writing does act as a specific form of intervention and to explore some of the limits of writing as a type of political action. In particular, I will look at Williams's Stecher trilogy of novels as an attempt to substitute a "proletarian style" for "proletarian propaganda" in the articulation of a theory of "creative democracy."

IV

In *The American Evasion of Philosophy,* Cornel West describes John Dewey as "the culmination of the tradition of American pragmatism. After him, to be a pragmatist is to be a social critic, literary critic, or a poet—in short, a participant in cultural criticism and cultural creation."[54] West explains that Dewey joins Emerson in an "evasion of epistemology-centered philosophy" that situates "philosophical reflection *and* poetic creation in the midst of quotidian human struggles for meaning, status, power, wealth, and selfhood." Dewey's philosophical reconstruction aims to "demystify and to defend the most reliable mode of inquiry in modern culture, namely, critical intelligence best manifest in the community of scientists" (*AEP* 72–73). That Williams and Burke both join Dewey in this genealogy of pragmatism should not be surprising. During Burke's brief stay at Columbia, he studied with Dewey, and Williams used Dewey as the basis for his own "philosophical" treatise, *The Embodiment of Knowledge* (1928).[55] Additionally, as we saw in Chapter 2, Williams openly agreed with Dora Marsden's anti-epistemology-centered philosophical project in 1917, and he admits in a 1944 letter to Horace Gregory that he took his notions of embedding general culture in the local from Dewey's essays that had appeared in *The Dial* between 1919 and 1920 (*SL* 224), though he later strongly disagreed with what he saw as Dewey's arrogance toward and separation from the masses.[56] Rather than engage in an extended comparison of Dewey and Williams, however, I would like to outline below the discursive space in which West locates Dewey—as part of West's own project of "prophetic pragmatism"—and show how Williams shares in the project of "creative democracy" through the somewhat negative example of his Stecher trilogy of novels.

West argues that Dewey rejects the "subjectivist turn of Descartes" to focus instead on

> . . . intersubjectivity—the multiform interactions of human organisms with nature
> and with each other. The problem is not whether there is epistemic justification

for the status of an external world outside the veil of ideas, but rather how one
goes about dealing and coping—less or more intelligently—with one's
environment.

(AEP 89)

This epistemological swerve is identical to the one Williams takes in both his
reworking of Dora Marsden's "philosophical algebra" and his redefining the "di-
agnostic space" established in the Enlightenment into the "intersubjective space"
of his poetry. Like Dewey, Williams stresses the "active, selective, and instru-
mental character of human experience," and he, too, follows Emerson in "high-
light[ing] the future, the forward-looking character" of life. In this way, as Dewey
says in "The Development of American Pragmatism" (1922), "Pragmatism, thus,
presents itself as an extension of historical empiricism, but with this fundamental
difference, that it does not insist upon antecedent phenomena but upon consequent
phenomena; not upon the precedents but upon the possibilities of action." For both
Dewey and Williams, "Imaginative recovery of the bygone is indispensable to
successful invasion of the future" *(AEP 91)*.

Dewey's "critical intelligence" and Williams's "imagination" share in an in-
strumental optimism toward human development that is the cornerstone of each
writer's attitude toward history, as well as of each writer's attitude toward the
creation of what West terms "an Emersonian *culture* of radical democracy in which
self-creation and communal participation flourish in all their diversity and plural-
ity" (West's emphasis). "For Dewey," as well as for Williams, "the aim of po-
litical and social life is the cultural enrichment and moral development of
self-begetting individuals and self-regulating communities by means of the release
of human powers provoked by novel circumstances and new challenges" *(AEP
103)*. This process takes place within the textual matrices of "history" and "tra-
dition" as part of what Dewey calls "experience" and what Williams calls "dis-
covery." This application of an inferential methodology, based on probability and
appeals to prior situations, is at the heart not only of Dewey's "scientific method,"
but also Williams's "diagnostic techniques" that were developed in Chapter 3. It
involves what Dewey himself describes as

> primarily a process of undergoing: a process of standing something; of suffering
> and passion, of affection, in the literal sense of these words. The organism has to
> endure, to undergo, the consequence of its own actions.
>
> Experience, in other words, is a matter of *simultaneous* doings and sufferings.
> Our undergoings are experiments in varying the course of events; our active tryings
> are trials and tests of ourselves. . . . Nothing can eliminate all risk, all adventure.
>
> The obstacles which confront us are stimuli to variation, to novel response,
> and hence are occasions for progress.
>
> If biological development be accepted, the subject of experience is at least an
> animal, continuous with other organic forms in a process of more complex organ-
> ization. . . . And experience is not identical with brain action; it is the entire organic
> agent-patient in all its interaction with the environment, natural and social. . . .
> Knowing must be described by discovering what particular mode—qualitatively
> unique—of doing and suffering it is.[57]

Dewey's description of "experience" should recall, in part, that "remark" that Burke says in *Attitudes Toward History* that his "friend William Carlos Williams had made to [him] in a moment when, as often, his duality as poet and physician spoke as one. . . . 'First, there would be the sheer physicality of life, the human organism as one more species of alimentary canal with accessories . . . digestive tract with trimmings' " (*ATH* 392)—and, as we will see in Chapter 5, the ways in which "the entire organic agent-patient in all its interaction with the environment, natural and social" is an apt description of the kind of "mapping" that takes place in *Paterson*. For now I would like to explore a few of the ways in which Williams's trilogy of novels—*White Mule* (1937), *In the Money* (1940), and *The Build-Up* (1952)—share in West's and Dewey's statement about "the aim of political and social life" by examining how the social and cultural forces of Joe and Gurlie Stecher's America corrupt these ideals of "cultural enrichment and moral development" (*AEP* 103).

The "new challenge" in these novels is the challenge of the new world itself—the climb to power and prominence of an immigrant family at the turn of the century. The story of the Stechers, based on Williams's wife's parents, Paul and Nannie Herman, moves from a small apartment on 104th Street in New York City to the building site of what is to be their "ancestral manor"—"like nothing in the neighborhood. Like nothing" (*BU* 334) in upstate New York. Still, the story of Joe's success in America forms neither the framework nor the telos of the trilogy. Instead, the first two novels follow the development of the infant Flossie during her first two years of life, where a walk in the park is as much the focus of a chapter as Joe's receiving financial backing for his own business. This attention to infant development brings out more of the ways in which Williams's ideas anticipate Jessica Benjamin's notions of "destruction" and "mutuality." Both parents serve as active models for their two daughters, though the daily care of the children often falls in the hands of a young servant girl, and neither Joe nor Gurlie's role as "active subject" is wholly positive. Still, nearly all the other children in the novels are either completely spoiled, and so "destroy" their often hapless mothers, or they are completely restricted and dominated by overbearing parents, while Joe and Gurlie both balance the girls' assertions of their wills and identities with their own ideas and examples.

At one point in *In the Money,* Williams has Gurlie take the children to a Fifth Avenue doctor who gives her a pamphlet he has written on child development during the second year—nearly the exact time that Benjamin focuses on in her work.[58] Dr. Mabbot—a kind of projection of what Williams himself might have been had he taken a more lucrative practice in New York instead of remaining in Rutherford—likes to write, though "not scientific studies so much" (*ITM* 140). Mabbot also combines the masculine and feminine in ways similar to Williams, as he explains his always wanting a daughter by saying, "there's a lot of women in most men . . . in doctors anyhow—a lot of woman" (*ITM* 138). Mabbot's pamphlet agrees with recent studies in asserting that at the age of two, the infant "begins to experience now its first independence" and that this time is a "larval" stage that "gives the mind its enduring form. . . . 'Not bad,' said Joe. 'So you like it.' 'It's all right" (*ITM* 155–56). Mabbot even includes his own version of "destruction":

"What the devil? the unformed mind seems to say. Two and two make four. When I do this I get that. I! Who is this 'I' that does things? Let's see if that's so. Crash! Whang. Quite so. Yes, two and two quite correctly make four. Well, what the devil, I knew that anyway."

"No. This is too silly," said Joe. "I think all doctors are crazy." But he went on reading.

(*ITM* 156)

The notion of "destruction" and "rapprochement"—where the parents' "survival" allows for the infant to differentiate her own unique identity in relationship to some other that lies outside herself—leads toward "mutuality" by holding in suspension ideas of identity and difference, and as such it provides a psychological grounding for a cultural notion of "intersubjectivity" that can hold in suspension ideas of racial, ethnic, gender, and economic "identities" and differences. It is interesting to note, in this regard, that Williams precedes the above with a chapter called "Introducing the Boys" that shows the oedipal world of Joe's business rivals and follows it with two-year-old Flossie's biting Joe's knee "out of an excess of emotion or the pure spirit of scientific investigation" (*ITM* 157). Joe, as active subject, kicks back.

But Williams by no means provides a purely positive model of "mutuality" in these novels. Joe's story of economic success is also the story of his gradual estrangement from his early involvement with Samuel Gompers and the labor movement, as well as from his family and friends. Joe trusts neither workers nor bosses, as he sees both forces as inevitably corrupt and interested only in making money. Initially a speechmaker and supporter of the AF of L, Joe cynically breaks a strike at his printing office—knowing the bosses will give him no credit—just so the "work" can be done. Joe begins with the "old world" value that "Everybody should work. Everybody should work the best that he knows how," but he knows that this valuation conflicts with the idea of "America . . . the United States of America—money" (*WM* 13). This conflict takes the form of confusing signifier with signified in Joe's mind, as the value of a man should be signified by the good work he does, not merely in how much money he makes. Money separated from material practices becomes an abstract good in itself, and as such, it is a corrupting source. It is interesting in this regard that Joe will begin to make his fortune by successfully bidding on a government contract to print money orders—signifiers of money in themselves, even further removed from any material signified.

Joe (and Williams) share in Emerson and Dewey's distrust of organizations on either the left or the right, but unlike Dewey (and Williams) Joe ultimately denies the need to operate within a community of individuals. Dewey's use of Emerson in *Individualism: Old and New* illustrates an important distinction that Williams makes in his figuration of Joe:

> "It is in vain," said Emerson, "that we look for genius to reiterate its miracles in the old arts; it is its instinct to find beauty and holiness in new and necessary facts, in the field and in the roadside, in the shop and mill." To gain an integrated individuality, each of us needs to cultivate his own garden. But there is no fence about this garden: it is no sharply marked-off enclosure. Our garden is the world, in the angle at which it touches our own manner of being. By accepting the

corporate and industrial world in which we live, and by thus fulfilling the precon-
dition for interaction with it, we, who are also parts of the moving present, create
ourselves as we create an unknown future.[59]

Joe's "self-creation" promotes a form of individualism that serves self-interest in
his own pursuit of money and his gradual separation from family and community.
The central chapter in *White Mule* is a Christmas party where family and friends
compare "all the color and so quiet" of Christmas in the "old country" with its
louder, more commercialized American counterpart. In it Joe openly displays his
ambivalence between old and new, work and money, by remarking at one point
that "*Arbeit macht das Leben süss!* . . . when you have a couple of million dollars
to shake around together" and by cynically observing that an American Christmas
may lack "real happiness," but that "you don't refuse the presents" (*WM* 137 &
143). The party ends warmly, however, with Joe playing "Ständchen" on the violin
for the crowd. In the second novel, Christmas is moved toward the end of the story,
with Joe nearly removed from all the festivities. Here it is Joe's brother Oswald—
a free-living romantic who at one point ran off with the wife of his former regi-
ment's commander—who hand-cuts all the decorations for the tree and breathes
life into the party. In the third novel, Christmas is merely noted in a paragraph
along with a box of "Armour products" that Oswald had sent from the factory he
works in. In *White Mule,* Joe visits the wife of a fired worker, and when he sees
the squalor and cruelty in which she and her children live, he gives her money and
promises to get the husband another chance at work. In *The Build-Up,* it is Gurlie
who comes to the rescue of a starving family in Riverdale, but she does so under
the mixed circumstances of having volunteered to represent "The Town Improve-
ment Association"—a group that "merely took up the women's time and gave
them something to talk about, according to Joe." Gurlie volunteers to help only
after one of the town's "matriarchs" has insisted that something be done, and her
act, while it is undeniably charitable, is further compromised in that it is an op-
portunity for Gurlie to establish her own authority over Father Kelley and the
influence of Catholic church in town (*BU* 131–45).

Joe's role in *The Build-Up* seems to go beyond little more than asking how
much the things cost that Gurlie and her daughters buy and providing the money
for their purchases. And by the end of the novel, Joe literally "cultivates his own
garden" in a secluded area on the large country property he has bought, isolating
himself further from both family and community. Joe calls his "fortress" after
"the legendary resting place of the Prussian State Treasurer, Spandau," and he
ensures his isolation by building a stone fence around it. "Everyone knew that that
pile of rocks was his private keep. It got to be ten feet around and as high as your
head, neatly piled, as he would do it, the stones fitted all about like the exterior of
a Gothic cathedral. 'Spandau!' he'd say, with his ironic smile and one never knew
quite what he meant" (*BU* 314–15). What Williams means here, I think, is that
Joe's "fortress" is a fitting emblem of the kinds of aristocratic, nationalistic, and
religious forces that his "making money" embodies. The trilogy ends with the
excavation for Joe's last home—"a big stone house of native-cut stone"—with
his only son dead from a hunting accident, his oldest daughter run off with a

disreputable but "well-known" artist, and Flossie having married a poor, somewhat contemptuous and self-involved young doctor-poet. Joe's story closes with this final, nearly mad speech:

> Let her have it! She wants it—for all it's worth. Let her have it. I've got the money, I made it, I made it by the sweat of my brow. It's mine. Now she can take over. I made it. I enjoyed making it. Now let her spend it. That's what she enjoys and I'm the man to let her do it. To hell with it all.
>
> The excavators started their work and ran into granite hard as flint after the first scoopfuls of topsoil!
>
> "No matter. Blast! Blast it out!" said Joe. "Blow the damned rock to hell and gone. We're going to have a house like nothing in the neighborhood. Like nothing," he said looking up toward the mansion of the tycoon on the mountain in plain view to the southward, "like nothing in the neighborhood. Expense be damned."
>
> (*BU* 334)

Joe's "self-creation" takes place within a matrix of power and ambition that is masculine, corrupt, exploitative, xenophobic, and completely self-interested. And while Joe successfully resists the forces of corruption and exploitation—he is scrupulously honest in his business and his employees are all fairly treated and incredibly loyal—there is a sense of the tragic, as well as the sentimental, in his ultimately succumbing to and participating in these forces. Even more so than Joe, however, it is Gurlie whose self-development is affected by those traditions that deny her own direct participation within the matrix of power. Gurlie is a forceful, ambitious woman whose identification with an old-world aristocracy—she can trace her roots back to the Vikings and dreams of reclaiming her ancestral estate-farm in the south of Norway—drives her to occupy an equal position among the American elite. As a woman, however, the only identity she can find within the world of money is the Lady Macbeth–like status of pushing her husband. "And I'll bet my britches," says one of the workers in *In the Money,* "that if you went to look it up, you'd damn well find there's a woman pushing old Stecher into this and make no mistake about that" (*ITM* 39). Gurlie becomes the convenient brunt for the displaced feelings of ambition that drive Joe to make more money and buy better houses—although as Joe's own pleasure in his success and his final speech attest, he has made his money as much for himself as for his family.

Gurlie is every bit Joe's equal as active subject in the trilogy, and she even refuses to wear a wedding ring because Joe won't wear one. Gurlie's self-creation, however, is doomed from the start, as the matrix of power in which she would carve her identity relies wholly on differences to make its distinctions. As an immigrant—much is made of Gurlie's speaking with an accent that never fully disappears—she will always be marked as other by those "matriarchs" who trace their roots to the Mayflower. Consequently, Gurlie's identity becomes tied to those possessions—particularly her houses—that signify her rise in society. "You should let me buy things for you when you want something good," she tells her sister Olga (*BU* 9). It is Gurlie who points out to Joe that "In America bluff is everything" (*WM* 22), and her own removal from a concrete world of material signifieds for a world of signifying materials distances her from family and community as well.

As a result of her participation in this social matrix of power and class, Gurlie gradually removes her family from the heterogeneous community in New York and the young black girls who look after her daughters for the all-white community of Riverdale. Gurlie hires only young Scandinavian girls to look after her children now, thus attempting to displace her own status as poor immigrant and relocate herself as part of an ancient Norwegian high culture that preempts an Anglo-American tradition—"The Norse were the first to have a culture, no matter what was said of others" (*WM* 25). The ultimate futility of this distinction is figured in *The Build-Up* when Gurlie visits a member of the old "Southern aristocracy" in order to speak about her visit to Norway in front of Mrs. Moore's "close friends" at a Grange meeting. Even though Mrs. Moore's property and belongings are more dilapidated and worn than those of the poor farmers Gurlie disdains in Vermont, she and her group are guaranteed a status that Gurlie can never achieve. And the violence and racial hatred this group was founded on is made clear in a brief exchange between Gurlie and "her hostess":

> "What was all that racket I heard last night?"
> "I didn't hear anything," said her hostess.
> "The dogs barking." She had dreamed of runaway slaves hiding in the swamp and bloodhounds.
> "Oh, I suppose it was some of the young bloods from hereabouts on a coon hunt with their dogs."
> "A coon hunt?"
> "Yes, there's lots of raccoons around here. The dogs tree them and then the men chop the tree down and the dogs finish them." Some time before she fell asleep Gurlie had thought she heard a chopping, axes striking regularly into the wood.
>
> (*BU* 224)

Gurlie's own dreams of integration lead her to romanticize the noises as "escaped slaves," as well as to miss completely the connection between the two kinds of "coon hunts." Her speech to the group ends up being a polemic on the rise of foreigners in America and the shared status of all Americans as immigrants, and it is drowned out by chatter about local sex scandals and derisive comments about ambitious foreigners who "when they get up in the world want to put everyone else down. Ha ha! That is the kind that want to marry their daughters into the English aristocracy" (*BU* 227).

Gurlie's relationship to her daughters is a strained one, and the assertion of her own will and "new-world" identity ultimately "destroys" her older daughter Lottie. Her abuse of Lottie takes the form of dismissing her as a "skinny little nothing" unlike the usually robust Norwegian girls. She also pushes her daughter, a talented but unambitious pianist, into a relationship with the infamous "Affinity Ives" because of the "artistic connections" he could provide. Ives is a well-known painter of the day and comes from an aristocratic, wealthy, Revolutionary-war family. At one point, he describes his own great-grandmother—the scandalous

Mme. Jumel—as "a brilliant woman. The morals of the time were such that she got a bad reputation. She was merely ahead of her generation. There are always women like that during periods of great stress. She understood what was going on and—profited by it" (*BU* 280). Sensing a tradition in which Gurlie would like to dream herself, she has Lottie play for Ives and sit for him to paint her portrait. Ives sees America as "a maimed environment out of which nothing wide and broad enough in the artist's experience could come to stand up against time" (*BU* 301). He leaves America to return to Europe, where Lottie joins him under the pretense of continuing her study of piano, which she abandons—as Ives abandons his fourth wife—to marry Ives and travel with him.

As the chronicle of the gradual abandonment of self, family, and community in the pursuit of wealth and status, Williams's Stecher trilogy maps out an important indictment of his father-in-law's, and his own, culture. And his novels do so by focusing always on the quotidian, familiar, everyday world of children, schools, and neighborhoods. Joe's own final mad detachment is the embodiment of the detached signifier—the money order—that brought him his wealth and that ultimately signifies the schizophrenic nature of commodity production itself. But Williams's novels do not proceed along the usually doctrinal lines of "social realism." Instead, it is the very act of producing his novels that embodies positively his social and cultural ideals. Williams wrote to Louis Zukofsky in 1936 about how his interests in Social Credit—a scheme that would make generally available the surplus value caused by technological improvements in production in the form of "social credit"—led him to write both a review of H. H. Lewis's poems for the *New Masses* and a paper on "The Attack on Credit Monopoly from the Cultural Viewpoint" that he read at the Public Affairs Conference at the University of Virginia. While we will look more closely at both of these pieces in the next chapter, it is important here to note that, according to his letter, the "one bright though[t]" that Williams says he was "able to relieve [him]self of was that what we must have in poetry today is not propaganda for the proletariat—but a proletarian *style*."[60] In other words, Williams recognizes literature as an act of cultural production, and just as Social Credit would make capital available to everyone, Williams's writings would make available forms of cultural capital (i.e., "literature") in their accessibility not only in price, but also in the development of that "proletarian style." Consequently, the simple, quotidian focus and form of these works becomes a conscious strategy to socialize "culture."

But even more important, Williams's novels follow two strategies in developing their "proletarian style." First, they recognize that most of us occupy a space at the margins of history, and so they concentrate on that part of the cultural matrix, the communal and the familial, that lies within our power to participate in and even influence. Next, Williams asserts his moral ideals of mutuality and intersubjectivity in the negative example of the Stechers' gradual removal from them. In this way, Williams follows Burke's principle that "Man" is the great "inventor of the negative" as a principle that embodies morality in a series of "Thou-shalt-nots" that lead to the formation of character (*LASA* 9–24). Consequently, the reader, by imaginatively re-creating that moral lesson, forms his own character not by following some authorial doctrine but by actively "identifying" the text itself.

In this way, Williams can give his reader a "proletarian style" that actively replaces "proletarian propaganda."

Another of Burke's maxims about "Man" is that he is "separated from his natural condition by instruments of his own making" (*LASA* 13–15). We have already seen how Joe Stecher's literally "making money" implicates him in a schizophrenic textuality of commodity production that relies more on acts of signification than it does on a relationship to some material signified. But this maxim also recalls that most common instrument to which Burke refers—our acts of symbol making and language itself—that both separates the Stechers from the very society in which they would participate and joins the reader with his own culture in "identifying" the everyday speech that Williams captures. As such, the language of Williams's novels becomes perhaps the most important instrument in his project of cultural production. And it does so by holding in tension a wide variety of dialects and cultures, as it negatively moralizes against their homogenization. The language, whether through a grammar of translation that retains the uniqueness of cultural differences or through a grammar of transference that demands a single pattern, is Williams's greatest focus for the creation of his personal and political ideals, as we will see by examining once again Williams's lifelong project—*Paterson*.

5

The Radiant Gist

As Burke himself would say at this point, "And now where are we?" In the previous chapters I have tried to show how the mechanism that Williams establishes in his writing between prose and poetry attempts to distinguish between a use of language that relies on a previously established grammar to determine meaning and one that attempts to create a new grammar, what Wittgenstein would call a "new form of life," in a moment of discovery. This act of discovery relies on a process analogous to an empathic identification with people, things, words, or ideas in an act of self-creation that maintains the integrity of both self and object. In using this mechanism both to re-create and to demonstrate an act of discovery, Williams also attempts to restructure cognitive, epistemological, psychological, medical, and political conventions by opposing what I have called a "grammar of transference" with a "grammar of translation."

To summarize briefly, a grammar of transference subsumes the unique particulars of the object or person before it into a previously established "grammar of signs" that determines the identity of that person or the meaning of that object, the way that the Puritan's grammar of signs in *In the American Grain,* for example, subsumes the unique identity of the Indians into their notion of the devil. In this way, language functions according to notions of allegory that rely on strict correspondences and differences like those found in the grammars of floral dictionaries or in the textual space of what we've called "scientific" diagnoses. In this spatial model—a space of "projection without depth, of coincidence without development"—the complex particulars of the individual patient are compressed into the universal signs of a particular disease, which are then made to coincide with the name of that disease. Here the idiographic qualities of the unique individual are subsumed by the nomothetic, regulatory law that reads particulars only in the scientistic terms of this grammar of signs. In similar fashion, an oedipal model of identity formation operates according to a strict grammar of signs based on gender polarity. Here the oedipal father tells his son—"You must be like me; you must not be like your mother; and you must wait to love her as I do"—and tells his daughter—"You must not be like me; you must be like your mother; and you must wait to love me as she does." Politically, notions of tradition and history can serve as just such a grammar of transference by determining the value of the members of a community in advance and limiting their access to forms of power through the adherence to a strict system of difference. Notions of identity in this system also rely on the limited particulars of specific individuals as they adhere to a grammar of signs that ensures both the continuation of the empowered and the subordination of the disinherited.

Williams violently opposes the prosaic force of this grammar of transference with the poetry of what he calls the "imagination"—the location for Williams of analogical, inferential thought that relies on a methodological empiricism for the creation of what Kenneth Burke calls representative anecdotes. The imagination orders signs according to a grammar of translation, linking through language objects that are apparent and determining their meaning by analogy with the objects of previous experience. By reading signs according to a "botany of symptoms"— a grammar that notes analogical similarity between unique particulars—this grammar of translation allows for the formulation of general conclusions or "universals" that are probable, but that are always subject to revision. Like Gadamer's notion of effective-historical consciousness, Williams's imagination interrogates the object or person before it, revising its own prosaic "prejudices" or predilections by recognizing and maintaining the unique particulars of that object. The act of the imagination is a textual act that seeks to retain the integrity of both subject and object, self and other, by holding in tension the paradoxical relationship of recognizing its own otherness. I have called this act, after Jessica Benjamin, seeing the self in the other and the other in the self. As such, this act of identification also involves a notion of identity like the one promoted in Benjamin's and Kohut's alternatives to the oedipal model. Here the infant gains his sense of a unique identity through a process of "destruction" and "rapprochement" that recognizes likeness and difference with both mother and father. This notion is embodied in the intersubjective space of Williams's writing, a textual space that moves beyond simple allegory or conceit to hold in suspension notions of identity and difference. This textual space—the space of Williams's own diagnoses—is what I have called a space of projection *with* depth, of coincidence *with* development. Here the cognitive moment of seeing the other in the self and the self in the other leads to the ethical development of struggles for equality and empowerment in an act of mutual recognition.

Seeing language as symbolic action, Williams attempts to embody this grammar of translation in the dialectic he creates between prose and poetry. In this act of translation, he seeks to maintain those particulars of the unique situation or individual in such a way that they also yield insight into the representative qualities of his "poetic reduction" of material circumstances. In this way, Williams quotes Dewey, "The local is the only universal, upon that all art builds" (*A* 391). But a grammar of translation, though it differs methodologically from a grammar of transference, is nonetheless a grammar. In order to ensure against its functioning as yet another form of domination, Williams valorizes the notions of conversation, empathy, and "mutuality"—the recognition of the other as active subject in his or her own right. These activities comprise Williams's "diagnosis"—an act of interrogation, exchange, and identification with another fully constituted subjectivity— where "the inarticulate patient struggles to lay himself bare for you," and in doing so "reveals some secret twist of a whole community's pathetic way of thought"

(*A* 359). This act of diagnosis, by recording "the actual words, as we hear them spoken under all circumstances" (*A* 362), articulates that patient's voice in an empathic identification of the social, psychological, and material circumstances of his or her condition. Williams's diagnoses also act according to what Wittgenstein calls a "philosophical grammar"—the means for analyzing the various ways in which we determine meaning or make sense of experience. In this way they serve as what Wittgenstein also calls "perspicuous representations"—an understanding of the ways in which we use words to "see connections."

By exposing those various grammars that we use to interpret experience, Williams also exposes those ways in which we participate in the construction and maintenance of power through our identification with those "symbols of authority"—those attitudes, allegiances, things, and ideals—that constitute the textual space in which self-creation occurs. This textual space is what Williams says history *is,* and the tradition we select from it codifies those grammars by which identity is formed and new texts are written. But this tradition must remain fluid and revisable. Once it hardens into a prosaic force that operates according to a grammar of transference, it no longer allows for notions of identity and difference to be held in suspension in a moment of discovery and identification. Instead, it reduces objects and people according to its own rigid grammar of signs. Consequently, the symbolic action of Williams's writing as embodied in his dialectic between poetry and prose performs three important functions: first, in its demand that the reader make his or her own act of discovery and identification within its discursive space, Williams's writing acts as a kind of cure for the reader by exposing and breaking down a grammar of transference. Next, it functions pedagogically by providing what Jameson calls "ideological analysis" by rewriting previous texts in such a way that it exposes that text as the revision of a prior ideological "subtext" that is contained both by and within the grammar that text establishes. In this way, Williams can oppose what history *is* with what history *should be*—a dialogue between texts that includes those voices that tradition has repressed or silenced. Finally, as I will argue in this chapter, Williams's writing functions politically by attempting to influence behavior at the level of what Pierre Bourdieu calls "the habitus"—those "systems of durable, transposable *dispositions,* structured structures predisposed to function as structuring structures" (Bourdieu's emphasis).[1]

For Williams, language provides us with both access to the world and our means of participating in it. As such, language provides us with both our identities in and identification with the world, just as it marks our separation from it. "To free the language"—Williams's project in *Paterson*—implies a personal, economic, and political freedom that is Williams's utopian goal. And while this goal is never reached in *Paterson*—it is, in fact, barely articulated positively—the act of diagnosis contained in this work provides us with a cognitive mapping of the textual space that constitutes our local position in the modern city. This notion of an "aesthetic of cognitive mapping"—what Jameson calls "a pedagogical political culture which seeks to endow the individual subject with some new heightened sense of its place in the global system"[2]—has its corollary in Burke's describing *Paterson* as kind of "Bædeker," one whose "esthetic or poetic aspects . . . by a medicine man like Williams . . . *complete*[s] his ideal of 'contact.' "[3] In this "Bædeker," Williams articulates those grammars of transference that seek to subordinate the individual within their own schizophrenic space—an atemporal, ahistorical, textual reduction of unique particulars to the materiality of signifiers that take their value from a system of commodification. Williams maps out these forces in his writing, but he also opposes them in the symbolic action of the dialectic he creates between the prose of history and the poetry of discovery and invention. *Paterson* was Williams's lifelong project, and as such I read it as fully embodying Williams's poetics in its capacity to cure as well as to delight and instruct.

What I will do in this final chapter, then, is "begin again" with *Paterson*, looking more closely at how the mechanism Williams creates by having prose interact dialectically with the poetry performs an "ideological analysis" that both exposes the machinations of what history *is* and identifies those voices silenced by it. In this way, I will argue, the symbolic action of Williams's writing actively demonstrates that "history lesson" that Jameson calls for in his critique of Burke by showing us what history *should be.* But Williams's history operates within a matrix of domination and gender polarity, and as such, it reveals the violence of those forces without attempting to reconcile them. Consequently, notions of identity in *Paterson* are split between acts of self-creation that depend on forms of domination and an imagined ideal of mutuality that sees both self and other as full subjectivities. I will examine this ideal of mutuality as it is dramatically represented in the "Cress" letters and implicitly figured in Williams's opposition to Eliot. Having distinguished Williams's psychic economy from Eliot's, I will next show how his political economy separates him from Pound's economic and political schemes. Finally, I will focus on *Paterson* as an act of cognitive mapping that attempts both to chart those local forces at work in Paterson and to locate the individual within them. I will also show how, in doing so, the symbolic action of Williams's writing acts developmentally in a project designed to promote "creative democracy," a program whose aim is "the cultural enrichment and moral development of self-begetting individuals and self-regulating communities by means of the release of human powers provoked by novel circumstances and new challenges."[4] The principal force of this action, I will argue, is what Williams calls "the radiant gist."

I

As we saw in Chapter 1, the dialectic Williams creates between prose and poetry in *Paterson* is implied in the work's first lines—" 'Rigor of beauty is in the quest. But how will you find beauty when it is locked in the mind past all remonstrance?' " (*P* 3). The quoted source here is Williams himself, and in the manuscripts of *Paterson* he provides the answer to this question—"'It is not in the things about us unless transposed there by our employment. Make it free, then by the art you have to enter those starved and broken pieces.'"[5] By exposing the ways in which the detached gaze of the historian or journalist freezes the particulars of people and things in the "facts" of its prose accounts of economic exploitation, silenced women, and incidents of murder, Williams's dialectic between prose and poetry performs what Jameson calls "ideological analysis" in its rewriting of what history *is*—the historical texts of Nelson and Barber, newspaper clippings, and Longwell's historical recollections from his grandfather about the town of Paterson—into what history *should be*. Williams's attitudes toward history in *Paterson* reflect that complex historical consciousness he had embodied in *In the American Grain*, though his attention here remains focused on the particulars of the city and people of Paterson. In this way, Williams both re-creates and actively participates in Burke's "unending conversation of history"—that conversation in the parlor that has gone on long before we arrived and will continue long after we leave (*PLF* 110–11)—in a representative anecdote that gives us the historical particulars of Paterson as they make up the process of historicity itself.

Williams's strategy here is to embody in the symbolic action of his writing both those prosaic forces that structure what history *is* and the resistant, poetic forces of discovery and invention that can create what history *should be*. The development of this strategy runs throughout the first four books of *Paterson*, the originally planned structure of Williams's work. For this reason I will limit my reading of *Paterson* to Books I–IV, though I do think Book V continues Williams's project in significant, if somewhat more personal, ways. In his opening description in Book I, Williams calls his work in part, "an identification and a plan for action to supplant a plan for action; a taking up of slack" (*P* 2), and my focus in this section will be on these three aspects of Williams's strategy. The latter term, "a taking up of slack," is from Burke, and it refers to those ways in which contradictions inherent in an ideological structure are made compatible (*ATH* 46). The former term, "identification," also has its Burkean meaning, though as we have seen, it implies for Williams the notion of an empathic act of discovery that involves seeing the other in the self and the self in the other. The middle term above, "a plan for action to supplant a plan for action," I will argue is Williams's pedagogical plan for *Paterson* to affect behavior at the level of the "habitus"—a term from Pierre Bourdieu that describes the "structured structures predisposed to function as structuring structures" of historically determined (but not necessarily determining) behavior.

Bourdieu explains that the "structures constitutive of a particular type of environment (e. g., the material conditions of existence characteristic of a class condition) produce *habitus*"—Bourdieu's term for those deep-seated predilections of behavior that act as "the strategy-generating principle enabling agents to cope with unforeseen and ever-changing situations."[6] Bourdieu claims that the habitus acts in a fluid manner, "always tending to reproduce the objective structures of which they are the product," and that "they are determined by the past conditions which have produced the principle of their production, that is, by the actual outcome of identical or interchangeable past practices, which coincides with their own outcome to the extent (*and only to the extent*) that the objective structures of which they are the product are prolonged in the structures within which they function" (Bourdieu's emphasis).[7] The habitus locates a mechanism of practice that is by no means mechanical. That is, the habitus acts dialectically within history as both the product of history and the means of continuing practices according to the principles of historicity, or what we have called tradition. Understood as "a system of lasting, transposable dispositions which, integrating past experiences, functions at every

moment as a *matrix of perceptions, appreciations, and actions,*" the habitus
"makes possible the achievement of infinitely diversified tasks, thanks to analogical
transfers of schemes permitting the solution of similarly shaped problems, and
thanks to the unceasing corrections of the results obtained, dialectically produced
by those results" (Bourdieu's emphasis).[8]

I want to use Bourdieu's notion of the habitus in order to help explain what
Williams describes as early as 1917 as "the democratic groundwork of all forms,
basic elements that can be comprehended and used with new force,'"[9] and as late
as 1951 as the principle embodied in "a new, a more profound language" that
underlies all "lying dialectics" (*A* 360–61). As Williams explains:

> What is the use of reading the common news of the day, the tragic deaths and
> abuses of daily living, when for over half a lifetime we have known that they
> must have occurred just as they have occurred given the conditions that cause
> them? There is no light in it. It is trivial fill-gap. We know the plane will crash,
> the train be derailed. And we know why. No one cares, no one can care. We get
> the news and we discount it, we are quite right in doing so. It is trivial. But the
> hunted news I get from some obscure patients' eyes is not trivial. It is profound:
> whole academies of learning, whole ecclesiastical hierarchies are founded upon it
> and have developed what they call their dialectic upon nothing else, their lying
> dialectics. A dialectic is any arbitrary system, which, since all systems are mere
> inventions, is necessarily in each case a false premise, upon which a closed system
> is built shutting those who confine themselves to it from the rest of the world. All
> men one way or another use a dialectic of some sort into which they are shut,
> whether it be an Argentina or a Japan. So each group is maimed. Each is enclosed
> in a dialectic cloud, incommunicado, and for that reason we rush into wars and
> prides of the most superficial natures.
>
> (*A* 360–61)

Two points need to be made here: first, Bourdieu's notion of the habitus relies on
studies made in preliterate societies, and as such, it forms an important corollary
to Williams's own practice among the poor, often illiterate immigrants and blacks
of Rutherford, with some important qualifications. For example, unlike the mem-
bers of a preliterate society, the illiterate will almost always be aware of, and made
subordinate to, the "literate" of their culture. Next, what Williams calls "dialec-
tic" in the above passage describes the action of our "grammar of transference"—
the swallowing up of objects into a fixed grammar of signs. By being based on
the same "hunted news" that Williams "gets from some obscure patients' eyes,"
this "lying dialectic" operates at the level of the habitus by the "taking up of
slack"—finding the means of incorporating or containing the dispossessed by
"awakening the habitus"—that is, by using "rules of customary law" to somehow
activate "the schemes of perception and appreciation deposited, in their incorpo-
rated state, in every member of the group."[10]

A good example of this kind of "taking up of slack" can be found in Klaus
Ehrens's "sermon" that runs throughout the second section of Book II, which
Williams describes as containing the "modern replicas" of those "giants" in Book
I who are "the elemental character of the place" (*P* 253). Ehrens is "A Protestant!
protesting—as / though the world were his own" (*P* 65). Born in "what we call

/ over here the Old Country,'' Ehrens claims that ''it's the same / people, the same kind of people there as here / and they're up to the same kind of tricks as over / here—only, there isn't as much money / over there—and that makes the difference'' (*P* 66–67). Originally from a poor family, Ehrens becomes a rich man in the New World—''I was born with a gift for that sort of thing''—and he says that he was ''as happy as money could make me. // But'', he asks his listeners, ''did it make me GOOD?'' (*P* 67–68). The answer, of course, is no, and the Lord comes three times to Ehrens, telling him to ''get rid of your / money. You'll never be happy until you do that'' (*P* 69). After a tortured period, where Ehrens realizes that his money ''did *not* make me good. (His clenched fists / were raised above his brows.) I kept on making / money, more and more of it, but it didn't make / me good'' (*P* 68), Ehrens throws his money away, embraces religion, and finds that ''There is no / end to the treasures of our Blessed Lord who / died on the Cross for us that we may be saved. / Amen'' (*P* 73).

Ehrens's speech is interspersed with, among other things, an account of Hamilton's plan to develop Paterson as an industrial capital—''a great Federal City, to supply the needs of the country'' (*P* 70)—along with his plan of ''Assumption'' and taxation to pay for the national debt, and a description of ''The Federal Reserve System [. . .] a private monopoly . . . (with power) . . . given to it by a spineless Congress . . . to issue and regulate all our money'' (*P* 73). In this way, Ehrens's speech becomes an interesting means of the ''taking up of slack'' for a system of capitalism and centralized credit by preaching its own ''prosperity of poverty'' designed to empower those who have no identification with the forms of power represented by Hamilton's ''Society for Useful Manufacturers'' (*P* 73) or the banking industry. For this disinherited group, the inheritance of heaven becomes their reward through their ''goodness'' in poverty. As we saw in Chapter 4, it was just such a deflection away from material conditions toward an abstract afterlife that formed the basis for Williams's condemnation of the Puritan religion in *In the American Grain*. And, if we consider Ehrens's evangelistic Protestantism in connection with the Puritan notion of an elect, his religion provides its own monopoly on salvation as well. Finally, it acts homeopathically to ''cure'' poverty by means of poverty, as it takes its very structure from the forms of power and money that it opposes.

But even more interesting is the way in which this ''prosperity of poverty'' exhorted by Ehrens's religion becomes absorbed into the very fabric of the structure of power that it paradoxically identifies both against and with. Burke explains:

> When the ''economy of plenty'' cannot abide by its own norms, they would ''take up the slack'' by restoring the ''prosperity of poverty.'' They can recommend the church's homeopathy with some plausibility because it is adequate *insofar as disease, sorrow, frustration, and death are ineradicable*. And they would try to extend the area of such plausibility so that men would resign themselves even to situations for which the remedies must be sheerly ''economic.''
>
> (*ATH* 46, Burke's emphases)

By having the condition of poverty explained by reasons as inevitable as death and sorrow, the ideology of capitalism has effectively ''moved in on'' the ''symbols of authority'' of the church. In this way, the "prosperity of poverty" becomes intimately identified with the very system of economics that it opposes. Moreover, if we equate Ehrens with an evangelist like Billy Sunday—mentioned in Book IV as ''—getting his 27 Grand in the hotel room / after the last supper (at the *Hamilton*)'' (*P* 172) for his role in breaking up the union movement by referring ''as a good Republican to 'the strike-maddened crowd' ''[11]—Ehrens's religion and its complicity with forms of power and exploitation become even clearer.

The ''success'' of Ehrens's speech relies on its ability to respond to a condition of crisis in such away that it will ''awaken the habitus'' of the members of the audience who, dispossessed by one structure of power, can identify with an opposition party that continues along the same principle of structuration. This scheme of perception operates as a grammar of transference in maintaining a strict set of differences—saved and damned—to establish the terms of its identity. It also operates on the level of what Jameson calls a ''textual act''—that is, this scheme acts with the purpose of containing a ''subtext'' made up of some person, thing, or idea, within its own ''context,'' or structures of domination, while at the same time it articulates that context, encouraging the ''illusion that the very situation never existed before it . . . that there never was any extra- or con-textual reality before the text generated it.''[12] In this way, the ''context'' of dispossession disappears into the new context of the saved, based on an analogous kind of ''monopoly credit,'' while it attempts to convince the poor that their poverty was the sign of their prosperity all along. It is also in this way, as Williams says, that ''given the conditions that cause them''—the conditions of domination and subordination— the ''common news of the day'' occurs ''just as they have occurred.'' The principle of the habitus to act as a ''structuring structure'' acts dialectically to ensure the continuation of those structures of power. Also, as Williams says above, since ''all men one way or another use a dialectic of some sort into which they are shut,'' there is no way to exist outside of this principle any more than there is a way to exist outside of history. For Williams, this principle *is* history, and the only means of resisting it is to use history against itself by rewriting ourselves *into* history in an act of self-creation that avoids the ''splitting'' of identity into good and bad, and instead holds in tension notions of identity and difference. This principle, we will see below, is why the inclusion of historical texts is such a vital part of *Paterson*. In order to understand how this principle operates, however, we need to further clarify that ''hunted news'' which Williams says he gets from ''some obscure patients' eyes.''

I read this ''hunted news'' as analogous to what Jessica Benjamin calls ''that point at which breakdown occurs''—a moment of heightened psychic tension caused by the disruption of our notions of identity. This moment, Benjamin explains, is usually resolved by ''splitting, the process by which tension is relieved by ''splitting off'' the good object or self from bad object or other. This process of splitting—the structuring principle of the oedipal model, is the result of what Bourdieu calls ''the awakening of the habitus,'' and it will remain in effect as long as ''the objective structures of which [it is] a product are prolonged in the structures within which [it] function[s].'' But the solution to influencing the habitus—like Benjamin's response to the notion of splitting—does not, indeed can not, rely on the idea that the actions of the habitus can somehow be reversed. Attempts to do so would only lead to the perpetuation of forms of domination with a different gender or party in control. This is one reason, we will see, why Williams claims to be both anti-Marxist and anti-Fascist. Instead, as Benjamin explains, we need to recognize that

> the logic of paradox includes the acknowledgment that breakdown occurs. A sufficient ground for optimism is the contention that if breakdown is "built into" the psychic system, so is the possibility of renewing tension. If the denial of recognition does not become frozen into unmovable relationships, the play of power need not be hardened into domination. As the practice of psychoanalysis reveals, breakdown and renewal are constant possibilities: the crucial issue is finding the point at which breakdown occurs and the point at which it is possible to recreate tension and restore the condition of recognition.[13]

Williams's antisystematic bias in *Paterson* ensures against either the denial or the act of recognition becoming "frozen into unmovable relationships" by embodying his own "dialectic" in the symbolic action of his writing according to a "grammar of translation" that reveals in its interrogation of history those Gadamerian "prejudices" or predilections that are part of the habitus. In this way Williams's "ideological analysis" actively demonstrates an alternative means of the "taking up of slack" by those who have been dispossessed by history. Rather than promote a means of identification through an act of splitting that repudiates the foreign other and identifies the good self with the "symbols of authority"—those empowered attitudes, allegiances, things, and ideals of what history *is*—Williams proposes an act of identification that maintains the paradoxical logic of seeing the self in the other and the other in the self. He demands that we "Escape from it—but not by running / away. Not by 'composition.' Embrace the / foulness" (*P* 103). This cognitive moment of identification with, by, and of the disempowered, Williams hopes, will lead to the ethical development of struggles for mutual recognition between two, equally empowered subjects.

But Williams is not naive enough to think that this relationship between cognition and ethics is a necessary one. Williams is all too aware that both power and the habitus will function to the extent that "the objective structures of which they are a product are prolonged in the structures within which they function." Consequently, his plan for *Paterson* includes a proposal to alter the economic structure of credit monopoly that underwrites the continuation and concentration of power. In the section of Book II that we looked at above, for example, Williams takes his information about the Federal Reserve system from a pamphlet written by Alfredo and Clara Studer, who were members of a group promoting the idea of Social Credit.[14] Williams's connection to this group, as well as his ideas about the Left, unions, and Fascism, are vexed ones, and I will deal with them more specifically with regard to his relationship with Pound in the third section below. The democratic principle of Social Credit—of making available the increases in productivity made possible by increases in technology in the form of credit to be used equally by all citizens—is one that I will argue always appealed to Williams, though the fascist, anti-Semitic fervor that grew around the groups who promoted the idea of

Social Credit became yet another example of the failure of a moment of discovery when allowed to harden into a system. Still, at this point in *Paterson,* it is important to note the inclusion of an implied economic system based on exposing the concentration of power in the form of a credit monopoly granted to banks. It is also important to remember that this section begins with ''Blocked. // (Make a song out of that: concretely)'' (*P* 62), and the blocks of quoted prose here most often describe those ''blocks'' that power uses to maintain itself, the way that ''the Senate, is trying to block Lilienthal and deliver 'the bomb' over to a few industrialists'' (*P* 62).

The mention of ''Lilienthal,'' along with the figure of ''Altgeld'' in Williams's parody of ''America the Beautiful'' marks the way in which Williams begins to use history against itself. By including their names as items for identification, Williams forces the reader to unearth the stories of those historical figures of resistance who have been buried by what history *is*—here the historical accounts of Hamilton's plans and his efforts to concentrate power in the hands of the few. But even these blocks of prose reveal the structures of domination and their reliance on notions of splitting, as Williams quotes:

> Hamilton saw more clearly than anyone else with what urgency the new government must assume authority over the States if it was to survive. He never trusted the people, ''a great beast,'' as he saw them and held Jefferson to be little better if not worse than any.
>
> (*P* 67)

Within this Hamiltonian splitting of private and public, David Lilienthal and John Peter Altgeld become figures of resistance written into the verse of *Paterson* who work against those blocks of prose that contain the blocks of centralized power. Lilienthal's ''background of TVA battles'' led to his struggles ''before the Senate Committee on [his] confirmation as Chairman of the Atomic Energy Commission.'' Altgeld was the governor of Illinois who had pardoned the surviving rioters of the Haymarket Riots in the 1890s, and who had ''refused to call out the National Guard 'to protect the rights of property' of the owners during the Pullman Strike.'' This latter effort proved futile as ''President Grover Cleveland (born in Caldwell, N.J.) a true believer in the sanctity of ownership, the right of an employer to do as he pleased, and the duty of the government to combat lawlessness by the working classes . . . used troops to break the strike'' and ultimately crushed Eugene Debs's American Railway Union.[15] When placed within the context of Williams's parody of ''America the Beautiful,'' written in the 1890s, around the time of Altgeld's term of office, these figures all call attention to acts of resistance during a period of American history that, as Alan Trachtenberg notes, marked ''the incorporation of America''—''the reorganization of perceptions'' along the lines of ''an industrial capitalist system.''[16]

The symbolic action of Williams's own uncodified dialectic between prose and poetry, power and resistance, performs several functions in this section. First, it provides us with historical figures who disrupt the prose of what history *is* and provide us with figures for identification in two ways: not only must we ''enter those starved and broken pieces'' that make up the texts of history in order to discover the identity of these figures, but also our identification of and with them exposes a force that resists those blocks of prose. Next, by including that resistance within the prose itself—in the descriptions of the Federal Reserve system and, perhaps most importantly, in the letter from "Cress" that ends this section—Williams forces us to discover the "poetry" of resistance and invention "hidden in the prose" as well as the "prose" of containment "hidden in the poetry" of Klaus Ehrens's sermon. Finally, by including all of these "voices" within his Burkean conversation of history, Williams maintains notions of identity and difference in his dialogic text of what history *should be*—the record of these antithetical forces and traditions. Much like his conversations in *In the American Grain,* these voices seem weighted toward "swinging the pendulum back" from what history *is;* still, no voice is silenced. And, as we will see in the next section, Williams's notion of identity here avoids the "splitting" inherent in Ehrens's distinctions of saved and damned, poor and rich—distinctions that attempt to repress their paradoxical interdependence on each other as "other" in their maintenance of strict notions of good and bad. We can best understand Williams's notion of identity in *Paterson* by looking more closely at two of the most important "dialogues" contained in Book II—Cress's strident, one-sided argument with the silent Dr. P, and Williams's own implicit harangue against T. S. Eliot.

II

Valéry Larbaud had said in *In the American Grain* that, "As with all histories, it begins with giants—cruel, but enormous, who eat flesh" (*IAG* 113), and Book I of *Paterson* gives us "The Delineaments of the Giants" that make up "the city who is a man." Interestingly, these giants include both the voice of "Cress," the thwarted female figure Williams creates from the letters of Marcia Nardi, and a description of "Dr. P," a figure for Williams himself. These letters play a prominent role in Book II, "Sunday in the Park," a book that Williams says "comprises the modern replicas" (*P* 253) of those giants. Gilbert and Gubar see Williams's use of Nardi's letters in *Paterson* as "transforming [Nardi] into a character whom he can control, a creature of his own imagination" and that in doing so Williams precludes the threat of the feminine by usurping her words.[17] While I agree with Gilbert and Gubar about the anxiety toward women that most modernists display in their writing, as well as about the usurpation of the feminine voice that Williams's appropriation of "Cress" embodies, I read this act of appropriation as a conscious exposure of the force of gender polarity and the forms of domination inherent in it. As such, Williams's distinction in Book I between "Two women, Three women. / Innumerable women, each like a flower. // But / only one man—like a city" (*P* 7) marks the delineaments of those giants whose principles of structuration have made "Divorce . . . / the sign of knowledge in our time" (*P* 17).

These distinctions of gender polarity mark for Williams a separation between that "male" and "female psychology" about which he had argued as early as 1917 that "It is the union of these elements, each separately contributed, that gives life to the whole."[18] Here the force of male abstraction must be united with a feminine adherence to the concrete that is linked to the experience of giving birth to and nurturing infants. We saw in Chapter 2 how Williams's thought shares in Jessica Benjamin's notion of "mutuality," where identity is formed through a process of differentiation that holds in paradoxical tension notions of likeness and difference to both mother and father, seeing both parents as fully constituted, active subjects. In the world of *Paterson,* however, both the psychic and the sexual economy are marked by structures of possession and domination that thwart the recognition of the other as anything but an object whose value is largely determined by exchange value. Moreover, as Benjamin points out, in such a system "freedom *means* fleeing or subjugating the other," as the oedipal father comes to represent freedom as the denial of dependency,[19] and the choices of avoidance or domination seem to be the choices Williams offers by the end of Book IV.

But as Benjamin also asserts, our goal is not to reverse the logic of "splitting"—the process by which tension is relieved by "splitting off" good object or self from bad—or to posit some utopian realm of intersubjectivity. Our goal instead must be to "find the point at which breakdown occurs and the point at which it is possible to recreate tension and restore the condition of recognition."[20] This point of breakdown runs throughout the first two books of *Paterson,* as one of the most crucial "delineaments" of the "giants" of Book I is the divorcement of male from female, self from self:

> Why even speak of "I," he dreams, which
> interests me not at all?
>   The theme
> is as it may prove: asleep, unrecognized—
> all of a piece, alone
> in a wind that does not move the others—
> in that way: a way to spend
> a Sunday afternoon while the green bush shakes.
>   (*P* 18–19)

A "way to spend / a Sunday afternoon while the green bush shakes" will be the "theme" of Book II, "Sunday in the Park," but before we look at this book, I want to note a few more "delineaments" drawn in Book I. First, Williams develops these "giants" in a series of analogical figures that all spill in and out of each other—the male figures of Paterson, Dr. P, Sam Patch, Peter the Dwarf, and even Edward Dahlberg, and the female figures of Paterson's wife, Cress, Sarah Cumming, "Billy" and "T" (Alva N. Turner), and the "9 women / of some African chief." Next, even the most "elemental" of these figures—Paterson and his unnamed wife—lie next to each other, silently figured in the landscape of the city. Additionally, both Sam Patch and Sarah Cumming—the next "giant" figures—end up as "a body found next spring / frozen in an ice-cake; or a body / fished next day from the muddy swirl—/ both silent, uncommunicative" (*P* 20). And they both share this condition despite the "fact" that "Patch leaped but Mrs. Cumming shrieked" (*P* 20)—that is, despite the fact that Patch's fall occurred before he could make a speech of victory about his exploits as active male subject ("Napoleon and Wellington can conquer men and nations, but only I can jump

over the Genesse''), and Mrs. Cumming's fall is related to the denial of her sub-
jectivity noted in her silence and, presumably, caused by her husband's ignoring
her.[21] Finally, the delineaments of all of these ''giants'' are drawn within the
boundaries of a gender polarity that not only separates male from female, but also
hints at the male violence and female fear inherent in this separation—''I / think
he means to kill me, I don't know / what to do. He comes in after midnight, / I
pretend to be asleep. He stands there, / I feel him looking down at me, I / am
afraid!'' (*P* 26).

My point here is that ''The Delineaments of the Giants'' are blocks of silence
and failed communication. An attempted identification between Paterson's
''thoughts, the stream / and we, we two, isolated in the stream, / we also: three
alike—'' ends in failure because ''I am aware of the stream / that has no language,
coursing / beneath the quiet heaven of your eyes // which has no speech'' (*P* 23–
24). With ''no speech''—no communication—acts of identification that maintain
the integrity of both subject and object, self and other, become impossible, and so
''the / silence speaks of the giants / who have died in the past and have / returned
to those scenes unsatisfied'' (*P* 24). But within the text of Book I, Williams still
hints at the ways in which this identification and discovery can occur. The first is
in that ''complex mathematic'' of Paterson's thought—the paradoxical ''equation
. . . beyond solution'' (*P* 10) that Williams articulates in his ''Reply to a Young
Scientist''—''one plus one plus one plus one plus one equals not five but one.''[22]
Here, notions of difference—and particularly in this section, of gender difference
between Paterson and the ''girls from / families that have decayed and / taken to
the hills'' (*P* 12)—are collapsed within a single identity. But with ''no speech''
or language—''the language / fails them / They do not know the words / or have
not / the courage to use them'' (*P* 11)—this act of identification can only become
the act of appropriation that Gilbert and Gubar note and that Williams, I have
argued, purposefully calls attention to.

On the back dust flap of *Paterson: Book III*, Williams is quoted as saying;

> Paterson is a man (since I am a man) who dives from cliffs and the edges of
> waterfalls to his death—finally. But for all that he is a woman (since I am not a
> woman) who is the cliff and the waterfall. . . . The brunt of the four books is a
> search for the redeeming language by which a man's premature death . . . might
> have been prevented.
>
> Book IV shows the perverse confusions that come of a failure to untangle and
> make it (language) our own as both man and woman are carried helplessly toward
> the sea (of blood) which by their failure of speech awaits them. The poet alone
> in this world holds the key to their final rescue.

While it will take the remainder of this chapter to show how the ''poet alone in
this world holds the key to their final rescue,'' Williams's identification of man
and woman demonstrates that ideal of mutuality that holds in tension notions of
identity and difference. But ''since'' Williams is ''not a woman,'' his separation
of male and female into self and other is none other than an honest re-creation of
his own historical situation. Moreover, his identification with the male as active
subject and his figuration of the feminine into the forms of nature merely follows

his own historically situated models, but with this important difference: the project of *Paterson* is by no means to make over nature-as-other into the self's own image, but rather to identify with the land in an act of mutual recognition. Nature in *Paterson* is ideally that textual space in which self-creation occurs, holding in tension notions of identity and difference, and recognizing the force of both male and female. The goal of an empathic identification is not some mystified fusion with the other, but rather the maintenance and recognition of a paradoxical relationship of dependence and independence between self and other. We will return to this last point below, but for now we can see how this ideal of identity formation is contained within the voice of the other—Cress.

In an often-quoted letter to Horace Gregory, Williams explains the Cress letters saying, "Here the tail has tried to wag the dog. Does it? (God help me, it may yet, but I hope not!)" (*SL* 266). Less quoted, however, are the immediately preceding lines: "And, if you notice, dogs run all through the poem and will continue to do so from first to last. And there is no dog without a tail." The Cress letters, Williams explains, are an integral part of *Paterson,* and they make up an important part of the tale of the dog/poet who begins the poem—"Sniffing the trees, / just another dog / among a lot of dogs. What / else is there? And to do? / The rest have run out—/ after the rabbits." "The rest" are poets like Pound and Eliot who have run off to Europe, chasing the rabbits of continental literature. "Only the lame stands—on / three legs. Scratch front and back. / Deceive and eat. Dig / a musty bone" (*P* 3). Williams's mongrel poet most often appears in opposition to some figuration of Eliot. For example, he follows a prose description of a "Collie bitch" leashed to "a stone bench" by "a man in tweeds"—"she stands patiently before his caresses in that 'bare sea chamber' "—with a letter about "Musty" whose sexuality cannot be tied down (*P* 53–54), and the next line of his opening verse above continues with "For the beginning is assuredly / the end" (*P* 3).

Eliot is also mentioned in the letter to Gregory quoted above, and in our next section we will see the connection between Eliot and Williams's use of prose, notions of identity, and definitions of culture. First, however, we need to understand the connections between prose and identity in Williams's use of Marcia Nardi's letters. Williams tells Gregory at the beginning of his letter:

> Glad to hear from you. The purpose of the long letter at the end is partly ironic, partly "writing" to make it plain that even poetry is writing and nothing else— so that there's a logical continuity in the art, prose, verse: an identity.
>
> Frankly I'm sick of the constant aping of the Stevens' [*sic*] dictum that I resort to the antipoetic as a heightening device. That's plain crap—and everyone copies it. Now Rodman. The truth is that there's an *identity* between prose and verse, not an antithesis.
>
> (*SL* 265)

We have already seen the "identity" inherent in the action of finding the poetry in the prose and the prose in the poetry in both Chapter 1 and the Klaus Ehrens section above, but there is another kind of "identity" within the Cress letters that embodies a notion of poetic identity as well as personal identity in the failed attempt at destruction and rapprochement between Cress and Dr. P.

As we saw in Chapter 1, in an excerpt from an essay entitled "How to Write" (1936), Williams describes the process of writing a poem in terms of "two great phases of writing without either of which the work accomplished can hardly be called mastery." He explains that the poet must "proceed backward through the night of our unconscious past" into the "ritualistic, amoral past of the race," using what he calls the "demonic power of the mind"—its "racial and individual past . . . the rhythmic ebb and flow of the mysterious life process." Tapping this dark source within the poet enables him to release the "unacknowledged rhythmic symbolism" that is poetry's greatest strength and that "makes all prose in comparison with it little more than the patter of intelligence." This process also puts the poet in touch with "voices" that are "the past, the very depths of our being." Once the writing is on paper, however, it enters that other "great phase" and becomes "an object for the liveliest attention that the full mind can give it. . . . It has entered now a new field, that of intelligence." The first phase, the voice of the imagination, is the voice of "the nerves, the glands, the very muscles and bones of the body itself speaking." The two phases together are, "in the phrase of James Joyce . . . the he and the she of it."[23]

The voice of the "she," the voice of the unsuccessful, feminine/poetic imagination in *Paterson,* finds its greatest avatar in the figure of "Cress"—a poet friend of Williams's named Marcia Nardi. As both Paul Mariani and Theodora Rapp Graham point out, Williams has purposely misrepresented both Nardi's character and his true relationship to her in his manipulation of her letters.[24] Also, as Graham points out, "Cress eludes simple characterization,"[25] but we can make a few generalizations about her function in the poem. We read her letters with "involved, embarrassed pity,"[26] as Randall Jarrell suggests, but, as Edward Dahlberg counters, "It is the letters in *Paterson* that are the sun and the blood, the human cry and the conscience absent in the shale and pickerel-weed."[27] For some, and especially it seems for Dr. P, this cry does cause embarrassment, and he separates himself from it.

Dr. P appeared in Book I as a somewhat removed figure who was

> more concerned, much more concerned with detaching the label from a discarded mayonnaise jar, the glass jar in which some patient had brought a specimen for examination, than to examine and treat the twenty and more infants taking their turn from the outer office, their mothers tormented and jabbering.
>
> (*P* 32)

Obviously we can no more assume that this is an accurate sketch of Williams than we can tell the exact nature of Nardi and her relationship with the poet from the Cress letters. In fact, this distinction between writing and identity will be a crucial part of Cress's complaint and of both her own and Dr. P's failure to communicate. Book II is meant to give us the "modern replicas" of the giants delineated in Book I, and as such Dr. P and Cress become smaller figures of Paterson and Garrett Mountain, who lie silently together. But having also appeared in Book I as "giants" in their own right, both figures become simulacra—replicas for which there is no original—a condition of identity that I will discuss more fully in section IV below. Also, if we accept that there is an analogical relationship among all of the poem's characters, both Dr. P and Cress are parts of the poet, and their relationship becomes a relationship within the poet's mind.

Cress's voice in these letters is a strident, emotional one, made desperate by Dr. P's silence. She is "more the woman than the poet" (*P* 7), and she is the kind of woman "who can speak only to one person" (*P* 64). Separated from Dr. P by a failure of language, she has "been feeling (with that feeling increasingly stronger) that I shall never again be able to recapture any sense of my own personal identity (without which I cannot write, of course—but in itself far more important than the writing)" (*P* 76). Further, she feels "blocked"—economically, sexually, and psychologically—and this blockage has lead to "exiling one's self from one's self" (*P* 45). She begins her longest attack with this accusation:

> My attitude toward woman's wretched position in society and my ideas about all the changes necessary there, were interesting to you, weren't they, in so far as they made for *literature*? That my particular emotional orientation, in wrenching myself free from patterned standardized feminine feelings, enabled me to do some passably good work with *poetry*—all that was fine, wasn't it—something for you to sit up and take notice of! And you saw in one of my first letters to you (the one you had wanted to make use of, then, in the Introduction to your Paterson) an indication that my thoughts were to be taken seriously, because that too could be turned by you into literature, as something disconnected from life.
>
> (*P* 87, original emphases)

By "wrenching [herself] free from patterned standardized feminine feelings," Cress has escaped the life of complete silence and suicide that we see in Sarah Cumming, and her voice is, in part, the feminine voice of the poem made audible. But her attack on Dr. P is more accurate than she knows. "Cress" was "*something* . . . to sit up and take notice of," and as a "thing" she is both "something disconnected from life" and the very connection to it, something that "could be turned by [Williams] into literature." With the Cress letters, Williams is trying to make clear the very nature of the poetic process, a process that, in its extreme form of the separation between Dr. P and Cress, is severely blocked. Cress and Dr. P are the "he and the she of it," and though at one time Williams had envisioned using David Lyle's letters as the "he" of the poem to play against Nardi's letters as the voice of the "she,"[28] he has given us a model of the blocked poetic identity by using himself in the thinly disguised figure of Dr. P.

"That kind of blockage, exiling one's self from one's self" is Cress's own description of her psychological situation in the first letter of Book II (*P* 45). She continues in her next letter:

> If that situation with you (your ignoring those particular letters and then your final note) had belonged to the inevitable lacrimae rerum (as did for instance, my experience with Z.) its result could not have been (as it *has* been) to destroy the validity for me myself *of* myself, because in that case nothing to do with my sense of personal identity would have been maimed—the cause of one's frustrations in such instances being not *in* one's self nor in the other person but merely in the sorry scheme of things. But since your ignoring those letters was not "natural" in that sense (or rather since to regard it as unnatural I am forced, psychologically,

to feel that what I wrote you about, was sufficiently trivial and unimportant and absurd to merit your evasion) it could not but follow that the whole side of life connected with those letters should in consequence take on for my own self that same kind of unreality and inaccessibility which the innerlives of other people often have for us.

(*P* 48, original emphases)

As we will see below, Williams himself uses these same terms of "destruction" in describing his decision to use Nardi's letters to Robert Pepper. For now, however, we need to keep separate real people and people as they are made into "literature." Cress's attack on Dr. P is an assertion of identity that does attempt to wrench her self "free from patterned standardized feminine feelings," and as such it is an act of "destruction" analogous to the infant's assertion of identity that we saw in Chapter 2. But in order to be successful, this destruction of the infant's world must not go unrecognized, otherwise there is no way for the infant to differentiate herself from a real, external world. Either response—the act of destruction going unanswered or the act of destruction being followed by the parent's overwhelming the infant with its own assertion of control—leads to a sense of self based on domination or submission. Consequently, Dr. P's "unnatural" silence leaves Cress with "that same kind of unreality and inaccessibility which the innerlives of other people often have for us" in that Dr. P's failure to enter into an empathic relationship that would recognize both Cress's independence as well as her dependence on that act of recognition precipitates the failure of her attempted act of destruction. Because she sees Dr. P's silence as personal and not part of "the inevitable lacrimae rerum," his failure to recognize this act does, as she says, "destroy the validity for me myself *of* myself" because in this case her "sense of personal identity" *is* "maimed," leaving her with the sense that "the cause of one's frustrations in such instances" is "*in* one's self" and not "in the other person" or "merely in the sorry scheme of things." As Cress writes at the end of the second section:

I have been feeling (with that feeling increasingly stronger) that I shall never again be able to recapture any sense of my own personal identity (without which I cannot write, of course—but in itself far more important than the writing) until I can recapture some faith in the reality of my own thoughts and ideas and problems which were turned into dry sand by your attitude toward those letters and by that note of yours later.

(*P* 76)

Cress's accusations against Dr. P mark his separation from the real Williams in many ways. First, she says he lacks that sense of empathy, servitude, and attention to the real as opposed to the abstract that Williams valorizes throughout his work and demonstrated daily in his own medical practice. Next, her attack on his separating literature from life both echoes Edward Dahlberg's attack in Book I— "With you the book is one thing, and the man who wrote it another" (*P* 28)— and leads to her own "real" relationship with her own symbol making:

Only my writing (when I write) is myself: only that is the real me in any essential way. Not because I bring to literature and to life two different inconsistent values as you do. No, *I* don't do that; and I feel that when anyone does do it, literature is turned into just so much intellectual excrement fit for the same stinking hole as any other kind.

But in writing (as in all forms of creative art) one derives one's unity of being and one's freedom to be one's self, from one's relationship to those particular externals (language, clay, paint, et cetera) over which one has complete control and the shaping of which lies entirely in one's own power; whereas in living, one's shaping of the externals involved there (of one's friendships, the structure of society, et cetera) is no longer entirely within one's own power but requires the cooperation and the understanding and the humanity of others in order to bring out what is best and most real in one's self.

(*P* 87, original emphases)

These two paragraphs could have been written by Williams himself, as they bring out both the connection with the concrete particulars of life that Williams associates with a "feminine psychology," as well as the struggle inherent in the acts of recognition and rapprochement. But Cress's emphasis on her writing as being "the real me in any essential way" separates her from Williams's notions of identity. Cress's understanding of an empathic relationship with others doesn't extend to the other of her own writing. By identifying completely with the material and materiality of her craft, she lacks that ability to maintain the tension between identity and difference that is at the heart of mutuality and the key to Williams's description of the poetic identity that interrogates itself as other. Cress's sense of self becomes a confused mixture of assertion and submission. She nearly demands that Dr. P become the kind of close friend "at whose apartment one is quite welcome to stay for a month or two, and whose typewriter one can use in getting off some of the required letters asking for interviews, and whose electric iron one can use in keeping one's clothes pressed, et cetera," though she realizes that "I couldn't turn to *you,* a stranger, for any such practical help on so large a scale" (*P* 89). Cress makes clear that "as a woman not content with woman's position in the world" she has had "to do a lot of pioneer *living* which writers of [Dr. P's] sex and with [his] particular social background do not have thrust upon them," and this lack of accepted social position as active female has left her "completely in exile socially" (*P* 90). Her confused sense of personal identity and dependence on others reflects this lonely position.

In a letter to Robert D. Pepper, Williams calls the Cress letters "a reply from the female side to many of my male pretensions. It was a strong reply, a reply which sought to destroy me. If it could destroy me I should be destroyed. It was just that it should have its opportunity to destroy." To hide the reply, Williams says, "would have been a confession of weakness on my part."[29] Williams's description of the Cress letter as "a reply from the female side to many of my male pretensions" is part of an explanation of why he left the *Cress* letters in Book II. He begins his letter to Pepper by describing *Nardi's* letter as "an attack, a personal attack upon me by a woman,"[30] There is, I will argue, a significant difference between the two. Williams recognizes Nardi's attack as a personal one, and he identifies with it in the Cress letters as an attack from the "female side" on his "male pretensions." In doing so it becomes not only an act of "destruction" to be handled by two unique subjectivities, but also an internal struggle within Williams's own psyche. Williams's correspondence with Nardi continued intermittently throughout the forties and fifties, with Williams giving advice, medical information, grant opportunities, and money to Nardi. His letters to her (some of them ripped apart and taped back together) mark the empathic struggle of their continued friendship long after the publication of *Paterson,* Book II:

> Your very moving letter rec'd. I do not reply out of politeness, as you put it, but out of a very deep respect for your extraordinary abilities and your tragic situation, tragic in that you cannot escape it. . . .
>
> As artists we do our best work when we are most moved, not when we are unhappiest, tho' it comes sometimes to that. We need close friends, surely, to whom to "confess" at times with a sure feeling that we shall be given unfailing sympathy and unquestioning support in our emotional agonies. I am that sort of friend to you. But the battle itself we must under go entirely alone.
>
> (from Williams to Nardi, September 22, 1950)

> You had no reason to expect that I would run off to New York to meet you last Thursday even if I could. You assume much too much. Therefore you have no occasion to be disappointed. It would have been pleasant to talk with you if it had been possible but it was not possible under the circumstances. I count on you to accept the fact accordingly.
>
> I hope some day to feel better and more free to go about as I used to do but I'm not sure thta [*sic*] such a time will ever come again. . . .
>
> What's going to happen in the future I cannot tell. At the moment I am depressed and do not wish to see anyone. My autobiography will be out in September, it was writing that that seemed to finish me. I don't know that it was worth it.
>
> I'm glad you're in better financial condition now than you were last year.
>
> (from Williams to Nardi, August 8, 1951)

> . . . By all means use my name with the Guggenheim Foundation people, may it bring you luck I'll give you as vigorous a recommendation as I am capable of. [*sic*]
>
> . . . You are one of the hardiest women and one of the most gifted and generous women I know, I am happy at your success.
>
> (from Williams to Nardi, October 5, 1956[31])

At the risk of having provided my own "tail that has wagged the dog," I have quoted all of the above not only to show how Marcia Nardi's act of "destruction" was survived by both Nardi and Williams, but also to document its leading to a rapprochement between two mutually recognized subjects. As part of Williams's cognitive mapping of the forces of gender polarity, "Cress" both is and is not Marcia Nardi as much as Williams is and is not Dr.P. And, in an act of identification that avoids the process of splitting, Cress and Dr. P also become identified with the two paradoxical sides of both Williams's poetic and his personal identity. In mapping out those forces, however, Williams as poet revises Cress as literature, having her submit to Dr. P, recanting her attempted act of destruction—"the anger which I imagined myself to feel on the previous pages, was false. I am too unhappy and too lonely to be angry''—and ultimately pleading for Dr. P's recognition of her "words" out of pity for her—"And if you don't feel like reading it even for those reasons, will you then do so, *please,* merely out of fairness to me—much time and much thought and much unhappiness having gone into those pages" (*P* 90–91, original emphases). In this way, Cress and Dr. P act as the "modern replicas" of those "giants" of *Paterson* as poem, place, and individual mind, where "Divorce is / the sign of knowledge in our time" (*P* 17).

As part of Williams's own "feminine psychology," Cress also identifies Williams's notion of "contact"—a lived relationship to his local surroundings—as well as his abiding concern with culture and the politics:

> And it's *writing* that I want to do—not operating a machine or a lathe, because with literature more and more tied up with the social problems and social progress (for me, in my way of thinking) any contribution I might be able to make to the wellfare [*sic*] of humanity (in war-time or peace-time) would have to be as a writer, and not as a factory worker.
>
> (*P* 89, original emphasis)

Cress's desire "to be *writing*" links these notions of identity and writing with their cultural and political import. It also brings us back to that letter to Horace Gregory, where Williams describes his use of the Cress letters saying, "The purpose of the long letter at the end is partly ironic, partly 'writing' to make it plain that even poetry is writing and nothing else—so that there's a logical continuity in the art, prose, verse: an identity." Williams uses *The Waste Land* in this letter as an example of a poem that uses prose that "is psychologically related to the text" (*SL* 265), and in another 1948 letter to Parker Tyler he clarifies this relationship between prose, poetry, and Eliot, by saying: "It *is* that prose and verse are both *writing,* both a matter of the words and an interrelation between words for the purpose of exposition, or other better defined purpose of *the art.* . . . Poetry does not *have* to be kept away from prose as Mr. Eliot might insist" (*SL* 263, Williams's emphases).

While Williams's dialectic between poetry and prose might seem far removed from his cultural opposition to Eliot, I will argue in the next section that they are in fact intimately related and integrally involved with opposing notions of identity formation. By examining the relationship between Eliot's poetry and his prose, I hope to clarify a definition of culture that both marks the boundaries of Williams's Paterson of the forties and fiftites and maps out those forces that Williams resists. I also will show how Eliot's ideas of poetic, personal, and cultural identity all rely on an act of splitting in order to create structures of difference that seek to contain sexual and economic forces that paradoxically both underwrite and undermine those very structures. By seeing how Eliot's notion of "impersonality" in poetry forms the basis for an act of self-creation that is an evasion of identity into the forces of history and tradition, we can also realize how Eliot uses this tradition to define a social identity that seeks to repress the economic conditions of its own formation in order to sanctify the idea of class. In this way we will also see Eliot's definitions of culture—as Eliot himself insists we must—as "a whole way of life" that Williams opposes.

III

Only dogs figure more frequently than Eliot in *Paterson,* as he is alluded to throughout the work. Even the excerpt from the *Journal of the American Medical Association* that begins Book II contains a subtle dig at Eliot and associates him with the blocked figure of Paterson:

> The body is tilted slightly forward from the basic standing position and the weight thrown on the ball of the foot, while the other thigh is lifted and the leg and opposite arm are swung forward (fig. 6B). Various muscles, aided
>
> *(P 45)*

The article, "Dynamic Posture," goes on to describe how "Precision and smoothness are essential to good muscle action and low energy output. . . . Crowded city pavements and dirty fume-laden air usually promote bad walking posture." Its author, Beckett Howorth, explains that "Dynamic Posture relates not only to walking, but is in a sense a way of life."[32] This notion of precision and following form as "a way of life" makes even walking in the park an exercise performed according to some grammar of transference, and this notion of following form or tradition is at the heart of Williams's opposition to Eliot. But if the connection between Eliot and the above lines seems too tenuous to hold all these ideas, the first line of the *JAMA* article also repeats the description of a painting of Eliot done by Wyndham Lewis that appeared in *Time* in 1949. Here the figure of Eliot is described by the line: "The body is tilted slightly forward in resigned anticipation of the worst."[33] Williams's own allusion to Eliot is made even more vocal in the verse that follows:

> *I asked him, What do you do?*
>
> *He smiled patiently, The typical American question.*
> *In Europe they would ask, What are you doing? Or,*
> *What are you doing now?*
>
> *What do I do? I listen, to the water falling. (No*
> *sound of it here but with the wind!) This is my entire*
> *occupation.*
>
> *(P 46)*

In the separation of America and Europe and in the echoes of the divided consciousness that make up both "Prufrock" and *The Waste Land,* Williams's parody here calls attention to the bifurcations and divisions that act as the structuring principle of Eliot's thought. We can see the way in which splitting operates both at the level of personal identity and as the structuring principle behind Eliot's notions of history by briefly examining a part of "Sweeney Erect":

> This withered root of knots of hair
>   Slitted below and gashed with eyes,
> This oval O cropped out with teeth:
>   The sickle motion from the thighs
>
> Jackknifes upward at the knees
>   Then straightens out from heel to hip

> Pushing the framework of the bed
> And clawing at the pillow slip.
>
> Sweeney addressed full length to shave
> Broadbottomed, pink from nape to base,
> Knows the female temperament
> And wipes the suds around his face.
>
> (The lengthened shadow of a man
> Is history, said Emerson
> Who had not seen the silhouette
> Of Sweeney straddled in the sun.)
>
> Tests the razor on his leg
> Waiting until the shriek subsides.
> The epileptic on the bed
> Curves backward, clutching at her sides.

It would be easy enough to read "Sweeney Erect" as an example of splitting that reveals its own fear of castration by punishing the threatening woman in the poem as well as taking oedipal revenge against the figure of Sweeney himself. But a letter from John Peale Bishop to Edmund Wilson about Eliot reveals an even more disturbing level of splitting at work here:

> Eliot is tubercular and disposed toward epilepsy; on one occasion he decided to kill himself in Pound's house but funked at the final moment. . . . Eliot it seems is hopelessly caught in his own prudent temperament. As EP says "I am too low for any steamroller to flatten me out; I can always creep out of the way. But Eliot is incapable of taking the least chance." As one would have surmised.
>   Mr. Eugenides actually turned up at Lloyd's with his pocket full of currants and asked Eliot to spend a weekend with him for no nice reasons. His place in the poem is I believe as a projection of Eliot however.[34]

Perhaps predictably, Eliot's most misogynistic poem is actually his poem of greatest self-loathing, as the "projection of Eliot" in "Sweeney" becomes the figure of the hysterical female epileptic. Here Eliot's abhorrence of his own sexuality—and depending how far we want to take Bishop's comment about Mr. Eugenides, the abhorrence of his own potential homosexuality—is split off, figured in the feminine, and brutalized. The threat to Eliot in this poem may be not only of the feminine but also of his own feminization, as oedipal fantasy and fear intersects with a splitting off of his own personal identity. If, as Eliot quotes Emerson above, history is "The lengthened shadow of a man," then Eliot's own figure casts a divided, shadowy history of splitting and repression that relies on strict gender distinctions to hide the contradictions of a bifurcated Eliot.

If for Cress, "*Only* my writing (when I write) is myself: only that is the real me in any essential way" (*P* 87), then Eliot's notion of impersonality represents the antithetical extreme of denying the act of writing as a form of self-creation and identification. We can read Eliot's famous definition of poetry towards the end of "Tradition and the Individual Talent"—written around the same time as "Sweeney Erect"—as a form of self-denial and repression:

> Poetry is not a turning loose of emotion, but an escape from emotion: it is not the expression of personality, but an escape from personality. But, of course, only those who have personality and emotions know what it means to want to escape from these things.[35]

It has been said that only those who have *Eliot's* "personality and emotions know what it means to want to escape from these things," and the joke may not be that funny any more. By seeing poetry as an escape from self, it also becomes an escape from self-discovery and identification into the "impersonal" forces of history and tradition. By living in "what is not merely the present, but the present moment of the past," Eliot's poetic identity relies on splitting the good into "what is already living" as a continuation of tradition and the bad into "what is dead."[36] In this way, we can read Eliot's anxious mentioning of "the dead" (the term appears nine times in various forms throughout the essay) not only as an oedipal anxiety toward his poetic predecessors, but also as a nervous distancing of an act of splitting that becomes repressed as an expression of the matrices of history and tradition. If for Williams the poetic space is a field of self-creation and identification in which both poet and reader must recognize their own otherness and identity, then Eliot's poetic space maps out a form of self-extinction and denial, whereby the forces of history and tradition—"the lengthened shadow of a man"—contain the shadowy figures of Sweeney, Doris, and the unnamed epileptic within the mythical tradition of Aeolus, Ariadne, Nausicaa, and Polypheme.

Eliot's history underwrites his notions of culture in ways that are equally antithetical to Williams's project. Eliot's culture is a unified ideal "of the people who live together and speak the same language: because speaking the same language means thinking, and feeling, and having emotions, rather differently from people who use a different language." The "dominant force in creating [this] common culture" is a unified religious-social code "in which the natural end of man—virtue and well-being in the community—is acknowledged for all, and the supernatural end—beatitude—for those who have the eyes to see it."[37] As Raymond Williams points out, "Eliot is essentially repeating Carlyle" by showing how the atomized societies of both liberalism and democracy "are movements away from something, and that they may either arrive at something very different from what was intended, or else, in social terms, arrive at nothing positive at all."[38] For Eliot, we have moved too far away from an "idea" of culture in the Coleridgean sense of "the knowledge of its ultimate aim" (*CC* 52). Instead, the forces of "profit" and industrialism have set the aims of a particular group or individual above the aims of the whole society, leaving us with the prospect of a future in which "it is possible to say that it will have *no* culture" (*CC* 91).

This idea of the aims of a whole society combines with Eliot's definition of culture as a "whole way of life" to underwrite a notion of class that maintains "that part of the total culture which pertains to that class" (*CC* 107). Eliot rightly sees a stratified culture as a "complex system of specialized developments" (*C&S* 238), and he attempts to redefine class away from a connection to economic function. As Raymond Williams explains, "there is, as he sees it, only one . . . obstacle to the acceptance of his general view." This obstacle involves a social restructuring according to a notion of "élites" that "rejects the idea of class based on birth or money" and substitutes a new class structure based on "achievement." Eliot argues that a substitution of elites for class will limit notions of culture to "certain specialisms" within a "doctrine of economic individualism" and "social *laissez-faire*." This social structure based on achievement both works against the continuation of cultural ideas and traditions—since the elite would presumably change with the achievements of each generation—and guarantees a "meager common culture," since what would be continued would be only those "élite's own specialisms" (*C & S* 239–41).

Instead Eliot recommends "a governing social class, with which the elite will overlap and constantly interact" (*C & S* 241), describing not only his own culture, but also William Carlos Williams's America of the forties and fifties and Raymond Williams's England of 1958. But in doing so, Eliot warns against the then popular "Equal Opportunity dogma." Eliot explains that a unified system of education would enervate the family structure and replace the continuation of cultural standards and inheritance—"of which we can never wholly be conscious"—with an "effective culture" that serves only economic interests and teaches "what will lead to success in the world" (*CC* 177–84). The continuity and development of Eliot's idea of culture can only be maintained by an adherence to a class structure that guarantees the continuance of the "responsibilities" of each class to a "whole way of life." But this "whole way of life" relies on the circumvention of the very economic system that paradoxically turns function into the property that underwrites those class distinctions while it works atomistically to disintegrate the "organic" quality of Eliot's "whole way of life."

As Raymond Williams points out:

> Against the actual and powerful programme for the maintenance of social classes, and against the industrial capitalism which actually maintains the human divisions that he endorses, the occasional observation, however deeply felt, on the immorality of exploitation or usury seems, indeed, a feeble velleity. If culture were only a specialized product, it might be afforded, in a kind of reserved area, away from the actual drives of contemporary society. But if it is, as Eliot insists it must be, "a whole way of life," then the whole system must be considered and judged as a whole. The insistence, in principle is on wholeness; the practice, in effect, is fragmentary.

(*C & S* 242)

Raymond Williams's final critique of Eliot brings us back to those contradictions inherent in Eliot's notion of personal identity that will enable us to see how culture combines with identity and writing. In saying that Eliot's "occasional observation, however deeply felt, on the immorality of exploitation or usury seems, indeed, a feeble velleity," Raymond Williams is implicitly condemning a statement that Eliot makes in *Notes towards the Definition of Culture,* and in doing so he locates for us that point at which prose and poetry, identity and culture, all coincide. In talking about the rise of "envy" that is the result of the dissolution of the family and class structure, Eliot says:

The envy of those who are "better born" than oneself is a feeble velleity, with only a shadow of the passion with which material advantages are envied. No sane person can be consumed with bitterness at not having had more exalted ancestors, for that would be to wish to be another person than the person one is. . . .

(*CC* 180–81)

"To wish to be another person than the person one is" is exactly the principle behind the act of splitting and repression that Eliot's poetry reveals. The shadow of Eliot's own passion betrays the "shadow of a man" that is both Eliot's history and the source of Williams's intense opposition to him. It also explains, in an unintentional way, why Williams writes to Parker Tyler that "poetry does not *have* to be kept away from prose as Mr. Eliot might insist" (*SL* 263). The "gist" of Eliot's poetry disrupts the prose of his definitions of culture and poetic identity, exposing their basis in domination, difference, and an economic system that both undermines and underwrites its "whole way of life."

Eliot begins *Notes towards a Definition of Culture* by defining "Definition" as "The setting of bounds; limitation (rare)—1483" (*CC* 79), and his attempt to define culture relies on an equally medieval definition of tradition and inheritance to set the boundaries against invasion of the ruling class by a new elite based on achievement and accumulation. As such, Eliot's idea of culture attempts to circumvent that modern history of economic development that led to the class structure of Eliot's London. In insisting that "the whole system must be considered and judged as a whole," Raymond Williams locates that point at which the contradictions of Eliot's notion of culture lead to its functional failure. He also points to the reasons why Eliot's poetry *does* have to be kept away from his prose. Eliot's attempt to circumvent history in order to establish a social identity is at one with his attempt to repress identity by escaping into history and tradition in two complex ways: first, it attempts to repress individual desire and subordinate individual identity to the idea of culture—the mystified knowledge of which no one group or individual is "wholly conscious." Next, it avoids recognizing an economic structure that led to the development of the modern replicas of those original classes in the 465 years that intervened between the wishful bounds of Eliot's 1483 "definition" and the conditions of his culture in 1948. Instead, it attempts to set its own boundaries around an idea of the ruling class, based on tradition and history, in order to split off as other that potentially disruptive, upwardly mobile elite that identifies the historical development of that very same ruling class.

Eliot's Coleridgean idea of culture is a knowledge so rarefied that no one part of the culture can ever be wholly conscious of it, though some classes are more conscious than others of this "ultimate aim" of culture (*CC* 52 & 107–22). Embedded in this "idea," of course, is some teleological notion of the final end of culture which we, as Christians, can only help to fulfill by allowing those who best perceive and perform that idea to continue to do so. But the "knowledge of the ultimate aim" of Eliot's idea of culture is nothing other than that same idea of culture—the continuation of particular structures and practices that empower the ruling social class. By maintaining the bounds of class, Eliot hopes to continue those objective structures that produce "habitus"—those systems of durable, transposable dispositions predisposed to function as structuring structures. This attempt to "awaken the habitus" also explains Eliot's insistence that schemes of education have little to do with the transmission of this knowledge, and it leads him to posit the family and other class members as the primary vehicles for transmitting and continuing these forms of knowledge. The continuation of knowledge in the form of inheritance is in this way linked inextricably to the continuation of those objective structures and customary laws that Bourdieu argues are necessary to ensure the functioning of habitus as a reproducer of those same structures.[39]

What Eliot is up against, however, is an economic structure that no longer functions to reproduce that class system that Eliot seeks to maintain. Instead, it reproduces a structure based on achievement and accumulation. But Eliot's circumvention of this economy, like his evasion of identity in "Sweeney," enables him to repress the material conditions that led to the structure of his culture and to claim that class structure as the expression of an idea. And it does so in act of splitting analogous to the one he performs in "Sweeney." Here, the good identity of a ruling social class is based on the expression of an idea known fully only to God, while the bad identity of an elite is empowered by a wrong-headed system of economic "Profit" whose aim is the material power known to all. Consequently, an elite can be accommodated if made subservient to the idea of class. Eliot admits that "in a vigorous society there will be both class and élite, with some overlapping and constant interaction between them," but he denies this elite the hereditary transmission of power, because then it would "lose its function as élite." It must not be allowed "to establish itself as a class" (*CC* 117).

But in seeking to contain this economic system within the voluntary bounds of his definition of culture, Eliot lacks those full "objective structures" necessary for continuance. Consequently, he coaches a return to religion—a return to the denial of the material and of desire itself—both to contain the effects of those economic forces within the objective structures of Christianity and to guarantee culture as the expression of an idea. At the end of *Notes towards the Definition of Culture* he claims, "The dominant force in creating a common culture between peoples . . . is religion. . . . I am talking about the common tradition of Christianity which has made Europe what it is, and the common cultural elements which this common Christianity has brought with it" (*CC* 200). This "idea of a Christian society" both sanctifies class as the protector of that idea and establishes those objective structures that allow for its continuation in history and tradition in two moves. First, it represses the link between economic forces and the production of the ruling social class. Next, it empowers that class as "more conscious" of the idea of culture and better able to transmit it. But in trying to subordinate economic interest to class interest, Eliot amounts to a kind of Klaus Ehrens who asks the elite to give up their material power to enjoy the spiritual riches of heaven and a social structure that deems them not fully conscious members. Ultimately, the contradictions inherent in Eliot's "whole way of life" become too great to allow it to function.

Another crucial part of Eliot's strategy of limitation involves language. Eliot claims that "it is obvious that one unity of culture is that of people who speak the same language: because speaking the same language means thinking, and feeling, and having emotions, rather differently from people who use a different language'' (*CC* 198), and the "obviousness" of this claim adds a sinister meaning to Eliot's original title for the first part of *The Waste Land* as "He Do the Police in Different Voices." If language is our primary means of identifying with our culture, then Eliot's insistence on a common language reiterates those differences that would fix our identity within that culture. And these different languages, for Eliot, would be a mark of class and a sign of function in culture, with a diversity of languages linked to particular classes unified in the common language that expresses those common feelings and thoughts. But if language marks the unity of culture, it also polices the differences between class, race, and gender. Language, in this way, becomes implicated in a scheme of differences that maintains the bounds of the class structure. "Speaking the same language" of a unified idea of culture would mean the policing of different voices as they adhere to class, function, and identity. And the goal of this language would be to subsume the particulars of the individual within the grammar of signs that constitutes both class and culture, making language function as a grammar of transference that suppresses struggles for recognition and mutuality. If "speaking the same language means thinking, and feeling, and having emotions, rather differently from people who use a different language," then this language succeeds only in communicating the unity of an idea; language fails those who wish to assert their own uniqueness.

Eliot's idea of culture relies on principles of structuration that are obviously antithetical to Williams's project of creative democracy, though the forces he articulates are very much a part of Williams's America, where—"the language! /— the language / is divorced from their minds" (*P* 12). Williams once wrote to Horace Gregory, "I don't know what it is, if I have not defined it, about Eliot that is so slimy" (*SL* 225), and what Williams may not have been able to define, but clearly felt, were those ways in which he opposed Eliot at the levels of personal identity, poetic identity, functions of writing, as well as ideas about culture, history, and tradition. Williams's most famous statement about Eliot was that he "gave the poem back to the academics" (*A* 146), and if we remember the academy in the early- to mid-twentieth century as a place of extraordinary wealth and privilege, where social connections and cultural grooming were among the most important lessons, we get a sense of the kinds of limitations Williams's poetics are designed to break down. In breaking up the blocks of prose and privilege, Williams's poetics seeks to release a "radiant gist" of culture that is also "a whole way of life." And it does so by considering the whole system and judging it as a whole.

If for Eliot we have gotten too far away from an idea of culture, then for Williams we have not gotten far enough away from the culture of an idea. Williams's dictum to "Say it! No ideas but in things" (*P* 6) means, among other things, to return ideas to the realm of the material and the quotidian and to avoid the worship of "God-terms" such as Eliot's idea of culture. His anti-epistemological swerve avoids the very notion of Eliot's idea, as it locates thought in the observable in order to avoid those empowering ideas of culture that divorce us from the real conditions of our world. By locating ideas in things, Williams shifts thought away from the unknowable abstraction of an idea of culture to concentrate instead on the problems of communication between subjects and interactions with the material. He also focuses our attention on those struggles with language that can either fix or formulate our individual sense of identity. To "release the radiant gist" is Williams's means for breaking down the blocks of silence, prose, and limitations that would fix our identity in the formulation of a phrase. Williams's desire in *Paterson* is to use the symbolic action of his dialectic between poetry and prose as a representative anecdote of the struggle to release this "gist." By forcing us to "use the art we have to enter those starved and broken pieces" of history and individuals, traditions and things, Williams forces our own act of self-creation and identification in a move toward a culture of empowered individuals that is "a whole way of life." But in order to get at the core of Williams's definitions of culture, we need first to begin with the analogical relationship he establishes between "credit : the gist" (*P* 184).

IV

As Mike Weaver points out, Williams's "only party affiliation, outside that of the Democratic Party, was with the American Social Credit Movement."[40] Led by Gorham Munson and based on the theory of Major C. H. Douglas, the group released its manifesto in 1938, declaring itself to be "unalterably opposed to totalitarianism and collectivism, social systems in which the individual exists only for the group."[41] While we need not go into the particulars of Douglas's theories, the aim of Social Credit was to break the monopoly that banks held in their control of credit and to make available to the individual, in the form of credit, the surplus value generated by increases in production. Williams saw Social Credit as a form of individual empowerment and a restructuring of the economic system that would provide the objective structures for greater control and power by individuals. As such, Social Credit became the "gist" of Williams's notion of culture as "a whole way of life." Williams explains:

> After all, a revolution, like any other mechanism or exercise of power, has a gist, a basis, a rationale—must have an accuracy and finely aimed direction to *win*. And this has changed with time, as knowledge has increased and power has taken the place of labor and credit the place of capital.
>
> This gist *is* the control of power by credit—in all states alike, whether affected or unaffected by revolution, past, present or future. The force of the Social Credit philosophy is a clear-sighted envisioning of this gist of a perhaps necessary revolution which some of the ardent fighters for it seem to have lost sight of.
>
> Is a man for or against the Revolution? The answer is, first, What revolution? And after that has been defined, then, certainly *not* for violence, bloodshed and a resultant tyranny if by the exercise of courage and acute intelligence the end can be obtained otherwise.
>
> (*RI* 116, Williams's emphases)

By calling "the force of the Social Credit philosophy . . . a clear-sighted envisioning of this gist" that is the principle underlying any "exercise of power," Williams recognizes something analogous to what we have called the habitus and its dependence on objective structures in both its determination and continuation of those same structures. In this way, "the exercise of courage and acute intelligence'' can bring about lasting change without the violence of a revolution that merely continues those forms of domination and submission. Williams's definition of culture considers the "whole system . . . judging it as a whole," by providing "a whole way of life" that is functionally consistent in ways that Eliot's idea of culture is not. As such, Williams's "gist" of credit and culture also marks the difference between his notion of social credit and its cultural articulation during the thirties and forties. While the A.S.C.M. had made it clear that they abominated anti-Semitism and were virulently anti-Marxist and anti-fascist, the scheme was inevitably associated with all three, and in 1943 the A.S.C.M. collapsed fighting "a rear-guard action against the encroachments of the proto-fascists."[42] In particular, Williams's sources for the antibanking material he includes in Book II (*P* 73–74) and his "Advertisement" by "August Walters" in Book IV (*P* 180) are all groups or individuals who have corrupted the "gist" of social credit with their relationship to fascism. As such, their prose maps out the containment of that "gist" within a grammar of transference that replicates those same forces of domination that it seeks to oppose.

Williams's resistance to these groups, along with his understanding of the relationship between economic structures and the role of the artist in culture, can be best understood if we place it in context with Pound's involvement with economics and art. Pound was a supporter of Douglas's scheme of Social Credit until 1935, when he wrote Williams about Silvio Gesell and his ideas of "Social Money."[43] Gesell was a strong influence on Gottfried Feder, Hitler's financial adviser, and as early as 1923 a group had been organized in New York in support of his ideas. Gesell's "stamp scrip" was a tax on uncirculated money that would fall due monthly at a fixed rate. Money that was in circulation would have a stamp attached to it in order to maintain its face value, while uncirculated money would lose the value of the tax. In this way, Pound maintained, only those who hoarded money would suffer from the tax because their money would remain unstamped.

In "Ezra Pound and the 'Economy' of Anti-Semitism," Andrew Parker explains how the stamp scrip acts in Pound's overall economy of poetics and politics to form a whole way of life of its own. Parker shows how Pound's Canto 45, "With Usura," adopts an Aristotelian view of usury as "unnatural" and how Gesell's system was to have "countered" this practice by making money "no more durable than commodities" and returning it to its "natural" function as a "transparent measure of 'real' values."[44] Parker links Pound's abhorrence of usury with his desire to fix money in a direct relationship to real goods and his hatred of the "excess" that Pound "identified as the primary characteristic of 'the Semite.'" For Pound, Parker explains, Judaism somehow effaced "both verbal and economic boundaries." The practices of Midrash and Cabala exemplified a Jewish suppression of "any interest in precision," Pound said, and their desire to do "anything to make the word mean something it does NOT say." Pound equated this Jewish "excess" with "forgery" in the way that Jews forged meanings and forged money out of nothing (EP 79).

Parker connects Pound's attraction to stamp scrip as "a 'money picture' of extant goods" with his idea of the ideogram as analogous means of fixing meaning by maintaining a "natural" connection between sign and referent in order to stave off the "Jewish excess of meaning" inherent in language. And while Parker's argument is persuasive, he misses here the real connection between stamp scrip and writing for Pound—their connection to the charismatic leader or poet as the determiner of taxes and the manipulator of thought. By controlling the signs of both the verbal and the monetary economies, this leader influences the thought of a culture directly by determining the ways these signs are read—eliminating the Jewish middleman and Cabalist. In this way, stamp scrip functions as a consistent part of Pound's poetics/politics based on the powerful individual who makes history. Parker rightly sees Pound's anti-Semitism and attraction to fascism as being at one with his poetics. We only need to add that charismatic leader/poet to make the list complete.

Pound's attraction to Gesell may have been part of the reason why Williams wrote Louis Zukofsky in 1935 that "Pound has gone nuts—I won't pay any more attention to him."[45] Though Williams obviously did continue to pay attention to Pound's poetry, the vigor of which he thought so superior to his own that it made him feel "like a boor, a lout, a synthetic artist" (*SL* 264), his separation from Pound's economic schemes marks an equally significant difference from Pound's notions of the artist and his culture. Williams's artist is not a charismatic leader, but rather an example of the unique individual. Williams believed that "the artist is the truthfullest scribe of society that is found when he is left free," and he maintained that "individual genius is the basis of all social excellence whether as inventor, organizer or governor" (*RI* 104). Williams feels that

> It is essential to good government that the poet, as an individual, remain at liberty to possess his talent, and answerable to no one *before the act* but to his own truth.
>
> On the other hand he *is* answerable to society for his survival and he knows it, has no other returns for what he does and is governed thus not indirectly by a political agency before the act but *directly* by society itself after the act. In this men differ from bees and ants since with man society must wait upon the individual and not the other way around. Therefore, Man.
>
> (Society seldom recognizes this essential relationship between itself and the individual typified in the artist whose works, at their best, have always been strong social forces, one way or the other.)
>
> (*RI* 105, Williams's emphases)

As the "preceptor" of society, the artist embodies both in his life and in his work the "gist" of that very same principle of individuality and servitude that disrupts the "antisocial" oligarchy of self-interest that subordinates the individual to the "good of the state" and its own investment in and control over it. Williams uses Poe as an example of the artist who made a "cryptogram of his time, in form and content—with the passionate *regenerative force* of the artist underlying it." In this way, even when the artist's "works are purchased by corrupt or tyrannical fools or institutions, nevertheless, in those very works of art are likely to lie the disruptive seeds which will destroy the very hosts who have taken them in—and preserved them for society against their will" (*RI* 104–06, Williams's emphases). But even though the work of the "free artist" contains this "disruptive principle," Williams argues, this power is most often suppressed by the artist's dependence on society to get his work published, making him "answerable" to society "before the act." It is this social control of artistic and individual production that Williams hopes to counter with his scheme of Social Credit. By freeing the individual from his dependence on institutions and the government to fund his work, Social Credit makes society instead depend on the democratic interaction of economically empowered individuals and artists.

While Williams sees art as functioning in the same pedagogic way as Pound does, he feels that its instruction through example should lead to the empowerment of all individuals and not just those powerful leaders and artists who make up Pound's history. We can see this difference by briefly looking at how the two writers agree in their attitudes toward prose but use it differently in their writing. Specifically, Williams's use of prose in *Paterson* provides an important comparison with Pound's working in of prose within the *Cantos*. In "Excerpts from a Critical Sketch: A Draft of XXX Cantos by Ezra Pound" (1931), Williams says of Pound's work:

> It is that the material is so molded that it is changed in *kind* from other statement. It is a *sort* beyond measure.
>
> The measure is an inevitability, an unavoidable accessory after the fact. If one move, if one run, if one seize up a material—it cannot avoid having a measure, it cannot avoid a movement which clings to it—as the movement of a horse becomes part of the rider also—
>
> That is the way Pound's verse impresses me and why he can include pieces of prose and have them still part of a *poem*. It is incorporated in a movement of the intelligence which is special, beyond usual thought and action.
>
> (*SE* 108)

Pound's interest, like Williams's, lies in the most intense uses of language, and for both poets these examples are as likely to be found in prose as they are in poetry. By incorporating these highly charged moments of prose into "a movement of the intelligence which is special," Pound is able to transfigure the language of the prose within a "master meter that wishes to come of the classic but at the same time to be bent to and to incorporate the rhythm of modern speech" (*SE* 109). For Williams, however, it is the movement from the measure of prose to the measure of poetry that reveals both a condition of the world in which that measure is found and a necessary, violent, cyclical action within the world of human thought. We can see this action most clearly if we recall that part of Book IV we looked at in the first chapter (*P* 192–97). Using the prose-like lines of Byron Vazakas to transform the language of Charles P. Longwell's *A Little Story of Old Paterson,* Williams finds a middle ground here between the frozen sections of historical prose and the intense moments of his three-stress lines. They become a moment of calm in the swing from "the exposition of fact" to "the crystallization of the imagination." These lines also operate within a grammar of translation that takes Longwell's story—"unchanged in all its deformity and mutilation"—and drops it into the movement of *Paterson.*

But what is more important is the recognition that in seeing the prose documents as both "facts" and "things," the entire poem becomes a movement from prose with the poetry hidden in it to poetry with prose hidden in it. In the middle of this cyclical movement are moments of the lyrical, ordinary beauty of "beautiful thing"—the "radiant gist," the "luminous" material of poetry—obtained by breaking down the blocks of uranium, the blocks of prose, and the blocks of silence. All of the figures in the poem can be seen as types of the poet who attempt to do just this—release the radiant gist of poetry that will enable them to free the language—and here again we can see the differences between Williams's and Pound's use of prose. Pound once praised Joyce by saying that, "Good writing, good presentation can be specifically local, but it must not depend on locality. Mr. Joyce does not present 'types' but individuals. I mean he deals with common emotions which run through all races. He does not bank on 'Irish character.' "[46] While both poets obviously attempt to deal with "common emotions which run through all races," Pound, in the *Cantos,* is more concerned with the specific voices of charismatic individuals. In Canto XXXI, for example, the particular voices of Jefferson and Adams, placed within Pound's "master meter," blend with Sigismundo's motto—"Tempus loquendi / Tempus tacendi"—to give us a series of historical figures who march contemporaneously through Pound's work. Williams, however, is intensely local, and in presenting his quasi-anonymous voices, some frozen silently in the historical prose while others are freed to speak in the prose letters, Williams gives us a series of poetic types who do not "depend on locality." In particular, in his use of the letters in *Paterson,* Williams gives us the voices of these poets in a range of characterization that reflects this movement from the cold facts of prose to the "emotional dynamization" of poetry, dramatically representing his own ideas about the nature of the poetic identity.

Pound's "inventors" are the "discoverers of a particular process," and much like Pound himself in his essay "How to Read," they teach us a variety of grammars with which we can read both the material of literature and the material world. The methods of reading and the final curriculum Pound includes in his essay are meant to be a "vaccine" that will cure a sick society and its diseased sense of literature, and Pound scrupulously documents the means for our recovery.[47] Williams, however, cures his reader through the homeopathic and allopathic treatment provided by the symbolic action of his writing, allowing the individual reader to create his or her own grammar of translation. That is, Williams identifies those forces that are the source of our condition—the gender polarity that separates male from female and forms of possession and commodification that lead to the attack on the "Beautiful Thing" (*P* 127) and the "cost" of the "locust tree / in bloom" (*P* 95)—and through our recognition of them, uses the imaginative act of our empathic identification with those battered individuals and objects to counter the condition of divorce and separation. By embodying that "regenerative force of the artist" (*RI* 106) in the discovery he forces us to make within the dialectic of his poetry and prose, Williams's "invention" in *Paterson* becomes an attempt to influence behavior at the level of the habitus. By frustrating those predilections with which we approach a piece of writing, Williams's work moves through time to promote our own discoveries and identifications both with and within the language of his work. In doing so, he diagnoses and recreates those psychic, poetic, and even monetary economies that structure the ways in which we read the material signs of our world, leading us to discover new means of symbolic identification with them.

In Chapter 3 we saw how Williams develops the diagnostic space of his writing in what we called "a space of projection with depth, of coincidence with development." Here Williams can contain an act of recognition—an act of identification that holds in tension notions of identity and difference—that leads to the ethical development of intersubjectivity—an act of sharing and communication between two fully empowered subjectivities. In *Paterson* this space expands to contain the particulars of Paterson, its history and its inhabitants, as a representative anecdote of Williams's America. Within this diagnostic space, Williams maps those forces of power and domination that have led to his city's divorced condition. But also within that space is the "regenerative force" of Williams's "radiant gist"—"a flower within a flower whose history / (within the mind) crouching / among the ferny rocks, laughs at the names / by which they think to trap it" (*P* 22). In his dialectic between poetry and prose Williams performs an "ideological analysis" that exposes the violence of those economic, psychic, and historical forces that create the textual space of Paterson. With this cognitive act, an act of recognition, Williams hopes to develop the kinds of ethical recognitions that will both oppose those prosaic forces he exposes and lead to struggles of mutuality. Williams charts the imaginative violence inherent in these struggles and focuses our attention on the particular individuals who are engaged in them.

In closing this chapter, I would like to read Books III and IV of *Paterson* as an act of the kind of cognitive mapping that Jameson describes in his "Postmodernism, or The Cultural Logic of Late Capitalism."[48] Jameson explains a cognitive map as a symbolic act that enables "a situational representation on the part of the individual subject to that vaster and properly unrepresentational totality which is the ensemble of the city's structure as a whole" (CLLC 90). Providing this map also charts out the forces of ideology defined as "the representation of the subject's *Imaginary* relationship to his or her *Real* conditions of existence" in a "properly representational dialectic of the codes and capacities of individual languages" that is "a new political art" (CLLC 90–91). By exposing the ways in which we negotiate between the factual knowledge of our world provided by grammars of transference and the poetics of new experiences and discoveries that resist being codified into those grammars, Williams's pedagogical project in Books III and IV sets out to re-create those "episodes—all that any one man may achieve in a lifetime" and to "seek a language to make them vocal" (*P* 253). In doing so, what Williams delineates in these books are both the contours of his cultural topography and a means of positioning himself within them as active subject.

Williams's writing maps out a modern economy in which shifts in the structure of capitalism—where "power has taken the place of labor and credit the place of capital" (*RI* 116)—become embodied in the schizophrenic space of his writing. Here, as in the section ending Book III, language is divorced from any clear chain of signification and reduced to the materiality of words strewn across a page (*P* 137). Words, like credit, become free-floating entities that lack a clear, observable grammar to fix their meaning. Williams follows this page with a long letter from Pound, suggesting one tradition, forged by Pound himself, in which language can be grounded. And on the following page we get the list of "SUBSTRATUM" from an "Artesian Well at the Passaic Rolling Mill, Paterson"—Williams's own, local ground in which "The fact that the rock salt of England, and of some of the other salt mines of Europe, is found in rocks of the same age as this, raises the question whether it may not also be found here" (*P* 138–39). This list—taken from Nelson's *Geological History of the Passaic Falls* (1892)—gives us the history of an American "ground" for language and culture that promises to match that of Europe, though it is followed by an abrupt sign, "FULL STOP," a clichéd bit of Gray's "Elegy"—"and leave the world / to darkness / and to / me," and the proclamation that *"American Poetry is a very easy subject to discuss for the simple reason that it does not exist"* (*P* 140).

Jameson claims this schizophrenic condition as the loss of a sense of the unification of past, present, and future, both at the psychic and at the linguistic level. This condition reflects and supports both "the breakdown of all previous paradigms" and the loss of a sense of continuation by the subject in history, all of which Jameson reads as the cultural expression of the logic of late capitalism (CLLC 70–84). Book III contains Paterson's search for a "redeeming language" in his reading of the history books and newspapers of the "The Library," and the history Paterson reads is a schizophrenic series of prose fragments that record the massacre of Indians by the Dutch (*P* 102–3), the haunting of "Sale" Van Giesen by a "spectral cat" (*P* 133–34), reports about tightrope walkers across the falls (*P* 103–4), and an account of native burial rites (*P* 114 and 132). As Paterson reads, the resisting forces of wind, fire, and flood, both outside the library and inside Paterson's mind, recreate historical disasters that destroyed the city of Paterson three times. This distinction between the real and the imaginative violence that runs throughout *Paterson* articulates a process of discovery and invention based on an empathic identification within the texts of history—a process that models a means of recovery from that schizophrenic condition of modern history. The real violence of acts of colonization, property battles, sexual domination, and commodification can only begin to be resisted when we have broken those violent habits of thought that lead to their perpetuation. The means of this resistance is described at the end of Book III, where Paterson says:

> The past above, the future below
> and the present pouring down: the roar,
> the roar of the present, a speech—
> is of necessity, my sole concern
> (*P* 144–45)

Williams's imaginative exposure of those historical subtexts of containment reinscribe the subject within history through the symbolic rewriting of the history of the present, though Paterson himself never fully engages in this act of identification:

> Not until I have made of it a replica
> will my sins be forgiven and my
> disease cured—in wax: *la capella di S. Rocco*
> on the sandstone crest above the old

copper mines—where I used to see
the images of arms and knees
hung on nails (de Montpelier)
No meaning. And yet, unless I find a place

apart from it, I am its slave,
its sleeper, bewildered—dazzled
by distance   .   I cannot stay here
to spend my life looking into the past:

the future's no answer. I must
find my meaning and lay it white,
beside the sliding water: myself—
comb out the language—or succumb

—whatever the complexion. Let
me out!   (Well, go!) this rhetoric
is real!

(*P* 145)

Williams points here to the use of forms of symbolic action to perform a ho-meopathic cure. Like worshipers who left images of their diseased limbs so that the saints would cure them, Williams's images must recreate the condition of the present in order to bring about his own recovery. In the schizophrenic detachment of wax limbs and replicas, like the replication of the chapel of San Rocco outside Rutherford, rhetoric becomes yet another act of symbolic recreation capable of giving meaning to the disjointed fragments of history and self. But Paterson sees "No meaning" in the "images of arms and knees / hung on nails," and his desire here—to "find a place apart from it" and to "find my meaning and lay it white, / beside the sliding water: myself—/ comb out the language—or succumb"— recalls the figure of Eliot we looked at earlier, who chained his "Collie bitch" to "a stone bench. . . . The deliberate combstrokes part the long hair . . . she stands patiently before his caresses in that bare 'sea chamber' " (*P* 53).

But the forces of codification and containment, embodied in the "stale litera-ture" contained in the library itself, have within them the "gist" of their own potential destruction in the very nature of their rhetoricity. Reduced to a free-floating image—a kind of simulacrum—both history and the identities of individ-uals within it can be rewritten in a new language. In this same way, we can reread the schizophrenic language of "*Salut à Antonin Artaud* "—who said that all li-braries should be burned—and "(10,000,000 times plus April)" (*P* 137) as a de-struction of "*The Book of Lead*" whose pages Paterson "cannot lift" (*P* 134). The flood that is "undermining the railroad embankment" (*P* 136) recalls the Pullman strike that took place five years after the "Artesian Well" was dug (*P* 139), and "Vercingetorix" and his opposition to the Roman domination of Gaul becomes "the only / hero" (*P* 143). In the original solution to the "riddle" that runs throughout Book III, Williams says "again is the magic word / turning the in out" (*P* 135) and to "Begin again" means "To make a start / out of particulars / and make them general, rolling / up the sum, by defective means" (*P* 3). The act of discovery requires an act of identification that Paterson may avoid in his inability to lift the pages of history, but Williams's own identification with the particulars of those individual texts that he lifts from *"The Book of Lead"* begins the symbolic action of that cure.

These notions of discovery, identification, and invention are clarified in the last two parts of Book IV, where the figures of Madame Curie and "A. G." combine with the figure of Paterson to articulate that whole way of life that makes up Williams's "radiant gist" of culture. Williams's "Curie" is based more on the image of her that he saw on the screen in the 1944 movie about her life, starring Greer Garson. She becomes, then, another image manipulated by the strategy of Williams's writing to figure a moment of discovery and birth. "Curie (the movie queen)," pregnant when she makes her discovery, is "—a furnace, a cavity aching / toward fission; a hollow, / a woman waiting to be filled //—a luminosity of elements, the / current leaping!" "Curie, the man, gave up / his work to buttress her" (*P* 174), and while Williams does say that "Woman is the weaker vessel," he also says that "the mind is neutral, a bead linking / continents, brow and toe / / and will at best take out / its spate in mathematics / replacing murder" (*P* 178). The rapprochement inherent in that "complex mathematics" of identification between active subjects replaces the murder and violence of domination and submission. Williams asserts this need to identify both male and female with the mind in the preceding lines:

> And so, with coarsened hands
> > she stirs
>
> And love, bitterly contesting, waits
> that the mind shall declare itself not
> alone in dreams   .
>
> A man like you should have everything he wants   .
> > not half asleep
> > waiting for the sun to part the labia
> > of shabby clouds . but a man (or
> > a woman) achieved
>
> (*P* 177)

Phyllis, the girl from Ramapo who appears in the first section of Book IV, interrupts the above lines, repeating her statement to Paterson and recalling the blocked triangle of desire she plays out with Corydon and Paterson. Curie, however, combines male and female both in the "love" that "declare[s] itself . . . a man (or / woman) achieved" and in her position as a pregnant woman in the usually male role of scientist. But the principle of the "radiant gist" has always been associated with the feminine—from the "first wife" who is "a flower within a flower whose history (within the mind) . . . laughs at the names by which they think to trap it" (*P* 22) to the figures of Sappho, Elektra, Artemis, and the Abbess Hildegard (*P* 178–79), to the battered "Beautiful Thing" of Book III—as Williams valorizes the feminine connection to the concrete particulars of the world. Curie embodies the "dissonance" inherent in the "luminosity of elements"—both male and female—that leads to an act of discovery (*P* 174). And her discovery becomes a model for the action of the poem, the city and the individual—"Uranium, the complex atom, breaking / down, a city in itself, that complex / atom, always breaking down . / to lead. // But giving off that, to an / exposed plate, will reveal" (*P* 177). Williams never names what is "revealed," as it is the moment of discovery that he is celebrating here, not the naming or containing of it.

If Curie releases the "gist" of poetic discovery, then "A. G." has discovered the gist of Williams's poetry:

> All that I have done has a program, consciously or not, running on from phase to phase, from the beginnings of emotional breakdown, to momentary raindrops from the clouds become corporeal, to a renewal of human objectivity which I take to be ultimately identical with no ideas but in things. But this last development I have yet to turn into poetic reality. I envision for myself some kind of new speech—different at least from what I have been writing down—in that it has to be clear statement of fact about misery (and not misery itself), and splendor if there is any out of the subjective wanderings through Paterson. This place is as I say my natural habitat by memory, and I am not following in your traces to be poetic: though I know you will be pleased to realize that at least one actual citizen of your community has inherited your experience in his struggle to love and know his own world-city, through your work, which is an accomplishment you almost cannot have hoped to achieve.
>
> (*P* 173)

In his attempt to capture "a new speech" that will be "a clear statement of fact about misery," A. G. represents the continuation of Paterson, both place and poem, in history. A poetic inheritor of Williams's "experience to struggle to love and know his own world-city, through your work," A. G. knows that the only way to be like Williams is *not* to write like Williams, not to follow "in your traces to be poetic." A. G. knows that "I may need a new measure myself" and he would "like to talk with you concretely on this" (*P* 173). A. G. embodies that empathic identification with his "world-city" and its inhabitants, and his valorization of "observations of *things*" leads up to the figure of Curie, creating a combined male/female poetic identity.

The kind of analogical thinking inherent in noting the likenesses and differences between these figures is made explicit further on in this section, where Williams connects the "gist" with his other essential cultural discovery of social credit in a series of loose analogies:

> Money   :   small time
>   reciprocal action relic
> precedent to stream-lined
>   turbine   :   credit
>
> Uranium   :   basic thought—leadward
>   Fractured   :   radium   :   credit
>
> Curie   :   woman (of no importance) genius   :   radium
>
>   THE GIST
>
>   credit   :   the gist
>
> (*P* 184)

Williams's writing here avoids the detached condition of schizophrenia by virtue of the grammar of discovery Williams has developed and in which we can translate the analogical relationship between "credit" and "gist." In articulating what he calls the "Difference between squalor of spreading slums / and splendor of renaissance cities," Williams makes clear his belief that "Credit makes solid / is related directly to the effort, / work: value created and received, / 'the radiant gist' against all that / scants our lives" (*P* 185). He also makes clear the necessity of creating the objective economic structures necessary for the continuance of a whole way of life that serves the unique individual. The empowerment of the individual is the radiant gist of Williams's culture, and as such, *Paterson* maps out the strategies to break down those forces that block the flow of communication, credit, poetry, and knowledge. Releasing the radiant gist means engaging in an act of discovery—the translation of a new event into a new grammar that maintains that event's uniqueness—that must resist resolving the tensions of the moment into structures of domination based on splitting. In this way, Williams hopes to influence behavior at the level of the habitus by maintaining those tensions and by providing the objective structures necessary for their maintenance.

At the individual and the cultural level, this radiant gist translates into a program of "creative democracy"—"the cultural enrichment and moral development of self-begetting individuals and self-regulating communities by means of the release of human powers provoked by novel circumstances and new challenges"[49]— and we can see this development in the final section of Williams's work. Book IV ends with an act of self-creation that takes place within and through history—the history of the city of Paterson, the history of American poetry, and the history of Williams's family. In "Revolutions Revalued," Williams says:

> ... but to smash everything is to learn nothing. Life is and must be continuous— for if it disappears we have no way of recreating it. So that we must always build upon the past, replacing the obsolete with the new. If we lose that basis which lies embedded in history we must remake it—or degenerate—a task which might prove impossible once the continuity had been lost.
>
> (*RI* 113)

The imaginative destruction in Williams's work must lead to rapprochement not only between individuals, but also with history and tradition. For this reason, the identity of Paterson includes an identification with a myriad of voices that maintain their own uniqueness as they make up the man who is a city. Burke describes irony as arising when "one tries, by the interaction of terms upon one another to produce a *development* which uses all the terms. . . . They are all voices, or personalities, or positions, integrally affecting one another" (*GM* 512), and Williams's dialectical development here includes those voices of self and other in an act of rapprochement that includes past, present, and future.

The voices that open this final section join Williams's wife—"Haven't you forgot your virgin purpose, the language?"—with his English grandmother— "What language? 'The past is for those who lived in the past,' is all she told me" (*P* 186)—and look forward to the birth of Williams's grandson—"Here's to the baby, / may it thrive! / Here's to the labia / that rive // to give it place / in a stubborn world" (*P* 192). The "virtue" contained within the moral development of these voices recalls the conversation with Valery Larbaud that made up "The Virtue of History" in *In the American Grain*. There the "unending conversation of history" revealed that effective-historical consciousness that identifies its own prejudices and predilections in its interrogation of and identification with past and present. Similarly, here "Virtue is wholly / in the effort to be virtuous . / This takes connivance, / takes convoluted forms, takes / time!" (*P* 188). Williams's pragmatism swerves from an idea of culture and history to explore the cultural development of self-begetting individuals and the struggles necessary for mutual recognition within his own unending conversation of what history *should be*—the "convoluted forms" of his dialectic between poetry and prose.

Williams returns to the use of historical prose in this section, and his inclusion of what history *is*—those violent acts of containment and destruction—is a vital part of what history *should be*—the continuation and development of struggles for mutual recognition. Within the grammar of discovery that Williams has created we can begin to "see connections" between the act of "private revenge" that causes the bloody murder of Jonathan Andries (*P* 186–87) and the virtue inherent in Pep West's sharing his bed and merely falling asleep with the "tall and rather beautiful young woman" who, like West, was "interested in literature. . . . They wakened later, simultaneously, much refreshed" (*P* 187). Here sexual domination disappears in an act of sharing while the political murder by a "party of Tories" continues the brutal flow of power. Even oedipal struggles are specifically condemned as Williams had told his son in section II "Norman Douglas (*South Wind*) said to me, The best thing a / man can do for his son, when he is born, is to die // I gave you another, bigger than yourself, to contend with" (*P* 170). The structure of the family, like the analogous structures of culture and history, all rely on that act of seeing the other in the self and the self in the other—the maintenance of unique voices and languages in unending conversation.

The unique voice of Whitman's poetic past links the deformed figure of "Peter the Dwarf" (*P* 192)—a figure for the genius of place and the "deformed verse" suited to its expression (*P* 10, 83, and 40)—with Williams's present and A. G.'s future in Williams's final "Run to the Sea." But Williams's identification with Whitman contains crucial differences from him. Unlike Whitman's final union with mother and death in the sea of "Out of the Cradle, Endlessly Rocking," Williams declares that "the blood dark sea . . . is not our home" (*P* 201). He joins with the voice of his grandmother in seeing that "The past is for those who lived in the past," and instead Williams gives us an extended identification with the past in his section of verse taken from the prose of Charles P. Longwell's *A Little Story of Paterson As Told by an Old Man* as part of a continued development in the poem's present and future. Here the particulars of Paterson live again in the rec-ollection of Indians, slaves, and settlers. "Many of the old names" are remembered (*P* 196), but not as part of some nostalgic project to recapture or live in the past. The past is in the present as much as the accounts of historical violence are present in A. G.'s political work on labor newspapers and the "taproom overhanging the river, filled with gas, ready to explode" (*P* 193), and in the murder of Nancy

Goodell—a chilling act of very real destruction by Goodell's father that occurred on Williams's sixty-seventh birthday in 1950.

It is fitting, then, that Williams ends Book IV with the figure of Paterson rising from the water and turning inland with his female dog, spitting out the local seed of continuation from a beach plum. Given the history of domination and power that continues in the tradition in which both Williams and Paterson find themselves, the only recourse is fleeing or submission. The spectacle of the hanging of "John Johnson, from Liverpool England" is a complicated moment of destruction that was the result of the first murder in the newly formed Passaic County in 1850, and as such it holds in abeyance the possibility of rapprochement or the continuation of a society of the spectacle in the maintenance of power. In this society, where "the image has become the final form of commodity reification,"[50] Williams can only figure within his images those forces he would resist and resist the reification of his images in the symbolic action of the dialectic he creates between the forces of prose and the force of poetry. Williams had said that "*Paterson IV* ends with the protagonist breaking through the bushes, identifying himself with the land, with America. He finally will die, but it can't be categorically stated that death ends *anything*" (*IWWP* 22, Williams's emphasis). What happens after "the blast / the eternal close / the spiral / the final somersault / the end" (*P* 202) depends upon our own identification of the poetic force of the radiant gist.

Notes

Introduction

1. Paul de Man, "The Rhetoric of Blindness: Jacques Derrida's Reading of Rousseau," in *Blindness and Insight* (Minneapolis: University of Minnesota Press, 1983), pp. 102–41. See also Burke in *LASA* 44–62.

2. While there are very few critics writing on Williams today who hold this view, it is a not uncommon opinion held by those both within and outside the academy who see Williams as a poet vastly inferior to Pound, Eliot, or Stevens. See, for example, Donald Davies' review of *The Collected Poems of William Carlos Williams: Volume I, 1909–1939,* "A Demurral" in the *New Republic* 196 (20 April 1987): pp. 34–39.

3. Letter to Kenneth Burke, 7 February 1947; in the Kenneth Burke collection, Pennsylvania State University Library.

4. Denise Levertov, "The Ideas in Things," in *Ezra Pound and William Carlos Williams: The University of Pennsylvania Conference Papers,* ed. Daniel Hoffman (Philadelphia: University of Pennsylvania Press, 1983); pp. 131–42. I would like to thank Chris MacGowan for bringing this statement to my attention.

5. In particular, see Paul Mariani, *William Carlos Williams: The Poet and His Critics* (Chicago: American Library Association, 1975), Peter Schmidt, *William Carlos Williams, The Arts, and Literary Tradition* (Baton Rouge: Louisiana State University Press, 1988), and Terence Diggory, *William Carlos Williams and the Ethics of Painting* (Princeton: Princeton University Press, 1991).

6. See J. Hillis Miller, *The Linguistic Moment: From Wordsworth to Stevens* (Princeton: Princeton University Press, 1985), pp. 3–58 and 349–89, and *Poets of Reality: Six Twentieth-Century Writers* (Cambridge: Harvard University Press, 1965), pp. 285–359, for a fuller display of Miller's textualist readings of Williams and his positioning of Williams within a romantic tradition.

7. See Diggory, pp. 3–44 and 103–26.

8. J. Hillis Miller, "Presidential Address 1986. The Triumph of Theory, the Resistance to Reading, and the Question of the Material Base," *PMLA* 102 (1987): 281–91. All further references will be abbreviated in the text as PA.

9. Textualist readings have been attacked as inadequate by critics as various as Charles Altieri, David Bromwich, and Frank Lentricchia, and my own reading of Miller relies, in some way, on each of these writers. In particular, see Charles Altieri, *Act and Quality: A Theory of Literary Meaning and Humanistic Understanding* (Amherst: University of Massachusetts Press, 1981), "Wittgenstein on Consciousness and Language: A Challenge to Derridean Literary Theory," in *MLN* 91 (1976), pp. 1397–1423, and "The Hermeneutics of Literary Indeterminacy: A Dissent from the New Orthodoxy," in *NLH* 10 (1978), pp. 71–99; David Bromwich, "Recent Work in Literary Criticism," in *Social Research,* 53

(Autumn 1986), pp. 411–48; and Frank Lentricchia, *Criticism and Social Change* (Chicago: University of Chicago Press, 1983).

10. Miller is by no means the only critic to read *In the American Grain* as a simple opposition of political or psychological forces. For a sampling of some of these readings see James E. B. Breslin, *William Carlos Williams: An American Artist* (New York: Oxford University Press, 1970), pp. 87–124; James K. Guimond, *The Art of William Carlos Williams: A Discovery and Possession of America* (Chicago: University of Illinois Press, 1968), pp. 78–92; Vera M. Kutzinski, *Against the American Grain: Myth and History in William Carlos Williams, Jay Wright, and Nicolás Guillén* (Baltimore: Johns Hopkins University Press, 1987), pp. 3–47; Carl Rapp, *William Carlos Williams and Romantic Idealism* (Hanover and London: Brown University Press / University Press of New England, 1984), 43–45; Stephen Tapscott, *American Beauty: William Carlos Williams and the Modernist Whitman* (New York: Columbia University Press, 1984), pp. 61–63; Mike Weaver, *William Carlos Williams: The American Background* (Cambridge: Cambridge University Press, 1971), pp. 149–58; Thomas R. Whitaker, *William Carlos Williams,* Twayne's United States Authors Series, No. 143 (New York: Twayne Publishers Inc., 1968; rev. 1989), pp. 77–91.

11. Paul de Man, "Literary History and Literary Modernity," in *Blindness and Insight* (Minneapolis: University of Minnesota Press, 1983), p. 165.

12. Hugh Kenner, *The Pound Era* (Berkeley: The University of California Press, 1971), p. 387, and Richard Ellmann, *James Joyce* (Oxford: Oxford University Press, 1959, 1982), p. 3.

13. Cornel West, *The American Evasion of Philosophy: A Genealogy of Pragmatism* (Madison, Wisconsin: The University of Wisconsin Press, 1989), p. 103.

Chapter 1

1. Ezra Pound, "How to Read," in *Literary Essays of Ezra Pound,* ed. with an introduction by T. S. Eliot, (London: Faber & Faber, 1954), p. 26.

2. Ezra Pound, "The Prose Tradition in Verse," in *Literary Essays,* p. 372.

3. Ezra Pound, "How to Read," p. 23.

4. Paul Mariani, *William Carlos Williams: A New World Naked,* (New York: McGraw Hill, 1981), p. 492.

5. See Paul Mariani, pp. 461–518, and *SL,* pp. 219–233.

6. Paul Mariani, p. 487.

7. While Book V of *Paterson* does continue Williams's original project in significant ways, I read it as being generated out of a different enough set of concerns to warrant limiting my focus to the first four books. The vast majority of critics who have written on Williams would agree that the circumstances of Williams's life mark a difference in the work leading up to the completion of *Paterson* and that which followed, though there is wide disagreement as to which stage of Williams's career is the most successful, as well as to how pronounced these differences are. For the circumstances surrounding these changes, see Mariani, pp. 630–739. For a good discussion on the kinds of changes Book V brings to a reading of *Paterson,* see Peter Schmidt, *William Carlos Williams, the Arts, and Literary Tradition* (Baton Rouge: Louisiana State University Press, 1988), pp. 173–205.

8. The call for criticism to "name the text rightly" and the reading of Williams's cultural ideal as a "natural," "magical," heliotrope-like culture that is "rooted in the ground" can be found in J. Hillis Miller, "Presidential Address 1986. The Triumph of

Theory, the Resistance to Reading, and the Question of the Material Base," *PMLA* 102 (1987): 282. See also the Introduction above.

9. Joel Conarroe, *William Carlos Williams' Paterson:* Language and Landscape (Philadelphia: University of Pennsylvania Press, 1970), pp. 54–55.

10. These are ideas that run throughout Burke's writing, but in particular see *Attitudes Toward History* (Berkeley: University of California Press, 1984), pp. 44–49 and 353–74; and *Language as Symbolic Action: Essays on Life Literature, and Method* (Berkeley: University of California Press, 1966), pp. 3–24. All further quotations from the works of Kenneth Burke will be made in the text according to the schema listed on p. x.

11. While Bernard Duffey's *A Poetry of Presence: The Writings of William Carlos Williams* (Madison: The University of Wisconsin Press, 1986) promises to do just this kind of comparison, Duffey does little more than read William's work according to Burke's dramatistic pentad developed in *A Grammar of Motives* (Berkeley: University of California Press, 1969). Paul Mariani's excellent biography, *William Carlos Williams: A New World Naked,* documents Williams's relationship with Burke very thoroughly but does not engage in a rigorous examination of either writer's thought.

12. Letter to Louis Zukofsky, 15 Sept. 1929; in the Louis Zukofsky collection, Harry Ransom Humanities Research Center, University of Texas at Austin.

13. Wallace Stevens, *The Necessary Angel: Essays on Reality and the Imagination* (New York: Vintage Books, 1951). Stevens's greater concern for the composition of fictions, as well as his ruminative search for "what will suffice" also account for this difference.

14. Williams, of course, ultimately agreed with Zukofsky's revisions. See *CP II* 454 and Mariani, pp. 480–83.

15. Stevens's "Preface" is reprinted as "Williams," in *Opus Posthumous,* ed. with an introduction by Samuel French Morse, (New York: Vintage Books, 1957), p. 252.

16. Ibid.

17. Ibid., pp. 253–54. It is interesting that Stevens uses *Lessing's* Laocoön here. Lessing's work uses the statue of the Laocoön as an example of spatiality that cannot be equaled in the temporal medium of writing, and it may be that Stevens is commenting here on Williams's work in combining the temporal element of his verse with its spatial form on the page. For more on this idea, see Henry M. Sayre, "Ready-mades and Other Measures: The Poetics of Marcel Duchamp and William Carlos Williams," in *Journal of Modern Literature,* 8, No. 1 (1980), 3–22; and *The Visual Text of William Carlos Williams,* (Urbana and Chicago: University of Illinois Press, 1983).

18. Ibid., p. 252.

19. Wallace Stevens, *The Collected Poems* (New York: Vintage Books, 1982), p. 411.

20. See "The Sources of Epicurean Empiricism" in *Philodemus: On Methods of Inference, A Study in Ancient Empiricism* ed. with translation and commentary by Phillip Howard De Lacy and Estelle Allen De Lacy, (Lancaster, Pa.: Lancaster Press, 1941), pp. 123–34.

21. Wallace Stevens, *The Collected Poems,* p. 120.

22. Stevens's review, originally published in *Life and Letters Today,* December 1935, is reprinted in *Opus Posthumous* as "A Poet That Matters," pp. 244–51; pp. 249 and 251.

23. Wallace Stevens, "Williams," p. 252.

24. De Lacy, p. 136; see also pp. 123–31 and 134–37. As DeLacy points out, much of the thought of both Epicurus and Philodemus owes a great deal to the medical writings of the Hippocratic school and others. For a fuller discussion of Williams's ideas about medicine and language, see Chapter 3.

25. See Ludwig Wittgenstein, *Philosophical Investigations,* trans. G. E. M. Anscombe

(New York: Macmillan, 1958), and *Studies in the Philosophy of Wittgenstein,* ed. Peter Winch (New York: Humanities Press, 1969), pp. 1–19. All further references to the *Philosophical Investigations* will be made in the text as *PI.*

26. The quotation cited is from Charles Altieri, *Act and Quality: A Theory of Literary Meaning and Humanistic Understanding* (Amherst: University of Massachusetts Press, 1981), p. 24. For a clearer statement of this shift in Wittgenstein's work than I could hope to provide, see pp. 41–52. Further references will be abbreviated in the text as *AQ.*

27. In Ernst Cassirer, *Language and Myth,* trans. Susanne K. Langer (New York: Dover Publications, 1946), pp. 17–18. See also Hermann Usener, *Götternamen: Versuch einer Lehre von der religiösen Begriffsbildung* (Bonn, 1896).

28. Letter from Kenneth Burke to Brian A. Bremen, July 21, 1987.

29. See Kenneth Burke, *A Grammar of Motives* (Berkeley: University of California Press, 1969), pp. 181–84 and David Hume, *Enquiries concerning Human Understanding and concerning the Principles of Morals* intro. by L. A. Selby-Bigge, 3d ed. with text revised and notes by P. H. Nidditch (Oxford: Clarendon Press, 1975) pp. 11–61.

30. See De Lacy, pp. 120–24.

31. For a more detailed exploration of the relationship between Williams's medical training and his writing, see Chapter 3. See also *A Voyage to Pagany* (New York: New Directions, 1970), pp. 147–59; and the *Autobiography,* pp. 127–33 and 286–89. Burke's discussion of *tactus eruditus* appears in "William Carlos Williams, 1883–1963," reprinted in *Language as Symbolic Action: Essays on Life, Literature, and Method* (Berkeley: University of California Press, 1966), pp. 282–91. His use of empirical thought appears in nearly all his works, but for his mention of Philodemus, see *A Rhetoric of Motives* (Berkeley: University of California Press, 1969), pp. 169–74.

32. De Lacy, p. 147.

33. See Burke, *Language as Symbolic Action,* pp. 25–44, and *The Rhetoric of Religion: Studies in Logology* (Berkeley: University of California Press, 1970), pp. 172–272; see also Philodemus's text in De Lacy, pp. 59–69.

34. De Lacy, pp. 139–40; see also Epicurus, *On Nature* XXVIII, ed. A. Vogliano (Berlin: Weidmann, 1928), pp. 15–17.

35. I am indebted to Richard Kroll for pointing out this similarity to me, and for much of the argumentation here. See his *Words and Acts: The Naturalization of Discourse in the Restoration and Early Eighteenth Century* (Ann Arbor: UMI Dissertation Information Service, 1984), pp. 16–83.

36. See Burke, *A Grammar of Motives,* pp. 505–11. For his notion of "entitlement," see *Language as Symbolic Action,* pp. 359–79.

37. Kohut's theory of narcissism is an untapped gold mine for literary studies, and I am indebted to Barbara Johnson for pointing me toward his works. See Heinz Kohut, *The Analysis of the Self: A Systematic Approach to the Treatment of Narcissistic Personality Disorders* (New York: International Universities Press, 1971); *The Restoration of the Self* (New York: International Universities Press, 1977); *The Search for the Self: Selected Writings of Heinz Kohut: 1950–1978,* ed. and intro. by Paul Ornstein, 2 vols. (New York: International Universities Press, 1978); *Self Psychology and the Humanities: Reflections on a New Psychoanalytic Approach,* ed. with an intro. by Charles B. Strozier (New York: Norton, 1984); and *How Does Analysis Cure?* ed. Arnold Goldberg (Chicago: University of Chicago Press, 1984).

38. Heinz Kohut and Philip F. D. Seitz, "Concepts and Theories of Psychoanalysis," in *The Search for the Self,* p. 340; see also "Introspection, Empathy, and Psychoanalysis: An Examination of the Relationship Between Mode of Observation and Theory," ibid., pp. 205–32.

39. Kohut, "Forms and Transformations of Narcissism," in *The Search for the Self,* pp. 428–29. All further references to this article will be abbreviated in the text as F&T.

40. T. S. Eliot, *After Strange Gods: A Primer of Modern Heresy* (New York: Harcourt Brace, 1934), p. 20.

41. The phrase, of course, is Jameson's. See Fredric Jameson, *The Prison-House of Language* (Princeton: Princeton University Press, 1972), as well as *The Political Unconscious: Narrative as a Socially Symbolic Act* (Ithaca, New York: Cornell University Press, 1981).

42. Ralph Nash, "The Use of Prose in 'Paterson,' " in *Perspective,* VI (1953), 191–99. In general, most critics support Nash's explanation of the purposes of the prose passages.

43. Nash, pp. 194–95.

44. See Mariani, p. 242–45, and Byron Vazakas, *Transfigured Night,* Intro. by William Carlos Williams, (New York: Macmillan, 1946), p. ix. It is also interesting to speculate just how much Williams was influenced by the forms of both Barber's *Historical Collections,* which contains different typefaces, and both Longwell's and Nelson's works, which contain lines of poetry quoted in unlikely places. See John W. Barber and Henry Howe, *Historical Collections of New Jersey: Past and Present,* (New Haven, Connecticut: n.p., 1868); Charles P. Longwell, *A Little Story of Old Paterson As Told By An Old Man,* (Paterson, New Jersey, 1901); William Nelson, *History of the City of Paterson and the County of Passaic, New Jersey,* (Paterson: n.p., 1901); William Nelson, and Charles A. Shriner, *History of Paterson and Its Environs: The Silk City,* 3 vols. (New York and Chicago, 1920).

45. "Reply to a Young Scientist," quoted in Sister M. Bernetta Quinn, *The Metamorphic Tradition in Modern Poetry,* (New York: Gordian Press, 1972), p. 104.

46. The story of Sarah Cumming originally appeared in Alden's Collections, but Williams's source was probably an "annexed account" quoted in John W. Barber and Henry Howe, *Historical Collections of New Jersey: Past and Present,* (New Haven, Connecticut, 1868), p. 412. The ellipses following "in the district of Maine . . ." do indicate an omission from the original—one that fixes the character of Mrs. Cumming—"She was a lady of amiable disposition, a well-cultivated mind, distinguished intelligence, and most exemplary piety; and she was much endeared to a large circle of respectable friends and connections." The ellipses after "caught him once more . . ." also indicate an omission, here the reason for her fall—"Mrs. Cumming had complained of a dizziness early in the morning; and, as her eyes had been some time fixed upon the uncommon objects before her, when she moved with the view to retrace her steps, it is probable she was seized with the same malady, tottered, and in a moment fell, a distance of 74 feet, into the frightening gulf!" The ellipses after "on the following day . . ." are simply Williams's addition, and along with the insertion of "(the Hundred Steps)", these additions do change the flow of the passage from the original rhythms (*P* 14).

Mike Weaver attributes these changes to Herbert A. Fisher, whose manuscripts and notes, Weaver claims, provided Williams with this material. All of the historical works cited above, however, are readily available in most New Jersey libraries, and given the ways in which these revisions work within the scheme of *Paterson,* I think it much more likely that Williams made these revisions himself. See Weaver, *William Carlos Williams: The American Background* (Cambridge: Cambridge University Press, 1971); pp. 118, 202, 205–07, and 211.

47. Benjamin Sankey, *A Companion to William Carlos Williams's 'Paterson',* (Berkeley: University of California Press, 1971), p. 41. Though Sankey feels that this piece is "undoubtedly Williams's own," I suspect it may be a compilation of several sources with some revisions made by Williams.

48. Sankey, pp. 40–43; see also *SE,* pp. 134–61.

49. Sister B. Quinn refers to this development as part of the "metamorphic quality" of

Paterson, but as Burke discusses in his *Grammar* on pp. 503–17, the trope Williams uses to attain this polyglottic "development" is irony, not metaphor. See Quinn; also John C. Thirlwall, "William Carlos Williams' 'Paterson': The Search for a Redeeming Language—A Personal Epic in Five Parts," in *New Directions 17* (New York: New Directions, 1961), pp. 258–267.

50. Unpublished material in the Williams papers, Lockwood Memorial Library Poetry Collection, State University of New York at Buffalo, quoted in Joel Conarroe, *William Carlos Williams' 'Paterson': Language and Landscape,* (Philadelphia: University of Pennsylvania Press, 1970), p. 55.

51. See Conarroe, pp. 134–138; also "On Measure—Statement for Cid Corman," in *SE,* pp. 337–340.

52. "Letter to an Australian Editor," *Briarcliff Quarterly,* III (1946), 208, quoted in James K. Guimond, "William Carlos Williams and the Past: Some Clarifications," *Journal of Modern Literature,* I (1971), 499.

53. From a conversation with John C. Thirlwall, quoted in Thirlwall, pp. 275–282.

54. See Sankey, p. 70.

55. Randall Jarrell, "A View of Three Poets," in *Partisan Review,* 18 (1951), reprinted in Charles Tomlinson, *William Carlos Williams: A Critical Anthology* (Baltimore: Penguin Books, 1972), p. 173.

56. See both Mariani, pp. 461–476, and Theodora R. Graham, " 'Her Heigh Compleynte': The Cress Letters of William Carlos Williams' *Paterson,*" in Daniel Hoffman, ed., *Ezra Pound and William Carlos Williams: The University of Pennsylvania Conference Papers,* (Philadelphia: University of Pennsylvania Press, 1983), pp. 164–193. The best documented, and perhaps most informative, account of Williams's relationship with Nardi is Elizabeth O'Neill's "Marcia Nardi: Woman of Letters," in *Rossetti to Sexton: Six Women Poets at Texas,* ed. and introduction by David Oliphant (Austin: Harry Ransom Humanities Research Center, 1992); pp. 73–111. These authors disagree, however, on the "real" nature of both Ms. Nardi's character and her relationship with Williams. See also Gilbert and Gubar's discussion of the Cress letters in Sandra M. Gilbert and Susan Gubar, *No Man's Land: The Place of the Woman Writer in the Twentieth Century. Volume 1: The War of the Words* (New Haven: Yale University Press, 1988), p. 153. Though I agree with their description of Williams's use of the letters as the masculine appropriation of the feminine voice, I disagree with their reading of Williams's motives. As I discuss above and in Chapter 5, I think Williams is purposefully using the letters to illustrate just such an appropriation of, and divorce from, the feminine.

57. Reprinted in Linda Welshimer Wagner, *The Poems of William Carlos Williams: A Critical Study,* (Middletown, Connecticut: Wesleyan University Press, 1963), pp. 145–147.

58. For more about Ginsberg and WCW, see Mariani, pp. 604–605 and 702–706.

Chapter 2

1. Paul Mariani, *William Carlos Williams: A New World Naked* (New York: McGraw Hill, 1981), p. 280.

2. William Carlos Williams, "Supplement: Belly Music," in *Others* (July 1919), p. 27.

3. See, for example, John Henry Ingram, *Flora Symbolica; or the language and sentiment of flowers* (London: Warne, 1869); Jean Marsh, ed. *The Illuminated Language of Flowers,* Revised version of Kate Greenaway's 1884 *Language of Flowers* (New York: Holt, Rinehart and Winston, 1978; and Nicolette Scourse, *The Victorians and Their Flowers* (London: Croom Helm, 1983).

4. Anatole France, "La Vie en Fleur," in *The Dial,* 71 (December 1921), pp. 691–92.

5. William Carlos Williams, "Supplement: Belly Music," in *Others* (July 1919), p. 27.

6. Erasmus Darwin, *The Botanic Garden* (1791), (Menston, England: The Scholar Press Limited, 1973), "Part I: The Economy of Vegetation," pp. v-vii.

7. See Chapter 1, pp. 20–27.

8. Charles Altieri, *Act and Quality: A Theory of Literary Meaning and Humanistic Understanding* (Amherst: University of Massachusetts Press, 1981), p. 47.

9. Bram Dijkstra, *The Hieroglyphics of a New Speech: Cubism, Stieglitz, and the Early Poetry of William Carlos Williams* (Princeton: Princeton University Press, 1969), p. 172.

10. See *Philodemus: On Methods of Inference, A Study in Ancient Empiricism,* ed. with translation and commentary by Phillip Howard De Lacy and Estelle Allen De Lacy, (Lancaster, Pa.: Lancaster Press, 1941), De Lacy, pp. 139–40; see also Epicurus, *On Nature* XXVIII, ed. A. Vogliano (Berlin: Weidmann, 1928), pp. 15–17.

11. See Burke, *A Grammar of Motives,* pp. 505–11. For his notion of "entitlement," see *Language as Symbolic Action,* pp. 359–79.

12. My other problem with Dijkstra's description is that as a "poetic reduction" of a painting, Williams's poem becomes a reduction of a reduction, a translation of a translation. Moreover, the presentation of the poem in its original context gives no mention of the fact that this poem is a description of a painting. If anything, we are meant to assume that these are the "flowers" that have "rooted" and begun "to awaken" in the preceding poem ("By the road to the contagious hospital"—*CP I* 183). Finally, considering Williams's close relationship with Demuth, along with Demuth's being cited in *Spring and All* as an exponent of the imagination and Williams's dedicating the work to him (*CP I* 178 & 500), it is not unreasonable to assume Williams and Demuth would "see eye-to-eye" when it came to viewing the pot of tuberoses. For these reasons I refer to Williams's re-presentation here as "the flowers."

13. Williams is wondering in his letter about what his inclusion in Zukofsky's poetry Anthology would have meant if someone else had edited it. He then says, "In fact, the book is you and it is magnificent so my question does not need answering—doesn't exist (as Dora Marsden would have said)." William Carlos Williams to Louis Zukofsky, Oct. 4, 1948, in the Louis Zukofsky Collection at the Harry Ransom Research Center, University of Texas at Austin. For more about Marsden herself, her writing, and her relationship with the rest of the contributors to *The Egoist,* see Carol Barash, "Dora Marsden's Feminism, the *Freewoman,* and the Gender Politics of Early Modernism," in *The Princeton University Library Chronicle* XLIX, 1 (Autumn 1987), pp. 31–56; Bruce Clarke, "Dora Marsden's Egoism and Modern Letters: West, Weaver, Joyce, Pound Lawrence, Williams, Eliot," in *Works and Days* 2, 2 (1985), pp. 27–47; Jane Lidderdale and Mary Nicholson, *Dear Miss Weaver: Harriet Shaw Weaver 1876–1961* (New York: Viking, 1970); Michael H. Levenson, *A Genealogy of Modernism: A Study of Literary Doctrine 1908–22* (Cambridge: Cambridge University Press, 1984), pp. 63–80; and Mike Weaver, *William Carlos Williams: The American Background* (Cambridge: Cambridge University Press, 1971), pp. 23–29.

14. For Marsden's full "Lingual Psychology," see *The Egoist* (1916–19). The quotations here are from "Lingual Psychology: A New Conception of the Function of Philosophic Inquiry," in *The Egoist* III, 7 (July 1, 1916), pp. 98–100.

15. Dora Marsden, "The Science of Signs," in *The Egoist* III, 8 (August 1916), p. 113.

16. Dora Marsden, "Lingual Psychology: A New Conception of the Function of Philosophic Inquiry," in *The Egoist* III, 7 (July 1, 1916), p. 97.

17. Max Stirner, *The Ego and his Own,* trans. John Byington (London: A. C. Fifield, 1912) and Otto Weininger, *Sex and Character* (New York: G. P. Putnam's Sons, 1906).

18. The particular articles are: Dora Marsden, "The 'I' and the 'Ego': A Differentia-

tion," in *The Egoist* III, 9 (September 1916), pp. 129–31 (this issue also contained an article by Williams called "The Great Opportunity," an essay about the rise and fall of the *Others* group); "Berkeley's Doctrine of Esse (Extracts from Notes on [*sic*] By Prof. C. Lloyd Morgan)," in *The Egoist* III, 10 (October 1916), pp. 145–48 (this entry is followed by Williams's poem "March"); "The Verbal Form 'Be,' " in *The Egoist* III, 11 (November 1916), pp. 161–64; and "Philosophy: The Science of Signs: XVII Truth (continued); IV The Measure of Authority which Egoism allows to the Science of External Nature," in *The Egoist* VI, 3 (July 1919), pp. 33–38 (this entry is followed by Williams's poem "The Late Singer").

19. Weininger, p. 286.

20. William Carlos Williams, "Correspondence: The Great Sex Spiral: A Criticism of Miss Marsden's 'Lingual Psychology,' Chapter I," in *The Egoist* IV, 3 (April 1917), p. 46.

21. William Carlos Williams, "Correspondence: The Great Sex Spiral: A Criticism of Miss Marsden's 'Lingual Psychology,' " in *The Egoist* IV, 7 (August 1917), pp. 110–11.

22. Ibid., p. 111.

23. Ibid., pp. 111 and 110.

24. William Carlos Williams, *Interviews with William Carlos Williams: "Speaking Straight Ahead,"* ed. with an intro. by Linda Welshimer Wagner (New York: New Directions, 1976), pp. 98–100.

25. William Carlos Williams, "Correspondence: The Great Sex Spiral: A Criticism of Miss Marsden's 'Lingual Psychology,' " in *The Egoist* IV, 7 (August 1917), p. 111.

26. Jessica Benjamin, *The Bonds of Love: Psychoanalysis, Feminism, and the Problem of Domination* (New York: Pantheon Books, 1988), p. 13. All further references to this work will appear in the text as *BL*. In support of her statement about the baby's recognition of the mother, Benjamin cites T. B. Brazelton, "Neonatal Assessment," in S. I. Greenspan and G. H. Pollock, eds., *The Course of Life: Psychoanalytic Contributions Toward Understanding Personality Development;* Vol. I: *Infancy and Early Childhood* (Rockville, Md.: NIMH, 1980); J. MacFarlane, "Olfaction in the Development of Social Preferences in the Human Neonate," in M. Hofer, ed., *Parent-Infant Interaction* (Amsterdam: Elsevier, 1975); G. Carpenter, "Mother's Faces and the Newborn," in *New Scientist* 61 (1974), pp. 742–46; and A. DeCasper and W. Fifer, "Of Human Bonding: Newborns Prefer Their Mother's Voices," in *Science* 208 (1980), pp. 1174–76.

27. See Heinz Kohut, "Forms and Transformations of Narcissism," in *The Search for the Self,* pp. 428–29; and Chapter 1 above, pp. 24–26. See also Heinz Kohut, *The Analysis of the Self: A Systematic Approach to the Treatment of Narcissistic Personality Disorders* (New York: International Universities Press, 1971); *The Restoration of the Self* (New York: International Universities Press, 1977); *The Search for the Self: Selected Writings of Heinz Kohut: 1950–1978,* ed. and intro. by Paul Ornstein, 2 vols. (New York: International Universities Press, 1978); *Self Psychology and the Humanities: Reflections on a New Psychoanalytic Approach,* ed. with an intro. by Charles B. Strozier (New York: Norton, 1984); and *How Does Analysis Cure?,* ed. Arnold Goldberg (Chicago: University of Chicago Press, 1984).

28. Edgar Allan Poe, "Mr. Longfellow and Other Plagiarists: A Discussion with 'Outis,' " in *The Complete Works of Edgar Allen Poe* Vol. VIII; *Criticisms* (New York: G. P. Putnam's Sons, 1902), pp. 143–219.

29. See Sigmund Freud, *Civilization and Its Discontents*(1930) in *The Standard Edition of the Complete Psychological Works* (London: Hogarth Press, 1953) vol. 23, p. 72ff.; see also Benjamin, pp. 131–45.

30. Altieri, *Act and Quality,* p. 47.

31. James Clifford, "Introduction: The Pure Products Go Crazy," in *The Predicament of Culture: Twentieth-Century Ethnography, Literature, and Art* (Cambridge, Mass.: Harvard University Press, 1988), pp. 1–17; the quotations are on pp. 3–4.

32. Ibid., pp. 4–5.

33. Ibid., p. 7.

34. See Mariani, pp. 176–84.

35. William Carlos Williams to Kenneth Burke, February 24, 1921; April 27, 1921; and January 26, 1921; in the Kenneth Burke Collection, Penn State University.

36. Kenneth Burke to Brian A. Bremen, July 21, 1987.

37. Frederic Jameson, "The Symbolic Inference; or, Kenneth Burke and Ideological Analysis," in *Critical Inquiry* (Spring 1978), pp. 507–23; pp. 507–9.

38. Ibid., pp. 511–12.

39. Ibid., p. 513.

40. Ibid., p. 510.

41. Ibid., pp. 520–21.

42. Frederic Jameson, "Postmodernism and Consumer Society," in *The Anti-Aesthetic: Essays on Postmodern Culture,* ed. Hal Foster (Port Townsend, Washington: Bay Press, 1983): pp. 111–25; pp. 119–20.

43. Ibid., p. 118.

44. Ibid., pp. 124–25.

45. Noam Chomsky, "The Task Ahead II: The Global System," in *Zeta Magazine* (July/August 1989), pp. 15–22; p. 20.

46. See Heinz Kohut, "Forms and Transformations of Narcissism," in *The Search for the Self,* pp. 455–58; and Chapter 1 above, pp. 24–26.

47. William Carlos Williams, "Correspondence: The Great Sex Spiral," p. 110.

48. William Carlos Williams to Louis Zukofsky, May 27, 1930, in the Louis Zukofsky Collection at the Harry Ransom Research Center, University of Texas at Austin. For more on Williams's "depression" and his situation at home, see Mariani, pp. 297–347.

49. See Mariani, pp. 9–14.

50. See Otto Weininger, *Sex and Character* (New York: G. P. Putnam's Sons, 1906), pp. 186–298, and William Carlos Williams, "Correspondence: The Great Sex Spiral: A Criticism of Miss Marsden's 'Lingual Psychology,' " in *The Egoist* IV, 7 (August 1917), p. 111. Weininger also thought that prostitution was the most "honest" form of feminine existence.

Chapter 3

1. David B. Morris, "Williams's Force," in *Literature and Medicine* 5 (1986), pp. 122–40.

2. See Jean Le Rond d'Alembert, *Preliminary Discourse to the Encyclopedia of Diderot,* trans. Richard N. Schwab and Walter E. Rex (New York: Bobbs Merrill, 1963), pp. 14–25.

3. See Philodemus, *On Methods of Inference: A Study In Ancient Empiricism,* ed. with translation and commentary by Phillip Howard and Estelle Allen De Lacy (Philadelphia: American Philological Association, 1941), pp. 120–29. For a concise description of the Hippocratic writings and ancient medicine in general, see G. E. R. Lloyd, *Early Greek Science: Thales to Aristotle* (New York: Norton, 1970), pp. 50–65, and *Greek Science After Aristotle* (New York: Norton, 1973), pp. 75–90 and 136–53.

4. d'Alembert, pp. 143–57.

5. See Michel Foucault, *The Birth of the Clinic: An Archaeology of Medical Perception,* trans. by A. M. Sheridan Smith (New York: Vintage Books, 1973) for a more detailed, if somewhat eccentric, account of the epistemic shift.

6. See Robert Darnton, *The Great Cat Massacre and Other Episodes in French Cultural History* (New York: Vintage Books, 1984), pp. 191–213. It remains an interesting project to discover just how much d'Alembert and the whole project of the *Encyclopedia* rhetorically owes to medicine, as well as just how "revolutionary" his reclassification of medicine as a branch of the physical sciences really is. Rousseau points out in his *Confessions,* that Diderot and d'Alembert had initially intended to write a "kind of translation of Chambers['*Cyclopaedia*], somewhat like that of James' *Dictionary of Medicine,* which Diderot had just finished" (quoted in d'Alembert, p. xiv).

7. John Milton, *The Complete Poetical Works of John Milton,* ed. Douglas Bush (Boston: Houghton Mifflin, 1965), p. 517; Puttenham quoted in Meyer H. Abrams, *The Mirror and the Lamp: Romantic Theory and the Critical Tradition* (London: Oxford University Press, 1953), p. 138; and Philodemus, *On Methods of Inference: A Study In Ancient Empiricism,* ed. with translation and commentary by Phillip Howard and Estelle Allen De Lacy, (Philadelphia: American Philological Association, 1941), pp. 120–37.

8. Philodemus, *On Methods,* pp. 113–19.

9. Philodemus, *The Rhetorica of Philodemus,* translation and commentary by Harry M. Hubbell, (New Haven: Yale University Press, 1920), p. 339.

10. See Keith Hutchinson, "What Happened to Occult Qualities in the Scientific Revolution?", in *ISIS* 73 (1982), pp. 233–53. See also Foucault, *The Birth of the Clinic,* and Douglas Lane Patey, *Probability and Literary Form: Philosophic Theory and Literary Practice in the Augustan Age* (London: Cambridge University Press, 1984), pp. 36–74.

11. Foucault, p. xviii.

12. Foucault, p. 6 and Hutchinson, pp. 243–53.

13. F. G. Crookshank, "Supplement II: The Importance of a Theory of Signs and a Critique of Language in the Study of Medicine," in C. K. Ogden and I. A. Richards, *The Meaning of Meaning: A Study of the Influence of Language upon Thought and of the Science of Symbolism* (New York: Harcourt Brace, 1923), pp. 520–521. While I do not know if Williams ever actually read this piece, Ogden and Richard's work was extremely important to Kenneth Burke.

14. See Chapter 2, pp. 47–48, and William Carlos Williams, "Belly Music," in *Others* (July 1919), p. 27. For the ideas of metonymy and synecdoche see Chapter 1, pp. 22–23, and Kenneth Burke, *A Grammar of Motives,* pp. 509–10.

15. P. P. Price, *A Treatise On the Diagnosis and Prognosis of Disease* (1791), and Erasmus Darwin, *The Botanic Garden* (1791), (Menston, England: The Scholar Press Limited, 1973), "Part I: The Economy of Vegetation," p. v.

16. Darwin, "Part II: The Loves of the Plants," "Advertisement" and p. vi.

17. Ibid., pp. 40–50 and 83–88.

18. See "Newton's Rainbow and the Poet's" in Meyer H. Abrams, *The Mirror and the Lamp: Romantic Theory and the Critical Tradition* (London: Oxford University Press, 1953), pp. 303–12.

19. Darwin, "Part I: The Economy of Vegetation," pp. vii–viii.

20. Darwin, "Part II: The Loves of the Plants," "Proem," p. v.

21. Ibid., pp. 41–42.

22. Darwin, "Part II: The Loves of the Plants," pp. 44–50 and 83–88.

23. Silas Weir Mitchell, *The Autobiography of a Quack and The Case of George Dedlow,* Illustr. A. J. Keller, (New York: Century, 1900). All further references to this work will appear in the text above as *AQ.*

24. Edgar Allan Poe, "Diddling: Considered As One of the Exact Sciences," in *The Complete Works of Edgar Allan Poe, vol. 12* (New York, G. P. Putnam's Sons, 1902), pp. 210–23.

25. See in particular Sandra M. Gilbert and Susan Gubar, *The Madwoman in the Attic: The Woman Writer and the Nineteenth-Century Literary Imagination* (New Haven: Yale University Press, 1979), pp. 84–92, Walter Benn Michaels, *The Gold Standard and the Logic of Naturalism* (Berkeley: University of California Press, 1987), pp. 3–28, and Elaine Showalter, *The Female Malady: Women, Madness, and English Culture, 1830–1980* (New York: Pantheon Books, 1985), pp. 140–44. Opinion remains somewhat divided as to the overall "heinous nature" of the "rest cure," though the most important, and most negative, opinion has to be Gilman's own as expressed in "Why I Wrote 'The Yellow Wallpaper,' " in *The Charlotte Perkins Gilman Reader,* ed. Ann J. Lane (New York: Pantheon Books, 1980), pp. 19–20.

26. Ludwik Fleck, *Genesis and Development of a Scientific Fact* (Chicago: University of Chicago Press, 1979), p. 10.

27. See Showalter, pp. 121–44.

28. S. Weir Mitchell, *Lectures on Nervous Diseases, Especially in Women* (Philadelphia: J. P. Lippincott, 1885), p. 47.

29. S. Weir Mitchell, *Doctor and Patient: A Series of Essays of Advice to Women* (Philadelphia: J. P. Lippincott, 1888), p. 13.

30. Charlotte Perkins Gilman, "Why I Wrote 'The Yellow Wallpaper,' " in *The Charlotte Perkins Gilman Reader,* ed. Ann J. Lane (New York: Pantheon Books, 1980), pp. 19–20. One beneficiary of these alterations was Edith Wharton, whose treatment by Mitchell was successful. Susan Goodman has told me that she attributes Wharton's cure to Wharton's being allowed to write during her treatment. I also wonder how much of a role the "passive associations" mentioned in the text above had to do with the more staid Wharton's expectations of both the nature of her illness and the means of its alleviation.

31. S. Weir Mitchell, *Doctor and Patient,* pp. 155–77.

32. Ibid., p. 143.

33. Ibid., pp. 101–04.

34. See James S. Terry and Peter C. Williams, "Literature and Bioethics: The Tension in Goals and Styles," in *Literature and Medicine* 7 (1988), pp. 1–21.

35. K. Danner Clausner, "Approaching the Logic of Diagnosis," in *Logic of Discovery and Diagnosis in Medicine,* ed. Kenneth F. Schaffner, (Berkeley: University of California Press, 1985), p. 42.

36. The different aspects of work in this field are explained in each of the essays in *Logic of Discovery and Diagnosis in Medicine.*

37. Quoted in Anne Hunsaker Hawkins, "A. R. Luria and the Art of Clinical Biography" in *Literature and Medicine* 5 (1986), pp. 4–6. In addition, see A. R. Luria, *The Making of Mind: A Personal Account of Soviet Psychology,* ed. by Michael and Sheila Cole (Cambridge, Mass.: Harvard University Press, 1979); Oliver Sacks, *The Man Who Mistook His Wife for a Hat and Other Clinical Tales* (New York: Harper and Row, 1987); Gerald Weissmann, *The Woods Hole Cantata: Essays on Science and Society* (New York: Dodd, Mead, 1985).

38. Oliver Sacks, *The Man Who Mistook His Wife for a Hat,* p. viii.

39. Hawkins, "A. R. Luria," p. 4.

212 *Notes*

40. Samuel Johnson, *Aristotle's Art of Poetry* (London, 1705), p. 80 and *The Preface to Shakespeare,* in Milton J. Bates, pp. 209–10.

41. See above, Chapter 1, pp. 24–27, and Chapter 2, pp. 54–61. See also Jessica Benjamin, *The Bonds of Love: Psychoanalysis, Feminism, and the Problem of Domination* (New York: Pantheon Books, 1988); and Heinz Kohut, *The Analysis of the Self: A Systematic Approach to the Treatment of Narcissistic Personality Disorders* (New York: International Universities Press, 1971); *How Does Analysis Cure?* ed. by Arnold Goldberg with Paul Stepansky (Chicago: University of Chicago Press, 1984); *The Restoration of the Self* (New York: International Universities Press, 1977); *The Search for the Self: Selected Writings of Heinz Kohut: 1950–1978,* ed. and intro. by Paul Ornstein, 2 vols. (New York: International Universities Press, 1978); *Self Psychology and the Humanities: Reflections on a New Psychoanalytic Approach,* ed. with an intro. by Charles B. Strozier (New York: Norton, 1984).

42. Kohut, "Forms and Transformations of Narcissism," in *The Search for the Self,* pp. 455–58.

43. Kohut, *How Does Analysis Cure?,* pp. 174–75. Kohut adds that, as such, self psychology has not introduced a "new kind of empathy," but merely "broaden[ed] and deepen[ed] the field of empathic perception."

44. Kohut, "Forms and Transformations of Narcissism," in *The Search for the Self,* p. 429.

45. Letter to Frances Steloff, March 15,1939; in the William Carlos Williams Collection of the Harry Ransom Research Center, University of Texas at Austin.

46. See Fredric Jameson, "Postmodernism, or The Cultural Logic of Late Capitalism," in *New Left Review,* 146 (July–August 1984), 53–92. For now, I will avoid jumping into the mass of literature on the "postmodern space."

47. Thom Gunn, "Inventing the completely new poem," in *TLS* (February 19–25, 1988), pp. 179–80. I disagree with Gunn's reading of "Queen-Anne's-Lace," however.

48. James E. B. Breslin, *William Carlos Williams: An American Artist* (Chicago: University of Chicago Press, 1975, rev. 1983), p. 58.

49. *Contact* 4 (Summer 1921), p. 5–8.

50. See Ludwik Fleck, *Genesis and Development of a Scientific Fact* (Chicago: The University of Chicago Press, 1979), especially pp. 1–20.

51. See Samuel Hahnemann, *Organon of the Rational Art of Healing,* trans. C. E. Wheeler, M.D. (New York: E. P. Dutton, 1913).

52. From Kenneth Burke, "re : W.C.W. on art as disease," n.d. the Kenneth Burke Collection, Penn State University.

53. *Contact* 4 (Summer 1921), p. 5–8.

54. William Carlos Williams, "Yours, O Youth," in *Contact* 3 (Spring 1921), p. 15.

55. William Carlos Williams, "Gloria" in *Others* (July 1919), p. 3.

56. William Carlos Williams, "Notes from a Talk on Poetry," in *Poetry: A Magazine of Verse* XIV (July 1919): 211–16.

57. William Carlos Williams, "Belly Music," in *Others* (July 1919), p. 27.

58. See Roland Barthes, *The Pleasure of the Text,* trans. Richard Miller (New York: Hill and Wang, 1975) and Chapter 2 of this work.

59. Sir Paul Harvey, *The Oxford Companion to Classical Literature* (Oxford: Oxford University Press, 1984), p. 345.

60. Ibid.

61. William Carlos Williams, "The Three Letters," in *Contact* 4 (Summer 1921), pp. 10–13.

62. Michel Foucault, *Discipline and Punish: The Birth of the Prison,* trans. Alan Sheridan (New York: Vintage Books, 1979).

Chapter 4

1. As Chris MacGowan pointed out to me, it was most likely David Wang who chose to translate Mao Tse-Tung's poem. Still, both the style of the translation and the types of poems Wang chose were most heavily influenced by Williams himself. For the story of Wang's collaboration with Williams, see both *CP I* 500–02 and Hugh Witemeyer, "The Strange Progress of David Hsin-Fu Wand" in *Paideuma* (1986), 191–210. For more about Williams's early politics and the equation of "politics" with "social concerns," see David Frail, *The Early Politics and Poetics of William Carlos Williams* (Ann Arbor, Michigan: UMI Research Press, 1987).

2. See Cornel West, *The American Evasion of Philosophy: A Genealogy of Pragmatism* (Madison, Wisconsin: University of Wisconsin Press, 1989), pp. 71–111.

3. See Chapter 2 above, and West, pp. 211–39.

4. William Carlos Williams to Louis Zukofsky, July 22, 1936, in the Louis Zukofsky Collection of the Harry Ransom Research Center, University of Texas at Austin.

5. Paul Mariani, *William Carlos Williams: A New World Naked* (New York: McGraw Hill, 1981), p.151. For a reading of the poem that links Williams's reading of Kandinsky's "spiritual pyramids" to the relationship between the modern artist and the "pressure of the 'energized past,' " see Christopher J. MacGowan, *William Carlos Williams's Early Poetry: The Visual Arts Background* (Ann Arbor, Michigan: UMI Research press, 1984), pp. 29–36.

6. Paul de Man, "Literary History and Literary Modernity," in *Blindness and Insight* (Minneapolis: University of Minnesota Press, 1983), p. 151.

7. Friedrich Nietzsche, *The Use and Abuse of History,* trans. Adrian Collins, (New York: Macmillan, 1986), p. 50.

8. "A Late Egyptian Sarcophagus," *Bulletin of the Metropolitan Museum of Art,* Vol.IX (1914).

9. de Man, p. 150.

10. Williams's use of simile is nearly always to be viewed with a suspicious eye. Steeped in the imagist tradition of the "direct presentation of the thing," Williams railed against the "bastardy of the simile" in its weakening of the "vividness which is poetry by itself" (*I* 247).

11. de Man, pp. 162 and 164–65.

12. Ibid., p. 164.

13. see Nietzsche, pp. 65–73; and de Man, pp. 145–52.

14. Nietzsche, p. 71 and pp. 12–13.

15. de Man, p. 151.

16. For a more complete critique of de Man's view of history, see Frank Lentricchia, *Criticism and Social Change* (Chicago: University of Chicago Press, 1983), pp. 38–52.

17. Hayden White, *Metahistory: The Historical Imagination in Nineteeth-Century Europe* (Baltimore: Johns Hopkins University Press, 1973), p. 372.

18. Paul de Man, "Reading and History," in *The Resistance to Theory* (Minneapolis: University of Minnesota Press, 1986), pp. 69–70.

19. De Man mentions the possibility of Baudelaire and Hegel sharing a knowledge of common occult sources, and it may be that, through Poe, Williams also indirectly shares in this knowledge. See "Reading and History," pp. 70–72.

20. Wassily Kandinsky, *Concerning the Spiritual in Art and Painting in Particular,* ed. Robert Motherwell (New York: Wittenborn, Schultz, 1947), pp. 23–40. MacGowan and others discuss Williams's use of Kandinsky's ideas in terms of his attempting to reproduce the effects of modern painting in his poetry, but they ignore the complications involved in Williams's using the medium of language as opposed to paint. See MacGowan, pp. 27–36;

see also Bram Dijkstra, *Cubism, Stieglitz, and the Early Poetry of William Carlos Williams: The Hieroglyphics of a New Speech,* (Princeton: Princeton University Press, 1969), pp. 15–46 and 63–81; Mike Weaver, *William Carlos Williams: The American Background* (Cambridge: Cambridge University Press, 1971), pp. 37–43; and Paul Mariani, *William Carlos Williams: A New World Naked* (New York: McGraw Hill, 1981), pp. 106–07.

21. See Jan Mukarovsky, *The Word and Verbal Art,* trans. John Burbank and Peter Steiner, with a forward by René Wellek (New Haven: Yale University Press, 1977) and de Man, "Reading and History,", pp. 63–67.

22. See Jacques Derrida, "Structure, Sign, and Play in the Discourse of the Human Sciences," in *Writing and Difference,* trans. Alan Bass (Chicago: University of Chicago Press, 1978), pp. 278–93.

23. William Carlos Williams, "America, Whitman, and the Art of Poetry," *The Poetry Journal* (Boston), 8.1 (November, 1917), pp. 27–36; reprinted in *The William Carlos Williams Review,* 13.1 (Spring, 1987), pp. 1–4.

24. Williams's relationship to both Whitman and Keats has rightly been the focus of a great deal of critical attention. Bloom himself briefly discusses this relationship in his "Introduction" to *Modern Critical Views: William Carlos Williams* (New York: Chelsea House, 1986), pp. 1–9. In the same volume, see Stephen Cushman, "The World is not Iambic: Measure as Trope," pp. 137–60; Joseph N. Riddel, "Williams and the Ek-stasy of Beginnings," pp. 77–100; and Donald Hall, "William Carlos Williams and the Visual," pp. 115–36. See also Carl Rapp, *William Carlos Williams and Romantic Idealism* (Hanover and London: Brown University Press / University Press of New England, 1984); Stephen Tapscott, *American Beauty: William Carlos Williams and the Modernist Whitman* (New York: Columbia University Press, 1984); and James E. Miller, Jr., *The American Quest for a Supreme Fiction: Whitman's Legacy in the Personal Epic* (Chicago: University of Chicago Press, 1979). The two best discussions of Williams's relationship to Whitman, in particular, are to be found in Peter Schmidt, *William Carlos Williams, the Arts, and Literary Tradition* (Baton Rouge: Louisiana State University Press, 1988) and in James Breslin, "William Carlos Williams and the Whitman Tradition," in *Literary Criticism and Historical Understanding: Selected Papers from the English Institute,* ed. Philip Damon (New York: Columbia University Press, 1967). Schmidt's book, in particular, presents a view of Williams's relationship to tradition in general that complements my argument in this chapter in several ways, though I became aware of his work after I had finished drafting my own.

25. Hans-Georg Gadamer, *Truth and Method,* trans. Garrett Barden and John Cumming (New York: The Crossroads Publishing Company, 1985), p. 273.

26. See Gadamer, pp. 267–74 and 305–41.

27. Williams, "America, Whitman, and the Art of Poetry," pp. 1–2.

28. Gadamer, p. 274.

29. Williams, "America, Whitman, and the Art of Poetry," p. 2.

30. Ibid.

31. James Longenbach, *Modernist Poetics of History: Pound, Eliot, and the Sense of the Past* (Princeton: Princeton University Press, 1987). See in particular pp. 3–28.

32. Fredric Jameson, "Marxism and Historicism," *NLH* 11 (1979), pp. 50–51.

33. Wilhelm Dilthey, *Selected Writings,* ed. and trans. H. P. Rickman (Cambridge: Cambridge University Press, 1976), p. 215. See also Benedetto Croce, *History: Its Theory and Practice,* trans. Douglas Ainslie (New York: Harcourt, Brace and Company, 1921); Ezra Pound, *The Cantos of Ezra Pound* (New York: New Directions, 1950), pp. 3–5; and Longenbach, pp. 14–18.

34. T. S. Eliot, "Tradition and the Individual Talent—II," in *The Egoist* 5 (December 1919); p. 73; see Longenbach, pp. xi–xii.

35. Longenbach, p. 22.

36. Ezra Pound, *The Spirit of Romance* (New York: New Directions, 1968), p. 6, and T. S. Eliot, "Tradition and the Individual Talent," in *The Egoist* 4 (September 1919): 55.

37. Eliot, p. 55.

38. The statement was part of a review of a group of American poets by George Barker entitled "Fat Lady at the Circus," *Poetry* (London) 13 (June–July 1948): 38–39.

39. William Nelson, *Geological History of the Passaic Falls* (Paterson, N.J., 1892). Nelson's historical works provide Williams with a great many of the historical texts used in *Paterson*. See my " 'The Radiant Gist': 'The Poetry Hidden in the Prose' of Williams's *Paterson*," *Twentieth Century Literature* 32 (Summer 1986): 221–41, for a closer look at how Williams shapes these passages to his own purposes.

40. Williams, "America, Whitman, and the Art of Poetry," pp. 1–2.

41. Van Wyck Brooks, "On Creating A Usable Past," *The Dial* LXIV (April 11, 1918): 337–41; reprinted in *Van Wyck Brooks: The Early Years,* ed. Claire Sprague (New York: Harper and Row, 1968), p. 223.

42. Waldo Frank, *Our America* (New York: Boni and Liveright, 1919) and *The Rediscovery of America: An Introduction to a Philosophy of American Life* (Westport, Connecticut: Greenwood Press, 1929, rpt. 1982); H. L. Mencken, *The American Language* 4th ed. (New York: Alfred A. Knopf, 1936); Lewis Mumford, *The Golden Day: A Study in American Literature and Culture* (New York: Boni and Liveright, 1926); Paul Rosenfeld, *Men Seen: Twenty-Four Modern Authors* (New York: The Dial Press, 1925), and *Port of New York* (New York: Harcourt, Brace, 1924); Harold Stearns, ed., *Civilization in the United States: An Inquiry by Thirty Americans* (New York: Harcourt, Brace, 1922). For an informative discussion of these and later writers in search of a "usable past," see Russell Reising, *The Unusable Past: Theory and the Study of American Literature* (New York: Methuen, 1986).

43. The action I am describing here is the action of what has become known as "cultural materialism." See Raymond Williams, *Problems in Materialism and Culture* (London: Verso, 1980), *Marxism and Literature* (London: Oxford University Press, 1977), *Culture* (Glasgow: Fontana, 1981); see also Jonathan Dollimore and Allan Sinfield, eds., *Political Shakespeare: New Essays in Cultural Materialism* (Ithaca: Cornell University Press, 1985); and Fredric Jameson, *The Political Unconscious: Narrative as a Socially Symbolic Act* (Ithaca: Cornell University Press, 1981). For a recent critique of this "new-historicist" thought, see Edward Pechter, "The New Historicism and Its Discontents: Politicizing Renaissance Drama," *PMLA* 3 (May 1987): 292–303. See also Cornel West, who recognizes his debt to Raymond Williams throughout *The American Evasion of Philosophy: A Genealogy of Pragmatism* (Madison, Wisconsin: University of Wisconsin Press, 1989).

44. Frank Lentricchia, *Criticism and Social Change* (Chicago: University of Chicago Press, 1978), p. 132.

45. Wallace Stevens, "Adagia," in *Opus Posthumous,* ed. Samuel French Morse (New York: Vintage Books,1982), pp. 168 and 159.

46. Ibid., p. 169.

47. See Frank Lentricchia, *Criticism and Social Change.* Though I agree with and admire much of Lentricchia's reconstruction of Burke's thought, I think he makes Burke more specifically Marxist than Burke actually is in *ATH*. In a somewhat coy "Afterword" to *Criticism and Social Change,* Burke himself says that Lentricchia's "reservations regarding my work do not strike me as radical—and we could say that he does not just write about

some of my works, he lets him and me in effect 'join forces.' " Burke sees Lentricchia's work as a further participation in the "conversation" of history, "though e'en between us there are disagreements." See pp. 165–66. Still, much of my own understanding of Burke relies heavily on Lentricchia's book, as well as on his "Reading History with Kenneth Burke" and Fredric Jameson's "The Symbolic Inference; or, Kenneth Burke and Ideological Analysis" in *Representing Kenneth Burke,* eds. Hayden White and Margaret Brose (Baltimore: Johns Hopkins University Press, 1982), pp. 119–49 and pp. 31–51.

48. Fredric Jameson, "The Symbolic Inference; or, Kenneth Burke and Ideological Analysis," in *Critical Inquiry* (Spring 1978), pp. 507–23; p. 509. All further references to this work will appear in the text above as SI.

49. Fredric Jameson, "Postmodernism, or The Cultural Logic of Late Capitalism," in *New Left Review,* 146 (July-August 1984), 53–92.

50. See Cornel West, *The American Evasion of Philosophy,* pp. 71–111, especially C. Wright Mills's criticism of Dewey on p. 101.

51. See Gadamer, pp. 267–74 and 305–41.

52. See Jessica Benjamin, *The Bonds of Love: Psychoanalysis, Feminism, and the Problem of Domination* (New York: Pantheon Books, 1988), pp. 159–81. See also Chapters 1 and 2 above.

53. See in particular Aldon L. Nielsen's views on Williams's treatment of race in both "Whose Blues?," *Williams Carlos Williams Review* (Fall 1989), pp. 1–8, and in his *Reading Race White American Poets and the Racial Discourse in the Twentieth Century* (Athens, Ga.: University of Georgia Press, 1988).

54. Cornel West, *The American Evasion of Philosophy,* p. 71. All further references to this work will appear in the text as *AEV.*

55. See Mariani, p. 336.

56. See Williams's "A Fault of Learning: A Communication" in *Partisan Review,* X.5 (1943), pp. 466–68.

57. John Dewey, "The Need for a Recovery of Philosophy," in *Creative Intelligence: Essays in the Pragmatic Attitude* (New York: Henry Holt, 1917), pp. 3–69; pp. 9–11 and 35; quoted in *AEV* 88–89.

58. See Jessica Benjamin, *The Bonds of Love,* pp. 100–10 and Chapter 2 above.

59. John Dewey, *Individualism: Old and New* (New York: Capricorn, 1929), p. 171; quoted in *AEV* 103–04.

60. William Carlos Williams to Louis Zukofsky, July 22, 1936, in the Louis Zukofsky Collection of the Harry Ransom Research Center, University of Texas at Austin.

Chapter 5

1. Pierre Bourdieu, *Outline of a Theory of Practice,* trans. Richard Nice, (Cambridge: Cambridge University Press, 1977), p. 72. My use of Bourdieu relies wholly on the value of his idea of "the habitus" as a "terministic screen" (see Burke's *LASA* 44–62).

2. Fredric Jameson, "Postmodernism, or The Cultural Logic of Late Capitalism," in *New Left Review,* 146 (July–August 1984), p. 92.

3. Kenneth Burke to Brian A. Bremen, July 21, 1987.

4. Cornel West, *The American Evasion of Philosophy: A Genealogy of Pragmatism* (Madison, Wisconsin: University of Wisconsin Press, 1989), p. 103. See also Chapter 4 above.

5. See Joel Conarroe, *William Carlos Williams' Paterson:* Language and Landscape

(Philadelphia: University of Pennsylvania Press, 1970), pp. 54–55 and Chapter 1 above.

6. Pierre Bourdieu, *Outline of a Theory of Practice,* p. 72.

7. Ibid., pp. 72–73.

8. Ibid., pp. 82–83.

9. William Carlos Williams, "America, Whitman, and the Art of Poetry," *The Poetry Journal* (Boston), 8.1 (November, 1917), pp. 27–36; reprinted in *The William Carlos Williams Review,* 13.1 (Spring, 1987), pp. 1–4; p. 2.

10. Pierre Bourdieu, *Outline of a Theory of Practice,* p. 17.

11. Williams takes this information on Billy Sunday from a pamphlet by John Reed. See Mike Weaver, *William Carlos Williams: The American Background* (Cambridge: Cambridge University Press, 1971), p. 213.

12. See Fredric Jameson, "The Symbolic Inference; or, Kenneth Burke and Ideological Analysis," in *Critical Inquiry* (Spring 1978), pp. 507–23; p. 509. See also Chapter 4 above.

13. Jessica Benjamin, *The Bonds of Love: Psychoanalysis, Feminism, and the Problem of Domination* (New York: Pantheon Books, 1988), p. 223.

14. See Mike Weaver, *William Carlos Williams: The American Background,* pp. 103–14 and 208.

15. Ibid., pp. 207–08. The quoted sources are Lilienthal himself and George Zabriskie, a friend of Williams's.

16. Alan Trachtenberg, *The Incorporation of America: Culture and Society in the Gilded Age* (New York: Hill and Wang, 1982), p. 3.

17. Sandra M. Gilbert and Susan Gubar, *No Man's Land: The Place of the Woman Writer in the Twentieth Century. Volume 1: The War of the Words* (New Haven: Yale University Press, 1988), pp. 152–53. See also Sandra M. Gilbert, "Purloined Letters: William Carlos Williams and 'Cress,' " *William Carlos Williams Review* 10:2 (Fall 1985), pp. 5–15.

18. William Carlos Williams, "Correspondence: The Great Sex Spiral: A Criticism of Miss Marsden's 'Lingual Psychology,' " in *The Egoist* IV, 7 (August 1917), pp. 110–11. See also Chapter 2 above.

19. Jessica Benjamin, *The Bonds of Love,* p. 221.

20. Jessica Benjamin, *The Bonds of Love,* p. 223.

21. I have unfortunately lost the reference for this speech that Patch was to have made. For Williams's revisions of the Sarah Cumming incident in order to make her the victim of her husband's ignoring her, see Chapter 1 above.

22. "Reply to a Young Scientist Berating Me Because of My Devotion to Words," in *Direction* I, 1 (Autumn 1943), p. 27.

23. Reprinted in Linda Welshimer Wagner, *The Poems of William Carlos Williams: A Critical Study,* (Middletown, Connecticut: Wesleyan University Press, 1963), pp. 145–147.

24. See both Paul Mariani, *William Carlos Williams: A New World Naked* (New York: McGraw-Hill, 1981), pp. 461–476, and Theodora R. Graham, " 'Her Heigh Compleynte': The Cress Letters of William Carlos Williams' *Paterson,*" in Daniel Hoffman, ed., *Ezra Pound and William Carlos Williams: The University of Pennsylvania Conference Papers,* (Philadelphia: University of Pennsylvania Press, 1983), pp. 164–193. The best documented, and perhaps most informative, account of Williams's relationship with Nardi is Elizabeth O'Neill's "Marcia Nardi: Woman of Letters," in *Rossetti to Sexton: Six Women Poets at Texas,* ed. and introduction by David Oliphant (Austin: Harry Ransom Humanities Research Center, 1992); pp. 73–111. These authors disagree, however, on the "real" nature of both Ms. Nardi's character and her relationship with Williams.

25. Graham, p. 166.

26. Randall Jarrell, "A View of Three Poets," in *Partisan Review,* 18 (1951), reprinted

in Charles Tomlinson, *William Carlos Williams: A Critical Anthology,* (Baltimore, Maryland: Penguin Books, 1972), p. 173.

27. Edward Dahlberg, "Word-sick and Place-Crazy," from *Alms for Oblivion,* (Minnesota: University of Minnesota Press, 1964), in Tomlinson, p. 201.

28. Mariani, p. 468.

29. Letter to Robert D. Pepper, 21 August 1951, quoted in Mike Weaver, *William Carlos Williams: The American Background,* p. 209.

30. Ibid., p. 208.

31. From the William Carlos Williams Collection at the Harry Ransom Research Center, University of Texas at Austin.

32. Beckett Howorth, "Dynamic Posture," in *Journal of the American Medical Association* CXXXI, 17 (24 August 1946), pp. 1398–404. Quoted in Mike Weaver, *William Carlos Williams: The American Background,* p. 206.

33. See *Time* (30 May 1949), p. 37.

34. From John Peale Bishop to Edmund Wilson, November 1922, in the Edmund Wilson Papers at Yale University.

35. T. S. Eliot, "Tradition and the Individual Talent," in *The Sacred Wood: Essays on Poetry and Criticism* (London: Methuen, 1920, reprinted 1980), pp. 47–59; p. 58.

36. Ibid., p. 59.

37. T. S. Eliot, *Christianity and Culture: The Idea of a Christian Society and Notes towards the Definition of Culture,* (New York: Harcourt Brace Jovanovich, 1968), pp. 198–200 and p. 27. All further references to this work will appear in the text as *CC.*

38. Raymond Williams, *Culture and Society: 1780–1950* (New York: Columbia University Press, 1958, 1983), pp. 228–30. All further references to this work will appear in the text as *C&S.*

39. See Pierre Bourdieu, *Outline of a Theory of Practice,* pp. 72–79.

40. See Mike Weaver, *William Carlos Williams: The American Background,* pp. 103–14.

41. *New Democracy* New Series, 19 (November 1938), quoted in Mike Weaver, *William Carlos Williams: The American Background,* p. 105. See also Gorham Munson, *Aladdin's Lamp: The Wealth of the American People* (New York, 1945).

42. Mike Weaver, *William Carlos Williams: The American Background,* p. 111.

43. Ibid., p. 109.

44. Andrew Parker, "Ezra Pound and the 'Economy' of Anti-Semitism," in *Postmodernism and Politics* ed. Jonathan Arac (Minneapolis: University of Minnesota Press, 1986), pp. 71–75. All further references to this work will appear in the text as EP. For a similarly illuminating discussion of Pound's "poetic economy," see Richard Sieburth, "In Pound We Trust: The Economy of Poetry / The Poetry of Economics," in *Critical Inquiry* (Autumn 1987), pp. 142–772.

45. William Carlos Williams to Louis Zukofsky, 14 May 1935, from the Louis Zukofsky Collection at the Harry Ransom Research Center, University of Texas at Austin.

46. Ezra Pound, "Dubliners and Mr. James Joyce," in *Literary Essays,* p. 401.

47. Ezra Pound, "How to Read," in *Literary Essays,* pp. 23–40.

48. Fredric Jameson, "Postmodernism, or The Cultural Logic of Late Capitalism," in *New Left Review,* 146 (July–August 1984), 53–92. All further references to this work will appear in the text above as CLLC.

49. Cornel West, *The American Evasion of Philosophy: A Genealogy of Pragmatism* (Madison, Wisconsin: University of Wisconsin Press, 1989), p. 103. See also Chapter 4 above.

50. See Guy Debord, *The Society of the Spectacle* (1967; Detroit: Red & Black, 1977), thesis no. 24.

Bibliography

Abrams, Meyer H. *The Mirror and the Lamp: Romantic Theory and the Critical Tradition.* London: Oxford University Press, 1953.

Althusser, Louis. *For Marx.* Trans. Ben Brewster. New York: Penguin Books, 1969.

———, et al. *Reading Capital.* Trans. Ben Brewster. London: New Left Books, 1970.

Altieri, Charles. *Act and Quality: A Theory of Literary Meaning and Humanistic Understanding.* Amherst: University of Massachusetts Press, 1981.

———. ''The Hermeneutics of Literary Indeterminacy: A Dissent from the New Orthodoxy. In *NLH* 10 (1978), 71–99.

———. ''Objective Image and Act of Mind in Modern Poetry. In *PMLA* 91 (1976), 101–14.

———. ''The Poem as Act: A Way to Reconcile Presentational and Mimetic Theories. In *Iowa Review* 6 (1975), 103–24.

———. ''Presence and Reference in a Literary Text: The Example of Williams' 'This Is Just to Say.' '' In *Critical Inquiry* (Spring 1979), 489–510.

———. ''The Qualities of Action: A Theory of Middles in Literature. In *Boundary 2* (Winter 1977), 323–50.

———. ''Wittgenstein on Consciousness and Language: A Challenge to Derridean Literary Theory. In *MLN* 91 (1976), 1397–1423.

———. ''Wordsworth's 'Preface' as Literary Theory. In *Criticism* 18 (1976), 122–46.

Barthes, Roland. *Elements of Semiology.* Trans. Annette Lavers and Colin Smith. New York: Hill and Wang, 1967.

———. *S/Z: An Essay.* Trans. Richard Miller. New York: Hill and Wang, 1974.

———. *Mythologies.* Trans. Annette Lavers. New York: Hill and Wang, 1972.

———. *The Pleasure of the Text.* Trans. Richard Miller. New York: Hill and Wang, 1975.

———. *Writing Degree Zero.* Trans. Annette Lavers and Colin Smith. New York: Hill and Wang, 1967.

Barber, John W., and Henry Howe. *Historical Collections of New Jersey: Past and Present.* New Haven, Connecticut, 1868.

Belsey, Catherine. *Critical Practice.* London and New York: Methuen, 1980.

Benjamin, Jessica. *The Bonds of Love: Psychoanalysis, Feminism, and the Problem of Domination.* New York: Pantheon Books, 1988.

Bernstein, Michael André. *The Tale of the Tribe: Ezra Pound and the Modern Verse Epic.* Princeton, N. J.: Princeton University Press, 1980.

Bloom, Harold, ed. *Modern Critical Views: William Carlos Williams.* New York: Chelsea House Publishers, 1986.

Bourdieu, Pierre. *Outline of a Theory of Practice.* Trans. Richard Nice. Cambridge: Cambridge University Press, 1977.

219

Breslin, James E. *William Carlos Williams: An American Artist.* New York: Oxford University Press, 1970.

Bromwich, David. "Keats's Radicalism. In *SiR* 25 (Summer 1986), 197–210.

———. "Recent Work in Literary Criticism. In *Social Research* 53 (Autumn 1986), 411–48.

Brooks, Van Wyck. *Van Wyck Brooks: The Early Years.* ed. Claire Sprague. New York: Harper and Row, 1968.

Burke, Kenneth. *Attitudes Toward History.* Boston: Beacon Press, 1937; rev. with new afterword, 1984.

———. *Counter-Statement.* Berkeley: University of California Press, 1931; rev. 1953, 1968.

———. *A Grammar of Motives.* Berkeley: University of California Press, 1945.

———. *Language as Symbolic Action: Essays on Life, Literature, and Method.* Berkeley: University of California Press, 1966.

———. *Permanence and Change: An Anatomy of Purpose.* Berkeley: University of California Press, 1935; rev with new afterword, 1984.

———. *The Philosophy of Literary Form.* Berkeley, University of California Press,1941; rev. ed. 1973.

———. *A Rhetoric of Motives.* Berkeley: University of California Press, 1950.

———. *The Rhetoric of Religion: Studies in Logology.* Berkeley: University of California Press, 1961.

Cassirer, Ernst. *Language and Myth.* Trans. Susanne K. Langer. New York: Dover Publications, 1946.

Clifford, James. *The Predicament of Culture: Twentieth Century Ethnography, Literature, and Art.* Cambridge, Mass.: Harvard University Press, 1988.

———and Marcus, Stephen, eds. *Writing Culture: The Poetics and Politics of Ethnography.* Berkeley: University of California Press, 1986.

Conarroe, Joel. *William Carlos Williams' 'Paterson': Language and Landscape.* Philadelphia: University of Pennsylvania Press, 1970.

Croce, Benedetto. *History: Its Theory and Practice.* Trans. Douglas Ainslie. New York: Harcourt, Brace, 1921.

Cushman, Stephen. *William Carlos Williams and the Meaning of Measure.* Yale Studies in English 193. New Haven: Yale University Press, 1985.

d'Alembert, Jean Le Rond. *Preliminary Discourse to the Encyclopedia of Diderot.* Trans. Richard N. Schwab and Walter E. Rex. New York: Bobbs Merrill, 1963.

Darnton, Robert. *The Great Cat Massacre and Other Episodes in French Cultural History.* New York: Vintage Books, 1984.

Darwin, Erasmus. *The Botanic Garden* (1791). Menston, England: The Scholar Press Limited, 1973.

Debord, Guy. *The Society of the Spectacle.* Detroit: Red & Black, 1977, thesis no. 24.

de Man, Paul. *Blindness and Insight.* Minneapolis: University of Minnesota Press, 1983.

———. *The Resistance to Theory.* Minneapolis: University of Minnesota Press, 1986.

———. *The Rhetoric of Romanticism.* New York: Columbia University Press, 1984.

Derrida, Jacques. *Of Grammatology.* Trans. Gayatri Chakravorty Spivak. Baltimore, Johns Hopkins University Press, 1974.

———. *Speech and Phenomena And Other Essays on Husserl's Theory of Signs.* Trans. David B. Allison. Evanston: Northwestern University Press, 1973.

———. *Writing and Difference.* Trans. Alan Bass. Chicago: University of Chicago Press, 1978.

Dewey, John. *Creative Intelligence: Essays in the Pragmatic Attitude.* New York: Henry Holt, 1917.

———. *Individualism: Old and New.* New York: Capricorn, 1929.

Diggory, Terence. *William Carlos Williams and the Ethics of Painting.* Princeton, N. J.: Princeton University Press, 1991.

Dijkstra, Bram. *The Hieroglyphics of a New Speech: Cubism, Stieglitz, and the Early Poetry of William Carlos Williams.* Princeton, New Jersey: Princeton University Press, 1969.

Dilthey, Wilhelm. *Selected Writings.* Ed. and trans. H. P. Rickman. Cambridge: Cambridge University Press, 1976.

Dollimore, Jonathan, and Sinfeld, Allan, eds. *Political Shakespeare: New Essays in Cultural Materialism.* Ithaca: Cornell University Press, 1985.

Duffey, Bernard. *A Poetry of Presence: The Writings of William Carlos Williams.* Madison, Wisconsin: University of Wisconsin Press, 1986.

Federal Writers' Project of the Works Progress Administration for the State of New Jersey. *New Jersey: A Guide to Its Present and Past.* New York, 1939.

———. *Stories of New Jersey.* New York, 1938.

Fleck, Ludwik. *Genesis and Development of a Scientific Fact.* Chicago: University of Chicago Press, 1979.

Foster, Hal, ed. *The Anti-Aesthetic: Essays on Postmodern Culture.* Port Townsend, Washington: Bay Press, 1983.

Foucault, Michel. *The Birth of the Clinic: An Archaeology of Medical Perception.* Trans. A. M. Sheridan Smith. New York: Vintage Books, 1973.

———. *Discipline and Punish: The Birth of the Prison.* Trans. Alan Sheridan. New York: Vintage Books, 1979.

———. *The History of Sexuality; Volume 1: An Introduction.* Trans. Robert Hurley. New York: Vintage Books, 1980.

———. *The History of Sexuality; Volume 2: The Use of Pleasure.* Trans. Robert Hurley. New York: Vintage Books, 1984.

———. *The History of Sexuality; Volume 3: The Care of the Self.* Trans. Robert Hurley. New York: Vintage Books, 1986.

———. *Language, Counter-memory, Practice: Selected Essays and Interviews.* Ed. Donald Bouchard. Trans. Donald Bouchard and Sherry Simon. Ithaca, New York: Cornell University Press, 1977.

———. *Madness and Civilization: A History of Insanity in the Age of Reason.* Trans. Richard Howard. New York: Vintage Books, 1965.

———. *Power/Knowledge: Selected Interviews and Other Writings 1972–1977.* Ed. Colin Gordon. Trans. Colin Gordon, Leo Marshall, John Mepham, Kate Soper. New York, Pantheon Books, 1980.

———. *The Order of Things: An Archaeology of the Human Sciences.* New York: Vintage Books, 1970.

Frail, David. *The Early Politics and Poetics of William Carlos Williams.* Ann Arbor, Michigan: UMI Research Press, 1987.

Frank, Waldo. *Our America.* New York: Boni and Liveright, 1919.

———. *The Re-discovery of America: An Introduction to a Philosophy of American Life.* Westport, Connecticut: Greenwood Press, 1929, rpt. 1982.

Gadamer, Hans-Georg. *Truth and Method.* Trans. Garrett Barden and John Cumming. New York: Crossroads Publishing Company, 1985.

Gilbert, Sandra M. and Gubar, Susan. *The Madwoman in the Attic: The Woman Writer and the Nineteenth-Century Literary Imagination.* New Haven: Yale University Press, 1979.

————. *No Man's Land: The Place of the Woman Writer in the Twentieth Century. Volume 1: The War of the Words.* New Haven: Yale University Press, 1988.

————. *No Man's Land: The Place of the Woman Writer in the Twentieth Century. Volume 2: Sex Changes.* New Haven: Yale University Press, 1988.

Goldberg, Jonathan. "The Politics of Renaissance Literature: A Review Essay. In *ELH* 49 (1982), 514–542.

Guimond, James K. *The Art of William Carlos Williams: A Discovery and Possession of America.* Chicago: The University of Illinois Press, 1968.

————. "William Carlos Williams and the Past: Some Clarifications. In *Journal of Modern Literature,* I (May 1971), 493–502.

Hacking, Ian. *The Emergence of Probability: A Philosophical Study of Early Ideas about Probability, Induction and Statistical Inference.* London: Cambridge University Press, 1975.

Hahnemann, Samuel. *The Lesser Writings of Samuel Hahnemann.* Collected and translated by R. E. Dudgeon, M.D. New York: William Radde, 1852.

————. *Organon of the Rational Art of Healing.* Trans. C. E. Wheeler, M.D. New York: E. P. Dutton, 1913.

Heinzelman, Kurt. *The Economics of the Imagination.* Amherst: University of Massachusetts Press, 1980.

Hoffman, Daniel, Ed. *Ezra Pound and William Carlos Williams: The University of Pennsylvania Conference Papers.* Philadelphia: University of Pennsylvania Press, 1983.

Hollis, Martin and Lukes, Steven, eds. *Rationality and Relativism.* Oxford: Basil Blackwell, 1982.

Hume, David. *Enquiries concerning Human Understanding and concerning the Principles of Morals.* Reprinted from the 1777 edition with intro. and analytical index by L. A. Selby-Bigge; 3d ed. with text revised and notes by P. H. Nidditch. Oxford: Clarendon Press, 1975.

Hutchinson Keith. "What Happened to Occult Qualities in the Scientific Revolution?" In *ISIS* 73 (1982), 233–53.

Ingram, John Henry. *Flora Symbolica; or the language and sentiment of flowers.* London: Warne, 1869.

Jameson, Fredric. *Marxism and Form: Twentieth-Century Dialectical Theories of Literature.* Princeton: Princeton University Press, 1971.

————. "Marxism and Historicism. In *NLH* 11 (1979): 50–67.

————. *The Prison-House of Language.* Princeton: Princeton University Press, 1972.

————. *The Political Unconscious: Narrative as a Socially Symbolic Act.* Ithaca, New York: Cornell University Press, 1981.

————. "Postmodernism and Consumer Society." In *The Anti-Aesthetic: Essays on Postmodern Culture.* Ed. Hal Foster. Port Townsend, Washington: Bay Press, 1983: 111–25.

————. "Postmodernism, or The Cultural Logic of Late Capitalism." In *New Left Review,* 146 (July–August 1984): 53–92.

————. "The Symbolic Inference; or, Kenneth Burke and Ideological Analysis." In *Critical Inquiry* (Spring 1978): 507–23.

Kenner, Hugh. *A Homemade World: The American Modernist Writers.* New York: Alfred A. Knopf, 1975.

————. *The Pound Era.* Berkeley: University of California Press, 1971.

————. "To Measure Is All We Know. In *Poetry,* XCIV (May 1959), 127–32.

————. "With the Bare Hands. In *Poetry,* LXXX (Aug. 1952), 276–90.

Koehler, G. Stanley. "A Gathering for William Carlos Williams." In *The Massachussets Review,* (Winter 1962), 275–344.

Kohut, Heinz. *The Analysis of the Self: A Systematic Approach to the Treatment of Narcissistic Personality Disorders.* New York: International Universities Press, 1971.

————. *How Does Analysis Cure?* Ed. by Arnold Goldberg with Paul Stepansky. Chicago: University of Chicago Press, 1984.

————. *The Restoration of the Self.* New York: International Universities Press, 1977.

————. *The Search for the Self: Selected Writings of Heinz Kohut: 1950–1978.* Ed. and intro. by Paul Ornstein. 2 Vols. New York: International Universities Press, 1978.

————. *Self Psychology and the Humanities: Reflections on a New Psychoanalytic Approach.* Ed. with an intro. by Charles B. Strozier. New York: Norton, 1984.

Kutzinski, Vera M. *Against the American Grain: Myth and History in William Carlos Williams, Jay Wright, and Nicolás Guillén.* Baltimore: Johns Hopkins University Press, 1987.

Laclau, Ernesto. *Politics and Ideology in Marxist Theory.* London: New Left Books, 1977.

————and Mouffe, Chantal. *Hegemony and Socialist Strategy: Towards a Radical Democratic Politics.* Trans. Winston Moore and Paul Cammack. London: Verso, 1985.

Lentricchia, Frank. *Criticism and Social Change.* Chicago: University of Chicago Press, 1983.

Levenson, Michael H. *A Genealogy of Modernism: A Study of English Literary Doctrine 1908–1922.* Cambridge: Cambridge University Press, 1984.

Lloyd, G. E. R. *Early Greek Science: Thales to Aristotle.* New York: W. W. Norton and Co., 1970.

————. *Greek Science After Aristotle.* New York: W. W. Norton and Co., 1973.

Lloyd, Margaret Glynne. *William Carlos Williams's 'Paterson': A Critical Reappraisal.* Cranbury, New Jersey: Associated University Presses, 1980.

Longenbach, James. *Modernist Poetics of History: Pound, Eliot, and the Sense of the Past.* Princeton: Princeton University Press, 1987.

Longwell, Charles P. *A Little Story of Old Paterson As Told By An Old Man.* Paterson, N. J., 1901.

————. *Historic Totowa Falls and Vicinity.* Paterson, N. J., 1942.

Lowell, Robert. "Paterson II." In *Nation,* CLXVI (June 19, 1948): 692–94.

Luria, A. R. *The Making of Mind: A Personal Account of Soviet Psychology.* Ed by Michael and Sheila Cole. Cambridge, Mass.: Harvard University Press, 1979.

MacGowan, Christopher J. *William Carlos Williams's Early Poetry: The Visual Arts Background.* Ann Arbor, Michigan: UMI Research Press, 1984.

Macherey, Pierre. *A Theory of Literary Production.* Trans. Geoffrey Wall. London: Routledge and Kegan Paul, 1978.

Mariani, Paul. *William Carlos Williams: A New World Naked.* New York: McGraw Hill, 1981.

————. *William Carlos Williams: The Poet and His Critics.* Chicago: American Library Association, 1975.

Marsh, Jean, ed. *The Illuminated Language of Flowers.* Revised version of Kate Greenaway's 1884 *Language of Flowers.* New York: Holt, Rinehart and Winston, 1978.

Martz, Louis L. "*Paterson:* A Plan for Action." In *Journal of Modern Literature,* I (May 1971), 512–22.

————. *The Poem of the Mind: Essays on Poetry / English and American.* New York: Oxford University Press, 1966.

Mazzaro, Jerome. *William Carlos Williams: The Later Poems.* Ithaca and London: Cornell University Press, 1973.

Mencken, H. L. *The American Language* 4th ed. New York: Alfred A. Knopf, 1919, 1921, 1923, 1936.

Michaels, Walter Benn. *The Gold Standard and the Logic of Naturalism.* Berkeley: The University of California Press, 1987.

Miller, James E., Jr. *The American Quest for a Supreme Fiction: Whitman's Legacy in the Personal Epic.* Chicago: University of Chicago Press, 1979.

Miller, J. Hillis. "Deconstructing the Deconstructors." In *Diacritics,* (Summer 1975), 24–31.

———. *The Linguistic Moment: From Wordsworth to Stevens.* Princeton: Princeton University Press, 1985.

———. *Poets of Reality: Six Twentieth Century Writers.* Cambridge, Massachusetts: The Belknap Press of Harvard University Press, 1965.

———. "Presidential Address 1986. The Triumph of Theory, the Resistance to Reading, and the Question of the Material Base," *PMLA* 102 (1987): 281–91.

———, ed. *William Carlos Williams: A Collection of Critical Essays.* Englewood Cliffs, N. J.: Prentice Hall, 1966.

———. "Williams' *Spring and All* and the Progress of Poetry." In *Ddalus,* 99 (Spring 1970), 405–34.

Milton, John. *The Complete Poetical Works of John Milton.* Ed. Douglas Bush. Boston: Houghton Mifflin, 1965.

Mitchell, Silas Weir. *The Autobiography of a Quack and The Case of George Dedlow.* Illustr. A. J. Keller. New York: Century, 1900.

———. *Doctor and Patient: A Series of Essays of Advice to Women.* Philadelphia: Lippincott, 1888.

———. *Lectures on Diseases of the Nervous System.* Philadelphia: Lippincott, 1885.

———. *Lectures on Nervous Diseases, Especially in Women.* Philadelphia: Lippincott, 1885.

———. *Little Stories.* Philadelphia: Lippincott, 1902.

———. *Wear and Tear; or Hints for the Overworked.* Philadelphia: Lippincott, 1891.

Mukarovsky, Jan. *The Word and Verbal Art.* Trans. John Burbank and Peter Steiner, with a forward by René Wellek. New Haven: Yale University Press, 1977.

Mumford, Lewis. *The Golden Day: A Study in American Literature and Culture.* New York: Boni and Liveright, 1926.

Nash, Ralph. "The Use of Prose in 'Paterson.' " In *Perspective,* VI (Autumn 1953), 191–99.

Nelson, William. *Geological History of the Passaic Falls.* Paterson, N.J., 1892.

———. *History of the City of Paterson and the County of Passaic, New Jersey.* Paterson, N.J., 1901.

Nelson, William, and Charles A. Shriner. *History of Paterson and Its Environs: The Silk City.* 3 vols. New York and Chicago, 1920.

Nielsen, Aldon L. *Reading Race: White American Poets and the Racial Discourse in the Twentieth Century.* Athens, Ga.: University of Georgia Press, 1988.

———. "Whose Blues?" In *Williams Carlos Williams Review* (Fall 1989), 1–8.

Nietzsche, Friedrich. *The Use and Abuse of History,* trans. Adrian Collins. New York: Macmillan, 1986.

Patey, Douglas Lane. *Probability and Literary Form: Philosophic Theory and Literary Practice in the Augustan Age.* London: Cambridge University Press, 1984.

Pearce, Roy Harvey. *The Continuity of American Poetry.* Princeton, N. J.: Princeton University Press, 1961.

Pechter, Edward. "The New Historicism and Its Discontents: Politicizing Renaissance Drama.

In *PMLA* 3 (May 1987), 292–303.

Peterson, Walter Scott. *An Approach to 'Paterson'.* New Haven and London: Yale University Press, 1967.

Philodemus. *On Methods of Inference: A Study In Ancient Empiricism.* Ed. with trans. and commentary by Phillip Howard and Estelle Allen De Lacy. Philadelphia: American Philological Association, 1941.

―――. *The Rhetorica of Philodemus.* Trans. and commentary by Harry M. Hubbell. New Haven: Yale University Press, 1920.

Poe, Edgar Allan. *The Complete Works of Edgar Allan Poe.* New York, G. P. Putnam's Sons, 1902.

Pound, Ezra. *The Cantos of Ezra Pound.* New York: New Directions Publishing Corporation, 1950.

―――. *Literary Essays of Ezra Pound.* Ed. with an intro. by T. S. Eliot. London: Faber & Faber, 1954.

―――. *The Spirit of Romance.* New York: New Directions, 1968.

Quinn, Sister M. Bernetta. *The Metamorphic Tradition in Modern Poetry.* New York: Gordian Press, 1972.

―――. "*Paterson:* Landscape and Dream. In *Journal of Modern Literature,* I (May 1971), 523–48.

Rapp, Carl. *William Carlos Williams and Romantic Idealism.* Hanover and London: Brown University Press / University Press of New England, 1984.

Reising, Russell. *The Unusable Past: Theory and the Study of American Literature.* New York: Methuen, 1986.

Riddel, Joseph N. *The Inverted Bell: Modernism and the Counterpoetics of William Carlos Williams.* Baton Rouge: Louisiana State University Press, 1974.

―――. "A Miller's Tale." In *Diacritics* (Fall 1975), 56–65.

Rosenfeld, Paul. *Men Seen: Twenty-Four Modern Authors.* New York: Dial Press, 1925.

―――. *Port of New York.* New York: Harcourt, Brace, 1924.

Sacks, Oliver. *The Man Who Mistook His Wife for a Hat and Other Clinical Tales.* New York: Harper and Row, 1987.

Sankey, Benjamin. *A Companion to William Carlos Williams's 'Paterson'.* Berkeley: University of California Press, 1971.

Sayre, Henry M. "Ready-mades and Other Measures: The Poetics of Marcel Duchamp and William Carlos Williams. In *Journal of Modern Literature* 8, No. 1 (1980), 3–22.

―――. *The Visual Text of William Carlos Williams.* Urbana and Chicago: University of Illinois Press, 1983.

Schaffner, Kenneth F., ed. *Logic of Discovery and Diagnosis in Medicine.* Berkeley: The University of California Press, 1985.

Schmidt, Peter. *William Carlos Williams, the Arts, and Literary Tradition.* Baton Rouge: Louisiana State University Press, 1988.

Scourse, Nicolette. *The Victorians and Their Flowers.* London: Croom Helm, 1983.

Showalter, Elaine. *The Female Malady: Women, Madness, and English Culture, 1830–1980.* New York: Pantheon Books, 1985.

Sieburth, Richard. "In Pound We Trust: The Economy of Poetry / The Poetry of Economics." In *Critical Inquiry* (Autumn 1987), 142–72.

Stearns, Harold, ed. *Civilization in the United States: An Inquiry by Thirty Americans.* New York: Harcourt, Brace, 1922.

Stirner, Max. *The Ego and his Own.* Trans. John Byington. London: A. C. Fifield, 1912.

Tapscott, Stephen. *American Beauty: William Carlos Williams and the Modernist Whitman.* New York: Columbia University Press, 1984.

Thirlwall, John C. "William Carlos Williams' 'Paterson': The Search for a Redeeming Language—A Personal Epic in Five Parts." In *New Directions 17*. New York: New Directions, 1961, pp. 252–310.

Tomlinson, Charles. *William Carlos Williams: A Critical Anthology*. Baltimore, Maryland: Penguin Books, 1972.

Trachtenberg, Alan. *The Incorporation of America: Culture and Society in the Gilded Age*. New York: Hill and Wang, 1982.

Usener, Hermann. *Götternamen: Versuch einer Lehre von der religiösen Begriffsbildung*. Bonn: n.p., 1896.

Vazakas, Byron. *The Equal Tribunals*. New York: Clarke and Way, 1961.

———. *Transfigured Night*. Intro. by William Carlos Williams. New York: Macmillan, 1946.

Wagner, Linda Welshimer. *The Poems of William Carlos Williams: A Critical Study*. Middletown, Connecticut: Wesleyan University Press, 1963.

———. *The Prose of William Carlos Williams*. Middletown, Connecticut: Wesleyan University Press, 1970.

Wallace, Emily Mitchell. *A Bibliography of William Carlos Williams*. Middletown, Connecticut: Wesleyan University Press, 1968.

Weatherhead, A. Kingsley. "William Carlos Williams: Prose, Form, and Measure. In *English Literary History* 33 (March 1961), 118–131.

Weaver, Mike. *William Carlos Williams: The American Background*. Cambridge: Cambridge University Press, 1971.

Weininger, Otto. *Sex and Character*. New York: G. P. Putnam's Sons, 1906.

Weissmann, Gerald. *The Woods Hole Cantata: Essays on Science and Society*. New York: Dodd, Mead, 1985.

West, Cornel. *The American Evasion of Philosophy: A Genealogy of Pragmatism*. Madison, Wisconsin: The University of Wisconsin Press, 1989.

Whitaker, Thomas R. *William Carlos Williams*. Twayne's United States Authors Series, No. 143. New York: Twayne Publishers Inc., 1968; rev. 1989.

White, Hayden. *Metahistory: The Historical Imagination in Nineteeth-Century Europe*. Baltimore: Johns Hopkins University Press, 1973.

White, Hayden, and Brose, Margaret, eds. *Representing Kenneth Burke*. Baltimore: Johns Hopkins University Press, 1982.

Whittemore, Reed. *William Carlos Williams: Poet from Jersey*. Boston: Houghton Mifflin, 1975.

Williams, Raymond. *Culture*. Glasgow: Fontana, 1981.

———. *Marxism and Literature*. Oxford: Oxford University Press, 1977.

———. *Problems in Materialism and Culture*. London: Verso, 1980.

Williams, William Carlos. "America, Whitman, and the Art of Poetry." In *The Poetry Journal*, Boston: 8.1 (November, 1917), 27–36. Reprinted in *The William Carlos Williams Review*, 13.1 (Spring, 1987), 1–4.

———. "The American Idiom." In *New Directions 17,* New York: New Directions, 1961, pp. 250–51.

———. "A Point for American Criticism." In *Our Exagmination Round His Factification For Incamination Of Work In Progress*. Beckett, Samuel, et. al. London: Faber & Faber, 1936.

———. *The Autobiography of William Carlos Williams*. New York: Random House, 1951.

———. *The Build-up*. New York: New Directions, 1952.

———. *The Collected Poems of William Carlos Williams: Volume I, 1909–1939*. Ed. A. Walton Litz and Christopher MacGowan. New York: New Directions, 1986.

————. *The Collected Poems of William Carlos Williams: Volume II, 1939–1962*. Ed. Christopher MacGowan. New York: New Directions, 1988.

————. *The Embodiment of Knowledge*. New York: New Directions, 1974.

————. *The Farmer's Daughters*. New York: New Directions, 1961.

————. *Imaginations*. New York: New Directions, 1970.

————. *Interviews with William Carlos Williams: "Speaking Straight Ahead."* Ed. with an intro. Linda Welshimer Wagner. New York: New Directions, 1976.

————. *In The American Grain*. New York: New Directions, 1925.

————. *In The Money*. New York: New Directions, 1940.

————. *I Wanted to Write a Poem: The Autobiography of the Works of a Poet*. Reported and edited by Edith Heal. Boston: Beacon Press, 1958.

————. "Notes from a Talk on Poetry. In *Poetry* XIV (July 1919), 211–16.

————. *Paterson*. Rev. ed. by Christopher MacGowan. New York: New Directions, 1992.

————. *A Recognizable Image: William Carlos Williams on Art and Artists*. Ed. with intro and notes by Bram Dijkstra. New York: New Directions 1978.

————. *Rome*. Ed. Steven Ross Loevy. Rpt. in *Iowa Review* 9, 3 (Spring 1978), 1–65.

————. *Selected Essays*. New York: New Directions, 1954.

————. *The Selected Letters of William Carlos Williams*. Ed. by John C. Thirlwall. New York: McDowell, Oblensky, 1957.

————. *Something to Say: William Carlos Williams on Younger Poets*. Ed. with intro. by James E. Breslin. New York: New Directions, 1985.

————. *A Voyage to Pagany*. New York: New Directions, 1970.

————. *White Mule*. New York: New Directions, 1937.

Peter Winch, ed. *Studies in the Philosophy of Wittgenstein*. New York: Humanities Press, 1969.

Ludwig Wittgenstein. *Philosophical Investigations*. Trans. G. E. M. Anscombe. New York: Macmillan, 1958.

————. *Zettel*. Ed. G. E. M. Anscombe and G. H. Von Wright. Berkeley: University of California Press, 1970.

Zabriskie, George. "The Geography of *Paterson*." In *Perspective*, VI (Autumn 1953), 201–16.

Index